FREAKS TALK BACK

FREAKS

The University of Chicago Press

TALKKDAB

Tabloid Talk Shows and Sexual Nonconformity

JOSHUA GAMSON

Chicago and London

Joshua Gamson is assistant professor of sociology at Yale University. He is the author of *Claims to Fame: Celebrity in Contemporary America* (1994).

The University of Chicago Press, Chicago 60637
The University of Chicago Press, Ltd., London
© 1998 by The University of Chicago
All rights reserved. Published 1998
Printed in the United States of America
07 06 05 04 03 02 01 00 99 98   1 2 3 4 5
ISBN: 0-226-28064-0 (cloth)

Library of Congress Cataloging-in-Publication Data

Gamson, Joshua, 1962–
    Freaks talk back : tabloid talk shows and sexual nonconformity / Joshua
Gamson.
        p. cm.
    Includes bibliographical references and index.
    ISBN 0-226-28064-0 (cloth : alk. paper)
    1. Talk shows—United States. 2. Talk shows—Social aspects—United
States. 3. Sex in television. 4. Homosexuality in television. I. Title.
PN1992.8.T3G35   1998
791.45′6—dc21   97-40577
                                                                      CIP

♾ The paper used in this publication meets the minimum requirements of the American National Standard for Information Sciences—Permanence of Paper for Printed Library Materials, ANSI Z39.48-1992.

For Gilad and Ari, as they enter talking

Contents

Acknowledgments   **ix**

1 Why I Love Trash   **2**

2 The Monster with Two Heads   **28**

3 Truths Told in Lies   **67**

4 Sitting Ducks and Forbidden Fruits   **106**

5 I Want to Be Miss Understood   **138**

6 Flaunting It   **170**

7 The Tight Rope of Visibility   **208**

Appendix: Methods   **227**

Notes   **241**

Works Cited   **265**

Index   **277**

Acknowledgments

I have paid some of them off with meals and flattery, but I still owe great debts of gratitude to a wide range of people who helped me afford, formulate, research, and develop this project. I would be in much greater financial debt, to begin with, without major support from the Wayne F. Placek Award of the American Psychological Foundation, which financed the first year of research, and a Yale University Junior Faculty Fellowship, which supported me during the year of writing. The Research Fund for Lesbian and Gay Studies at Yale, and the Yale Provost's Office (thanks to Associate Provost Arline McCord) also provided research funding.

As I began the research, a number of people were crucial in helping me locate interview contacts: Tim Bruno, Xavier Carrica, Dallas Denny, Emily Eldridge, Marilyn Fletcher, Molly Fowler, Garrett Glaser, Elise Major, Robert Morrison, Karen Nakamura, Peter Nardi, Robyn Ochs, John Siceloff, Susan Stryker, Donald Suggs, Craig Waldo, and John Wentworth. As I proceeded, others helped make the data collection possible in a variety of ways: Hailyn Chen-Gallagher, Shelly Donow, Morgan Gwenwald, Jeanne Heaton, David Leonard, Manhattan Gender Network, Dave Mulryan, Carole Smith, Sandy Starr, and Donna Vallone. I am especially grateful to Ann Fitzpatrick for her transcription work, to Hazel Kahan for her wonderful guidance and company in the focus-group process, and to Baris Gumus, without whose research assistance, sense of humor, and intelligence I would not have been able to complete the content analysis. The many people who took the time to speak with me in interviews have, in a literal sense, given life to this book, and I hope the result is at least some reward for their time and openness.

A number of friends, in addition to the members of my Yale University classes in mass media and mass culture, proved themselves fun talk show companions and very insightful talk show researchers, accompanying me to tapings: Bonnie Adrian, Carla Eastis, Laurie Ginsberg, Laura Kirks, Deborah Levy, Pam McElwee, Karen Nakamura, Shanti Parikh, and especially my appropriately nosy fellow fan Anne Herlick. Many people have also given time and brainpower to commenting critically on my work as the writing progressed, pushing the ideas and the expression along: Amy Aronson, Craig Calhoun, Corey Creekmur, Jimmy Dawes, Steven Epstein, Larry Gross, David Kirp, Jack Levinson, Wayne Munson, Geri Sawicki, Beth Schneider, Michael Schudson, Verta Taylor, and the members of the Workshop on Politics, Power, and Protest at NYU. Doug Mitchell, whose generosity as an editor and a human and whose taste in food have amazed me over and over, has been a key supporter, sharp commentator, and able nourisher. For this project as always, my parents, William and Zelda Gamson, have been my central sources of astute feedback, wise mentoring, and just plain nurturing.

FREAKS TALKKƆA

1 WHY I LOVE TRASH

One can only imagine what this constant attention to the fringes of society, to those who break rules, is doing to our society's ability to define and constrain deviance. One thing seems fairly certain: law-abiding, privacy-loving, ordinary people who have had reasonably happy childhoods and are satisfied with their lives, probably won't get to tell their stories on Phil, Sally, or Oprah. . . . Television talk shows are not interested in adequately reflecting or representing social reality, but in highlighting and trivializing its underside for fun and profit.

PROFESSORS VICKI ABT AND MEL SEESHOLTZ[1]

Nobody wants to watch anything that's smarmy or tabloid or silly or unseemly — except the audience.

TALK SHOW HOST SALLY JESSY RAPHAEL[2]

Doesn't she look like a weird, scary drag queen?

FILMMAKER GREGG ARAKI, ON TALK SHOW HOST SALLY JESSY RAPHAEL[3]

Let's begin here: talk shows are bad for you, so bad you could catch a cold. Turn them off, a women's magazine suggested in 1995, and turn on Mother Teresa, since watching her "caring feelings" radiate from the screen, according to psychologist Dr. David McClelland of Harvard, has been shown to raise the level of an antibody that fights colds. "It stands to reason," reasons the *First* magazine writer, "that viewing threatening, confrontational images could create an opposite reaction." In fact, given that talk shows "create feelings of frustration" and fear, "shatter our trust and faith" in our expectations of people's behavior, and "give us a false perception of reality," it is perhaps best to watch game shows or soaps while nursing that cold. Watching daytime talk shows could conceivably send you into a decline into pathologies of all sorts: scared, angry, disgusted, convinced that you are abnormal for not fitting in with the "cast of misfits and perverts," susceptible to both perversion and more colds.

While the Mother Teresa versus Jerry Springer matchup is out there enough to be camp, the hand-wringing it represents is only an exaggerated version of the many criticisms and political rallying cries aimed at talk shows over the last few years. Experts of all sorts can be found issuing warnings about talk show dangers. Before bringing out Dr. McClelland, for instance, the *First* article quotes George Gerbner, dean emeritus of the Annenberg School for Communication ("These shows are virtually destroying the goodness of America"), Harvard psychiatrist Alvin Poussaint ("It does not bode well for the future generation of young people growing up on a steady diet of this drivel"), and Fred Strassberger, once chair of the media task force of the American Psychological Association ("It's now becoming alarmingly clear that talk shows are adding greatly to the fear, tensions and stress in our society"); later, TV critic Tom Shales joins in ("These shows are portraying

Americans as shallow monsters"), along with psychologist Robert Sim-mermon ("cruel exploitation of people's deepest wounds to entertain view-ers who could very well wind up believing such aberrant behavior is nor-mal").[4] Goodness, normality, and stability, if we buy these arguments, are all threatened by the drivel, exploitation, and monstrosities of daytime TV talk shows.

One person's trash, though, is another person's gold mine. Sure, I some-times hate these shows. What's not to hate? They can be among the most shrill, mean, embarrassing, fingernails-on-the-blackboard, one-note, point-less jabber. But I can't help it, I love them just the same. In part, I love them because they are so peculiar, so American, filled with fun stuff like "relationship experts" (who are not actually required to have any creden-tialed expertise; it's almost enough just to declare "I'm a people person") and huge emotions, and hosts who wear their hypocrisies on their tailored sleeves, shedding tears for the people whose secrets they extract for profit while attacking them for revealing secrets on national television, riling up their guests and then scolding them for being so malicious. Silly as they can be, daytime TV talk shows are filled with information about the American environment in which they take root, in which expertise and authenticity and rationality are increasingly problematic, and in which the lines between public and private are shifting so strangely. And they embody that infor-mation with Barnumesque gusto. I like what talk shows make us think about.

But there's more to my affinity. Although you might not know it from looking at me, and although in many ways my behaviors and tastes are embarrassingly conventional—a good story, a comfortable pair of jeans, hugs—I identify with the misfits, monsters, trash, and perverts. From that perspective, talk shows look rather different. If you are lesbian, bisexual, gay, or transgendered, watching daytime TV talk shows is pretty spooky. (Indeed, it must be unnerving and exciting for pretty much anyone whose behavior or identity does not conform to the dominant conventions of good-ness, decency, and normality.) While you might get a few minutes on na-tional news every once in a while, or a spot on a sitcom looking normal as can be, almost everywhere else in media culture you are either unwelcome, written by somebody else, or heavily edited.

On television talk shows, you are more than welcome. You are begged and coached and asked to tell, tell, tell, in an absurd, hyper enactment of what Michel Foucault called the "incitement to discourse," that incessant modern demand that we voice every this-and-that of sexuality.[5] Here you are testifying, dating, getting laughs, being made over, screaming, performing, crying, not just talking but talking back, and you are doing these things in front of millions of people. The last few years have seen shows on "lipstick lesbians," gay teens, gay cops, lesbian cops, cross-dressing hookers, transsexual call girls, gay and lesbian gang members, straight go-go dancers pretending to be gay, people who want their relatives to stop cross-dressing, lesbian and gay comedians, gay people in love with straight ones, women who love gay men, same-sex marriage, drag queen makeovers, drag kings, same-sex sexual harassment, homophobia, lesbian mothers, gay twins, gay beauty pageants, transsexual beauty pageants, people who are fired for not being gay, gay men reuniting with their high school sweethearts, bisexual teens, bisexual couples, bisexuals in general, gays in the military, same-sex crushes, hermaphrodites, boys who want to be girls, female-to-male transsexuals, male-to-female transsexuals and their boyfriends, and gay talk shows—to mention just a few. Watching all this, be it tap-dancing drag queens or married gay bodybuilders or self-possessed bisexual teenagers, I sometimes get choked up. For people whose life experience is so heavily tilted toward invisibility, whose nonconformity, even when it looks very much like conformity, discredits them and disenfranchises them, daytime TV talk shows are a big shot of visibility and media accreditation. It looks, for a moment, like you own this place.

Indeed, listening closely to the perspectives and experiences of sex and gender nonconformists—people who live, in one way or another, outside the boundaries of heterosexual norms and gender conventions—sheds a different kind of light on talk shows.[6] Dangers begin to look like opportunities, spotlights start to feel like they're burning your flesh. Exploiting the need for visibility and voice, talk shows provide them, in distorted but real, hollow but gratifying, ways. They have much to tell about those needs and those contradictions, about the weird and changing public sphere in which people are talking. Just as important for my purposes, talk shows shed a different kind of light on sex and gender conformity. They are spots not only of visibility but of the subsequent redrawing of the lines between the normal and the abnormal. They are, in a very real sense, battlegrounds over what sexuality and gender can be in this country: in them we can see most clearly the kinds of strategies, casualties, and wounds involved, and we can think most clearly about what winning these kinds of battles might really mean. These battles over media space allow us to get a grip on the ways sex and gender conformity is filtered through the daily interactions between commercial cultural industries and those making their lives within and around media culture. I watch talk shows for a laugh and a jolt of recognition, but also for what they can tell me about a society that funnels such large questions—indeed, that funnels entire *populations* nearly wholesale—into the small, loopy spectacle of daytime talk.

Defecating in public

It is a long, twisted road that takes us toward insight, but the controversy over the talk show genre in general—a genre itself largely composed of controversy and conflict—is a promising first step. On the one side, cultural critics, both popular and scholarly, point adamantly toward the dangers of exploitation, voyeurism, pseudotherapy, and the "defining down" of deviance, in which the strange and unacceptable are made to seem ordinary and fine. On the other side, defenders both within and outside the television industry argue that talk shows are democracy at work—flawed democracy but democracy nonetheless—giving voice to the socially marginalized and ordinary folks, providing rowdy commonsense counterpoints to elite authority in mass-mediated culture. Beneath each position, and in the space between them, is a piece of the puzzle with which this book is playing.

The list of dangers is well worth considering. There is, to begin with, concern for the people who go on the shows, who are offered and accept a deal with the devil. They are manipulated, sometimes lied to, seduced, used, and discarded; pick 'em up in a limo, producers joke, send 'em home in a cab. They are sometimes set up and surprised—"ambushed," as critics like to call it—which can be extremely damaging, even to the point of triggering lawsuits and murderous impulses, as in the case of Scott Amedure, who revealed his secret crush for Jonathan Schmitz on a never-aired *Jenny Jones Show,* including his fantasy of tying Schmitz up in a hammock and spraying him with whipped cream and champagne. Amedure was murdered several days later by Schmitz, who, after receiving an anonymous love note, went to his admirer's trailer home near Detroit and shot him at close range with a 12-gauge shotgun. Schmitz complained that the show had set him up to be humiliated. "There was no ambush," a spokeswoman for *Jenny Jones* owner Warner Brothers said; "that's not our style." Amedure, Schmitz proclaimed, had "fucked me on national TV."[7]

Although most survive without bodily harm, guests often do considerable damage to themselves and others. They are offered airfare and a hotel room in New York, Los Angeles, or Chicago, a bit of television exposure, a shot of attention and a microphone, some free "therapy." In exchange, guests publicly air their relationship troubles, deep secrets, and intimate life experiences, usually in the manners most likely to grab ratings: exaggerated, loud, simplified, and so on. Even more disturbing, perhaps, it is those who typically do not feel entitled to speak, or who cannot afford or imagine therapy, who are most vulnerable to the seduction of television. This is, critics suggest, not a great deal for the guests, since telling problems and secrets in front of millions of people is a poor substitute for actually working them out. Not to mention, critics often add, a bit undignified. "Therapy is not a spectator sport," says sociologist and talk show critic-at-large Vicki Abt. Telling secrets on television is "like defecating in public." [8]

While it is worth challenging the equation of talking and defecating, all this, we will see, is basically the case. But it is also the easy part: talk shows are show business, and it is their mission to exploit. They commodify and use talkers to build an entertainment product, which is then used to attract audiences, who then are sold to advertisers, which results in a profit for the producers. Exploitation thus ought to be the starting point for analysis and not, as it so often is, its conclusion. The puzzling thing is not the logic of commercial television, which is well documented, well understood, and extremely powerful, but why so many people, many of them fully aware of what's expected of them on a talk show, make the deal.

Yet it is not really the guests, generally dismissed as dysfunctional losers on display, who concern talk show critics most centrally. It is the audience, either innocent or drawn in by appeals to their most base interests, that preoccupies critics the most. For some, the problem is the model of problem solving offered. Psychologists Jeanne Heaton and Nona Wilson argue in *Tuning in Trouble,* for instance, that talk shows provide "bad lessons in mental health," offer "bad advice and no resolutions for problems," and wind up "reinforcing stereotypes rather than defusing them." "Credible therapeutic practice aimed at catharsis or confrontation," they point out, "is quite different from the bastardized Talk TV version." Indeed, they suggest that viewers avoid "the temptation to apply other people's problems or solutions to your own life," avoid using "the shows as a model for how to communicate" or as tools for diagnosing friends and relatives, and so on. [9] The advice is sound, if a bit elementary: talk shows are not a smart place to look for either therapy or problem solving.

Beyond the worry that audiences will adopt therapeutic technique from daytime talk, critics are even more troubled by the general social effects of talk shows. Here and there, a critic from the Left, such as Jill Nelson writing in *The Nation,* assails the casting of "a few pathological individuals" as representatives of a population, distracting from social, political, and economic conditions in favor of stereotypes such as "stupid, sex-addicted, dependent, baby-makers, with an occasional castrating bitch thrown in" (women of all colors) and "violent predators out to get you with their penis, their gun, or both" (young black men).[10] More commonly, though, critics make the related argument that talk shows indulge voyeuristic tendencies that, while perhaps offering the opportunity to feel superior, are ugly. *"Exploitation, voyeurism, peeping Toms, freak shows,* all come to mind in attempting to characterize these happenings," write Vicki Abt and Mel Seesholtz, for instance.[11] "For the audience," *Washington Post* reporter Howard Kurtz adds in *Hot Air,* "watching the cavalcade of deviant and dysfunctional types may serve as a kind of group therapy, a communal exercise in national voyeurism."[12] These "fairground-style freak shows" are just a modern-day version of throwing Christians to the lions, psychologists Heaton and Wilson assert: in place of Christians we have "the emotionally wounded or the socially outcast," in place of lions are "psychic demons," in place of blood there is psychological damage, in place of crowds yelling "Kill, kill, kill!" we have crowds yelling "Why don't you cut his balls off?"[13] Even if such events serve to unite the Romans among us, offering what Neal Gabler calls "the reassurance of our superiority over the guests and over the programs themselves,"[14] they do so at significant costs. "Perhaps the sight of so many people with revolting problems makes some folks feel better about their own rather humdrum lives," Kurtz argues, but "we become desensitized by the endless freak show."[15] Talk shows are pruriently addictive, the argument goes, like rubbernecking at car wrecks: daytime talk shows are to public information what pornography is to sexual intimacy.

I will have more to say about the ceaseless characterization of talk shows as "freak shows," but for now it is enough to note that the lines are drawn so starkly: between Christians and Romans, between "deviant and dysfunctional types" and "some folks," the guests and "us," between "the fringes of society, those who break rules" and "law-abiding, privacy-loving, ordinary people who have had reasonably happy childhoods and are satisfied with their lives." These are important lines, and plainly political ones, and the ones critics most fiercely act to protect. And as one who falls both within and outside the lines, I find the confidence with which critics draw them in need of as much careful consideration as the genre's alarming exploitations.

In fact, the lines of difference and normality are the centerpiece of the arguments against talk shows: talk shows, critics repeat over and over, redefine deviance and abnormality, and this is not a good thing. "The lines between what is bizarre and alarming and what is typical and inconsequential are blurred," point out psychologists Heaton and Wilson; talk shows "exaggerate abnormality" by suggesting that "certain problems are more common than they are, thus exaggerating their frequency," and by embellishing "the symptoms and outcomes of problems, thus exaggerating their consequences." Viewers are left with images of "drag queens getting makeovers and transsexuals' surprising transformations blended together with normal adolescent development."[16] Kurtz, himself a regular on political talk shows, is a little less clinical in his assessment: "This is more than just harmless diversion. It is, all too often, a televised exercise in defining deviancy down. By parading the sickest, the weirdest, the most painfully afflicted before an audience of millions, these shows bombard us with sleaze to the point of numbness. The abnormal becomes ordinary, the pathetic merely another pause in our daily channel surfing."[17]

This boundary between the normal and the abnormal, tightly linked to those between decent and vulgar, sacred and profane, healthy and unhealthy, and moral and immoral, is the key not only for critics in journalism, but for those in politics as well. "This is the world turned upside down," former secretary of education William Bennett complained of daytime talk.[18] "We've forgotten that civilization depends on keeping some of this stuff under wraps."[19] As a reminder, Bennett offered his own tamer, secularized version of the Mother Teresa versus the freaks argument: this place is owned by perverts, and decent people must retrieve it. Launching a campaign to "clean up" the "cultural rot" of daytime TV, pressuring advertisers to withdraw from shows that "parade perversity into our living rooms,"[20] Bennett, with Connecticut senator Joseph Lieberman and the public-interest group Empower America, emphasized the degenerative moral impact of talk shows, which "increasingly make the abnormal normal, and set up the most perverse role models for our children and adults." The entertainment industry, Lieberman told a press conference, is "degrading our culture and ultimately threatening our children's future," through both "sexual deviancy" and "constant hyperemotional confrontations." "The reality is that these shows are at the, at the front lines," he continued, echoing the *Post*'s Kurtz nearly word for word, "of distorting our perceptions of what is normal and acceptable," adding to "the tendency of our country to define deviancy down."[21] Our living rooms, our children, our normality, all under threat.

The interesting thing here is not just that talk shows are seen as a threat to norms and normality—as we will see, they are indeed just that, and the

Figure 1 Maps to talk show guests' homes.
Drawing by John O'Brien; © 1996
The New Yorker Magazine, Inc.

Figure 2 Congressionally mandated themes for the daytime talk shows. Drawing by Crawford; © 1996 The New Yorker Magazine, Inc.

fight is often between those who think this is a good thing and those who think it is not—but just who threatens whom here, who is "us" and who is "them." Sexual nonconformists are only the most obvious specter. Consider the common strategy of listing topics to demonstrate the degraded status of talk shows: "Maury Povich has done women who leave husbands for other women, student-teacher affairs, and a woman who says she was gang-raped at fourteen. Geraldo Rivera has done transsexuals and their families, teen prostitutes, mud-wrestling women, swinging sexual suicide, power dykes, girls impregnated by their stepfathers, serial killers, kids who kill, and battered women who kill."[22] One need not deny the prurience and sensationalism of talk shows to see the connections being made by critics. Serial killers and bisexual women, transsexuals and mud wrestlers, dykes and battered women: "the sickest, the weirdest, the most painfully afflicted." New York *Daily News* columnist Linda Stasi, not shy about telling us what she really thinks, provides a further, complicating hint of the threatening categories: talk shows, she says, have become "a vast, scary wasteland where the dregs of society—sociopaths, perverts, uneducated lazy scum who abuse their children and sleep with anyone who'll have them—become stars for fifteen minutes."[23] That list is a typical and fascinating mix: perverts and those lacking education, lazy people and people who have a lot of sex. Kurtz backs up Stasi, for instance, asserting that, "after all, middle-class folks who work hard and raise their children in a reasonable fashion don't get invited on *Donahue* or *Geraldo*. They do not exist on daytime television. Instead, we are bombarded with negative images of the sort of losers most of us would avoid at the local supermarket."[24]

The "dregs of society" argument, in fact, almost always lumps together indecency, sexual difference, lack of education, and social class—though class is typically coded as "uneducated" or "inarticulate," or, when linked to race, as "trash" or "urban." Take this passage from a book on talk shows and mental health: "Pulitzer Prize–winning author David Halberstam used to call *Donahue* a 'televised Ph.D. course.' Now he says that *Donahue* has 'lost its soul.' Likewise, Art Buchwald used to receive regular invitations to talk about his essays and books on *Donahue*. But now 'Buchwald claims he can't get an invitation . . . unless he gets a sex-change operation.' "[25] You used to be able to get an education, listening to men like Halberstam and Buchwald; now, talk shows have replaced educated men with transsexuals, resulting in the loss of the talk show soul. The examples continue, but after even just a taste the equations start to come clear: uneducated is lazy is sex-loving is sexually perverted is non-middle-class is soulless losers.

Puzzle pieces begin to emerge from these criticisms. How exactly do poverty and lack of education, sex and gender nonconformity, and race come to be lumped together and condemned as monstrosities? What are we to make of these equations? Are they the result of exploitative programming that scripts and markets weird people most of "us" wouldn't talk to in a supermarket, selling the middle-class audience its own superiority? Are they the result of willful distortions by guardians of middle-class morality and culture, part and parcel of the ongoing "culture wars" in the United States? Are they, as defenders of the genre suggest, the result of a democratization process that threatens those who are used to the privilege of owning and defining public discourse?

The chatter of the dispossessed

Audiences and participants sit in a circular form and—this is the only TV format in which this happens—speak out, sometimes without being called on. They yell at each other, disagree with experts, and come to no authoritative conclusions. There is something exhilarating about watching people who are usually invisible—because of class, race, gender, status—having their say and, often, being wholly disrespectful of their "betters."

PROFESSOR ELAYNE RAPPING[26]

Audience discussion programs adopt an anti-elitist position which implicitly draws on . . . alternative epistemological traditions, offering a revaluation of the life-world, repudiating criticisms of the ordinary person as incompetent or ignorant, questioning the deference traditionally due to experts through their separation from the life-world and their incorporation into the system, and asserting instead the worth of the "common man."

PROFESSORS SONIA LIVINGSTONE AND PETER LUNT[27]

As long as they speak the King's English, we say it's OK. But then you get someone who isn't wealthy, who doesn't have title or position, and they come on and talk about something that's important to them—all of a sudden we call that trash.

TALK SHOW HOST JERRY SPRINGER[28]

Just as exploitation is an obvious component of talk shows, so is democratization. Where critics choose one Greco-Roman analogy, defenders tout another: in place of the Christian-eating spectacle, they see, although not always so simply, a democratic forum. Where critics see "freaks" and "trash," defenders see "have-nots" and "common people." These are important counterpoints, and raise important questions suppressed by critics, of voice, visibility, and inclusion. But this line of thinking, too, on its own tends to run in an unhelpful direction, simplifying the conditions of visibility, the distortions of voice, and the restrictions on inclusion that daytime talk involves. Just because people are talking back does not mean we are witnessing democratic impulses and effects.

It is easy enough to discern the elitism in criticisms of talk shows, or any other popular genre, and defenders of talk shows from within the industry push up against it with a defense of the masses, painting themselves as both defenders of free speech and friends of the common folk.[29] "I think it's a shame that we've got so many people who claim to talk to God every day," Phil Donahue complained to Larry King, "coming down from the mountain to tell their neighbors what they ought to see."[30] Charles Perez, a young former *Ricki Lake Show* producer who had a short stint as host of his own show, while perhaps not quite as impressed with the tastes of his neighbors, took a similar "the people have chosen" approach to talk. "I put this a lot in the hands of the public," he said. "The same way you have a corner grocer and he should be selling mostly vegetables, but he's selling Hershey candy bars because that's what all the kids on the block want."[31] Talk shows may not be nutritious, but viewers should not be faulted for wanting what they want.

This populist defense of talk shows, familiar from arguments about popular culture in general, is taken many steps beyond the shoulder-shrugging, "it's a free country" line. Talk shows, defenders claim, give voice to common folks and visibility to invisible folks, and it is this characteristic that elicits such hostility. Indeed, Donahue and others assert, the talk show genre was and is a "revolutionary" one. "It's called democracy," Donahue argues, "but [before my program] there were no shows that—every day, let just folks stand up and say what-for. I'm proud of the democracy of the show."[32] Ellen Willis, writing in *The Nation,* makes a similar, although much more complex, point: "Social conservatives have been notably unsuccessful at stemming the democratization of culture, the breakdown of those class, sex and race-bound conventions that once reliably separated high from low, 'news' from 'gossip,' public from unspeakably private, respectable from deviant. Talk shows are a product of this democratization; they let people who have been largely excluded from the public conversation appear on national

TV and talk about their sex lives, their family fights, sometimes their literal dirty laundry. . . . On talk shows, whatever their drawbacks, the proles get to talk."[33] When the proles get the microphone, when the excluded become included, there is always a fight. The nastiness of critics toward talk shows, the argument goes, is simply a veiled anxiety about cultural democratization—and especially about the assertive, rowdy space taken on talk shows by usually silent classes of people. Talk shows "operate at the level of everyday life, where real people live and breathe," Donna Gaines writes. "Bennett's morality squad may see talk shows as carnival freak shows, but all that means is that the shows have the power to drag us statistical outcasts in from the margins."[34] "Do you ever call a Congressman trash?" asks Jerry Springer. "It's a euphemism for trailer park, minorities, space between their teeth. We all know it. They don't want to hear about them, they don't want to see them."[35] Springer argues that he is giving unpopular people "access to the airwaves" ("as if embarrassing them before millions," snorts Howard Kurtz, "were some kind of public service").[36] Princess Di with bulimia is news on *20/20* with Barbara Walters, Yale-educated host Richard Bey complains, but his own show—which, on the day I attended, included a "freeloader" named Rob lying on his back on a spinning "Wheel of Torture" while his dorm-mates poured buckets of paint and baked beans on him—is trash. "They don't think these people deserve to be heard or seen," he suggests, taking a sort of working-person's-hero pose. "Mine is a working class audience. It's very representative of America."[37]

Many academics echo this line of thinking, emphasizing the democratic aspects of the genre. Audience-participation talk shows, Sonia Livingstone and Peter Lunt claim, for instance, "are a forum in which people can speak in their own voice, which . . . is vital for the construction of a gendered or cultural identity."[38] Oprah Winfrey herself, Gloria-Jean Masciarotte suggests in the journal *Genders,* is "a device of identity that organizes new antagonisms in the contemporary formations of democratic struggle."[39] Talk shows "constitute a 'contested space' in which new discursive practices are developed," Paolo Carpignano and his colleagues argue in the journal *Social Text,* "in contrast to the traditional modes of political and ideological representation." "The talk show can be seen as a terrain of struggle of discursive practices. . . . [What] is conceived as a confrontational device becomes an opening for the empowerment of an alternative discursive practice. These discourses don't have to conform to civility nor to the dictates of the general interest. They can be expressed for what they are: particular, regional, one-sided, and for that reason politically alive. . . . The talk show rejects the arrogance of a discourse that defines itself on the basis of its difference from common sense."[40] Talk shows embrace everyday common sense against elite expertise, privileging "the storied life over the expert guest," emphasizing " 'ordinary' experience," and the " 'authentic' voice of the everyday people, or street smarts of the working class."[41] They provide "a space in which ordinary experiences are collected together as grounding for a decision."[42]

Indeed, daytime talk, as a woman-oriented genre, is arguably rooted in social movement–generated changes of the sixties and seventies, especially those pushed by feminism. Defenders point to the genre's predominantly female audience, and in particular to its feminist-inspired reworking of what counts as legitimate public discussion, as evidence that it is a genre of "empowerment." Most significantly, TV talk is built on a radical departure from what has traditionally been seen to belong in the public sphere: drawing on "the personal is political" charge of feminism, talk shows move personal lives to the forefront of public discussion. Their popularity, Carpignano and others argue, are a symptom of "a transformation in the nature of the political," and "the means of expression of these new areas of political struggle are quite different from those of formal politics."[43] Talk shows, such arguments suggest, are politics by other means.

Moreover, such talk show analysts claim, the political effects are empowering for those who have traditionally been defined as outside of public discussion, whose lives were, until recently, kept private by both choice and coercion—in particular, women and sex and gender minorities. Phil Donahue argues, for instance, "these programs cumulatively make a contribution toward the empowerment of women especially";[44] *Village Voice* writer Richard Goldstein points out that talk shows "were the first mass-cultural arena where homosexuals could get beyond polemics and simply justify their love."[45] The same basic claim comes through in the sparse academic literature on TV talk: that talk shows "afford women the political gesture of overcoming their alienation through talking about their particular experience as women in society," promote "an unnatural or perverse sexual identity,"[46] and can be seen as "a celebration of outlaw culture"[47] (a point, of course, on which the critics concur). Daytime TV talk shows are thus "the lever in the dislocation of universal, natural difference," disrupting traditional sex and gender categories. "It is to that epic dislocation in categories and knowledge," Masciarotte claims, "that the talk shows' most recent, combative forms speak."[48]

Previously silenced people speaking in their own voices, spaces for "alternative epistemologies" opening up, common sense battling the politics and ideology of traditional elites, political arenas expanding, "epic dislocations" and rethinking of social categories: these would all seem to be significant, healthy contributions of the talk show genre to democratic practice. Indeed, it would seem, talk shows, even if they aren't exactly good for you, are at least good for us—especially those of us with an investment in social change. Yet even setting aside the tendency to romanticize "the masses" and the near gibberish of claims such as "*The Oprah Winfrey Show* functions as a new bildungsroman that charts the irritant in the system through an endless narrative of discomfort" and so forth,[49] something seems a bit fishy here. If you have ever actually watched a few hours of talk shows, they seem about as much about democracy as *The Price Is Right* is about mathematics. Sniffing around this territory more closely, digging through some of its assumptions, clarifies further where we have to go.

Two claims in particular hide within the defenses of talk shows, even the critical defenses: that talk shows "give voice" and that they operate as some kind of "forum." Pushing at them a little uncovers more interesting questions. It is certainly true that, more than anywhere else on television, talk shows invite people to speak for themselves. But do people on daytime talk really wind up speaking in a voice that they and others recognize as somehow authentically their own? How do the medium and the genre structure the "voices" that come out? What sorts of speaking voices are available, and in what ways are they distorted? How could we even tell a "real" voice from a "false" one? Second, there is the question of the "forum." It is certainly true that talk shows come closer than anywhere else on American television to providing a means for a wide range of people, credentialed but especially not so credentialed, to converse about all sorts of things. But is daytime talk really a forum, a set of conversations? How do the production and programming strategies shape the capacity for discussion, and the content of conversation? If, as Wayne Munson has put it, talk shows are simultaneously spectacle and conversation,[50] what is the relationship here between the circus and the symposium, and what is the political significance of their combination?

It is tempting to choose sides in all of this, and often I do. Depending on my mood, I might be annoyed by the paternalistic moralizing critics and tout defiant perversity, or I might find myself overwhelmed by the willful, wasteful stupidity of TV talk and recommend V-chip brain implants. But I have now gone a different route, guided by the Big Issues running through the talk show debates and by my own gnawing ambivalence, both as scholar and as just a guy.

What critics and defenders, both inside my brain and outside of it, agree upon is that talk shows are consumed with blurring old distinctions (while often reaffirming them), with making differences harder to tell (while often asserting them with ease): the deviant isn't readily distinguished from the regular person, class stereotypes melt into the hard realities on which they rest, what belongs in private suddenly seems to belong in front of everybody, airing dirty laundry looks much like coming clean. Talk shows wreak special havoc with the "public sphere," moving private stuff into a public spotlight, arousing all sorts of questions about what the public sphere can, does, and should look like.[51] In doing so, they mess with the "normal," giving hours of play and often considerable sympathy to stigmatized populations, behaviors, and identities, and at least partly muddying the waters of normality. And since those brought into the public sphere of TV talk are increasingly distant from the white middle-class guests of earlier years, talk shows wind up attaching class difference to the crossing of public/private and normal/abnormal divides. It is around this stirred pot, in which humdrum and freaky, off-limits and common property, high status and low, sane and crazed, all brew together, that the anxious flies swarm. This seething brew, and not just the talk shows themselves, is what is so powerful and intriguing, and it is this brew on which I myself am feeding, using the close study of TV talk to investigate the broader, linked activities of line-drawing between public and private, classy and trashy, normal and abnormal.

I have long been especially interested in how the lines between normal and abnormal sexual beings are drawn and redrawn: the ways those lines restrict me personally, from the question of whom I can touch to the question of where I can work; the dilemmas confronted by social movements trying to gain rights by claiming the mantle of normality, even as they are also celebrating their "queer" difference and criticizing the oppressive constraints imposed by a hetero-as-normal society;[52] the ways sexual categories intersect with others (race, class, gender) with their own hierarchies of natural and defective people, and the permutations of perversion pile up and multiply.[53] The mass media are plainly very central to these processes of sexual meaning-making, and talk shows are hot spots for the processes, and so my attention is driven toward them.

Indeed, many of the key terms of talk show controversy—the themes of health and pathology, of sacred and profane—speak with special force to people who cross or have crossed gender lines, and to people who form same-sex partnerships, who have been deemed ill or immoral for most of recent history, and who have been subject to often brutal forms of medical and religious control. But if talk shows speak to us, they certainly speak with forked tongues. Listening to them means living with the fact that they never quite make sense. On this trip into their country, as I offer a translation of their noisy, eager language into my own, you will see that it turns out to be a dialect filled with the syntax of savage contradiction. With careful listening, an ambivalence about talk shows begins to sound just about right. At the heart of this book, where sexual meaning-making, sexual politics, and the redrawing of key social boundaries meet up, are the *paradoxes of visibility* that talk shows dramatize with such fury: democratization through exploitation, truths wrapped in lies, normalization through freak show. There is in fact no choice here between manipulative spectacle and democratic forum, only the puzzle of a situation in which one cannot exist without the other, and the challenge of seeing clearly what this means for a society at war with its own sexual diversity.

The way in

How do we push our way into this weird world? Other people's ideas have certainly helped pave the road. There is by now much scholarly writing about both the construction of sexuality and gender,[54] and the media representation of sexual minorities.[55] Put simply, from theory and research on sexuality construction, I lift the idea that sexual categories and statuses are under continual negotiation, and the question of when and how these categories and statuses become open to change and challenge. From theory and research on mass media, I take the notion that media representations are part of a more general system of oppression of nonheterosexuals, operating most commonly to justify continued prejudice, violence, and discrimination against lesbian, gay, bisexual, and transgendered people, and the question of when and how media institutions become sites at which oppression can be combated.

"Sexuality is as much a human product as are diets, methods of transportation, systems of etiquette, forms of labor, types of entertainment, processes of production, and modes of oppression," Gayle Rubin wrote fifteen years ago.[56] Although still subject to debate, the premise that sexuality and gender are "socially constructed," rather than simply reflecting categories and beings found in and fixed by nature, has become commonplace in academic analysis since the 1980s.[57] Sexual categories and gender categories, theorists and researchers have persuasively demonstrated, vary dramatically across time and across cultures.[58] Moreover, social scientists have suggested that within any given social structure, sexual attitudes, behaviors, and roles are produced and reproduced through everyday interactions and social "scripts."[59] "Gender is a human invention, like language, kinship, religion, and technology; like them, gender organizes human social life in culturally patterned ways," as Judith Lorber put it recently.[60]

This general framework has yielded an important set of questions, both intellectual and political. If sexuality is indeed constructed and negotiated through social processes, how exactly do these processes work? Under what conditions do sexual categories and meanings change? If we wanted to intervene in this process, where and how might we go about it? While the first question has been effectively approached, the latter two have not been terribly well answered, mainly because sexuality has typically been analyzed in abstraction from its institutional and organizational carriers. Studies of the construction of sexuality only rarely look in detail at the opportunities and constraints associated with *particular institutional settings,* proceeding instead as if sexual categories and meanings exist in free-floating "discourse";[61] the everyday, practical activities through which sexual meanings are produced and reproduced tend to fade into the background.

Sociologists of culture, however, have long argued that cultural attitudes and cultural content cannot be understood divorced from the organizational contexts in which they are produced.[62] One cannot understand the homogenization of much television culture, for example, without understanding the political economy of television entertainment production; one cannot understand the tip of television news toward the "official story" without understanding the norms and routines of journalists.[63] The same goes for public discourse on sexuality and gender: in order to understand how sex and gender categories, and conformity to those categories, are put together, it helps a good deal to look at the concrete, structured settings where they are being negotiated. Daytime TV talk shows, with their unusual and tremendous attention to sex and gender nonconformity, are rich, juicy places to look at the link between cultural production and sexual meanings.

Partly because they are attentive to the relationship between institutional practice and cultural discourse, studies of commercial media's roles in reproducing and justifying antigay prejudice have also lent a helpful, rattling hand here. Taking off with Vito Russo's ground-breaking *The Celluloid Closet,* in fact, studies of the portrayals of gay men and lesbians in film and television have soundly demonstrated how homosexual lives have been subject to systematic exclusion and stereotyping as victims and villains, how "aspects of gay and lesbian identity, sexuality, and community that are not compatible or that too directly challenge the heterosexual regime are excluded" from mainstream television, how television has produced "stereotypical conceptualizations of AIDS that vilify gays and legitimate homophobia," how even "positive" portrayals of lesbians "serve as mechanisms to perpetuate hetero/sexism." At best, Larry Gross suggests of network television, the constraints of "public pressure and advertiser timidity" lead to "well-meaning approaches that plead for tolerance" but require "complete asexuality."[64]

These studies have congealed into conventional, often sacred-cow ways of thinking about media visibility that are now begging for challenge. Vito Russo's "invisibility is the great enemy," for instance, is still the going line in lesbian and gay media activism: more exposure is the answer.[65] Yet at a time when a major sitcom character and the lesbian playing her have come out amidst a coterie of gay and lesbian supporting characters, when a drag queen has her own talk show on VH-1, when big movie stars no longer see gay roles as career poison, when one soap opera has had a transsexual storyline and another, thrillingly, a gay talk show–murder story line, it may no longer be enough to think so simply about invisibility and stereotyping. With their extraordinary interest in gay, lesbian, bisexual, and transgender topics (which predates the recent miniexplosion of gay visibility in commercial media by two decades), talk shows are a fabulous chance to see what happens when lesbian, gay, bisexual, and transgender people *are* highly visible subjects in a commercial cultural arena.

The most arresting challenge comes not just from the exceptional visibility daytime television brings to sex and gender nonconformity, but even more from the potential *agency* of gay men, lesbians, bisexuals, and transgendered people within the genre. "Gays have always been visible," after all, Russo argued in the afterword to the revised edition of *The Celluloid Closet.* "It's *how* they've been visible that has remained offensive for almost a century."[66] Russo was right: until very recently, lesbians and gay men had little input into our own representation. Almost without exception, the literature on homosexuality and the media has therefore treated the process of representation as one-sided. Larry Gross captures this approach very well.

> *Representation in the mediated "reality" of our mass culture is in itself*
> *power; certainly it is the case that nonrepresentation maintains the*
> *powerless status of groups that do not possess significant material or*
> *political power bases. Those who are the bottom of the various hierar-*
> *chies will be kept in their place in part through their relative invisibil-*
> *ity; this is a form of symbolic annihilation. When groups or perspec-*
> *tives do attain visibility, the manner of that representation will itself*
> *reflect the biases and interests of those elites who define the public*
> *agenda. And those elites are mostly white, mostly middle-aged, mostly*
> *male, mostly middle- and upper-middle class, and (at least in public)*
> *entirely heterosexual.*[67]

They annihilate us, or deform us, because it serves them well—and because
they can.

It is not so much that this perspective is wrong, but that it sidesteps some
of the most telling complexities. Missing from these analyses of lesbian and
gay media representation is precisely what is interesting about talk shows:
what happens to media representations of nonconforming sexualities when
lesbians and gay men are actively invited to participate, to "play themselves"
rather than be portrayed by others, to refute stereotypes rather than simply
watch them on the screen? That is the twist talk shows provide. They allow
us to witness tightly linked, media-generated battles over sexual norms and
morality—struggles themselves closely tied to class cultural and public-
private divisions—in which transgender, lesbian, gay, and bisexual people
are vigorous, visible, sometimes agile, participants. They mess up our thinking about the difficulties and delights of becoming visible—and, in a more
general sense, about the political benefits and dilemmas of cultural representation. And as the dust settles, they can clear up our thinking.

My takes on other people's ideas have planted not only these intellectual
guideposts but also methodological ones, leading me to a wide range of
places to dig for the information that feeds this book. The charge that discourse and institutional practice are not separable phenomena, for instance,
prompted me to study the practices of talk show producers, organizations,
and guests alongside the thematic, narrative, and representational content
of the programs. Thus I wound up in studios, where I sat in the audience
at least once in most of the New York–based programs, watching the production of the shows from that perspective; in offices and restaurants in
New York and Los Angeles, where I interviewed production staff; in cafes
and in people's homes in New York, Washington, Boston, San Francisco,

and Los Angeles, and on the phone to smaller towns, where I interviewed people who had appeared as talk show guests. The details are all in the appendix, but here are the vitals: I interviewed a total of twenty production staff and forty-four guests. (In an ironic, if unsurprising, reversal of their daily routine, almost all of the production staff spoke on the condition that they not be identified, and I therefore sometimes use pseudonyms in the discussion. Almost all of the former guests spoke on the record.) Taken together, these interviews cover experiences on just about every topic-driven daytime talk show that has had a life: *Bertice Berry, Richard Bey, Carnie, Donahue, Gordon Elliott, Gabrielle, Mo Gaffney, Geraldo, Jenny Jones, Ricki Lake, Leeza, Oprah, The Other Side, Charles Perez, Maury Povich, Jane Pratt, Sally Jessy Raphael, Joan Rivers, Rolonda, Jerry Springer, Tempestt, Mark Walberg, Jane Whitney,* and *Montel Williams.*

At the same time, I collected all the available transcripts in which lesbian, gay, bisexual, and gender-crossing subjects made a significant appearance, for the years 1984–86 and 1994–95; with the assistance of interview subjects, the Gay and Lesbian Alliance against Defamation, and my own VCR, I collected as many videotapes on these subjects as I could get my hands on. Although not all programs are transcribed, the sample of more than 160 transcripts includes *Bertice Berry, Donahue, Geraldo, Jenny Jones, Oprah, Maury Povich, Susan Powter, Dennis Prager, Sally Jessy Raphael, Rolonda, Jerry Springer, Jane Whitney,* and *Montel Williams.* The 100-odd hours of videos include most from that list, along with *Richard Bey, Danny Bonaduce, Carnie, Gordon Elliott, Gabrielle, Jenny Jones, Ricki Lake, Leeza, Marilu, The Other Side, Charles Perez, Jane Pratt, Joan Rivers, Tempestt,* and *Mark Walberg.* The transcripts were coded on a number of key dimensions—guest composition, program topic, thematic content, and so on—from which an outline of talk show content began to emerge; those outlines were then filled in with close readings of all of the transcripts and videos.

I swamped myself with more than enough data about talk show production and content, and much of the book teases out connections between these two strands of research: how producers' needs for both spontaneity and predictability lead to contradictions in the sexual politics of talk show programming, how some guests covertly strategize to change the framing of shows in which they are being used, and so on. But linking talk show content to institutional practices still leaves an important set of actors out of the loop: audiences and viewers who, as much recent work on "cultural reception" has demonstrated, encounter cultural products with their own practices and interpretive lenses, often shaped by their location in the matrix of social hierarchies.[68] The insufficiency of assertions about content is illustrated nicely in the debate over talk shows, in which critics and defenders alike assert that talk shows have this or that effect on viewers, or that viewers are getting such and such from them, but never actually *talk* to the people who are allegedly affected.

With that in mind, and backed also by my periodic participant-observation among talk show audiences, I facilitated thirteen group discussions with regular talk show viewers (a total of about seventy-five people). The first nine, conducted in suburban New Jersey, were with heterosexually identified viewers; some groups were mixed, and others were organized according to educational background and/or gender. The next three, which met in Manhattan, were with lesbians and gay men (one group of lesbians, one of gay men, and one mixed men and women). I also visited the Manhattan Gender Network, a transgender organization, and spoke with the group's members about their understandings of television talk shows. There are limits on this information, for sure: nearly all participants were middle-class, and the lesbian and gay viewers were all urban and mostly highly educated. Still, much of what I heard allows me to check the unanchored contentions running through the talk show debates, bouncing the content of the programming off the way viewers think about talk shows, and audience practices and thoughts off producers' routines and claims.

What has emerged from all this watching, reading, questioning, listening, and participating is the curious story of how talk shows and sex and gender nonconformity interact, how gay, lesbian, bisexual, and transgender people make their ways through the genre as subjects and objects, how what seems to be, and often is, a world of goofy lightness turns out to be heavily enmeshed in complicated, contradictory processes of social change. For now, a brief preview. Chapters 2 and 3 offer both a critical grounding in the history and production practices of television talk shows and important evidence of the complex, crisscrossing tracks on which queer visibility rides. Chapter 2 traces the history of TV talk, and the subhistory of sex and gender minorities within them, demonstrating that the genre is built on an awkward combination of class cultures; thus the visibility of lesbian, gay, transgender, and bisexual people is always shaped by the class friction that inheres in daytime TV talk. Chapter 3 takes up the vexed questions of truth and reality on talk shows, and in the process exposes the ins and outs of TV talk production: producers simultaneously pursue big moments of truth and revelation, and scramble, often to the exclusion of anything recognizably "real" or "true," to control the direction of a show; performance and dishonesty are built into the production of talk television, yet the shows are shot through with jarring breakthrough moments. Sex and gender nonconformity topics ride this wave, largely by fitting into a rhetoric of truth telling ("be true to yourself") which dovetails with both producers' needs and the coming-out strategy of bisexual, gay, lesbian, and transgender movements.

The next chapters move more explicitly onto political tracks. Chapter 4 wanders through the struggles over sexual morality playing out on talk shows, and especially the fate of the political and moral right on the shows. The shows, loosely guided by a combination of liberal, therapeutic, and bottom-line ideologies, wind up for the most part turning the tables on the antigay right, so that the bigots become the freaks; the result is an unusual, conditional, and unstable acceptance of gay and lesbian, and to a much lesser degree transgender and bisexual, people. Chapter 5 turns to the pulling apart and putting together of sex and gender categories, which are both a source of oppression and a resource for empowerment. Talk shows make a habit of raising the issue of "telling the difference" (between gay and straight, male and female), encouraged by their production needs both to raise the possibility that such differences are spurious and to then close down that possibility in a variety of ways; yet the issue is raised more often, and more frequent opportunities are given to talking "monsters" or "freaks" who defy categorization, than anywhere else in media culture.

Chapter 6 watches the disparate ways political battles are encouraged and reworked by TV talk: the often-successful attempts by activist guests to gain some control over the production process; the exacerbation of internal tensions within lesbian, gay, transgender, and bisexual political organizing, in particular the sharpening of lines between those pursuing "mainstream" assimilation and those emphasizing "queer" difference; and the amplification of larger battles over the lines between public and private, into which sex and gender nonconformists, often interpreted as "flaunting" on talk shows, are swallowed. In chapter 7, I bring together these funny dilemmas, ripe and sometimes rotten, squeezing out their implications for the important, dangerous, and necessary changes in the cultural representation of sex and gender differences.

But that is the end, where my mind left me after countless hours devoted to the somewhat unlikely, dangerously cold-inducing task of talk show immersion. As host, it seems only fair to start by telling you, in a nutshell, what I really think of talk shows. As gayman, I think they're a wretched little place, emptied of so much wisdom and filled, thank God, with inadvertent camp, but they're the place most enthusiastically afforded us—a measure of our cultural value. We are taking, and are being given, much more public media space now, but only because talk shows forged a path in there, and we had best understand what we can from the wretched little space where we were once honored guests. As scholarman, I think they're rich and interesting, like a funny, lively, slightly frightening room in a museum: dwell in them for a bit, think about their significance from a bunch of different angles, and you come out knowing more about the world, this current one, in which so much of how people see and feel themselves oozes into shape inside the sticky, narrow walls of commerce. Scholarman and gayman meet, for sure, in their common desire for a collective life in which, on a good day, people really take care of one another, and laugh; but it is really the restless coexistence of the two, one measured and the other lacking the luxury of distance, one concerned with culture in general and the other just trying to survive intact within it, that juices up this book. Talk shows are filled with such odd couplings, packed with paradox, with double-edged swords, with painful pleasures and vapid depths and normal perverts. This book cavorts on the tips of those swords.

2 THE MONSTER WITH TWO HEADS

The wonderful Two-Headed Girl is still on Exhibition in New England. She sings duets by herself and she has a great advantage over the rest of her sex, for she never has to stop talking to eat, and when she is not eating she keeps both tongues going at once. She has a lover and the lover is in a quandary, because at one and the same moment she accepted him with one mouth and rejected him with the other. Now is she her own sister? Is she twins? Or having but one body (and consequently one heart) is she strictly but one person? Does she expect to have one vote or two? Has she the same opinion as herself on all subjects, or does she differ sometimes? Would she feel insulted if she came to spit in her own face?

BOSTON NEWSPAPER, NINETEENTH CENTURY[1]

Sometimes I watch talk shows with the sound off, and I pump up the volume on Chick Corea, or Mozart, or Joni Mitchell, thrilling to the class clash. Strings move delicately in and around each other, or the piano goes places I can't even understand, or Joni poetically admonishes herself for old-fashioned longings, and on the screen people suddenly pop out of their seats, coming at each other with chests thrust forward, mouths wide open in silent, monstrous screams. Sometimes they are big people, fat, and sometimes their teeth are bad. My teeth are well dentisted, I avoid potato chips and stick to frozen yogurt, and am sure to punish fatty transgressions with a trip to the gym where, of course, I see again, from my moving perch on the tread-mill, the silent screamers on the TV monitors, drowned out by the hip-hop in my headphones.

Trailer-park trash and ghetto kids, one talk show producer told me, that's our joke about the guests we get. Very little in that remark was undisturbing: not the notion that the human-garbage analogy makes any sense, nor the idea that poverty and disposability are related, nor the racial coding, in which trailer-park stands for "poor white" and ghetto stands for "poor black," nor the image of producers laughing all the way to the bank, heads thrown back, as they take down eager messages from people living on not very much. Yet while I can certainly get all superior about it, I knew what the producer meant. We live in the same America, and we speak the same language of class—not class in any strict sociological sense, but we at least roughly know what poor and uneducated, or suburban middle-class, or highly educated and quite well off, look like and sound like.

It is certainly true that, over the past few years, the look and sound of daytime talk TV has gotten increasingly poor, white, and rural and poor, black or Latino, young, and urban. But that's not entirely the case. Flipping the channel, I might get the urge for a different soundtrack if I happened to stumble onto, say, the Los Angeles-based *Leeza,* hosted by squeaky clean, bright-toothed *Entertainment Tonight* veteran Leeza Gibbons. Everyone there looks a lot like Leeza, like they've just finished shopping at the Beverly Center and have stopped by to chat a bit before heading back to the Food Court. The host, the guests, the audience, everyone looks like they smell good. ("They look beautiful and they're all beautifully dressed, they're in sports jackets and they look pretty and they look good," a former audience coordinator for the show told me. "She pays for that. That costs a lot of money." On another show, *Marilu,* he said, they sometimes paid models $150 for up to two hours to sit in the audience.) Watching these folks, I long for someone in the audience—a young black woman, maybe, in sunglasses and a jogging suit—to stand up and point at people and slice through the plastic, maybe even using what my friend Jimmy once pointed out is an all-purpose *Ricki* or *Jenny Jones* applause line: "Girl, you got to get some self-respect."

In fact, the talk show genre has always operated as an oddball combination of middle-class coffee-klatch propriety and rationality and working-class irreverence and emotional directness. Talk shows, in a general sense, stretch back to earlier public traditions emerging from different, and sometimes opposed, class cultures, and they still operate with the awkward tension between sensation and conversation growing from these roots. Propriety, of course, is not a middle-class property and working-class and underclass people certainly do not own irreverence and emotion, but the talk show genre is fashioned from particular cultural pieces historically associated with different classes: relatively sober, deliberative, "polite" middle-class forms of participating in and presenting public culture embodied in literary circles and the lyceum, for instance, and irreverent, wild, predominantly lower-class public leisures such as the carnival, the cabaret, the tabloid, and the nineteenth-century theater.[2] That history and the talk show's status as a commercial genre aimed at women are a crucial backdrop to the story of sex and gender nonconformity on daytime talk.

Yet, while those tapping talk show history always note the obvious connection to female audiences and women's "empowerment," its intertwined class cultures are generally ignored. Instead, the story is told as a morality tale, going something like this. In 1967, Phil Donahue removed the desk from the *Tonight Show*-style talk show, accidentally discovered that the women in his audience had great questions, and took his microphone into the audience. (One day during a station break, the story goes, a conversation took off between an audience member and a guest, Noxzema model Gunilla Knudsen, famous for saying the ad line "Take it off, take it all off." When the show went back on the air, the woman from the audience was on stage braiding Ms. Knudsen's hair. "The response was electric," write Jeanne Heaton and Nona Wilson. "From that moment on the audience was an integral part of the show's format. Talk TV would never be the same. Like so many others in America, the women watching finally had a place in the conversation, and they were determined to be heard."[3]) Donahue became king of daytime.

He was a good king, allowing women to speak and bringing topics into public view that had previously been considered unfit for public discussion. Women, still largely excluded from the public sphere, were given voice. (*Donahue* provided "useful information and dialogue that had been largely unavailable to housebound women. It afforded them the opportunity to voice their opinions about everything from politics to sex, and even the politics of sex."[4] Or, as Gloria Steinem herself said, oddly implying a link between intelligence and nighttime, "Donahue really understood that women in the daytime are smart, and he put the full range of subjects, from foreign policy to safety in the home, you know, on a time slot that had previously been treated as it if were only for, as someone once put it to me, mental defectives with curlers in their hair. And he always said, too, that if he did his job really well, that the next big talk show host would be a black woman."[5]) He reigned for nearly two decades, largely by bringing social conflicts to the stage, until 1986 when black woman Oprah Winfrey joined him nationally and then surpassed him, matching his cognitive style with her therapeutic one. ("Phil was driven to uncover and explore. Oprah came to share and understand," say Heaton and Wilson.[6] "We used to say people watch Phil to think," a television producer from this period told me, "and they watch Oprah to feel.")

With talk shows inexpensive to produce and now proven popular and profitable, others joined in, and the timeworn mantle of sensationalism, reborn in Phil's conflict-and-taboo strategy and Oprah's personal-and-taboo one, was taken up by new shows such as *Sally Jessy Raphael* and *Geraldo*. And so, the tale continues, the bad began to drive out the good. So began the era of mothers who hate their daughter's boyfriends, transsexuals and female impersonators, and so on, as serious topics began to be replaced by freak shows and exaggerated emotional displays. ("It appeared that having opened the door to private life," write Heaton and Wilson, "nothing was sacred and everything was up for grabs."[7]) Donahue's "illegitimate children,"[8] as he proudly called them, began to propagate like rabbits. With the growth of cable television in the 1980s, the number of talk shows grew, reaching a high point of nearly thirty syndicated talk shows in the mid-1990s; with such stiff competition for ratings and revenue, the sensationalism on single-topic programs also grew, solidifying in 1994 and 1995, when Ricki Lake and her imitators successfully captured a younger audience with fast-paced, rowdy, "kick him to the curb girlfriend"–style programming. The shows had been finally dumbed down and pumped up, the story goes, so that not only was rational discussion precluded but the pursuit of truth abandoned, in favor of anything, including fraud, that worked. ("There was a growing sense that the shows were ridiculous and that they had covered just about every truth, leaving fakery as the only option to make things wilder," Heaton and Wilson suggest.[9]) In 1996, *Donahue,* the mother of all talk shows, was canceled. Heat, at least for the time being, had replaced light.

Regular folks and Very Special People: Class cultures and public life

It is not so much that this version of history is wrong, but that it misses the important features: the ways in which different class cultures have been continuously competing, represented, and sold, on and through television talk shows. To get hold of this, we need to briefly dig at the roots. Of course, people have been talking to each other in public for a long time—think ancient Greek oratory, think Native American storytelling, think gossip—but here we are looking at a somewhat more specific history of public, participatory culture. While informal public talk of all kinds, particularly the informal talk of women, certainly plays into the development of television talk in the United States, it is the practices of organized, participatory public leisure that provide the heftiest building blocks of the genre. Talk shows, to put it most simply, are built from middle-class traditions of organized rationality-driven discussion and service-oriented presentation, on the one hand, and urban and rural working-class traditions of emotionally driven participation and spectacular mass entertainments, on the other. Those class cultures solidified originally by being defined *against* one another, primarily as middle and upper classes sought to distinguish themselves from those "below" them, with whom, until the late nineteenth century, they had often shared public leisure space. Talk shows, in which these class traditions mix and mutate, have reinstated a strained mix of politely "high" and unruly "low" cultures.

One pile of building blocks, Wayne Munson suggests, was inherited from public-sphere traditions initiated by new European middle classes in the seventeenth century, such as the English coffeehouse, a "salon-like setting for intellectual talk focusing on Enlightenment philosophy and the arts."[10] In the American colonies, the coffeehouse was joined by the philosophical society, the literary circle, and the lyceum (originated as "moral and fraternal" instructional associations aimed at young working men, eventually becoming a "celebrity lecture circuit"), all part of a "public sphere in which the common good could be rationally debated by the new middle class, free from private (market) interests and prior to implementation by the state."[11] Although some of these traditions were geared toward "raising" working people, they shared a basic model of middle-class public talk as the rational, deliberate, often formalized exchange of ideas. This is the model from which *Donahue*-style talk is primarily drawn. We sit together in a familiar room, take an issue or an idea ("homophobia"), and respectfully submit our thoughts for the benefit of those participating and listening ("My son is homosexual and that doesn't mean he's a bad person"); we ask questions ("What has a homosexual ever done to you to cause you to have this kind of hatred?"), we answer questions ("If God wanted homosexuals he would have made all one sex, you know"), we argue. We applaud or withhold applause, but we do not shout out. And whatever we're trying to figure out, we figure it out together, just us folks sitting around talking.

In fact, a sort of "folk wisdom" pervaded one of the earliest participatory media genres, the women's magazine of the early nineteenth century. Magazines such as the *Ladies' Home Journal* constructed a strategic intimacy with female readers at a time when face-to-face local cultures were fast being replaced by national, impersonal ones, in "an early mediated attempt at what the talk show is so often accused of doing: simulating local, interpersonal communication as an antidote to national and corporate institutions." By the turn of the century, women's magazines had effectively commodified both participatory tendencies (through the solicitation of readers' letters, for instance) and "enlightened self-improvement" (albeit in large part by replacing everyday wisdom with the advice of experts, a strategy also picked up by television talk).[12] Even as the possibilities for back-fence and town-meeting talk became more remote, these earlier middle-class models were built into the commodified versions of public participation: rational talk for self-improvement, either through the simple, commonsense wisdom of "regular" folks, or through the counsel of professional authorities.

Ways of getting together in public, and what we might do there together, were also developing in another direction with the growth of industries and cities in the mid- to late nineteenth century. New forms of leisure, especially public, commercial ones, brought quite a different model of what everyday participation in nonpolitical public life might look like. New public settings such as dance halls, amusement parks, and nickelodeons "extended the private—leisure having once been domestic—into the public." The cabaret, for instance, "introduced the interactive space that put performer and spectator in intimate proximity" and "opened the door to greater expressiveness through the intimacy, spontaneity, and informality of its performance."[13]

While these urban entertainments in part gave shape to "a new, expressive, working-class public life," one "that rejected the domesticity of middle-class mores associated with Victorianism, the Protestant ethic, or Old World immigrant culture,"[14] until the late nineteenth century public culture often crossed class lines. As historian Lawrence Levine shows in his fascinating study of Shakespeare as pop culture in the nineteenth century, for example, earlier traditions of theatergoing brought patrons of many statuses together in a boisterous, participatory show. Social classes mixed in a class-specific seating division, and noisy, active responses to the show were extremely common—led by the "gallery" occupants, those who either could not afford the better seats in "the pit" or the boxes ("apprentices, servants, poor workingmen") or were not allowed elsewhere ("Negroes and often prostitutes").[15]

Indeed, descriptions of audiences of the time may sound remarkably contemporary to a talk show watcher, not just for the cacophonies they describe but for the class anxiety submerged within them. The noise in the gallery, Washington Irving wrote in 1802, "is somewhat similar to that which prevailed in Noah's Ark; for we have an imitation of the whistles and yells of every kind of animal"; when roused, those in the gallery "commenced a discharge of apples, nuts & ginger-bread, on the heads of the honest folks in the pit." ("Cabbages, carrots, pumpkins, potatoes, a wreath of vegetables, a sack of flour and one of soot, a dead goose, with other articles," the Sacramento *Union* reported of another performance, "simultaneously made their appearance upon the stage.") Englishwoman Frances Trollope, attending a Shakespearean performance in America in 1832, reported spitting men smelling "of onions and whiskey" and complained that "the applause is expressed by cries and thumping with the feet, instead of clapping," and spontaneous choruses of "Yankee Doodle." "When it is considered here are assembled the wildest and rudest specimens of the Western population," Tyrone Power wrote a few years later of a New Orleans audience, "men owning no control except the laws, and not viewing these over submissively, and who admit of no *arbiter elegantrium* or standard of fine breeding, it confers infinite credit on their innate good feeling, and that sense of propriety which here forms the sole check on their naturally somewhat uproarious jollity."[16] Thumping, uproarious, whistling working people in the gallery and their quietly applauding, somewhat appalled neighbors of "fine breeding": both have a familiar ring.

The rambunctious participatory behavior, the quick and immediate responses to happenings on stage, much as it does on talk shows, made the audience part of the show. As Levine describes it, nineteenth-century theater has more in common with contemporary sporting events than with contemporary theatrical ones, in that the audience is "more than an audience." "They are *participants who can enter into the action on the field, who feel a sense of immediacy and at times even of control, who articulate their opinions and feelings vocally and unmistakably.* . . . These frenetic displays of approval and disapproval were signs of engagement in what was happening on the stage—an engagement that on occasion could blur the line between audience and actors."[17] That description, and its analogy to sporting events, could be as easily applied to late-twentieth-century TV talk audiences as to theater audiences a century prior.

These early commercial entertainments contributed, then, a second blueprint for how public participation might happen: with intimacy, immediacy, expressiveness both vocal and physical, spontaneity, informality, a blurring of the line between performer and audience. We hear echoes in the contemporary talk show, as well: in the unrestrained expressions of audience response ("If there was a prize for attitude, honey, you in the vest, you'd win it, and you, you should have had respect for yourself and kept your legs closed, and to you, you've had your five minutes of fame, so just move on") and rambunctious guest performances ("I don't talk to her no more, she says I'm a ho"), in the willingness to say and do things way outside the bounds of middle-class "propriety" ("Penis, penis, penis!" "I'll spit in your mouth!"), in the distrust of scientific rationality ("I believe there have been some scientific studies—but I just know it in my heart, so regardless of the scientific studies—that you are born gay").

But these earlier forms were not just parallel cultural developments, polite and rowdy cultures moving side by side. Early on, Shakespeare had been offered as "part of the same milieu inhabited by magicians, dancers, singers, acrobats, minstrels, and comics. He appeared on the same playbills and was advertised in the same spirit." By the turn of the century, theater audiences were "tamed" and fragmented into class-specific entertainment settings.[18] Indeed, much like in the recent outcry over talk shows, early- and mid-nineteenth-century commercial entertainments—mixed-class events in which high-expression working-class participation provided the tone—prompted a process of class distinction. By the late nineteenth century, participatory culture had become largely class-segregated, in part through the efforts of urban middle classes and elites to distinguish themselves from the boisterous rabble. For instance, those John Gilkeson calls "recreational reformers," aiming to "remodel working-class amusements so that they would be purposive, restrained, and above all respectable," began to abandon the ideal of a homogeneous, classless society in favor of "self-supporting and self-governing clubs among segments of the working class."[19] Indeed, the very distinction between "high" and "popular" culture emerged, Paul DiMaggio argues, out of the efforts of the activities of urban elites to draw a line between "their" culture and that of nonelites. Bostonians of working-class and upper-middle-class statuses before 1850, for example, attended venues that mixed fine art with mutant animals, and "exhibited works by such painters as Sully and Peal alongside Chinese curiosities, stuffed animals, mermaids, and dwarves"; by the early 1900s such mixing of cultural forms, and cultural participants, was much less frequent.[20] Politeness and gentility and distance in public settings were emphasized in part as a means of marking off the "higher" from the "lower" forms of public culture, gallery culture from box-seat culture.

Even so, the late-nineteenth-century milieu of inexpensive, spectacular entertainment contributed an even more specific tradition of public culture that has found its way to the talk show: the circus and its sideshows traveling rural America, and their counterpart "dime museums" in cities, which offered "an explosion of amusements and frenzied spectacles" with great popularity from the late nineteenth through the mid-twentieth century.[21] The freak show in particular offered the opportunity, for a small price, to be a spectator of oddities. "All for the insignificant price of one dime, two nickels, one-tenth of a dollar—the price of a shave or a hair ribbon," a freak show "talker" would call, "the greatest, most astounding aggregation of marvels and monstrosities gathered together in one edifice."[22]

Here, in shows large and small, banners and barkers announced the appearances of Lobster Boy ("24 in. long"), Snake Girl ("No Arms No Legs

No Bones, Alive"), Knotty ("World's Ugliest Man, Alive"), Sweet Marie ("643 lbs."), Cyclops Pig with Elephants Trunck, Penguin Boy, Frog Boy, the Double-Bodied Girl, the Two-Faced Man, the Woman Changing to Stone, the Mother Who Shocked the World, Boy Change to Girl, Tattooed Girl, Strange Little People.[23] As cultural critic Leslie Fiedler put it, these shows made money by selling public access to beings who challenged "the conventional boundaries between male and female, sexed and sexless, animal and human, large and small, self and other, and consequently between reality and illusion, experience and fantasy, fact and myth."[24] This freak-show challenge, we will see, also found its way into the contemporary talk show.

It was the promoter-showman P. T. Barnum who brought the art of the freak show to its height. Barnum's American Museum of Living Curiosities accompanied his Greatest Show on Earth. His popular "Marvelous Assemblage of Strangest Human Beings, a Wondrous Study of Nature's Wildest Vagaries, a World of Oddest, most Amazing Physical Exceptions" included "the tallest and bulkiest of giants; the tiniest and prettiest of dwarves; phantom-like living skeletons; most enormous fat folk; living galleries of tattooing art; the only full-bearded lady, and so on. These were all the curiosities which nature can devise, on exhibition before the public: they were sometimes referred to as the Very Special People."[25] And they were always, banners and promoters declared, alive. "After all," as the authors of a book on freak-show banners point out, "these advertisements so stretched the human imagination that the word 'alive' was almost always added to confirm the attractions' authenticity. If the audience could be convinced that the sideshow attractions were alive, then they must also be real, although this was not always the case."[26]

These elements of the brash, exclamation-pointed sideshow entertainment—its barkers, its "believe it or not" promotional strategy, its exhibition of anomalous beings and behaviors to a half-believing audience—are recreated quite plainly in the contemporary talk show. Like sideshows, talk shows are aimed primarily at less educated, less moneyed populations. In some of the more outrageous programs, one can also see the same "it's alive!" strategy at work: if the guests are alive, talking on stage in spontaneous-seeming ways, perhaps they must also be real. "Jo-Jo, the Dog-faced Boy, the greatest an-thro-po-log-i-cal mon-ster-os-i-ty in captivity," a freak-show promoter called decades ago, "brought back at great expense from the jungles of Bary-zil. Walks like a boy. Barks like a dog. Crawls on his belly like a snake."[27] Geraldo Rivera speaks in the same over-the-top

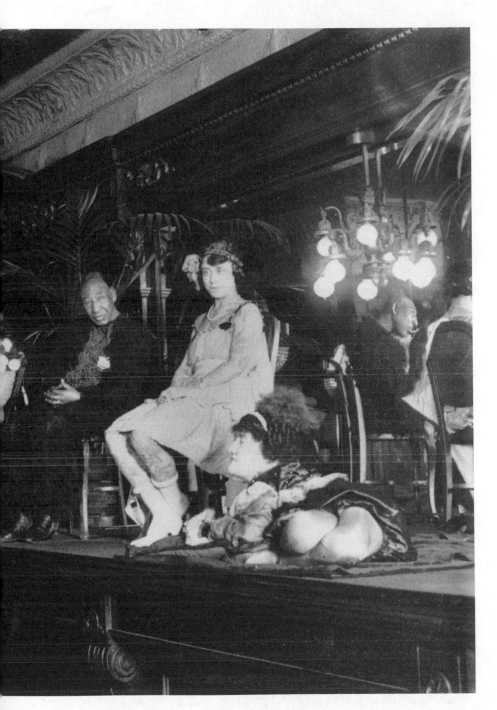

Figure 3 Freaks on exhibit, 1920. UPI/Corbis-Bettmann.

cadences. "Today you are going to see something that will shock and amaze you," he promises. "It's a bizarre and incredible trip to the tiny town of Trinidad, Colorado. I'm taking you there so you will have a front-row seat to the first-ever televised sex-change operation in talk show history!"[28] "Oh, it's not another show about transsexuals," Geraldo's barker cries at the start of another show about transsexuals. "This time it's the alternate side to the alternate lifestyle. Women Who Became Men! They went From Girly to Burly! Today's *Geraldo*!"[29] Walks like a boy. Talks like a girl. Brought back at great expense from the surgery rooms of Tri-ni-dad, Co-ly-ra-do.

The sensationalist impulse of sideshows was further institutionalized in print, around the same time, in tabloids and "true confession" magazines. Magazines such as *True Story* targeted young, working-class women through a formula of "women's personal, confessional accounts of temptations, love triangles, and tragic adventures," backed not by the "idealized art style" of fiction magazines but by "dramatic photographs of models in menacing poses or love clinches." *True Story*'s motto, in fact, could as easily be the credo of much daytime talk television: "Truth Is Stranger Than Fiction."[30] "Sob sister" journalists, women writers at the beginning of early-twentieth-century "yellow journalism," dug out and exaggerated the human-interest story behind social injustice. As Jane Shattuc points out, like television talk shows, the tabloids were cheap, were born of new inexpensive technologies, grew up around and were consumed by lower classes, and combined "a populist emphasis on the injustices done to the 'average' American with the allure of the extremes of vividly told stories."[31] Talk shows inherit much from these presentational strategies, in which everyday emotion is transformed into entertainment, and in which firsthand experience is elevated above abstract knowledge—importantly, it should be noted, characteristics historically associated with working-class and women's genres of popular culture.

There are undoubtedly more cultural elements feeding into the talk show genre, but the point of this loose cultural history should be clear: talk shows are class mutants. Much like Very Special People, they were born of unremarkable stock (civic meetings and theaters, sideshows and women's magazines) yet emerged a combination of odd, even paradoxical elements. The talk show, as Wayne Munson points out, "conflates the sensational, the advisory, and the political in a promiscuous hall-of-mirrors inclusiveness, mixing cheap amusement with reformist highmindedness, celebrity with anonymity, fulfillment with its lack, progress with regression, promotional

Figure 4 "Boy change to girl" sideshow banner, by Jack Sigler, c. 1950. Courtesy of Carl Hammer Gallery.

'humbug' with the seminar, the conventional with the exotic, expertise with the amateur, the clinical with the emotional." Munson and others read "postmodernism" in this mix, in that the genre "uses the very contradictions it exposes, bringing together a constellation of voices," tends to "juxtapose rather than integrate multiple, heterogeneous, discontinuous elements" and "explodes the notion of any one authentic self or of any single developmental mode."[32] These contradictions, heterogeneities, and discontinuities are certainly an important part of the picture, as we will see, structuring the visibility of sex and gender nonconformists. But an emphasis on the postmodern risks obscuring the degree to which the talk show is an awkward patchwork of old-fashioned class cultural fragments.

This beast, that is, has at least a couple of heads. The "respectable," middle-class head, even when it is rudely interrupting, speaks in a reasonable voice, as though it were in an eighteenth-century town meeting or some such thing, to persuade minds or help its neighbors. The "vulgar," poor people's head speaks less carefully, and much more loudly, happily shouting its response, whatever it may be, to the topic at hand, telling any and all who will listen what it thinks, booing and hissing if that gets the point across, as if in the gallery watching Shakespeare. Each head claims the space of the talk show as its own, and of course the two are constantly at odds, but they are joined at the hip, sisters and twins, sharing the same heart, disagreeing with their self, spitting in their own face. At the talk show's true birth within electronic media, however, the bickering was initially not very audible, until the talk show's second head sprouted once again.

The mother of all talk shows

Talk television's actual parents, of course, were its precursors on radio and television: listener-participation radio shows of the 1930s and 1940s such as *Ted Mack's Original Amateur Hour* (a talent show with "real" people), *Truth or Consequences* (in which audience members answered questions mailed in by listeners, often accompanied by public humiliation of one sort or another), and *Vox Pop* (person-on-the-street interviews), which broke open the notion of "ordinary people" as profitable subjects of electronic attention; late-night shows, originated by Sylvester "Pat" Weaver with 1950's *Broadway Open House,* and continuing with *The Steve Allen Show* and *The Tonight Show* with Jack Paar (and, taking over in 1962, Johnny Carson), which provided a model for the "loose, mostly unscripted program devoted to comedy and casual conversation," with some measure of both spontaneity and the host's personal opinions;[33] and prime-time shows such as the issues-oriented, audience-participation *America's Town Meeting* (1948–52) and *Queen for a Day,* the late-1950s show in which women competed for the crown by telling emotional stories of need.[34] By the 1950s, local talk shows were expanding rapidly, often appearing to be hosted, as Brian Rose describes it, "by anyone who could gain access to a camera." New Yorkers in 1959 could watch talk shows hosted by David Susskind, writers Fannie Hurst and Ben Hecht, New Jersey's governor Robert Meyner, even entertainer/former stripper/*Gypsy*-inspirer Gypsy Rose Lee.[35]

From these starting gates, electronic talk went off in a couple of directions—most simply, one for the boys and one for the girls—until, pulled along with various cultural shifts in the 1960s, Phil Donahue combined the two into a sort of bad-boy show for good women. Significantly, these gendered programming styles mapped roughly onto the class cultural elements of earlier times: women's programming picked up on the quiet, civility-oriented, middle-class traditions, while men's programming made use of the working-class conventions of tabloid, high emotion, and immediacy.

On the one hand, most talk radio (and a few TV brothers) pursued, and continues to pursue, a predominantly male audience through an emphasis on political debate, loud controversy, and shock; they quickly became "outposts for the disaffected."[36] When talk radio became a distinct format in the early 1960s—by the mid-1960s, 80 percent of radio stations carried some talk programming—its approach was tabloidesque, built on contention and big emotion, "to exploit news-generated controversies and contemporary problems about which people were emotionally charged—and therefore vulnerable—so as to get their deeper attention and more effectively sell them something."[37] In addition to the politically oriented call-in programming that continues to dominate talk radio today, this took forms such as "topless radio" with callers, mostly female, exposing "intimate details of their lives and fantasies over the airwaves," and the shock-jock, insult-and-outrage strategies currently embodied in the wildly popular Howard Stern.[38] Both political programming (such as *The David Susskind Show,* which ran in syndication for twenty-six years) and controversy-driven "loud talk" (eventually reproduced for a period in the 1980s by Morton Downey, Jr.) also found their way onto 1960s television, in the short-lived programs hosted by Les Crane, Alan Burke, and the "combative, edgy" Joe Pyne, "who, to the shock and delight of his audience, insulted his bizarre assortment of guests whenever he disliked what they said (which was often)."[39]

On the other hand, programming oriented toward women took a kinder, gentler direction, in the forms of "service talk" focusing on home and personal lives, and celebrity chat. *The Home Show,* for instance, hosted by Arlene Francis, offered advice about making a home and raising children, while *The Dr. Joyce Brothers Show* was described in 1962 as having "a flair for making private areas public without being embarrassing or offensive."[40] Celebrity variety shows hosted by Dinah Shore, Merv Griffin, and Mike Douglas, very popular among female audiences (and with at least one elementary school boy, who really should have been doing his homework instead), set themselves up as generic, suburban living rooms, and invited audiences in for a bit of cooking, friendly chitchat, and a song or two.

While in real life, of course, men are not born to the "political" and the loud and women to the "personal" and the tame, these were, and continue to be, the simple assumptions guiding the programming strategies on talk television and radio. Phil Donahue's innovation was to bring these two threads together—and in doing so, to stitch together middle-class salon and lower-class gallery. He was always controversial: atheists, feminists, Nazis, homosexuals, all kinds of unpopular figures got the microphone and the stage; Phyllis Schlafly met Eleanor Smeal, GM president Edward Cole met Ralph Nader, and so on.[41] He was often especially explicit about sex, showing the birth of a baby, an abortion, a vasectomy, inviting *Screw* magazine editor Al Goldstein and sex researchers Masters and Johnson (all shows that were censored in one city or another),[42] talking about condoms, penis size, nudists, masturbation, sex therapy, impotence, gender reassignment surgery, and of course homosexuality—so much sex-related stuff that Dr. Ruth Westheimer declared at the twenty-fifth anniversary of *Donahue* that "whenever I think of sex, I think of Phil Donahue."[43]

Yet his program did all of this with a touch of Dinah, not just by adapting the comfy living room, but also by adding "the dimensions of service" and "the compassion of an in-depth sharing of personal experience," so that "unlike the other 1960s controversial talk shows *Donahue* and its host could be confrontational yet sensitive and caring, still somehow 'polite' in the Merv Griffin mold."[44] Mixing "men's" programming with "women's," Donahue was both tough-political guy and sensitive-listener guy.

Perhaps more importantly, he expanded the living room outward at the same time as he moved personal, experiential knowledge and issues of personal life into the center. On talk radio, audience members were asked to speak but were not, of course, seen; on early television talk shows, they were seen but not asked to speak. On *Donahue,* audiences got both camera and sound. The set was still generic middle-class homey (pared down to a few chairs, sometimes a table, glasses of water for the guests) populated by polite, middle-class audiences, often older women, but the platform and its few guests were no longer the stationary focal point of the cameras. As Paolo Carpignano and his colleagues point out, since Donahue the studio audience itself has become a major player, so that "the living room gives way to a sort of town assembly," with "a compact amphitheater where the visual planes are not defined by the back and front of the camera," where "in a sort of democracy of lighting everybody is brought on stage and given their share of illumination."[45] *Donahue* was a staged town meeting: while the citizenry was mainly tourists whose next likely stop was the Empire State Building, and while the point was neither deliberation nor decision making, the genre became one in which "ordinary people" stepped up to the microphone to say what they felt like saying, often telling us how they thought things were and should be. This minor democracy of lighting and speech gave the largely female studio audience some degree of actual control over the conversation, for one thing, and even more importantly changed the televised *representation* of women from passive recipients to active participants in discussion.

It worked. The target viewer for daytime TV advertisers and therefore for broadcasters was and remains women between the ages of eighteen and forty-nine—the "frequent users" of daytime TV. Very quickly, Donahue was "delivering" huge numbers of such women to advertisers. The formula flourished, a number of analysts have pointed out, partly because it matched some of the overarching countercultural themes of the time: a distrust of technologically disseminated objective knowledge, and an emphasis on orally generated, personal, experiential wisdom, along with a stress on personal involvement in public life. *Donahue*

related personalized knowledge and expression in a way that echoed the decade's "lust for deep experience" and emphasis on the personal element at work in a history now regarded as "lumbering" and "out-of-control," and in which the "fetish of objectivity" had collapsed. [The genre] was a revolt against impersonal authority, the stodgy, and the forbidden; it also affirmed authentic selfhood—another key quest of the decade—over objectified knowledge in a social order in which "the arbitrary, the terrible, the irrational" had become routinized.[46]

This revolt, into which *Donahue* tapped and on which it rode, was tied tightly to the new roles for women in United States public life. Largely through the entry of women into public arenas more generally (work, politics), and strongly pushed by the various wings of the women's movement, issues that had previously been seen as domestic and personal (parenting, marital relations, sexual expression) were becoming public agenda items. Donahue, often quite self-consciously, embodied one of the feminist movement's rallying cries: the personal is political. The popularity of these shows, in fact, as Carpignano and his colleagues explain, "is not only due to the transformation of the social agenda during the past twenty years, following the changes in the role of women in the family and in society and the awareness brought about by women's struggles, but also to the fact that women's struggles have redefined the relationship between the public and the private."[47] Not only was the "personal" becoming a generator of newly relevant public issues, it was also becoming an alternative means to evaluating claims: I am convinced that such-and-such is true not so much because of deductive logic, but because it measures up to my experience. Thus *Donahue*, in appealing to a female demographic, took up "public" issues that had heretofore been private and, drawing on a long tradition in women's popular genres, when dealing with these and other more conventionally "public" issues spoke less the language of objectivity than the language of subjective, firsthand, "authentic" knowledge.

That language, as Donal Carbaugh argues in his sophisticated investigation of "cultural discourses on *Donahue*," also drew most prominently from the codes of liberal individualism. The "spoken system of symbols" on *Donahue*, that is, constructs persons as individuals with rights and choice-making selves to be treated with honesty and respect; the code "operates to create a kind of respect for persons as individuals, and a respect that reaffirms this stature," providing persons with "both the inalienable right to speak, and the freedom to choose." Carbaugh sums up the basic rules of the *Donahue* talking game like this:

> First, the individual has the right to speak opinions and that right
> must be respected. Second, opinions which apply to an individual are
> not to be judged unless the judgment is by God, or preceded by a
> proper acknowledgment of respect for another's right to speak. Opin-
> ions which impose on others may be critically judged if they violate
> others' rights to speak opinions. Third, and consequently, since individ-
> uals have the right to state their own opinions, and these opinions are
> not generally judged, speakers must tolerate a range of views. The
> norm could be stated: It is right to be tolerant of others' rights to

*speak opinions; the proper tone to maintain is a righteous tolerance
where it is right to tolerate a range of views.*[48]

This is a code, of course, that fits the programming requirements very well:
in a general sense, if speech is restricted, if the individuals' right to speak
and the tolerance of a range of opinions are eliminated, there isn't much of
a talk show left.

More specifically, the *Donahue* strategy, of creating and televising controversy while also maintaining the "niceness" of women's service genres,
benefits from the norm of "respect." ("Class, we will show respect to all
of the members," said Donahue, scolding his audience.) In an unspoken,
pragmatic way, the code of liberal individualism—the core set of middle-
class values, as Robert Bellah and his colleagues reminded us in *Habits of
the Heart*[49]—was a built-in requirement of the *Donahue*-created talk show
mix. And for a while the code would also serve to put a cork in the mouth
of the unruly, emotion-driven, gallery-sitting twin, invited to feed on sensational social conflict while sucking on the pacifiers of tolerance and respect
for individuals.

What are we going to do with all these homosexuals?

Given this history, it should not be terribly surprising that Phil Donahue
turned out to be one of the most important allies those pushing for gay
visibility could have imagined. It's safe to say that *Donahue* was not only
the mother of all talk shows, but also the father of American middle-class
gay media visibility. Not that the gay liberation movement of the time was
not making some inroads—gay life was making it to the cover of *Time* ("The
Homosexual: Newly Visible, Newly Understood") and the pages of *Newsweek* ("Policing the Third Sex"),[50] and urban gay communities were going
strong. But the movement's visibility strategies were both long-term and
episodic: encouraging people to come out of the closet, so that more heterosexuals would know more lesbians and gay men and fear us less, and generating media coverage of marches and protests, coverage only minutely controlled by gay activists. Moreover, as Edward Alwood documents well in
Straight News, the coverage at the time was very rarely in line with activists'
own views of gay life, often uncritically reproducing notions of homosexuality as individual and social pathology, or, in the case of tabloid journalism,
using it as an opportunity for some "fun" reporting. The voices of openly

gay men were trumped by the reliance on experts at outlets such as the *New York Times,* which reported in 1964, for instance, with no refutation whatsoever, on the work of psychiatrists Irving Bieber and Charles Socarides, who claimed that homosexuality "can be both prevented and cured." Five years later, reporting on the Stonewall riots in Sheridan Square, the New York *Daily News* simply mocked: "Homo Nest Raided, Queen Bees Are Stinging Mad," said the headline, while Jerry Lisker's article opened with the image of an angry woman sitting, legs crossed, "the lashes of her mascara eyes beating like the wings of a humming bird." "She was so upset she hadn't bothered to shave. A day old stubble was beginning to push through the pancake makeup. She was a he. A queen of Christopher Street. Last weekend the queens had turned commandos and stood bra-strap-to-bra-strap against an invasion of the helmeted Tactical Patrol Force. . . . Queen Power reared its bleached blonde head in revolt." The rioters were described as "princesses and ladies in waiting" and "honeys turned Madwomen of Chaillot," and the riot as taking on "the aura of a homosexual Academy Awards Night," with prancing queens blowing kisses and waving, and "a beauty of a specimen named Stella" wailing because she was afraid her "new beau" might see her hair in curlers.[51] Although activists protested such coverage, without much access to the microphones and steno pads, there was little anyone could do about it.

Television talk shows went one better than protest: they invited activist and nonactivist gender-crossers and homosexuals to sit down in front of millions of people, with almost an hour of attention in which they were heavy contributors to the content of the discussion, as opposed to seconds on news broadcasts or short blurbs in print. In 1967, *The David Susskind Show* (a national, late-night syndicated program) featured antigay psychiatrist Lawrence Hatterer and Dick Leitsch, the president of New York's chapter of the homophile Mattachine Society; in 1970, *The Dick Cavett Show,* after a protest by the Gay Activist Alliance, interviewed Leitsch, and the GAA's Marty Robinson and Arthur Evans, "touching on many of the most essential elements of being a [male] homosexual in the early 1970s."[52] Even with *Donahue* on the case, the opportunities were still occasional—a few shows a year devoted to homosexuality-related issues, a few more if you add gender-crossing into the count—but they were many more than elsewhere. And they often provided moments of recognition or relief for individual viewers living with a sense of sex or gender difference. "Those early shows that Donahue did on transgender issues, those were sensitively done, and they were informative and educational," says a member of the Manhattan Gender Network. "As someone who was 12 or 13 years old, this was very helpful and very important." A New York stage manager remembers a show "before the therapists" about parents and children. "It was all about parents who had no problem with the fact that their son was gay," she recalls. "I just remember the son and the mother, and I was just amazed that this mother had no problem with her son, and I couldn't even imagine that there was a family where there wouldn't be a problem." In a world with so little available information about sexual and gender differences, and so much hatred directed toward the different, these shows—watched with the volume down, perhaps, and with a mixture of shame and excitement—were oases for many.

Indeed, sex or gender nonconformity and the early talk show genre seemed almost made for each other. Homosexuality and gender-crossing at the time were simultaneously poorly understood (thus fitting the show's public-education profile), sexual (thus fitting the show's titillation needs), taboo (thus fitting the show's hook-them-by-shock strategy), in the realm of the domestic and private (thus fitting the show's larger reworking of the personal-as-public), controversial (thus fitting the show's needs for conflict), and newly politicized (thus fitting the show's talk radio–like focus on hot-button social issues and public policy questions).

The *Donahue* environment, on the flip side, was remarkably consonant with the predominantly white and middle-class gay movement's agenda. A late 1970s *Donahue* in which sex researchers William Masters and Virginia Johnson talked for an hour with Phil and his audience about their book *Homosexuality in Perspective*, for example, played like scientific backing for the ideological battles being fought by the movement at the time, packed with myth-bashing rationality and the assertion of homosexual-heterosexual similarities. "The only thing that is uniquely different" about homosexuals, Johnson claims, "is the way they express themselves sexually": "there's simply no difference in ability to respond to sexual stimulation between the homosexual and the heterosexual" (indeed, as Donahue summarizes it, "the homosexual lover is more likely to be a more effective lover than the heterosexual"); we should not be "measuring one life style to the other" but thinking about what the information "tells us about human sexual needs"; both homosexuals and heterosexuals commonly experience "cross-preference fantasy," no one "starts out as a homosexual or starts out as a heterosexual," and one out of every three men and one of every five women in this country "has had at least one homosexual experience" by age fifty ("we are born man or woman and sexual beings and we learn homosexuality and we learn heterosexuality and we learn bisexuality," says Masters); "the greatest mistake we can make is the cultural concept that the man with feminine characteristics is indeed homosexual," "we have absolutely no information that homosexuality is an illness or a disease," heterosexuals are more likely to seduce children into sexual activity than homosexuals, and so forth. Homosexuality is "a natural form of sexual expression," Masters argues. "We're not saying normal, we're not saying preferable, we're not saying most valuable," Johnson adds. "We're just saying natural form."[53]

I will have more to say later about the matches and mismatches between talk shows' requirements and rhetorics and those of gay, lesbian, bisexual, and transgender politics, but for now, it is worth simply noting how close were the philosophies of coming out and of *Donahue*'s early TV talk. Politically active gay men and lesbians were primarily arguing that coming out was revealing one's true self, an act of liberation enacted through speech, that antigay sentiment was born of ignorance and intolerance of individual difference, and involved the violation of individual rights; love is love. We know these things, they said, because we experience them, just as you experience yourself, and your love and desire. *Donahue*'s protolerance, individual-centered, test-of-experience, freedom-of-speech, authentic-self rhetoric was simply a more general version of the specific coming-out impulse. If being somewhat titillating objects of controversy was part of the price for guests, it was tempered by the push for understanding and tolerance. When Johnny Bonck ("gay man") and Lisa Heft ("friend of gay man") went on a 1987 *Donahue* to talk about their "strange and complex relationship," for example, "it was kind of like 'America, yea or nay,' and then that's it," Bonck recalls. "And we were just sitting there being homosexuals." They mainly went for the free trip to see friends in New York, but if there was any agenda at all, Heft says, it was "just to be real people, to be a full person." With *Donahue,* this was not much of a battle. "It was much more about taking this slightly unusual thing and making it a little more normal. That was really the energy in those days." "Everyone was so nice," Heft adds. "Everyone was so *nice.*"

Even then, things were not necessarily always as nice for gender "minorities" such as transvestites and transsexuals. Donahue's infamous skirt-wearing during his show on cross-dressing, in which he appeared in a cute little pink number, was, according to Donahue, "the program that caused the most controversy, the most comment, the most press attention, the most hysteria."[54] Yet despite this tendency toward the visually sensational, the calls for tolerance, understanding, and living the true self were consistent on these shows as well.

In fact, rarely did guests have to even bother making the argument for acceptance, since Donahue or his audience would nearly always step in. "You have been together it says for fifty-four years," Donahue says, introducing 76-year-old Gean Harwood and 74-year-old Bruhs Mero in a typical show in 1985 (already, it should be noted, about fifteen years after the Stonewall rebellion). "In a homosexual relationship that is mutually gratifying, loving, accepting, and all the things we hope for our sons and daughters." Yes, Gean answers, and "we have finally decided to put that aside and to tell the world about our relationship and that we're very proud of it." The audience applauds, as they do later for the "grandmother who came out at age 72" (the "gay granny," she says), and for an audience member's comment that "those that discriminate against people because they are gay and feel that they don't have the right to love another of the same sex is the same thing as discriminating against someone because of their race, their religion, whatever."

Donahue, as he was wont to do in evoking a controversy, takes the other side, warning that his audience is atypically liberal, whereas, he points out, hours earlier the city of Houston had voted to condemn an effort to outlaw discrimination against homosexuals. "I don't know where we got you," he says to his audience, with the common and perhaps mistaken implication that either Texas or Iowa is the real America, "but you do not speak for mainstream America. We do not like gay people in this country. We don't want them teaching school, we don't want them working at daycare centers. Some of us are afraid of them." Of course, Donahue has just shown that *he* is not afraid, that he *likes* his guests. He might articulate the antigay position, but one never gets any sense, despite the antigay "we" of which he so often spoke on these programs, that it is his own. Later in the gay seniors show, for instance, having reminded his viewers a few minutes earlier that "the testimony we've heard on this program is that [coming out] is a very liberating experience," Donahue states flatly that "there is more antisocial behavior at the hand of heterosexuals than homosexuals. So the gay community wants you to know that it's not fair to suggest that sex status or preference necessarily predisposes anybody toward child molestation. That, however, remains, I think, one of the biggest emotional roadblocks to equal status for all citizens." Donahue was there to knock out those roadblocks. "What are we going to do," he took to asking on these sorts of programs, "with all these homosexuals?" It was more of a disidentifying question—

the "you crazy, ignorant, bigoted asshole" address buried somewhere below its surface—than one linking Donahue to its "we." What do *you* want to do, the question really seems to ask, lock up the gay granny and throw away the key? Burn these people at the stake? "You are the witches of the 80s," he declares out of the blue toward the end of the program. Donahue is there to pour water, or more accurately some gasoline and then the water, on the flames.

Even gasoline was a boon for gay speakers, however, who got ample opportunity to speak their piece, opposed on the gay-and-gray show, for instance, only by the occasional audience member complaining that "being gay is too easy now" and "the Lord says that you will burn in hell about this." Buffy, Ruby, Ken, Gean, Bruhs, and William wind up testifying about their family's responses to their coming out, about the "fight throughout the world for legal marriage" for same-sex couples, about antigay discrimination, about the charge of gay "recruiting," about the relationship between homosexuality and religion, even getting in several plugs for Senior Action in a Gay Environment (SAGE, an organization for lesbian and gay seniors). The lover of one of the guests has the last word. "It was very good," he says of the show, "and I think it has opened a lot of people's minds to the fact that we are here and we will always be here. And I think it's great that you had us on."[55] We are here, we are everywhere, and this proves it.

Yet who we were and where we were proved to be quite narrow. *Donahue* recruited guests primarily from organizational networks—networks that were, especially among the lesbian and gay population at the time, run by and serving white, educated, middle-class people, predominantly male people. The two other homosexuality-related shows the year that the SAGE members appeared, for example, had this "respectable," we're-like-you-except-for-our-sexual-preferences profile: a show on gay parenting (again, *Donahue* was ahead of the curve on the issue) featured Don Harrelson, chairman of Los Angeles Gay Fathers (and his son Jon), Kevin Cathcart from Gay and Lesbian Advocates and Defenders, and Bill Jones, the first single male to adopt a child in the United States (and his son Aaron), while a program on controversial gay activism at Southern Methodist University featured a female student organizer, a male student opposition leader, a reverend and founder of a predominantly gay church fellowship, and a Presbyterian Church leader.

Of course, this selection of guests had nothing much to do with deliberate privileging of a stratum of the gay population, and everything to do with the daily needs of producers and the profile of the program (and the limited pool of openly gay people willing to risk national television appearances). Donahue's was meant to be a smart show, and one that took up social issues: get people who can speak well, and if possible, get the leaders. Producers, devising multiple shows at once on a tight schedule, needed to find guests quickly and efficiently: go to organized settings, see who's available from the leadership or from the social or membership network. Producers wanted viewers to identify with and respect guests: get guests who look and speak like the target audience of middle-class women. Finally, when it came to social issues, Donahue had a genuine commitment to bashing stereotypes: when looking for guests from stigmatized groups, get the ones who seem the most normal. "They didn't want somebody who acts crazy and crawls the walls and carries on—in plain language, a screaming faggot," says Bruce Spencer, who appeared on a *Donahue* show in the late 1980s. "They wanted to shock people by interviewing people from portions of the gay community in the business world, in various fields, where if you walk into the room nobody would look at you twice and say, 'Aha.' They wanted us to be as normal as we are in everyday life."

Again, these production needs dovetailed nicely with the agendas of mainstream gay organizing. In the decades when *Boys in the Band* and *Cruising* and *The Killing of Sister George* set the stereotypes for homosexuals—campy, self-hating sissies or twisted, predatory self-hating sex monsters or suicidal/homicidal lesbians[56]—here was an invitation to put out as "normal" and adjusted a face as possible. Here was also an opportunity to demonstrate, against the stereotypes, that "we are everywhere": in churches and not just in bars, in the medical profession and not just hairstyling and gym teaching, in the suburbs and not just the urban ghettos, and so on. In fact, the shows invited exactly the people organizers wanted them to invite, often simply pulling the already-designated spokespeople of gay politics or of organizations of gender-crossers: articulate about the issues not only because they lived them and had the educational tools to speak well about them, but also because they had experience speaking publicly about them. The symbiosis between mainstream movement organizations and talk show production was tight and direct.[57]

It remained so even as several other hosts arose to compete with *Donahue* in 1986 and 1987. It was as though Donahue's head split open, and out popped his chattering children, *Oprah* and *Sally,* who wanted to help us talk through our problems, and *Geraldo,* who wanted to go into battle for us. Oprah Winfrey—African American, in a large and then famously yoyoing body—made personal intimacy her central selling point, unlike the somewhat distant Donahue, making her own personal life public. She took the personal, emotional elements that Donahue's let's-debate-the-issues style suppressed, brought them out, and turned up the volume on them. "She too performs as a talker," as Gloria-Jean Masciarotte puts it. "She was always already one of her own guests." "Oprah routinely talks about her life as abuse victim, substance abuser, black person, single working woman, and girlfriend of Stedman. . . . Oprah Winfrey's use of emotionalism moves Donahue's original practice of making the issues of the day everyday issues to its furthest extent by making issues of the everyday. In a sense, then, on *The Oprah Winfrey Show* there is no area of politics that is not personal and no space where the personal is exempt from politics."[58] While Sally Jessy Raphael was more mother than buddy, more authoritative (in her trademark serious-person eyeglasses) than down-home, more golly and gosh than uh-uh and c'mon girl, her show took essentially the same strategy as Winfrey's: turning everyday emotions into show material, hosting through empathy more than intellect. "I had to come across as warm, comfortable, and feminine," Raphael herself said, "the kind of friend you'd like to chat with over coffee."[59] Raphael, critic Walter Goodman claimed a few years into her show's run, hosts "an encounter group for people who can't afford encounter groups."[60]

Indeed, Winfrey and Raphael were part of a more general trend in television toward confession and therapy. Talk shows took the "talking cure" and, combining it with the tabloidism of the "true confessions" magazine genre, moved it in front of the cameras. "Only silence, like turning off the television, is anathema to the new networks of communication," Mimi White explains. "The therapeutic ethos is an incitement to talk, to talk constantly, of oneself to others."[61] Like the code of individual freedom of speech so dominant on *Donahue,* the confession-as-therapy rhetoric of *Oprah* and *Sally* gave the genre a raison d'être: spill it for the cameras, it's good for you.

In the meantime, former *20/20* reporter Geraldo Rivera harked back to the not-so-nice, not-so-tolerant confrontational talk that had made brief appearances in early radio and television—but with righteous indignation for the victimizer, a tear for the victims, and a kiss for the ladies. "I'm Walter Winchell, Edward R. Murrow, Merv Griffin," said Rivera. To Oprah's tough but soft empathy, and Sally's I'm-a-mother listening, Geraldo played the lawyerly guy's guy ("Is it not the case," he often began, and "Did you not state, sir") who can also cry. And fight like a man: in one of his most

Figure 5 Oprah Winfrey and her audience, February 1987. AP/Wide World Photos.

famous episodes, Rivera broke his nose in an on-air, chair-throwing fight with neo-Nazis. "It's rock-and-roll television," he said of his show.[62]

While the therapeutic, we-all-got-troubles style was growing through *Sally* and *Oprah,* and while *Geraldo* was carving out a spot for his semimacho, fist-fighting-investigative-reporter-with-heart shtick, when it came to homosexuality (and many other "social issues") these shows all looked more or less like *Donahue*s with a substitute teacher. In her first year, for example, Oprah Winfrey hosted a show on homophobia, which pitted Rick Fox (who went "fag bashing" because "there was nothing to do on a Friday or Saturday night" and "it was fun"), Cheryl Hook ("two homosexual men stalked my then 4-year-old twins"), and *Washington Times* writer John Lofton ("the fact of the matter is that the greatest amount of violence that's been committed against homosexuals has been committed by other homosexuals . . . through sodomy, causing AIDS") against Cathy Sarris (raped and beaten by a man who said "he was doing this for Christ, somebody had to stop what was going on in terms of the gay movement"), Cleve Jones (stabbed by a man "laughing and shouting, 'Queer, queer,' and a few things I can't say on television"), and Kevin Berrill of the National Gay Task Force ("I'm tired of the people debating the alleged sin of homosexuality while gay people are being thrown off bridges and gay churches are being burned down and gay lives are being destroyed").

The debate-the-issues structure is here simply transferred from *Donahue,* as is the use of gay and lesbian guests recruited through mainstream organizations. The audience, as it often was and is, is quite hostile, much less tolerant than the host, talking about sin and Adam and Eve and "flaunting" and AIDS as punishment, and suggesting that "they should take all the gays and put them on an island, like they did with the lepers in the old days." Meanwhile, the well-spoken, nicely dressed gay and lesbian guests, along with a few audience members, make calls for tolerance, and Oprah herself echoes Donahue's tag line: "So what should we do with this population that is gay?" she asks Ms. Hook. ("I don't really think we know how to solve the problem," Hook answers, perhaps but not for certain missing Oprah's point.)[63] The pattern is a *Donahue* cutout: antigay sentiment aired by conservative guests and audience members, protolerance and individual-rights ethics espoused by liberal audience members, sometimes the host, and articulate, regular-looking, reasonable-sounding, educated guests. Same discussion, different channel.

"Normal" and articulate and counterstereotypical as the guests were, however, they were also something quite specific. Sissy men and butch women, uneducated and lower-class, people who were not white or from an urban gay center, were still almost nowhere to be seen on the panels. It was as though all the boys in the band and psycho lesbians and queen bees, and their uneducated, working-class, and dark-skinned gay siblings, had gone and killed themselves as programmed by Hollywood, replaced by the serious, sometimes angry, sharp but smiling faces of the New Homosexuals. Until, as we will see in a little bit, the African American queens and rural dykes and sex-happy club kids took the stage: that is, until the other talk show head got the mike.

Go Ricki: Talk as a sport

At one of the last tapings of *Donahue,* although our white faces blended in with the crowd, my thirtysomething friends and I stood out for our youth; at a taping of *The Ricki Lake Show,* my friend and I were as ancient and white as could be in a crowd that was about one-quarter white and one-eighth over thirty. There, a security guard announces that you have to be at least eighteen years old to enter, and that IDs will be checked, that you will go through a metal detector—"to check for guns, weapons, and beepers," a young African American intern tells us. "I need your attention for just two minutes please," another young woman, this one a redhead in black leggings and a brown blazer, calls out, and repeats the information about the metal detector. "No weapons," she announces, "and that includes no mace and no pepper spray, which we'll take and then return to you when the show's over." Later, when she is ready to begin "loading" us into the studio, leggings-woman reminds us to put our beepers on vibrate, turn all cellular phones off, and to take off any baseball hats and sunglasses. We are assumed, that is, to be wearing the equipment of young, urban street life. During the taping, the two big-earringed, teenaged African American women behind us are dying to ask questions, and make loud comments about the guests, who are apologizing to each other for various misdeeds (stabbing an ex-husband with a butter knife, blinding a friend with a sparkler on the Fourth of July, saying nasty things to an overweight, mentally disabled friend). "She's not sorry, she's a bitch," pronounces one. "You're fat yourself," blurts the other. Later, before the segment with the mentally disabled guest, the supervising producer comes out and makes a little warning speech. "We are committed to putting all kinds of difference on this stage, and all of our guests, whatever kind of background they have, get treated with respect," Stuart says, reminding us of the rules that, for all those in the audience who have watched the show, seem made to be broken. Beepers? Weapons? Sunglasses and baseball caps? Comments about bitches and fatsos? Instructions in decorum? At *Donahue,* there were chocolate chip cookies, and people held up their hands as if in an algebra class.

By 1995, not only could you suddenly see shows where the rowdy, not very genteel, poor and working-class talk show twin was holding forth with vim and vigor, you could, as one writer put it, get bedsores from watching them.[64] In the course of a couple of years, sores of various types were being brought about by a new mutation of the *Donahue* model. Several new shows had joined the fold in 1991, hosted by former *Current Affair* anchor Maury Povich, former motivational speaker Montel Williams, former stand-up comedian Jenny Jones; a few more started up in the two years following, including shows hosted by former serious newspeople Richard Bey and Jane Whitney, former mayor of Cincinnati Jerry Springer, *Entertainment Tonight*'s Leeza Gibbons, and former Australian Gordon Elliott. (Archconservative talk radio king Rush Limbaugh also joined the scene, but his show, unlike the others, featured neither a single topic nor audience participation.) While each of these shows sought to carve out their own host-driven niche, they were not serving up anything terribly different. It was the success of another 1993 talk show, however, hosted by former fat girl, honorary drag queen, and John Waters protégée Ricki Lake, that pushed the genre into new territory, spotlighting and manipulating a different kind of class culture than that of the share-debate-respect culture highlighted and exploited on earlier programs.

The man behind *Ricki* was Garth Ancier, once the frighteningly young program head at Fox Broadcasting, who at Fox had "found an untapped market in so-called 'urban' viewers," targeting "kids, men, blacks, Latinos, and city dwellers."[65] Along with Gail Steinberg, who had been a producer at *Donahue* and other shows and became *Ricki*'s executive producer, Ancier was looking to "take the Donahue format and age it down to attract 18-to-34-year-olds."[66] He started with teen-magazine founder Jane Pratt, who crashed quite quickly, and after auditioning future talk show host Carnie Wilson and daughter-of-a-talk-show-host Melissa Rivers, Ancier eventually turned to Lake, then twenty-four, who had recently lost her job on television's *China Beach*. ("It's not the destiny I would have chosen," Lake said later, for her part. "I needed the pilot money—$5,000. I wasn't thinking any further than that. I was just thinking I had to pay my rent next month."[67] Who knew?) The "breakeven barrier" for talk shows was a 3 rating, and most shows were not even doing that. With quasi-famous Lake at the helm, a young woman who had shown that big girls rule in *Hairspray*, who talked and reacted to things like a relatively hip but down-to-earth 24-year-old, the show had a rating of 4 by January 1994. By 1995, *Ricki* had become the number two talk show on television, bringing in an estimated 5.8 million viewers to Oprah's estimated 9.4 million, and the industry leader among the juicy, desirable market of 18-to-34-year-old women. It was delivering, in short, "the kind of demographics that quicken the heart rates of advertising executives."[68]

Not surprisingly, *Ricki* begat many clones, also eager to make advertising executives clutch their chests. Charles Dabney, who had been the gay roommate's boyfriend on an early season of MTV's *Real World,* and had worked with Ancier at *Jane Pratt* and then at *Ricki,* became suddenly "straight," took his mother's maiden name Perez, and tried his own show ("as a talk show host," one critic suggested, "he made a great flight attendant"[69]). Along with fellow unknown pretty-boy Mark Walberg, more seasoned semi-celebrities joined Perez in the fray: *Partridge Family* child-star Danny Bonaduce, *Beverly Hills 90210* vet Gabrielle Carteris, *Cosby* kid Tempestt Bledsoe, and schmaltz-pop singer and aptly named Carnie Wilson, who looked to me like a drag queen doing Ricki Lake before the weight loss and to another writer, who encountered her in flocked velvet, like "a badly stuffed couch."[70]

The new shows all mimicked the *Ricki* strategy: a near-exclusive focus on personal relationships (betrayals, dating, surprise crushes, and so on); a revved-up pace combined with a huge increase in the number of guests per show, so that nearly every segment involved new guests and the stage wound up filled with people competing to speak; titles told from the point of view of the young viewer. "Everyone on the show is young, and everyone in the audience is young, and the topics are young," says David Roth, who was a supervising producer on one of the newer shows.

It's all from the vantage point of the young person, you know. Instead of "Kids having sex in the house, what can parents do?" it's "My mom won't let me have sex in the house!" Where Donahue might do "Put in jail for a crime they didn't commit," we would do "I get stopped by cops for no reason at all!" And our audience seems to get bored quicker, so we'll have three times as many guests on one show than Donahue would have on the same topic. Donahue might have six people on who were all thrown in jail, we'll have twelve, thirteen, fourteen. Just a little bit younger, more attitude, things fast-paced, visual. And screaming, yelling, louder.

Ricki and the *Ricki* wanna-bes also attracted a young, urban studio audience composed largely of people of color. "I call it a subway audience," says Roth. As *Spin* writer Mark Schone describes it, "part of the Ancier-Lake 'urban' formula was an upfront appeal to black audiences, with the expectation that people of color would tune in to see their own, while the white kids would come along because black = street = hip."[71] Indeed, Roth's nephew's bar mitzvah demonstrates just this kind of equation:

> One summer, when the guests would say something, the audience would start saying, "Whoop, there it is," you know, and just singing that song, which was a big song that summer. Like a row of fourteen black and Spanish women, and guys or whatever, standing up and go-ing, "Whoop, there it is," you know. I would sit there and think, "Oh my god, like white America's going to tune out." But then I go to my nephew's bar mitzvah six months later and what song do all those kids want us to dance around to. And they all wear their pants like to their knees. It's almost like six months lag time, like to be cool and ahead of its time was something that always worked for our studio audience.

In addition to the bar-mitzvah-boy attraction, *Ricki* and her clones pushed forward another very significant departure from the *Donahue* mode, recruiting guests almost exclusively through "cart calls" (named for the ma-chine on which they are produced), in which a request for guests is posted along with a toll-free number: "Do you hate your sister's boyfriend? Call 1-800-GO-RICKI. Does your mother stop you from having sex in the house? Call 1-800-GO-RICKI." These 800 numbers are an easier way to recruit: rather than coming up with an issue and searching for those most informed about it, or discovering a story in a newspaper or magazine and tracking down its key figures, you just post a topic, see who calls, and build a show around the most interesting, funny, dramatic, good-storied, good-storyteller callers. This recruiting practice meant a very non-*Donahue*, even non-*Oprah*, pool of guests, drawn not so much from predominantly white, middle-class organizational and personal networks as from the population of viewers—in this case young, often poorly educated, often unemployed or underemployed, disproportionately people of color.

The a-talk-show-for-every-minor-celebrity party, with more than twenty talk shows on at once in the 1994–95 season, was only really fun for one season, as the new shows began cutting into each other's ratings sustenance and even pushing *Ricki*'s ratings down considerably, until most dropped like flies. The effects were nonetheless strong and lasting: established shows such as *Jenny Jones* and *Jerry Springer* survived by "younging" themselves like *Ricki*. Jenny Jones "reinvented herself as an inner-city icon."[72] Jerry Springer went from Donahue-like issues-and-commentary to a show that, in its host's words, "is *about* outrageousness, outrageous relationships."

"Nobody cared about Jerry Springer talking to Jesse Jackson," says Burt Dubrow, the Multimedia Entertainment executive who oversaw the *Jerry Springer* makeover.

We made Jerry real comfortable, and then took new subjects. We all decided that every woman has a fantasy at one time or another to strip, even if it's just for her husband. So we took that concept and we said, "Anybody who wants to do this write us and blah, blah, blah," and then we flew these people in based on their letters, with their husbands. We hired a stripper to teach them. The husbands were not allowed to see anything. And on the show we bring the husband out and put him on a big stage in a strip club, interview him, "You ready to see your wife, here we go, dah, dah, dah, here's Melinda." She comes out and does her act in front of an audience, men screaming, and the camera watching the husband watch his wife. It was great. That's when it turned. From issues to relationships. We younged it up. We made it contemporary. And we raised the rating about 30 to 35 percent.

Phil Donahue, whose show "skews old," as they say, was dropped in 1996.

Shows with something else in mind, unless they were an industry leader such as *Oprah*, pretty much faced the choice of go *Ricki* or die. Jane Whitney, for instance, who came from a background in news, hosted a show envisioned by its creators as "a cross between *Oprah* and *Nightline*." The production company, Telepictures, "did try to hang onto the original vision, but the pressures and rigors of the marketplace were such that they couldn't." When the show moved from a late-night show taped in Boston to a New York–based daytime slot, she says, "I saw the future in the first taping." And, as she tells it, it wasn't pretty.

It took me a lot longer, of course, to catch up. I was a fighter—they would probably say I was a pain in the ass—because I kept trying to stay true to the original mandate. But the tone of the studio audience changed just so significantly when we came to New York. It was almost like somebody blinked and it was a different audience. The first shows we taped I broke down crying afterwards. I think the first show we taped in New York was a show with people who had called in on 800 numbers, "My husband's best friend is trying to steal him." Husband and wife couple, husband was allegedly gay, unclear what his sexuality was, and was allegedly having an affair with his best friend but wouldn't admit to it. I mean, it was a screamfest. The company loved it, the staff loved it, and I was in tears. To me what had always been important was people being heard. In Boston you had a very sort of civilized—opinionated, but emphasis on civilized—audience. And it really was a forum for lots of different points of views. And this New York audience was like suddenly being thrust into a mud-wrestling match. Everybody seemed to be wearing their underwear and baseball caps. That in itself is not significant, except that they also became exceedingly judgmental and mean-spirited. Obviously not all of them, but there was a different feeling in that room. It sounds dramatic to say it, but it was like they were coming to watch an execution. I mean, if somebody didn't get hit, they were disappointed. I once had a kid say to me during a commercial break, you know, "These guys on the set going to mix it up? Is somebody going to get hit?" I'm like, "Probably not." You know, appalled just at the idea. He said, "Well, this is really boring." I actually once did step in to stop two men from hitting each other, and some of the audience was like disappointed. The shows were suddenly of a different temperament, a different identity than what we started out to do. And we couldn't be competitive unless we got our feet wet in that pool.

While the trauma of dealing with audience members there for a sporting match rather than a forum is still evident when she talks about it years later, what is especially revealing in Whitney's comments is the sense that suddenly someone else *took over*. Of course, there was no change at all in who really owned and profited from talk shows, but in a more symbolic way they did change ownership. Sitting in audiences, you can feel this sense of ownership, the sense of entitlement to speak, the sense of being at home: once, during a break at *Gordon Elliott*, the Fugees hip-hop remake of Roberta Flack's "Killing Me Softly" was playing very, very quietly over the studio speakers, and the group behind us, a crowd of black women in their thirties, began singing along, joined by people in various sections of the studio until the whole place was singing. Culturally, the shows changed hands. "They found us," claims producer Roth. "A lot of people in the studio audience would say, 'Thank you so much. Thank you, this is the first time that like we're going to be seen on TV.' It's a lot of people who grew up in the inner city and have a very expressive culture—I mean, black, white, Hispanic, it doesn't matter, it's just pretty much inner city, urban kids. They really saw themselves in the show, on the panel, and in the studio audience." As programs began targeting a younger demographic, they did so by inviting people onto the set with different interests, different rules about talking, different relationships to television; in short, they did so by both representing and exploiting different class cultures. In the preferred euphemisms of the industry, they became "urban" and "ethnic." That is, black people and Latinos became prominent, along with poorer white folks, and the educational level of guests and audience members came down along with their age and economic status.

There are all sorts of revealing problems and effects of this change that will come clear as we move onward, and it creates all sorts of interesting difficulties for those populations becoming visible. Conflict bumps controversy, performance outweighs testimony, spectacle overshadows discussion, speed trumps content, and so on, and this makes a big difference for what can get across. For now, though, it is worth previewing some of the ways bisexuals, lesbians, transgendered people, and gay men fit into this newer brand of programming.

It is quite plain that an increased circus atmosphere has, on many shows, meant that "freak" treatment has increased: rather than the normal-as-can-be spokesmodel types of *Donahue* years, many shows, using outrageousness to attract audiences, have simply reinstated over-the-top flamboyance of various kinds, playing up old stereotypes of gender reversal and hypersexuality, and conflating homosexuality and gender-crossing. A less obvious, but equally striking, change, however, has been the degree of "leveling" that is bought through the higher decibels, urbanized studio audiences, increased circus atmosphere, and lazier guest-recruiting strategies. *Ricki*fied talk shows, ironically, quickly went much further than their predecessors in demonstrating that "we are everywhere," since now we are not only middle-class, fancy-schooled, professional, and white. Before the younged-down shows, when homosexuality and gender-crossing and bisexuality were programmed primarily as embodied social issues, it was as though all other topics and people were straight; after, when a social issue could make its way to the screen only through the door of personal conflict, gay, lesbian, bisexual, and transgender guests could be found in the midst of generic interpersonal dramas. In addition to a few shows each year devoted to gay issues, "the presence of gay people on our show," says one openly gay producer, for instance, "usually occurs on a topic that can be any topic."

It could be, you know, "I'm in love with somebody and I've never told them before," or it could be "I stole my best friend's boyfriend," and it happens to be three men in that segment. The audience re-

*sponds, to the point that every single show that we run an advertise-
ment for, unless it's an issue involving a heterosexually specific thing
like pregnancy [sic]—even with those, lesbian stories slip in—we get
gay story responses. Because the young audience is a diverse audience,
and an audience that has no problem accepting diversity. You know, if
Donahue put on two gay people, he'd say, "Joining me now are so-
and-so. They're in an openly gay relationship and dah, dah, dah, and
they are also," he would always explain it. The idea here was to not
explain it. So we just throw them on there for no reason at all other
than that their story is a good story.*

Not surprisingly, same-sex relationships are not treated as simply equivalent
to heterosexual ones: although they make the same entrance as other guests
on an "I stole my best friend's boyfriend" show, popping out of some door
or sashaying out from behind some curtain, they typically do so without
names or pronouns, becoming "this person" or "so-and-so's best friend"
until they appear in person. Nonetheless, out they come to join the fracas,
just like their straight copanelists: stealers of other people's boyfriends and
girlfriends, secret admirers, exhibitionists, sisters of women who dress like
sluts, and so on. Not only are we everywhere, apparently, we are also just as
loud, goofy, dysfunctional, funny, nasty, emotional, and combative as everyone else. Gay and lesbian and bisexual, and to some degree transgendered
people as well, get pulled along in this staged democracy of troubled lives.

Although all these drastic, nutty transformations in the talk show genre
are certainly significant, the history I have sketched should also suggest that
they are not "declines" in any simple sense. When the older female audience
was abandoned for the younger one, quite simply, the expressive, irreverent,
rude, laughing twin took control. With such different guests and studio audiences, styles of expression changed accordingly, as producer Roth explains.

*We didn't ask them to scream, it's just that is the way this young audi-
ence relates to one another. The guests came on and started doing
stuff and saying stuff and acting a certain way that is reflective of cultures that already exist out there. I mean, no guest on the show has
ever been told, "Put your hand in the other guest's face and hold it
right in front of their face and look away," which is a common motion now among the talk shows. It's called "talk to the hand," which
is short for "talk to the hand because the face don't understand." It
didn't start on talk shows, it started somewhere in the street, somewhere in urban life. Actually, my audience is saying the same thing*

that Sally's audience is saying to the person on stage, except the person in the Sally audience is going to be a middle-aged white woman from Middlebury, Connecticut, with white, you know, polyester stretchy pants on, probably she's eaten too many donuts in her life, and is going to say something very well thought out, something along the lines of, "Well, I really think that you're in a very bad relationship and I think you should really think about getting some help working on your self-esteem." Where someone in my audience will say, "Girl-friend, your self-esteem is in the toilet," one snap, and then sit back down. It's much more expressive but the sentiment is the same. Look at the Donahue audience. I mean, those people have thought about what they're going to say. My audience, if [the host] throws a mike in somebody's face, that person is standing up and saying something great without even—I mean, a few weeks ago someone on the set said something really ass-backwards, the kind of thing where like every-body in the audience has a sort of open mouth. And this one guy looks at [the host], and she says, "Stand up, sir, what do you want to say?" He just looked her in the eye, white guy, looked her right in the eye and said, "She's cuckoo for Cocoa Puffs," and the audience lost it. Not a beat was missed. In all the time I've worked with studio audi-ences, it's the only time I've ever seen people jump up and say things almost as they're thinking them.

The earlier irreverent working-class cultures from which talk shows partially sprung echo here: their immediacy and spontaneity, their emotional expres-siveness, their humor, their quick beat, their impatience with "respectable" etiquette.

More than a new creation, this is a shift in balance between the monster's warring heads, a resprouting, in the old gendered soil, of one set of class cultural seeds. The vulgar twin has always been around, cuckoo for Cocoa Puffs, making brash comments and asking rude questions, and in the newer shows the respectable twin is also around, asking everybody to be civilized and spouting authoritative commentary and pop-psychological insight; the "masculine," rational style has always been joined at the mouth to the "fem-inine," emotional one. The talk show genre has *always* been a two-headed monster, and, taken as a whole or in its episodic and programmatic parts, it continues to be one today. If it's scary, especially to people who have gotten used to having the microphone to themselves, perhaps that is one of the main reasons why.

3 TRUTHS TOLD IN LIES

We did Geraldo three times, and each time they lied to us about what we were going to do and how we were going to do it. It's just like Lucy and Charlie Brown and the football. They kept promising, "We're going to hold the football for you this time." The last time we went on they really conned me. They said, "Wouldn't you like to sit down and have a one-on-one with Geraldo?" I said, "You have no idea how badly I'd like to do that." And she said, "Well, this is your chance." And that's the time we went on with the weightlifter and the tallest man in the world, the strongest woman in the world, you know, that sort of thing. It was a freak show. There must have been twenty people on that stage. We said, "We're not going to go on," but when we checked all of the stuff that they had sent us, we found out that all we had was an airline reservation, not a ticket. And the assistant producer comes by and we ask about our return tickets, and she looks at us and she says, "You'll get them when you come off the stage."

TRANSGENDER TALK SHOW GUEST LINDA PHILLIPS

At first one wonders what really made Cindy vomit, since by the time she got to *Sally,* joining a panel on "my husband left me because he's gay," she was so filled with venom it was hard to imagine her keeping a whole lot down. She had seen the warning signs, she says: her husband, Byron, had not only "got drunk and came home dressed as a woman," he had also "redone all my cupboards, he had cleaned my whole house, rearranged all my furniture." But when she found out her husband was seeing another man, she says, "I was like nonstop vomiting."

A visceral physical reaction to the revelation of homosexuality—or transsexuality, as the talk show–worn example of the puke-inducing penis in *The Crying Game* makes clear—is certainly not unusual. But what really seems to sicken Cindy, the other panelists, Sally their host, and a lot of the audience, is not so much homosexuality as deception. In a genre that fixates firmly on victims, and that for commercial reasons typically approaches its issue from the heterosexual woman's vantage point, a married gay man, generally painted as a *deceiver,* is transformed quite easily into a victimizer. "I was used as a cover," Cindy says. "Nobody told me, 'This man is gay.'" Byron denies it, saying that "at that time I didn't know I was gay," but no one seems to be buying that. "That's like being a little pregnant," says one audience member. "Either you are or you aren't. Hello. You should have gotten to know yourself before you married someone else." Sheryl, a wife Sally introduces as "ashamed and humiliated that her husband turned out to be gay," and who describes her ex-husband's lover as "a flaming faggot," demonstrates the way the transgression of dishonesty trumps that of homosexuality in the moral world of TV talk. (Although they push up against one another, antigay and antideception sentiments sometimes do coexist, the "faggot" and the "deceiver" both vilified.) "He not only used me to cover up his true feelings, to cover up his true identity for sexual feelings," she complains, "but he used the *Sally* show to get a free trip to New York" and then skipped out—for "a gay rally," she thinks. Sally herself adds the final nail in his coffin. "And today," she reports indignantly, "when we called he lied to us once, twice, three times, four times. He lied to us all morning."[1]

An old association between gayness and untrustworthiness is being reproduced here, as is the questionable notion that being left for someone of the opposite sex is more humiliating than being left for someone of one's own sex. But at the heart of this kind of treatment is the irresponsibility of the closet, the damage done by men who *are* gay (a fixed, ahistorical state, according to most of the beholders) but enter straight relationships. As an ex-wife of a gay man says on *Rolonda,* "If you're gay, then say it, be it. And if you don't know whether you are fully gay yet, just wait."[2] The ultimate stigma is attached not so much to homosexuality as to deceit. The ultimate slime ball is not so much the gay man as the man who *lies* about his sexual desires, first to his wife and then, even worse perhaps, to *Sally,* demonstrating his indifference to the contracts of both heterosexual marriage and televised talk shows. Both, the shows seem to suggest, require you to be who you are, your real, true, normal self, to come out sooner rather than later, to tell the truth, even if who you are makes some people vomit nonstop.

It is not just the "low road" shows that promote this line. "High road" *Oprah,* taking the same topic a year earlier, wound up making the same honesty-as-therapy sounds. There are, Oprah suggests, describing the value of a show on gay husbands to one of the men, "many, many men who are masquerading the same way you did for years" who will "see you today and can eliminate a lot of the years of lies for themselves." Eliminating the lies is in fact the ethical push of the show, both in general and on this particular day: "For me, always the issue is how you can be more truthful in your life," she tells us at one point in the gay husbands show, a point she has repeated in various forms consistently throughout the years. The wife gets much audience support when she criticizes her husband for keeping "the truth" from her (he had not yet "come to terms" with his homosexuality, he says); another guest, a gay man who was "up-front with her from the very beginning" because "it's all about honesty," also generates applause. All the guests, in various ways, support the "be who you are" ethic. Matthew, one of two sons who accept their father's homosexuality, says he doesn't want "people to have to hide what they really feel because it's not fair," and he wants "people to be who they are." His mother similarly locates the problem in dishonesty, rather than in sexual status: "I have no

difficulty with the fact that Steven is a *homosexual,*" she says, "I have difficulty with the fact that Steven *married me.*" Oprah weighs in periodically
along the way: making the move from ethics to health, she suggests that "if
nothing else comes out of this show, the truth of the matter is, you can't
love anybody else unless you accept and love yourself first." Psychologist
John Musser, whom we are told "counsels gay men and their wives on how
to reach the point of acceptance," picks up on this, emphasizing "the importance of loving ourselves and being honest and authentic and real in our
lives. We see the healing effect that happens."[3] While *Oprah* in general operates with "hetero-sensibilities," celebrating heterosexuality in myriad ways,[4]
it is even more committed, at least rhetorically, to the "healing effect" of
talking which is, after all, its business. When the disease is seen as inauthenticity, the cure for homosexuality is embracing homosexuality.

Thematically, that *Oprah* show was simply a repeat of an episode several
years earlier. In 1992, it was Norman and Diane and Paul who were the
central triangle. At first, the folks tell their story with some animosity and
coldness, but without much audience response. Norman, white and vested,
talks about having always had a feeling of loving men, but thinking he could
marry it away, while Diane, a large white woman in a pink dress, asks him
why he kept denying it; Norman's lover Paul, who had also been married
for many years, in his thick New England accent accuses Diane of making
his life hell. But after a time, the show turns, as Oprah follows up Diane's
charge that "you should have told me." Says Oprah to Norman, "I don't
know how the audience thinks, but I know what I think and I usually think
like the audience. I think we all think you should have told her." Immediately the camera pans the audience, which has exploded into applause and
nods and chirps of Yes. Paul and Norman try to explain themselves—in a
small town in New England you do what you have to do to conform, they
say—but Oprah's studio audience backs her up. "None of this would have
taken place if you had been honest with yourself, honest with her, never married her," says a pink woman in a pink striped shirt. "You've been using her
for thirteen years," says a white guy in a white shirt and tie. "You took her
trust, you took her caring, and you threw it all away." As Norman starts arguing back, another woman stands up and vehemently shouts, "You ruined
her life, and you ruined your own life by not admitting it." She points her
finger at him, yelling, ironically, the mantra of the gay liberation movement:
"If you're gay, be proud of it, be proud of it and say it." Like most formerly
married gay men on talk shows, these ones are attacked (almost exclusively
by straight-identified women) not for being gay, but for not being gay *enough.*

"If nothing else," Oprah says toward the end of that show, quietly echoing the finger-pointer, "I hope this show, for all the men and women who are out there carrying a secret, will find a way to come out and be truthful about it." Her expert guest, this time the author of a book on gay-straight married couples who found out her own husband was gay after twenty-four years, repeats the truth imperative. "Today's a new day," she says. "Let's start from here by telling the truth."[5] Same-sex desire is here simply a personal truth, and *lying* is the problem. The talk shows are there to stop the lying, to encourage and facilitate—one might even say enforce—the telling of truths. Homosexuality on talk shows is the love that is required to speak its name as quickly, clearly, and continuously as possible.

Talk shows frequently make their money by programming the revelation of personal truths, and hosts, guests, audience members, and two-minutes-at-the-end-of-a-show relationship experts often drive home what the shows themselves embody and support: honesty is the best policy, and the key to mental health. Yet truth and honesty and deception in the talk show world are anything but simple. TV talk shows, and commercial nonfiction media in general, operate in a world where truth is both imperative and impossible. On the one hand, shows want people who are who they say they are; on the other hand, shows want people who are what the producers want them to be. On the one hand, honesty as an ideology is crucial to the talk show genre; on the other hand, multiple truths cut across each other, as any authority but the personal is suspect. While the cameras are rolling, guests are told to tell the truth, be true to themselves, reveal previously unspoken truths; off camera, guests and audiences are encouraged to perform narrow and sometimes flat-out dishonest versions of themselves to fit the script. Sometimes they agree, sometimes they do not, but the result is always the same: a strikingly dishonest little world that is littered with highly charged moments of truth, a world intensely focused on the virtues of honesty yet pockmarked with lies. For sex and gender nonconformists—for anyone really, but especially for those whose lives are so often inflected by secrets—this is tricky territory.

Everybody Lies

Leeza *called and said, "We're going to do a story about bisexuality. We know you're the bisexual poster boy. We want you to come on and talk about it." I'd been on a few talk shows already talking about bisexuality, and I train people in coming out as bisexual on television,* and Leeza Gibbons and I had worked together, so when they called, I had no problem. And Lani [Ka'ahumanu, another bisexual activist] was going to come down to be on it, sleep on my couch. It was going to be fun.

And then they said they needed an "anti" person. They wanted me to have a gay friend who was against my being bisexual. The couple of people I asked didn't want to do it, and then the producers called me and said, "How about Ant?" Ant is a comedian and an actor, and he used to do the warm-ups for Leeza, and he's also a good friend of mine. He's one of my great friends. So we were supposed to be set up against each other. Ant didn't want to trash me, but he called me up right away and said, "Mike, I want to go and do this show." He gets SAG [Screen Actors Guild] wages. I didn't get a cent, but he gets enough for his mortgage to go on the show. He got nine hundred bucks for it. I said, "Ant, I know you don't think that way about bisexuality. I know you have no problems with it." Ant's dated women. I said, "You know what? No problem. Let's just set up a few ground rules." I knew that whatever arguments he could come up with I could counteract, and we could at least show that he has one opinion and I have another opinion, and we could argue successfully and make a point.

So when we came in there they told us suddenly that they didn't want us to be totally set up against each other, that Ant was going to attack some other people on the show instead. Whatever. I didn't understand what was going on, but I didn't have enough time to think about it or talk to him about it. Then they brought in this other young girl who Lani knew of. She was a runaway and she was lesbian and then she came out as bisexual. Well, Lani said, "You know what, this girl is just a media whore. She's just going on talk shows and she's totally making up stories. We've tried to help her up in San Francisco, and I know that her story's full of shit." So then I started going, "Uh-oh, what's going on here?" Then there was this other guy who was wandering around not talking to anybody, being very gruff and nasty, and dressed up kind of like a skinhead. I went up to him and I said, "What's going on?" And he said, "I don't want to talk to you fags." And I thought, "Uh-oh, what's going on here?" Suddenly there were all these other people appearing out of the woodwork that were not told to me, and this guy was a plant in the audience to get up and say, "My girlfriend was given AIDS by a bisexual man." Well, it was a total fabrication once again. Ant told me later that the guy was a producer who asked him out on a date after the show.

Still, I thought maybe it could work. Everything was set up so that the "anti" person was a friend of mine, someone I had worked with. We had even made parameters. I did everything that I taught people to do. I knew Ant's wit, I knew his sharpness and I thought I could fight right back and maybe get a point across. Well, I didn't know that he was just going to do his act. That's what happened. He did his act. He was very funny, and he just fell into his stand-up comedy routine. Ant had total control of the show; Leeza let him control the show.

The audience just used the fact that this openly gay guy was criticizing bisexuals. The audience initially was very open-minded but became fueled by Ant, and therefore instead of asking questions, they threw accusations. It was okay for them, the audience, to hate bisexuals because they were doing it through this gay guy. It was politically correct to identify with the gay character who's criticizing bisexuals. All the liberals in the audience, all the conservatives, whatever, the Nazi skinheads, could all identify with Ant and fuel their anger toward us, because it was okay to do it through that PC way. So he riled up the audience like nothing else could, because he was funny, he was glib, he was on. And he ripped us to shreds. And they knew he was going to do that. He told me later it was a total setup. It was actually a brilliant move.

I was pretty devastated, but I wasn't as devastated as the married [bisexual] couple who came from Atlanta, who had never been on a talk show before. I spent almost three hours afterwards with them, Pat and Anita, as they were blubbering in tears on my back porch. They were not prepared for the personal questions, the personal attacks, the vitriol they would get from the audience. They were attacked from the very beginning. They were like deer in the headlights. They were so devastated after that happened, and because of Ant's picking on them, that they went back home and were very embarrassed. They dropped out of the bisexual community there, which they had actually formed, and they have since split up. They blame the talk show. Then the show had the nerve to call them up and say, "We're doing a story about people who have had bad experiences on our talk show, and we want you to come be on the talk show to talk about your bad experience."

WRITER AND BISEXUAL EDUCATOR MICHAEL SZYMANSKI

The easy but ultimately not entirely satisfying way to map this territory is to start with this fact about talk show producers: they lie. Talk show producers are widely known to stretch the truth a lot, not because they were raised without morals but because they have a show to put on, and getting guests quickly and cheaply who will create the kind of show you need isn't always the easiest thing in the world to do. Nor do they have any particular commitment to the actual pursuit of "truth," whatever one thinks such a creature might look like; their commitment is obviously to entertainment and ratings, and the truth isn't always terribly interesting.

One home remedy, something akin to the quiz-show fixing in the 1950s, is fraud. Stories of "con jobs" abound: of an out-of-work actress who pretended to be a sexual surrogate out to help a young, impotent married man (another actor) on *Sally,* then appeared on *Geraldo* as a sexual surrogate who had taken up the case of a 35-year-old virgin (the same actor), then later the same year on *Oprah* as a married woman who hated sex; of a couple who appeared as married cousins on *Ricki,* then on a *Jenny Jones* show about men who don't want their wives to dress sexy, then played a mother and son-in-law on *Jerry Springer* arguing about whether he had beaten her daughter; of a guest on two consecutive *Montel Williams* shows in 1993 claiming he was an HIV-positive serial rapist of prostitutes, only to quickly recant.[6] Former host Jane Pratt tells of a guest who knocked on her car window after a taping. " 'We did a good job, eh?' he said, putting his arm around his supposed Ex-Girlfriend Who Thinks He's a Big Jerk. 'We're acting students at NYU. Coming on this show was a great break for us.' " As the guests were thanking her for the big break, the show's limo drove them off toward home.[7]

The companies, of course, claim ignorance, innocence, and outrage. If shows are "duped," however, it is hardly because those producing them leave no openings for deception. "As long as I have a guest who talks well, looks well, and represents himself well, it doesn't matter whether he's real or not," a "stringer" who claimed to have booked people on several different shows told the *New York Post* in 1995. "The initial conversation I had with a producer at *Charles Perez* was 'We'd like it to be as legitimate as possible, but the bottom line is the segment has to be filled.' . . . I come up with a plot, teach it to them, rehearse them." Against shows' denials of this kind of deal making, Ray Nunn, a former *Perez* executive producer who had also worked at *Oprah,* confirmed the stringer's claims. "There's no doubt about it, some of the guests are just fake," he said. "Sometimes they're young actors and actresses who find their way to talk shows. The worse scenario is that producers actually solicit actors to play roles. 'Can you be so and so?' " TV producer Rich Ornstein similarly backs up the claim that fraudulent guests are an "open secret" in the talk show industry, reporting a call from a casting agent, who had been called by a talk show producer, looking for actors and actresses to appear on talk shows as AIDS patients, lesbians, or bikers. "They rented out a studio for a cattle-call audition," Ornstein claims. "It was like putting together a movie."[8]

Most guests, though, are "civilians," and many of them also report either suspicions of fake guests or actual contact with them. In the hallway before their appearance on a *Mark Walberg* program on bisexuality, for instance, Barry Long and Sheri Carter had met a ponytailed man named Alex. By the time his segment started, "Alex" had become "Kevin." As Barry recalls it,

> *His first thing was, you know, "You bisexuals, you're spreading AIDS. Bisexuals just bridge between the heterosexual and the gay communities, and you're going to be the death of humanity." And he's standing up, and his finger's right in front of Sheri's face. Then a little later Mark [Walberg] asked him, "But Kevin, do you have a personal beef with this?" and he says, "Yeah, I was seeing this girl and things were going really well, and she comes one night and she tells me she don't want to see me any more because she started seeing this other girl, you know. What am I supposed to tell my friends? They're asking me like, 'So what's going on? Where is she?' What am I supposed to tell them, that she's dating this other girl?" He was really out there. Loud and angry. So during one of the breaks I leaned over Sheri's shoulder and said, "Kevin, you know, I'm sorry to hear about your experience. Let me just ask you this. How would you feel if she had left you for another guy?" And he was really calm. He said, "I'd probably be pissed off. I might be more pissed off." I said, "Well, I mean, is it worse that she left you for a woman?" He said, "No, I guess not." Seemed like a nice guy, a lot calmer during the commercial breaks. So after the show, downstairs, I went up to Kevin and I said something like, "I just wanted to talk to you. Sounds like you're really angry about all this." And he said, "Yeah, not really." I said, "Well, the things you were saying," and he says, "Well, you know, they told me to say that." I say, "Well, you seemed really," and he said, "Oh, you believed it? I guess I did my job well." He seemed really flattered. "I'm*

an actor, they paid me a couple hundred dollars. They told me to say
that stuff. I was good? Really, I was good. I was good."

Barry's story, like the remarkably similar happenings on the other coast
described by Michael Szymanski, holds a clue to the manipulation and lying
that is so common among talk show producers. The production arrangements encourage it, making it seem quite rational, or at least unavoidable,
to producers, who cannot be confident that the likes of Barry and Sheri
(who wanted to talk about the way they had worked out being married and
bisexual, with which they were quite happy) will make a show people will
want to watch. They need heat, and the easiest thing to do is to find people
to espouse readily recognizable conflict packages: in this case, slotting in the
widely disseminated images of bisexuals as AIDS conduits and as sexually
predatory relationship-busters. And rather than spending the scarce resource
of time trying to *find* people with other points of view, occasionally producers simply hire them.

Indeed, many shows' obvious dependence on conflict as the major key
to attracting an audience means that sometimes even getting good talkers
is not enough, and increases the pressure to treat booking as "casting." It
is no longer enough to find a couple of married bisexuals; you need their
angry ex-lovers or jealous current lovers, or angry lesbians who think there's
no such thing as bisexuality, or a straight guy who has been jilted by a
bisexual woman. Historian and transsexual activist Susan Stryker tells a
typical story of being approached by *Geraldo* producers.

They were looking for a transsexual for a show on "Women Who
Have Left Marriages to Pursue Lesbian Relationships." I would have
had a blast with that. They called me up, and I said, "Oh yeah, that
would be good." I was going to get a free ticket to New York, they'd
put me up, you know, get a little stipend for it. I thought that would
be a great way to get to New York for a party. And they said, "Now,
we want your ex to come along with you." And I said, "No, she
wouldn't be into that at all. I don't think my ex will be willing to
come along." And as soon as I said that they started being really bellig-
erent. "What do you mean? Don't you understand we're offering you
a plane ticket to New York?" It was like, "Yeah, so?" And they really
started trying to put the screws on. I said, "No, wait a minute. I just
said I don't think my ex would do it, she's a very private person. We
had a lot of conflicts over the breakup, over the transsexuality stuff,

*and it's like, not only would she not want to be that public about her
life, but I wouldn't be interested in being on the show with my ex."
Then they started getting really bitchy and trying to put on this
high-pressure salesmanship. Without her, they weren't interested in
me.*

Women who have left marriages to pursue lesbian relationships, great; a
woman born male who left her wife to pursue a lesbian relationship, even
better; a transsexual lesbian and her ex-wife, there's the ticket.

This mentality is simply the working equipment of a competent talk show
producer. "When you're booking guests," a former *Jane Whitney* producer
said, "you're thinking, 'How much confrontation can this person provide
me?' The more confrontation, the better. You want people just this side of
a fistfight."[9] One former *Ricki* producer complained about a couple who
were "fighting like cats and dogs" the day before, but arrived from the air-
port "all lovey-dovey." "They're like, 'Oh, everything is fine now, we're
going to keep the baby and, you know, I'm never going to hit her again.
We made up at 30,000 feet.' I was like, 'Oh, shit, come on, you're kidding
me!' "[10] On some shows, the fistfight requirement comes directly from owners. "We were told by the corporate people we had to put conflict in every
segment, and the conflict has to be wild," says a former producer of the
short-lived *Charles Perez Show.* " 'Get a fight going in the first segment or
you're going to lose [the audience].' Those are the guidelines."[11] Although
not every talk show is so heavily dependent on conflict, any producer will
tell you its value. "You have to have extremes," says Jason Walker, a producer for the more clean-cut *Leeza;* even *Oprah* producers talk about the
need for "direct conflict," with both or all of the relevant parties, even if
for them the ideal is to have heroic resolution as well. "It all comes down
to conflict," says Steven Goldstein, who had brief stints as a producer at
Oprah, Jerry Springer, and *Montel Williams.* "Two extremes fighting each
other, that's entertainment."

One producer, Goldstein reports, had a sign in her office. "Elements of
a great show," it said. "(1) Emotion, (2) Conflict, and (3) Visual." Of course,
it is preferable to find guests who can provide those characteristics—and
preinterviews, sometimes called "blind dates" since producers "claim to
know within the first minute whether the relationship is worth pursuing,"
are geared toward finding them.[12] But when all else fails, purchasing them
if one can get away with it, or allowing oneself not to question a guest who

seems too good to be true and then claiming to be outraged at the con job, makes more sense than risking a low rating.[13]

Yet paying actors without letting anyone in on the trick, although unethical to be sure, is not so much common practice as a tip-of-the-iceberg symptom of the whacked-out production routines of talk show entertainment. As Laura Grindstaff points out, "The very physical and emotional theatrics that make the genre popular and compelling are the most difficult to produce."[14] Treating the occasional hiring of actors as some aberrant threat to truth, thinking that if only the producers saw the error of their ways they would create "responsible" television, is to miss the fact that talk shows are role-driven to begin with, that even when they are working with "real people" (the vast majority of the guests), producers are casting and directing. For a number of reasons, in fact, actors are not the most efficient route to a good show. Fake guests, when revealed, are a major public relations threat, whether or not the company was complicit in the fraud. Besides, they cost more money than real ones, who often receive a stipend of one or two hundred dollars ("compensation for lost wages" is the industry euphemism), and more often than not will appear for free, seduced by the celebrity stint, the plane ticket to New York or Chicago or Los Angeles, the limousine, and the hotel room. ("A lot of the shows that need the more outrageous stories pay almost all the guests, even though they say they don't," reports a producer for *Leeza* who has worked for a number of other talk shows. "They do. And a few hundred dollars means a lot to some people.") The cheapest, by far most common route is therefore to cast a show with ordinary people, mustered either through organizations or through toll-free call-ins, or pursued because they are part of a sensational news story, and mold them into good guests. That is, producers have in mind what the cast will look like, and they recruit and then manage the cast according to those roles. As ex-producer Goldstein says, exaggerating the case a bit, "You book whoever you can, and it's just cheaper to tell them what to say."[15] Wandering down the hallway into *Sally*'s studio on a cold winter morning, past pictures of Sally Jessy Raphael and the cast of *Star Trek,* I catch a glimpse of this strategy. A producer holding what looks like any other TV script is talking to another woman, who later emerges on stage as one of the guests. Pushed along in the flow of the line, I catch only one clause of conversation, but a telling one, from the about-to-be-guest: "Should I say . . . ?" The story of Liz, a 22-year-old from Appalachian Ohio who went on a *Ricki* show about parents who are fed up with their children sponging off of them, fleshes out this kind of scene.

The first taping we were nice to each other, because we didn't want to go on there and embarrass everybody, you know, and each other. So we taped one taping, and the producer was screaming about it. She didn't like it because we were too nice, and she just cut the whole show. She took my dad and my sister back somewhere, and she took me back to where I was, and she just totally, this lady was like, "You need to beef it up. They don't want to see this. You guys are acting like you have no problem at all, and this isn't what the audience wants to see, and you have to beef it up." And I said, "Oh, you want me to be a bitch, that's what you want me to be, right?" And so she said, "Yeah, kinda." And I was like, "Fine." So we started all over again, a new taping, and the audience had to act like they didn't remember the first taping. So at first I was calm again, cause I wasn't really going to be ignorant, and then I heard him saying this stuff out there what we said we weren't gonna say. So he went on about the bad checks, and "she got in trouble for welfare fraud," and all this kind of stuff, and everybody was like, "Oh, my God," in the audience, and I was pissed. They were making it like it was all my fault, and I was the bad person, and I was no good, and I was having my sister do all kinds of bad stuff, so I just turned the tables. I said, "Well, he's not any better than me. He ran around with my 18-year-old friend that used to stay overnight at my house, while him and my mother was in the other room. Does that make him any better?" Then everybody turned around, and we just went on and on and on for the whole show. That was it. I didn't shake Ricki Lake's hand, I didn't even get to meet her. That was it.[16]

It should be clear by now that talk show producing is not brain surgery, but the production conditions actually make it quite high-pressure work, and most of the manipulative activities are designed to relieve the pressure. Multiple shows are being programmed at once, for one thing, with between five and eight shows taped each week; one producer, typically answering to a supervising producer, who is answering to an executive producer, will be responsible for constructing one or two shows a week, aided by associate and assistant producers. Especially since the expansion of the number of guests per show, that is an awful lot of guests to line up, and an awful lot of scrambling. Not just any guest will do, of course: producers are looking for people who can express themselves forcefully, who can tell a good story in an animated way, who will look good on camera. And all of this is done with an eye to a tight budget, quite often by people with very little experience. The sheer quantity of guests to be recruited, with little money, and prepped in a short period of time—guests are being called for a taping tomorrow, or three days from now—makes it rational to assign "roles" and then fill them with guests, even if they are not quite real.

Not only is it cheaper to book guests and *then* shape their performance, but the manic pursuit of guests and the messiness of decision making also at times precludes any more thoughtful approach. Lawrence Randall, who has worked on several national talk shows (including one of the industry leaders) over his seventeen years in television, describes the guest-recruiting process on many shows as constantly messed up by the whims of those in charge.

You come in and they don't know what the fuck they want, you know. You come today, your topic is people with green hair. Okay, so you go and you spend all that day, you work on people with green hair. Come in the next day. "Wait a minute. Hold off on the green hair, let's get people with yellow hair and blue hair today. See what you can do on that," you know. So you're like, "Fuck, I finally got some green hair, now they want yellow and blue." You come back the next day. "Well, I don't know about the yellow and blue," you know. "Take a couple of more yellows, and look for some purple too while you're at it." This goes on nonstop. It's a mess, because they don't know what topics work. These people are clueless.

"They have trouble booking anything," adds another veteran talk show producer, now at *Leeza*, of many of the producers on the copycat shows of the 1990s.

They'll book anything to get a show on. They're like frantic just to get a show on the air. So they don't really think about, you know, it's not like they thought out, "I want somebody who will say this. And then it makes sense to have somebody who will say this." They're just frantic because they're having trouble doing their job. I know one of them who used to work on a game show, and he'll just call up his Rolodex of game-show people and say, "Don't you want to sleep with such and such?" Sort of lead them into making up a story. Some shows are set up so that it's almost impossible to get the real thing, because they have very low budgets to fly people in and they try to do such out-there topics. There aren't that many people who fit into that who are going to watch the show and call in.

When you cannot get who you want, get somebody anyway. If their hair is not quite purple—maybe it's a bit on the blue side, or too dark—you can always try dying it at the last minute.

Texas Cheerleaders and Sickly Posses

As a booker, you're supposed to be there at like five or six in the morning, reading the papers and calling. So one morning I read in the New York Times *about how in some small town in Texas, four cheerleaders were kicked off the cheerleading squad because they were all pregnant. And there was this huge controversy in this town, because it was the three black girls didn't have abortions, and the one white girl did have an abortion and she was allowed back on the team. But the school wasn't giving names, nobody was giving names. But as a booker you're trying to be a little creative, so what I thought of was, okay, these mothers, these fathers, they must work somewhere, and I bet they work at a fast-food restaurant. So I called all the fast-food restaurants in the area and it turned out the mother of one of the girls worked at the Dairy Queen, and I got her on the phone that morning, and two hours later I was on an airplane. Little did I know that* Current Affair *and* People *magazine and* The Jerry Springer Show *were all following me. It turns out that she told someone, and they found out what flight I was on, and they were following me because they knew I had the lead.*

And I mean this tiny, podunk, trailer-park town, was all of the sudden deluged by everybody. The town just had a four-way stop sign, and you saw all these people and limousines and TV crews. The hotel was like this dinky hotel that was full to capacity from all media people, and like the room I was in, the last weekend there was like a trucker brawl murder. That town was like attacked by sharks, and they didn't know what hit them. Now I wasn't going to go into the high school and wait outside their classrooms. That's what they wanted you to do, the producers, they wanted you to go into the high school. They were on the phone, like, "Get the biggest limousine you can find, like impress these people with your money." Montel Williams' producers got a big limousine and paraded his money around the school.

So anyway I went to the woman's house. She was having second thoughts, she was all nervous. I was told this woman lives on a big house on the corner. The house didn't have a screen door, it didn't have a door. I mean, it was the big house next to all the trailers. It was sad. I had dinner with them. We got chicken, and there were like cockroaches walking across my hands as I was sitting on their floor. I finally left them at 11 o'clock, and I was coming back with my car to pick them up at six in the morning. I got there at 5:30 in the morning to find Jerry Springer's people there with a limousine and $1,000, taking them into the limousine. And they stole my guests. The reason why Jerry Springer *got the interview is because they went into the school and found the cousin of the girl that I got, and said, "I'll take your cousin and you, and your boyfriend, and give you money to come on our show." And I never was so upset in my life. I was shaking. I couldn't believe it. I mean, I was going to get fucked, I was going to lose my job. And I couldn't believe it. All of a sudden it wasn't what's* the good story, *it became* get the booking.

And when you're one of these people, and you've got all that attention, and all these people, and all this business, you lose your sense of like what am I doing. It's like you go from never leaving town—like Houston was the biggest city they ever went to, and some of these people had never been there—and it's like you're offering them this vision of grandeur, and it's to exploit them. You tell them what they want to hear. You lie to them so convincingly.

Former talk show producer Mike Kappas

A good deal of dishonesty is simply built into the way talk shows are produced. Shows that rely primarily on letters from potential participants, and "cart calls" requesting guests on a particular topic who then call in on toll-free lines, are virtually requests for people to mold themselves in advance. "Half the guests are making up a story just to be on TV," says the *Leeza* producer. Although that percentage is rhetorical rather than literal, the motivation of television exposure, and the subsequent molding of oneself to the expressed needs of talk show producers, is commonplace. The guests Patricia Priest calls "moths," those "lured by the flickering light of the screen" toward their fifteen minutes, many of whom write letters to talk shows pitching their own story (another common source of guests), are especially beckoned by the recruit-by-promo strategy. "If I'm on TV, I'm worthy of something," one such participant told Priest, for instance, "because there's a lot of people watching me." Another said she simply wanted to be able to say, "I'm on television."[17] A viewer like this who wants to be on television, and who regularly watches talk shows, will not only know the rules of the game (be lively, have good one-liners, and so on) but can also cast herself in the advertised role. Much like the game-show-Rolodex producer's "Don't you want to sleep with such and such?" questioning, this method of recruiting leads the witnesses. You may not hate your grandmother's new husband *that* much, or have *that* much trouble with the way your wife looks at other women, but if you want to be on television, and if Jenny Jones is looking for people who hate their grandparents' spouses or suspect their wives of being attracted to women, it is not a huge stretch.

Shows in which guests are pursued (rather than invited to pitch their stories), on the other hand, place the burden of deception on the producers, who must persuade these guests to come on the show. Randy Tanner, a former talk show production-company vice president and occasional producer, puts it this way.

> *You do this dance with them in the beginning. It's like, "Oh, you have obsessive compulsive disorder? I have obsessive compulsive disorder. You know, I wash my hands uncontrollably. You hate your sister's husband? You know what, I hate my sister's husband, too. That son-of-a-bitch." It's like, "Oh, you're a transvestite? You know, once I dressed up in a dress. I just wanted to see what it felt like and I still kind of like it. It still kind of turns me on a bit. Yeah, I wear panties underneath my suit, but don't tell anyone." You're trying to seduce a person who's on the other end of a telephone. Because if you can get them, that's how you make your money. And how else are you going to do that other than trying to make them feel comfortable, trying to make them feel like you understand, that you're one of them?*

"You have to say exactly what they want to hear," says Mike Kappas, who worked as a talk show booker. "You've got to say whatever it is to get them on your show." When he saw a story in *USA Today* about a woman whose 5-year-old daughter was raped by her brand new husband, for instance, Kappas knew what to do.

> *You've got somebody on your back saying "Did you make the call? Did you get the booking?" The story was that during the wedding reception, the husband took the daughter, now his stepdaughter, upstairs and raped her, and then told his new bride and the daughter that he*

was HIV-positive. And I remember being on the phone with the mother, saying, you know, "The best thing for you to do is to come on this show and tell your story," that whole bullshit. It was going to be therapeutic, everybody's going to learn from it. I'm a good liar. I mean, I was convincing this woman to talk about the fact that while she was getting married to this guy, he was upstairs fucking her 5-year-old daughter and giving her HIV. And I was on the phone going "Why don't you come on our show and talk about it?" You know, let me exploit you even more. You've been through hell, come on TV and talk about it. But if you wanted to keep your job, you had to book it.

That woman did not in the end do the show, but she fit the profile of most of the other people Kappas pursued: "uneducated, or very, very simply educated, not very worldly, often a minority"—like the pregnant Texas cheerleaders pursued by media mobs. In a booking war like that one, even cash isn't a guarantee that guests will stick with a show. When one show booked the "spur posse," boys who kept score of their many sexual conquests, for example, another show stole them, only to have the first show steal a few of them back. As one staff member who was in on these negotiations tells it, his show took them for a night on the town, dinner, and a strip show, and gave them cash; presumably with that cash, some of the boys hired a prostitute ("they thought it was really cool when they asked the prostitute to have anal sex cause she wasn't tight enough"), and ended the evening by "puking and cumming all over their clothes." The show, in order to retain them and make sure they were presentable on national television the next day, did the logical thing: they bought them new clothes.

Of course, in a booking war you are looking at out-and-out purchase rather than any subtle deception, but the point remains the same: the game of Get the Guest means that pretty much any strategy goes, including sweet talk about altruism and fame and panties, flashing wads of cash, providing vomit-free clothing, and lying.

Dancing Transsexuals and Quivering Grandmothers

In the beginning, I still held the belief that the talk shows were useful tools for education. It really did give people an opportunity to have a voice that otherwise wouldn't have been heard. You could see as you watched the people in the audience reacting in positive ways and actually learning things. So when Charles Perez called, and they said they wanted to do a show that tells the truth about sex reassignment, I said fine, okay. The producer that I spoke with was a very genial woman, and she seemed very sincere about making sure that people understood that this was something that people didn't take lightly, that it was something that people don't do on a whim. I mean, that this is not something for everyone, and some of the surgery is very, very bad, and that needs to be talked about. So, you know, we had this nice long conversation on the phone, and she also told me another person who was going to be on the show, who was a transsexual man that I knew well and respected and felt was intelligent and articulate, and that this would be great to be on the show together. I did not know how many other people were going to be on the show, she was very vague about that, but she said there would be at least two male-to-females. We had two, maybe three, conversations, and I agreed to do the show. But I didn't know how devious they could really be, and I had never seen the show before. Was I stupid.

At the last minute I found out that the guy that I thought was going to be on had been told that they were over budget, and they were not going to take him. I thought, "Hmm, I don't have such a good feeling," but I agreed to go, so I went. When we arrive at the studio, there's a bunch of strange-looking people standing around in the lobby, and they call a bunch of names and it turns out these were the people gathered for the show. But when we were on the elevator, there were three, you know, male-to-female young women there, and they looked at me and said, "What are you doing here?" And I said, "I'm going to be on the show." And they said, "Do you know what this show is about?" And I said, "Yes, I do," and they said, "Well, why are you going to be on this show?" I said, "Because I'm a female-to-male transsexual." "What?" They were totally blown away. They'd never heard of such a thing. I thought, "Great, I'm going to be on a show with people who have never heard of female-to-male transsexuals." They were transsexuals, just uneducated. They basically looked like funky high school girls, street walker types, you know, and they were real characters. Actually, on the air a couple of them said some pretty good things, because they were street smart, but they had no context for all of this, it was just their life and that was it.

So anyway, they divided us up and took us into separate dressing rooms, and they put me in a dressing room with a male-to-female cross-dresser I had actually met before, and we had a really good time.

And when the producer came in and talked to me about what I was going to say, she said, "Let's go out in the hallway and talk about it." She didn't want me to talk about it in front of the other person. She was just very excited about the way I looked, and how masculine I looked. Like, "You're going to play really well." I felt like, "This is great, you're a piece of meat." She said stuff about, you know, "You'll have a big chunk of time for yourself and you can get your message across." And she said stuff about how you have to speak up, you have to really get in there, and all this stuff.

Now I thought the topic was "The truth about surgical sex reassignment," and I didn't find out what it was really about until about half way through the taping, which was "Transsexuals with regrets." I never saw any part of the first segment, so I had no idea what was said. I was in the dressing room and they had something else on the monitor. So they brought us out, and it was a pretty long segment and I was very relaxed and matter of fact.

Then we broke for a commercial. When they come back the music starts up, and a door opens behind the audience and out come these three girls I'd met in the elevator and they come parading down, to like stripper music. As soon as I heard the music and saw the door open and saw them, which was just like a split second, I thought, "Oh my God, I've got to get out of here." But I sat very quiet for the next segment. At one point, they came back from commercial break, and Perez says, "We're here talking about transsexuals with regrets." By that time there was a total of nine people on stage. So another guest and these three girls got into a big fight, and I'm just covering my eyes and shaking my head, making it as clear as possible that I am not connected here. I just thought I would bide my time.

I don't know if it was commercial breaks or what, but one of the guys working the stage would come by and crouch down behind me and say, "Come on, you've got to yell, you've got to get your point out, you've got to yell, you've got to yell." As they're setting up for the next shot, he'd say, "Come on, get in there," you know. I couldn't even see him. "You're not going to get your message out. Get in there. Come on, fight for it." Then as soon as I was off the stage, I was dropped like a hot potato. Escorted back to the dressing room, bum's rush out the door.

JAMES GREEN, CONSULTANT, WRITER, TRANSSEXUAL ACTIVIST,
AND DIRECTOR OF FTM (FEMALE-TO-MALE) INTERNATIONAL

For their part, many more educated guests, offered what appears to be a major forum, describe classic bait-and-switch con jobs. Often, they say, they fell for it because they had had a successful, satisfying experience on another program, or because they were taken in by an apparently sympathetic producer's claim that this would be an opportunity to educate—often the primary motivation for activist guests, for instance. The guests Patricia Priest calls "evangelists," who seek a "pulpit" from which to deliver a message both to mainstream America and people like themselves,[18] are left especially vulnerable to the bait of education and the switch of entertainment. They talk about wanting to reach, say, gay kids in Indiana who think they are the only ones, or some former self who could not name its transsexual feelings, or about redressing ignorance and stereotypes; producers offer them "a big chunk of time to get your message across," and sometimes cast them instead in a role that does not fit them.

Whether they have gotten guests by tricks, treats, or straightforward, scrupulous means, producers face two nightmares: a guest who clams up, and a guest who says things that are radically different from the preinterview—that is, who doesn't play his or her role predictably. Preinterviews, in which talking abilities and basic roles are flushed out, and pretaping minisessions, in which talking abilities are inflated and basic roles reinforced, are designed to reduce the risk of nightmares. As James Green's story makes clear, when necessary guests are coached and goaded into playing the role they've been assigned; like Barnum and Bailey unicorns, they may come in looking like goats, but by the time they go out on stage, producers want them to be creatures with horns in the middle of their heads. They are often kept in separate waiting rooms, for example, ostensibly so they are not stale by the time they are on camera, but also obviously so they cannot reduce the tension on which the production depends, or coordinate their efforts against the interests of the program. Like male porn stars being "fluffed" into an erect state for their scene, Laura Grindstaff suggests, guests are aroused by producers "so they can go out there and 'show wood' " and hopefully "climax in the appropriate way."[19] On some shows (*Donahue,* for example, before its demise), the coaching is minimal, and seldom is there much more than a loose scripting of content; but on most talk shows there is coaching for televisually grabby behavior, some version of the faceless guy whispering "Come on, you've got to yell" in a guest's ear. Don't wait to be called on, it's going to go by very quickly so just jump right in; what you told me on the phone about such and such, that might be really good to talk about; it's a talk show, so we need you to talk. "There's a producer before you get on the air pumping you up with what they need you to say," says ex-producer Kappas. "The producer's going 'Remember you said you're going to punch them in the head if they say that! Remember what she's going to say! If she tells you that, you're going to tell her this!'"

Interestingly, the longer talk shows are on the air, the less necessary even this kind of grooming becomes. "For a good portion, you don't even need coaching or manipulation for the shows," says former producer Goldstein. "It's a self-contained system with people who watch talk shows. They know what the shows want. You don't have to tell them. They're real people who act." By now, that is, many guests and audiences behave according to some larger template of "talk show behavior." Explicitly or unconsciously, they seem to recognize the needs of the program (emotional displays are very good, for instance; long thoughtful pauses are not), and they are certainly reminded of this before the taping begins and throughout it. Therefore, by the time they get on the air, says Kappas, "they are parodies of themselves."

The same might be said of studio audiences, who are often subject to elaborate warm-ups and coaching. At *Gordon Elliott,* the song "To Be Real" comes roaring out of the speakers, and the audience begins to sing and dance along until a young man named Jimmy, who is young and dimpled and very effective with the crowd, tells us what he needs from us (applause and enthusiasm so that the audience at home will know "you're having the time of your lives"), jokes about how people from Brooklyn are always on camera with their fingers up their noses, has us practice our applause, chant "Go Gordon! Go Gordon!" and so on. "This is a job," the woman behind me jokingly says to her friend. As at most of the shows, the pitch is this: if you behave the way I'm asking, you're more likely to be on TV. "Who wants to be a talk show host?" the warm-up guy at *Ricki* asks, and a young Latina named Farrah volunteers; she enthusiastically serves as a stand-in Ricki Lake, asking questions from a set of blue cards so that we can practice applauding. We end with a round of "Go Farrah! Go Farrah!" At *Sally,* after an hour and a half wait, a small, blonde woman in a black outfit and lots of dangly jewelry introduces herself to us; she is Amy, the supervising producer. "You seem kind of low energy," she says in her strong, whiny Long Island accent. "Okay, so you've been waiting half an hour. Get it out of your system." She tries to help us a bit, telling us "I need you to be obnoxious" and "I need your energy about 75 times higher" and "you're not here to see *Meet the Press*" for a serious discussion, you're here to have a good time. Then she tells us the title of the show, always a secret until arrival: "He Cheated on Me and Now I Can't Trust Him." This gets a big response from the audience, which has found its obnoxious energy. "The men on this show are unbelievable," Amy says, taking no chances on allowing us to make our own judgments. "They are so cocky. These men cheat on women and are proud of it. Can you believe that? You know what one of them said? He actually said"—and here she mimics a stupid man's voice—"he said, 'I'd do Sally.'" The audience whoops. Amy keeps along this men-are-dogs track, telling us if we really "want to yell" and "tell these men that they're assholes," we should wait in line at the standing mikes. During the show, cued by Amy (who gives hugely exaggerated model responses and hand signals from the sidelines, when she is not yelling instructions at the guests or whispering in Sally's ear), those audience members who want to be on TV stand up and tell the cartoonlike men what dogs they are.

This is not so much lying as performance: guests and audiences are mostly playing some exaggerated or truncated version of themselves, not unreal, but not real either.[20] They play themselves as they might be if they were one of those people on a talk show. They bring to mind Lily Tomlin's parody of a late-night local TV ad: I am not an ac-ter-ess, I am a real person, just like yourself.

Once, for example, I sat in the audience of a sober, engaging, and quite moving *Maury Povich* show, in the front row looking directly up at a rather large woman in pink and a frail blonde woman in blue. We the audience had already been warmed up, having waited around with hip-hop music playing in the studio ("Everybody dance now!"). "Are you awake? Are you hyper? Let me hear you scream!" a young female producer had screamed, caricaturing dissatisfaction at our screaming abilities, initiating a second round of screaming, and then bringing up an audience member to do a little dance with her. But the mood changed abruptly when Povich arrived and, after a brief shmooze, launched into the show, about killer fathers in prison (cheaply tied by the show to the O. J. Simpson case through shots of Simpson's kids). The women on stage are both grandmothers, it turns out, battling for custody of their grandchildren, since pink's daughter was killed by blue's son, who is now serving time in jail. Maury's first question is to the victim's mother, and in what seems to me like a split second, the woman begins shaking and almost-crying, lifting a trembling hand to her face, lips quivering. Though the tears take a while to match the crying sounds, her emotion seems real enough—I have no doubt she lost her daughter—but it also seems made for television. ("Smile, Maury," the blonde grandmother later says quietly, and perhaps bitterly, between segments, "you're on television.")

After this first segment, in which the women tell their stories and argue a bit, we break, and a producer announces that they want to reshoot the opening. Povich reads the opening teasers off the teleprompter, ending in the same way he did the first time, by asking the pink shaking woman to tell her story. She looks briefly confused, unsure if she is expected to tell her story again, and for a moment, before a producery voice calls, "Great, Maury," I see a trembling hand start to lift, a lip begin to quiver, as if she is willing herself back into the character she knows herself to be. She is not a professional, not an act-er-ess, but if the job calls for another take, she knows what is expected. "People want fake real," ex-producer Goldstein claims, "and that's what they're getting."

The point here is not just that guests are sometimes faking it or that producers are often manipulating and deceiving, although those are both the case. The point is that performance and dishonesty are built into the *production arrangements* of television talk; they result from its logic, not from its corruption. Producers and bookers mislead and manipulate, if that gets them the booking; guests exaggerate and role-play, sometimes because they are told to do so, sometimes because they know it works. For the most part, transsexual and gay and lesbian and bisexual guests fit like any other guests into the generic framework in which they are used: if they go on for a hoot, they tend to recognize and ride the express roles given them; if they go on to get across a message, as until recently most such guests did, they are either lucky enough to fit the role they are invited to play, or butt up against a role they are uncomfortable playing.

Little of this is lost on viewers, it seems. The suspicion that the whole thing is performed, or parts of it falsified for their benefit, runs spontaneously throughout discussions with viewers. "It's sort of to me like watching a comedy," says Rachel, a 30-year-old Latina secretary, of *Ricki*. "They make me laugh, but I can't believe the things I see sometimes." Joni, a 59-year-old white homemaker, agrees. "They told them how to act. The audience is the same way. You don't think they tell them how to act? I think they're told to yell and scream." Jim, a 37-year-old white truck driver in another group, makes the same claim. "Some of them are like sitcoms," he says. "It's just like they're set up, they're so absurd, you can hardly believe what happens. It's just like watching to laugh." Reality does not always matter: "I'd rather it be real," says Debbie, a 27-year-old white bookkeeper, "but if it's a strange enough show and it's not real, then okay." And people disagree on which shows have more truth-telling in them, as when Oliver, a 40-year-old African American administrative assistant, argues that "the people on the new shows will tell you to your face, 'You're a mess, you came on TV to discuss being a mess, so you better be willing to listen to the fact that you're a mess,' and that's reality, that's true realism." But the awareness of staging and artifice—as with, one presumes, talk shows' cousin genre of professional wrestling—is a constant. That awareness can serve as a sort of buffer, in fact, for the potential damage of manipulative, stereotyping, vitriolic programming. Ironically, the more outrageous a show is, the more unbelievable it seems, the less damage it may be doing simply because it cannot be taken seriously. "It doesn't affect my attitudes at all because it's not reality," says Debbie, the bookkeeper, for instance. "I don't look at it as the place I get my information from. It's the place I get my entertainment." When truths could just as easily be lies, when you can't tell whether someone is screaming because they're angry or because they have been instructed to scream, there is not much reason to treat talk show guests as representative of much more than the comedy of television.

Moments of truth

Despite all the maneuvering, however, talk show production—again, like "reality" television more generally—depends on a large degree of honesty and spontaneity; in fact, the maneuvering is the *result* of the extra value of "real" moments. Like the circus sideshow banner, much of the appeal of the genre is its claim that audiences are witnessing something nonfictional. Like game and quiz shows, or infotainment programs such as *Inside Edition* and *Dateline,* the pleasures being offered rest on a belief in the realness of what is being represented.[21] If the emotions and opinions and situations on display are read as prepackaged and scripted, a talk show has little advantage over a soap opera; the goal is to be soap operatic and believable, fun as fiction but familiar as life, at the same time. Frank N. Magid Associates, the firm that does the bulk of the audience research for television talk shows, found that "viewers say that what is most attention-holding and thus grazer-resistant is programming that is either unusual *or* familiar," Wayne Munson reports. The challenge, then, is to design "shows and formats that strive for not just one or the other but *both.*" "The talkshow, in its combination of the familiar-yet-different—its constantly shifting, news-oriented focuses and guests; its highly charged, ad-libbed performance; its unpredictable, change elements intensified by spontaneity and audience interactivity—seems calculated to meet this challenge. . . . If 'uncanned'-looking programming is the grazer-resistant fare of the 1990s, the audience participation talkshow is among the best at generating or exploiting the productive instability that has become vital to gaining and keeping spectatorial attention."[22] Indeed, it is exactly because "unpredictability connotes a sense of credibility vital to the talk show's effectiveness" that producers are in the position of coaching guests in the first place;[23] coping with this "productive instability" at the genre's heart, talk show producers seek out the spontaneous and unpredictable, and then scurry around trying to reduce their risks, managing spontaneity and channeling unpredictability.

For one thing, this means that, speaking with former guests, for every horror story there seems to be a happy one, in which a guest reports an experience of breaking through, of saying what she wanted to say, of "enlightening" or of representing a life approximating the one she recognizes as her own. Beyond the general windows they provide on unseen lives—even if the windows are quite dirty, they are not entirely opaque—producers seek out unforeseeable moments of *emotional truth,* even more than the canned mimicry of talk show behavior. (Indeed, the attorney for talk show guest/confessed murderer Jonathan Schmitz, in his attempt to exonerate his client by impugning *Jenny Jones,* suggested to Jenny Jones on the stand that one of her special skills was provoking emotional responses—including, presumably, murderous impulses—from guests. She pleaded maybe guilty: "I'm not sure if I'm good at that," she said.) Although behind the scenes honesty is useless at best, honesty is always good on camera: it plays much better, for one thing, than the canned storytelling that goes with much dishonest self-presentation. Especially when it is fresh, when a new truth is being uncovered, it can be gripping to watch. Revelation shows—surprise crushes, long-lost loves, secrets of all kinds—are a staple precisely because they offer a low-risk, controllable route to the jackpot. It is not the revealer who provides the payoff, but the revealed to; the pot of gold is not the planned moment when the husband divulges that he is a cross-dresser but the instant just following, when the wife reacts without planning. For a moment, there's a sense that *anything might happen,* that *something really real is going on here.* When a fight breaks out during a commercial break, the cameras go on immediately to capture it not just because it is conflict, but because it looks to be, and most likely is, spontaneous and authentic. When the executive producer (sometimes in "the control room" with monitors and taping

equipment and other staff, sometimes on "the floor" with the show's producers) decides to "go long," taping beyond the roughly allotted segment
time, she often does this because she senses a moment of emotional truth
coming up and she is willing to spend the money for the chance to catch it;
later, she can edit the show down to the length she needs, and highlight that
moment.[24] Talk shows go for what Grindstaff, in an analogy to pornography, calls the "money shot," the raw-emotional orgasm scene of television.
Talk shows demand

> external, visible proof of a guest's inner emotional state, and the
> money shot—the dramatic climax when the lie is exposed, the affair
> acknowledged, the reunion consummated—is the linchpin of the dis-
> course. The money shot is also the linchpin of production efforts, in-
> forming the activities of producers at every stage of the process. All
> the work behind the scenes—choosing topics, finding, interviewing,
> and rehearsing guests, coaching audience members—is done in the ser-
> vice of its display. Depending on the show, the money shot might be
> "soft-core," prompted by grief or remorse and consisting primarily of
> tears . . . or "hard-core," involving bickering, shouting, screaming,
> and, occasionally, physical blows.[25]

In the control room during a taping of a show on gang girls, for instance,
while the director instructs the camera operators and the executive producer
chats with her producer over headsets, while two lawyers watch for problems and several other people staff various machines, most of the attention
is on camera shots, details like chyrons (captions) and segment lengths. The
energy in the room changes toward the end of the taping, though, when one
of the many monitors we are facing picks up a change in the demeanor of
one these hard-faced, tough-talking, unapologetic, bandana-wearing gang
girls: she looks like she might cry. The camera shot is switched, the director
calls for a close-up, and suddenly the girl's face is on the central monitor,
and we zoom in as she begins to break. "Yeah," the executive producer says
to me. "We live for those moments. They're like gold to us."

The risk of too much manipulation and control is that these moments
will not emerge. Throwing a show to the audience, you can predict some
of what will happen: someone will stand up and denounce each guest in
rapid succession, probably, or someone will mention self-respect. But the
audience is the wild card, and the messier the show, the wilder the card. In
fact, the cleaner, less sensationalistic shows can often have a tinny, white-
washed, infomercial tone, like the 1995 episode of the short-lived *Marilu*

on gay parents, in which everyone pretty much agreed that love is a good thing. The answers there are easy and cheesy. Jeff, a white gay man in a suit and tie, an amiable cantor, talks about his adopted daughter ("a little Gemini," crows host Marilu Henner) and the women who help raise her, jokes about prejudice ("I don't make eggs in a gay way"); Marilu explains her belief that children do not become judgmental if they don't see prejudice at home, and informs the audience that "it's not politically correct to say 'sexual preference,' you're supposed to say 'sexual orientation' "; Debra, a blonde lesbian in a smart suit and pearls, talks about finding a "darling guy" to donate sperm in a Beverly Hills hair salon, quotes Thoreau, and praises her children's school ("the parents know we're gay, and nobody cares, and that's beautiful"), and explains that the "only negativity I feel is from Lou Sheldon and Newt Gingrich," and so on.[26] It is not so much that all the talk of spiritual paths and praying before dinner and normal families and journeys of learning is dishonest—although it embodies a particular politic I will discuss later—but that it is bland, emotion-free, easy to swallow, dull.

On shows in which unpredictability is allowed freer reign, the moments of truth, like truths of any length, are harder to swallow. Audience members, like guests, are often performing—with the lights and all the doting production staff, it is difficult to pretend you are just having a conversation—but they are also often expressing genuine anger, disgust, sadness, pride. Of course, it is hard to distinguish "real" emotion from a performed version, but it is easy enough to find moments of unexpected, spontaneous expression. When, for instance, on a *Donahue* show on bisexuality, a middle-aged, suburban-styled white woman stands up and suggests, in a thick Long Island accent, that "I think you all should go in closets and stay there," Donahue knows he has a live one, and interviews her a bit. "What should we do with these homosexuals?" he asks her, of course, and while a panelist responds to her comments, the woman is shown in close-ups, and Donahue, known for his good instincts, sticks with her. What would she do if her son came home and said he was gay? "Throw him out," she says defiantly, then suddenly lights up, in ways that even the most cunning producer couldn't have invented. She goes to Fire Island, she says, and sees "them kissing and stroking" each other. "We don't do that, do we?" she asks rhetorically, to a bit of laughter, not nearly enough to stop her. "We don't take our clothes off and walk around with flaccid penises and show everybody." More laughter, both nervous and amused. "Flaccid penises?" Phil asks, and the woman grabs the mike, serious as a heart attack, as though she has been stewing on Fire Island for years, waiting for this very opportunity to air her bitter, raunchy grievances. Her voice is filled with a loathing jarringly at odds with her department-store appearance. "Yeah, flaccid, for a while, until the other guys rub it." She sits down, then impulsively stands back up. "With oil and everything, and they're kissing." ("You've got to stay away from Fire Island," Donahue concludes, to a final round of laughter.) For me, this is a funny and frightening performance but a true and familiar one: her disgust is palpable, unrehearsed, hysterical.[27]

That same year, Jenny Jones is interviewing lesbian teenagers. She and the audience probe in all sorts of ways: Jenny wants to know how it felt to have sex with boys ("boring, pretty gross," says Kimberly), audience members want to know "why do you always try to look like guys if you're attracted to the female thing?" and so on. The show proceeds according to plan, with one screaming match, a proud mother, self-possessed young women, and a beautiful young woman named Amy crying as she explains her suicide attempts. At first, she talks as she must have in the preinterview. "I just couldn't be myself," she explains. "But it's dangerous to come out," Jones suggests, and again, Amy begins with tame emotion, acting the coming-out poster child. "I feel so much better," she says. "I'm so much happier. I mean, all those people who stand up and say 'I hate you' "—and suddenly, as she begins to mimic the people who hate her, some of whom have just stood up in the audience, it is as if a switch is flipped. She speaks with hatred, pointing her finger at her imaginary self, and the camera operator, recognizing the sudden intensity, zooms in. "All those people who stand up and say, 'I hate you, because you're a homosexual I hate you, because you like a girl, because you do this, because you do that, because you're different.' That's wrong. And I will be who I want to be," she says, her voice strong but breaking, "and I'm proud to be gay." The fact that the producers undoubtedly saw the moment in terms of its usefulness, that they cynically did what they could to increase the possibility of provoking deep feeling, does not alter its intensity; for a moment, watching Amy, you could actually *feel* what it meant to be hated, *feel* what the poster-child rhetoric conveys more safely, the pain in which lesbian pride resides.[28]

Talk shows leave openings, sometimes tiny, sometimes rather gaping, but typically more than elsewhere in mass culture, for honest expressions like these to burst through, little shots of something like the truth, through the walls of distortion. These appear at first like insignificant flashes, especially given the machinations that surround them; but it is exactly because they are so rare elsewhere in media culture, because they are wrapped in the falseness and control to which television has made us accustomed, that they are powerful. And when it is *your* identity being cried over or loathed or exalted, these emotion bolts can sometimes bring a lump to your throat that you thought you had long since swallowed.

Speech therapy and the secret under your skirt

I grew up a quiet, observing boy, sometimes almost mute, and find myself now especially sensitized to the virtues and deficits of silence. In Israel, as a 9-year-old visitor, I spoke one concise sentence to my Israeli classmates over the course of a full year. "Nafalti," I said, to explain the cast on my leg, "I fell." There was certainly much more to the story (a bone-baring hole in my knee filled with pebbles, arguments in the emergency room, an electric scrub brush moving toward my flesh, a backward count to sleep), but that one word was all I could extract from myself. That was it. At the end of the year, when they threw me a going-away party and called for a speech, I ran from the room, leg fully healed, all the way home. The forgiving call to speech, after so much glaring silence, seemed like a rebuke, like throwing a bash for a cripple and asking him to dance. Ashamed afterward, I told myself that had I only brought myself to speak, I would be healed. Even then, as a shy kid, I believed in the restorative effects of talking. Although since then I have become an occasional chatterbox, and although I have always been critical of the notion that talking is the best form of therapy, this ideology is the water in which I, and many, many others in this society, are used to swimming. I do not live with very many secrets. Where I come from, talking is both *mitzvah* and *mikveh*: always a good thing to try, a required ritual of cleansing.

This is exactly the belief system on which talk shows depend, and which despite their habits of forgery they vigorously promote, and which has made them especially interested in and open to gay, lesbian, bisexual, and trans-gendered people: speech and disclosure are cleansing and healthy, confession is good for the soul. Tell the truth, get it off your chest, free your speech; at all costs, talk, you'll feel better. It is an ideology that borrows most heavily from psychotherapy,[29] but also from American values of free speech, from religious traditions of confession, and from cultural traditions that value firsthand, personal knowledge. Patricia Hill Collins, for instance, argues that black feminist thought involves "concrete experience as a criterion of meaning"—the talk show criterion exactly—as opposed to "the Eurocentric masculinist knowledge validation process," which emphasizes decontextualized, detached observers generating "objective" knowledge.[30] Talk shows, of course, commodify the call to reveal personal truths, giving it a curiously populist television-age twist: the more public the confession, the greater the absolution. The publicly oriented ideology of free speech, in fact, is joined in talk shows to the privately oriented traditions of confession and therapy, blowing the walls off the confession booth and the doctor's office. Even without the walls, talk shows, at the rhetorical level, root out and root for truth in an old-fashioned way, reinforcing the search for stable, discernible realities. "Oddly, in the age of postmodern simulacra," Jane Shattuc points out, "talk is consumed in corroborating the authenticity of lived experience as a social truth. It relies on the tangible or physical signs of the experience of its audience: testimonials, emotions, and the body."[31] They are going to get to the bottom of things, stop the masquerades, shed light in dark corners, help people tell each other what they really feel.

As I noted earlier, the logic behind this rhetoric of truth-telling-as-therapy is exactly that which informs the call to leave the closet. Despite occasional "Can gayness be cured?" topics, TV talk shows on gays and lesbians (and to a lesser degree, on bisexuals and transgendered people) are typically pro-grammed as stories about overcoming self-hatred, being true to oneself, and building relationships based on that revealed truth. To the degree that a coherent message is structured into the shows—and, as I have pointed out, the shows are simultaneously structured and open-ended—it is textbook liberal "essentialism":[32] we all have sexual cores, and some of us have gay ones; social pressure encourages those of us with stigmatized sexual desires to hate ourselves, and to develop our lives around the pretense of heterosex-uality; that lie is damaging to our mental health; leaving the lie behind is the key to liberating the true self, and therefore to mental health. One seeks the truth about oneself, adjusts to it, and communicates honestly to bring relationships into line with that truth as much as possible. Given this logic, it is often those who cannot accept the truth of a gay person's life, their own or somebody else's, to whom therapeutic talk is directed: the pathology is homophobia, not homosexuality. This is true not just on the early shows, which popularized the notion of homophobia as a disease, but also, even more so, on the newer ones. The objects of the "relationship experts," for instance, on *Ricki*'s "I'm Gay . . . It's Not a Phase . . . Get over It!"—the twisted ones, the ones in need of the show's therapeutic assistance—are the family members who cannot accept their gay and lesbian relatives. "How would you like it if he said to you, 'I don't believe you're straight, all you need is a good woman?' " Tempestt Bledsoe asks her guests on her version of the same show, "I'm Gay, Get Used to It!"[33] In these cases, it is not the normality of gayness that is at issue. In fact, when placed as part of a therapy or honesty storyline, as it so often is,[34] gayness takes on a status not only of normal difference but of ultimate truth.

The assertion that we all have sexual cores to which we must be true does not work nearly as sympathetically for transgendered people as for gay ones. While gay people are asked to bring their lives into line with their "real" essence, transgendered people are typically programmed in ways that emphasize anatomy as the only *true* gender marker, and thus any dissonance between genital status and gender identity as a sign of inauthenticity. Transsexualism, for instance, is often framed as a monstrous secret to be revealed to nontranssexuals—what would you do if you found out your girlfriend was a man?—and transsexuals not so much as gender-crossers but as *gender-liars.* "You're terrible. You're fooling people. You're deceiving people," one audience member tells a transsexual woman on *Sally,* although there has been no evidence of deception presented. "I mean, that would be very scary. Let's say you go to a bar, a disco, wherever you go, and all of a sudden, you got out to the parking lot, you escort this girl wherever you're going to go. All of a sudden, surprise! I mean, you know."[35] The story of Brandon Teena, a young transgendered person who lived as a man for a period before being raped and murdered, is programmed by *Geraldo* as one of several "secret lives revealed."[36] In another program called "bizarre" over and over by its host, Dona, married for two years to Bobby, a man who "turned out to be a woman," describes what Geraldo calls "the terrible day when you discovered that the man you married was, in fact, a woman." "My world collapsed. When she dropped her pants—and I don't mean to be crude—when a man takes his penis out, I don't care how big or little it is, they take it out, they don't do this. My world went black. I was looking at my own death. It was the most disgusting, vile, filthy, degrading thing that's ever happened to me in my life. I'd rather been raped by a herd of donkeys. . . . Her whole life is a lie, every single day." Later, asked by an audience member if she can trust enough to love again, Dona assures the audience that "I have a wonderful boyfriend, and he's all man. I checked his plumbing out, I'll guarantee you that," she says, as the audience applauds.[37]

As on the shows about married homosexuals, an underlying dichotomous "truth" is protected: there are only gay and straight, male and female. But in contrast to the way "living a lie" themes play out on shows about married homosexuals—come out so you don't hurt people, in short—with transgendered people, it is the *transgender status itself,* not just whether or not it is revealed, that appears as deception. Often, in fact, transsexuals insist that there is nothing misleading about their behavior, since they live in accordance with their gender identity; the host and the audience insist that current (or sometimes even prior) genital status outranks all others, and that to operate otherwise is to lie. Introducing Conrad to the audience for her tellingly titled show "I Was Fooled," for instance, Sally Jessy Raphael says he "has been living a lie for the last 13 years," and announces that he will now be confronted by some women who "can't really forgive the fact that Connie, dressed as a man, seduced them into a romantic relationship that included sex." All of these ex-girlfriends, and Sally herself, refer to Conrad using male pronouns, while he argues that "all I'm doing is being myself." Yet the show is structured as an argument between the deceiver and the deceived, and there is little that can take it off course. "The whole point," as one ex-girlfriend put it, "is you're not who you pretended to be." [38] Similarly, on a *Jerry Springer* episode called "My Boyfriend Turned Out to Be a Girl," 19-year-old Sean, whom Springer announces "was masquerading as a boy so he could date young girls," explains that to him it was never a masquerade. "I'm not sitting there saying, 'Oh, yeah, I'm going to trick her. I'm going to trick her,' you know. It's a matter of, you know, I'm sitting there, living my life as a boy. . . . I never thought about it, you know. To me, it was just a boy-and-girl relationship. That's it." While his ex-girlfriend and others continue to refer to him as "he" ("It's way beyond me that underneath him he's got the same parts I do, you know," ex-girlfriend Andrea says), a series of guests are brought on to denounce the "masquerade," including his ex-best friend Justin ("What am I going to tell my kids?" he asks, apparently very confused; "'I grew up and my best friend was a faggot'? See, I wouldn't have minded if he was a girl and he knew he was gay"), Andrea's mother ("There's a lot of people that's had a tough life, okay, but they don't go out and perpetrate other people"), and Justin's father ("You don't know exactly what people are all about anymore"). [39] In these "masquerade"-themed shows, it is the very existence of an inconsistency between genitals and gender presentation that gets framed as deception: to be transsexual is to *be* dishonest. Indeed, it is the rare sort of talk show revelation that may only go to show that some secrets are best kept, that rape by a herd of donkeys may be preferable to this kind of "truth."

Queer authority

Yet despite all the emphasis on telling it, "the truth" is terribly vexed and unstable on talk shows, and not just because so many of the people involved with the shows have so much invested in performance. With its postmodern "constellation of voices," its tendency to "juxtapose rather than integrate multiple, heterogeneous, discontinuous elements," and to "explode the notion of any one authentic self," the genre multiplies and destabilizes truths.[40] That is, there are so many different, competing, contradictory voices, none much privileged over the other, all apparently "true," that truth and authenticity are in some serious disarray. As Franny Nudelman points out in her discussion of *Oprah,* the genre, by "insisting on the indeterminacy of subjective experience" and bringing together competing narratives that mushroom endlessly, makes a generalized or unified point of view next to impossible: "While imitating a courtroom setting in which a jury listens to the testimony of a variety of witnesses in an effort to discern the truth, the program ultimately exalts personal experience as the only measure of veracity, thus obviating consensus."[41]

The case is overstated; the programs do not so much refuse patterns of meaning as propose overarching patterns while making "proof" impossible. They want to say what a show is about, they want to uncover or assert a clear, underlying truth, a moral of the story, and much of producers' activity is geared toward doing so: good guys and bad guys are explicitly cast, hosts push for honesty and offer end-of-the-show homilies telling audiences how things are or ought to be. Hosts step in as temporary authorities ("That is not the fact, sir," Ricki Lake tells a guest who has asserted that homosexual behavior is the easiest and most common way to get AIDS), and shows routinely use statistics, mostly pulled from magazine articles—percentages of women who have fantasized about having sex with another woman, according to *Cosmopolitan,* or percentages of Americans thinking homosexuals do not make good role models for children, according to *Time.* But the need for indeterminacy and conflict, and the emphasis on the trump veracity of individual, experiential knowledge, cuts away at any confidence in universal truth. In a setting so accustomed to personal truths as the only ones, most attempts at offering "facts" fall flat, looking like just another personal opinion.

"Tell the truth, tell the truth," a conservative right-winger from the Catholic Defense League ("Says gays are sick," says his chyron) repeats to gay activists on a *Richard Bey* show, but his charge only calls attention to its own impossibility. He proposes several facts to consider, including, as proof that "the homosexuals are destroying America," the claims that "the largest group of serial killers in Los Angeles, next to the Zebra killers, were the trash bag killers, a group of homosexuals that went around slaughtering and mutilating after sodomizing" and that Queer Nation advocates spreading HIV to other people, that "these people have infiltrated Hollywood to the top," and that "you can't even make an antigay joke today or you could lose your job." "Tell the truth," he repeats. His copanelist, an older man from the Family Defense Council with a busy shirt and a slight speech impediment, proposes that there is absolutely no proof that homosexuality has biological roots. "It's a behavioral perversion," he says (although it comes out "behavyowal puhvuhsion"). "Biologically, it's an abnormality, a man trying to have sex with a man, a woman with a woman." A lesbian from the Gay and Lesbian Alliance against Defamation and a gay attorney try to refute these claims, but the damage has already been done.[42] The conservatives know the game: they can claim pretty much anything as fact, since this is an arena in which subjectivity rules, in which every speaker and none is an authority, every fact an opinion. Blanketed as the arena is in the rhetoric of truth-telling, one can speak the language of truth without any possibility of being held accountable for truth claims. Who knows, maybe one claim will stick.

Even the ubiquitous (if fleeting) presence of "experts" does little to settle questions of truth, since, as Gloria-Jean Masciarotte argues, "the storied life" is typically favored over the "expert guest," the "cacophony of narratives" over analytical deliberation. "No matter who is featured up on stage—Ph.D. from Harvard, presidential candidate, head of the Nuclear Control Commission, or incest survivor," Masciarotte suggests, "the real expert on the issue at hand, the 'true' voice, is the storied voice of the audience and the caller" and the nonexpert guest.[43] The expert "is treated much like any other speaker—she is interrupted, challenged, and frequently silenced," Nudelman adds. "The expert voice, deprived of its authority, contributes yet another point of view."[44] Isabelle Richards, for instance, a marriage and family therapist who has appeared on about twenty daytime talk shows ("as seen on *Oprah, Sally Jessy Raphael* and *Ricki Lake*," reads her business card), recalls trying to talk about "dysfunctional families" on a *Sally* show featuring a transsexual woman named Dana whose husband had allegedly killed their son in a trash compactor. "When I was preparing, I said, 'Well, I feel like these women probably come from dysfunctional families.' My husband said, 'Do not use that language. People do not understand what that means.' But being a little stupid, I made that comment on the show. Well, Dana went crazy. She started to threaten me. I have scoliosis, and she said, 'You want to talk about dysfunctional? Look at you. You look like a hunchback.' She went crazy. She's pretty big, and she's telling me she's going to take me outside and show me what dysfunctional means."

Usually, the threat to experts isn't nearly as physical, of course, but expert claims rarely survive with the status they have on, say, *Nightline*. On one of his many antigay talk show appearances, this one on *Ricki*'s "You're Gay, How Dare You Raise a Child," the Family Research Institute's Paul Cameron gets caught up in a characteristic exchange. The two "experts," Cameron and gay *Newsday* columnist Gabriel Rotello, have already canceled out each other's facts: Rotello reading from a *New York Times* summary of psychological studies showing that children of lesbian or gay parents show no significant differences from those of heterosexual parents, Cameron claiming those are not the real studies and talking at length about his own institute's studies, which Rotello retorts are "like asking the Nazi party to do studies about Jews."

But the real fight, the real clash of authorities, comes between Cameron and Helen, a black lesbian bartender from Illinois who has already turned the audience against her by appearing unsympathetic to her daughter's suicide attempts. "You do not need a man to raise a child," Helen says, and Cameron, looking placid and self-satisfied, cuts her off, saying "The evidence is actually quite clear on this." Helen, with long hair, black leggings, and a sparkly blazer, talks over his words, which he calmly shoots like pellets. "Just because you got on a suit and a tie, and you got what they call a manhood down there," she yells at Cameron, "what make you so normal?" Marie, her lover, a Latina woman in tinted glasses, no longer holds her tongue. "What's your career?" she asks Cameron. "Psychologist? Good. I work in construction."[45] Period, end of story. You're a credentialed white man in a suit and tie, and you think that gives you authority here? Think again: I'm a Latina lesbian in pants who works in construction. In talk shows, the degree-flashing expert is as eligible as anybody else, if not more so, to be "schooled" by guests and audience members, who know "real life."

Paradoxically, both the ideology of speaking-the-truth, which camouflages all sorts of untruthful practices, and the primacy of personalized authority, which shakes any confidence in truths beyond the individual, are exactly what makes realities of sex and gender easier to find on talk shows than almost anywhere else this side of fiction. Regardless of whether people appearing on talk shows consistently tell the truth, and regardless of the blatant way in which it serves as a justificatory scheme for the genre's prying excesses, the overarching ideology of therapeutic truth speech has made talk shows, in a general sense, a particularly welcoming spot for sex and gender nonconformists.

Gays and lesbians, bisexuals and transgendered people, for one thing, are not just different. They have a talk show sort of difference: they live taboos, they embody secrets. According to most of them, moreover, it is a difference hidden in their core, an essential truth—exactly the kind of thing that must be brought out into the light, according to the talk show trutherapy imperative, that will only fester and cause pain all around if left in the dark. Unusual sexual behaviors and various controversial statuses are certainly talk show fodder, but homosexual, bisexual, and transgender statuses, at least as they have typically been elaborated in our lifetimes, are an even better fit with the speech-therapy and sex-confession ideologies underwriting the shows: unlike most skin colors, they are often invisible, kept secret; unlike extraordinary sexual practices, they are, according to the shows and many appearing on them, truths of the inner self.

Even more than that, ours are secrets of sex, desire, body—favorite subjects for contemporary discourse. "From the Christian penance to the present day," Michel Foucault demonstrated in *The History of Sexuality,* "sex [has been] a privileged theme of confession." In the confession, in fact, "truth and sex are joined, through the obligatory and exhaustive expression of an individual secret." Western cultures over the last three centuries have made speech about sex a primary preoccupation; contrary to the notion that our cultures have repressed sex talk, Foucault documented a "steady proliferation of discourses concerned with sex." As he put it, in what could also serve as a dead-on description of TV talk's approach to sex, since the seventeenth century there has been a growing "incitement to speak about it, and to do so more and more; a determination on the part of the agencies of power to hear it spoken about, and to cause *it* to speak through explicit articulation and endlessly accumulated detail. . . . Sex was driven out of hiding and constrained to lead a discursive existence. . . . What is peculiar to modern societies is not that they consigned sex to a shadow existence, but that they dedicated themselves to speaking of it *ad infinitum,* while exploiting it as *the* secret."[46] Talk shows partake of this "discursive explosion," this constitution of sex as a secret to be told, an ultimate truth to be endlessly discussed, dissected, and disclosed. They, their guests and their audiences, are part of the active *creation* of sexual realities, poking around for the true self that must be exposed, inviting its testimony, even if sometimes only to make fun.

Of course, given the crisis in which authority beyond the personal and individual finds itself on talk shows, certain kinds of key aspects about sex and gender nonconformity are hard to get across: what one might call the truths of political power, for instance, and not just of the individual self.[47] That trade-off is not always such a terrible one for sex and gender nonconformists, however, for whom, in this particular time and place, operating in a place where personal experience is trump has its appeals. The distrust of impersonal authority that talk shows have loudly embraced comes at the tail end of a period in which gays and lesbians and bisexuals were spoken for by science and medicine, and in the midst of a period in which transgendered people continue to be. (Indeed, when it comes to shows about transsexuals, scientific authority often makes an unusual TV talk show comeback.) Part of the cost of a history in which nonconforming sexual desires and gender identities have been medicalized is that gay and transgendered people have been deemed too "sick" to speak with authority about much, least of all about sexuality and gender. "For all our lives, we've always seen ourselves refracted through other people's prisms," Leslie Feinberg, who identifies as a passing woman, says on a 1993 *Joan Rivers* show. "We've always heard people analyze us, describe what our feelings are, what our thoughts are."[48]

Much of the political battle has thus involved assembling a platform from which to authoritatively challenge the voices of "objective" science which diagnose and devalue us. Typically that has been done by claiming the same kind of expertise: highly educated gay and lesbian professionals, for instance, mobilizing in the 1970s against the American Psychiatric Association classification of homosexuality as mental illness or challenging AIDS drug approval procedures in the 1980s.[49] Talk shows provide a very different basis for authority, in which the voice of personal expertise, now often coming from people whose education is largely informal, rules. Even if generalized claims about the "facts" of sexuality and gender carry little weight— and they are always circulating, albeit floating unanchored—on talk shows everybody is certified as an expert on their own experience. Being an expert on you is not nearly enough, but this is far more cultural power than most gay people had been granted in the past (and many even now are still spoken for by doctors and scientists), far more expertise than transgendered people have ever been granted publicly.

On *Joan Rivers* with Leslie Feinberg, transsexual writer, performer, and activist Kate Bornstein makes exactly this point. Rivers brings out a balding,

bespectacled sexual counselor named Dr. Roger Peo for the last two segments, and for a while he talks knowledgeably if uneventfully about the
costs of surgery, the necessity of counseling, and so on. But when Rivers
asks him to assess the situation of Kate and her transsexual lover David,
who had been her lesbian lover Catherine before beginning his own gender
transition, Dr. Peo suggests that "one of the things that they're working on
is the issue of gender roles." Kate shoots a here-we-go-again, they're-talking-
about-us-like-we're-not-even-in-the-room look at David, whose hand she is
holding, and calmly interrupts the esteemed doctor.

> *Excuse me, no, we're not working on the issue of gender roles, we're
> working on the issue of attraction and do we love each other and do
> we still love each other as people. Gender roles we worked out very
> early in our relationship. So I don't think that's it. [She turns to Joan,
> who is shown listening with furrowed brow.] This is what I was talk-
> ing about earlier. The three of us have lived this life, right, and it's be-
> cause of shows like yours that we're able to talk about this life and
> get this life out so that other people can see that we are now talking
> about our own lives.*[50]

What seems like a simple opportunity, and a compromised one, "talking
about our own lives," is actually a large shift: a chance to break the monopoly on "truth" held by those who would talk about us. Amidst all the hub-
bub and the coaching, there is a tremendous amount of testimony. *We who
have lived this life will tell you its truths.*

The cultural effects of these opportunities are uneven, for sure, but striking. While the rhetoric of truth-telling corresponds closely to the ideology
of coming out, the push built into talk show practice toward multiple, individual truths coincides with another queer practice: dislodging the confidence in a natural, universal order to all things sexual. For populations
whose oppression has been so closely tied to assertions of a single order of
the normal, who have been told that their bodies and desires are against God
and nature, talk shows' suspicion of traditional authority and disinterest in
the normal can be a refreshing invitation to bring forward new, disruptive,
destabilizing experiences. On talk shows, the authoritative voices of the natural order—religious and scientific authorities, primarily—are just so many
in a pile of claims about how things really are. In fits and starts, through a
foggy veil, important pieces of lives *as they are lived by the stigmatized* come
through, different and startling versions of the truths of sex and gender.
They come through details and vocabularies: *pre-op* and *post-op, gaydar*

and *fag hag*. They come through in simple, extraordinary visuals: here are two African American men in tuxes exchanging wedding vows, here is a Latina lesbian construction worker and her African American bartender lover yelling at a white doctor-man in a suit, here is a transsexual man crying with his parents, a bisexual woman who looks like the housewife she once was. They come through even more in the ongoing testimony of all kinds of people, the individual storytelling that remains the most common talk show format: here is what it was like for me to come out in Tennessee, here is what testosterone does to your clitoris, here is what it means to me to be bisexual and committed to a relationship. Often, the show is not just a spectacle of difference but a spectacle of talking back, in which the different duke it out with those who judge, label, and dismiss them.

Although, as we will later see in even greater detail, they continually manage to shut down exactly the doubts they crack open about sexual order, talk shows have made it at least quite a bit more difficult to hold onto a single framework—a true world order of sexuality and gender—into which all of these words and images and testimonies can be fit. There is no single story, and different truths pop up one after another; none is the truest, none is demonstrably false. Even the manipulation and the performing cannot keep a lid on the deeper reality finding body in all of these appearances, a reality that, we will see, triggers all sorts of anxieties and hostilities: these are humans, of all kinds, strange and boring, whip smart and dumb as doorknobs, from all kinds of places, who know what it has been like to live the lives they have been living.

4 SITTING DUCKS AND FORBIDDEN FRUITS

What I believe is that there is one way, God's way, the way of the Lord, Jesus Christ, who is the way, the truth and the light. I feel a tendency to want to ridicule at first, but then I feel great compassion for these people because these people are made in the image of God, and they are mocking God by mutilating and destroying the image. It's a very sad thing that we're seeing here. . . . Most people know that our sex is God-given and that it's not nice to try to fool Mother Nature. . . . God makes the person. God determines their sex. There are two very distinct sex roles — two only, only two. . . . They're freaks. They're freaks. We live in a fallen world.

JOURNALIST AND ONWARD CHRISTIAN SOLDIER *RADIO HOST JOHN LOFTON,*
ON JERRY SPRINGER, *"TEEN TRANSSEXUALS"*

When you think of all the things that could go wrong at birth or at least not be as they ought to be, from blindness to mental retardation to cystic fibrosis to, indeed, the entire litany of possible birth defects, why do we assume that the one thing that can never be out of sync is our gender identity? And yet, though we are quick to heap our love and compassion and charity on any of these disabilities, if it has something to do with sex, suddenly we don't want to hear about it. "What's wrong with that weirdo?" And we rail against this human as if he's the ultimate sinner. Come on. If a baby is born partially deaf and we give him a hearing aid, we don't say we're playing God or altering what God intended. If your daughter comes into this world with a defective heart, and perhaps doctors put in a valve, is that messing with the body God gave us? Of course not. And so with the same compassion that we offer to those who are trying to fix other parts of their body that perhaps aren't working as they should, why not a word of understanding to those whose gender seems out of whack? It's not a sin to want to be happy. You don't go to hell in the hereafter simply for trying to avoid hell here on Earth.

TALK SHOW HOST JERRY SPRINGER[1]

On nearly every talk show in which homosexuality makes a showing, some audience member stands up and mocks a guy named Steve. He is spoken of in dismissive, derisive tones, since he apparently receives no mention whatsoever in the Bible. "God made Adam and Eve," the mantra goes, "not Adam and Steve." No one seems to tire of saying or hearing this line; in fact, people seem to be competing to be the one to say it, disappointed when someone else gets to it first, since its rhyme gets a response every time. Applied to women, the saying is a bit more awkward and goofy. "It was Adam and Eve," I watched a woman tell a panel of femme lesbians on *Sally*, "not Jane and Eve." But the meaning is the same: you are not right, you are not loved, you were not created, you do not even really exist.

By now, imagining Steve and Adam making out in the Garden of Eden, fig leaves dropping gracefully to the ground as Eve runs off with Jane or Marilyn or Sharisse, has become something of a voyeuristic, subversive fantasy for me. I can have these fantasies not just because I myself have been known to partake of forbidden fruit, but also because I have very little connection to fundamentalist versions of religious morality. I come from Jewish humanist roots (bar mitzvah speech: was Joseph a dream-reading prophet or a savvy social climber?), and the religious arguments against homosexuality have never carried much weight with me. My roots carry their own fundamentalism, of course: for a good long time the whole homosexual thing did seem unnatural to me, male and female designed only for each other, and where I come from, natural and morally correct are right up next to one another. But the you're-breaking-God's-rules argument, and the cruelty and violence that so often accompany it, have rarely appeared to me much more than cowardice.

While I can have all the sordid biblical fantasies I want, they do nothing to diminish the strength of the rigid sexual morality often showing itself on talk shows, or the significance of the conversations and battles over sexual moralities taking place there. For one thing, these public fights are important because of the deep wounds they rip open for many lesbian, bisexual, transgender, and gay people, wounds we carry with us from early on: the experiences of being distilled into a single characteristic and denied full humanity, of being abandoned, of being privately disappointing and publicly embarrassing, and most of all, of being unloved and unlovable, so much so that even God cannot stand us. For another, moral discussions on talk shows take their place in a crucial hearts-and-minds battle for public opinion. They are one important piece of a public conversation over sexual moralities taking place in multiple, interacting sites—educational institutions and electoral politics, most obviously—which sets paths for sexual freedoms or their denial.

On talk shows, these moral disputes are especially significant because they are especially constant. A recent Michigan State University study, for instance, found that the theme of sexual propriety was prominent in half the programs sampled;[2] although a concern with propriety is not the same as moral condemnation, the two often go together. A few rough percentages from my own sample of talk show transcripts begin to tell the story. We collected all of the available transcripts from national, daytime, topic-oriented talk shows in which gays, lesbians, cross-dressers, bisexuals, and transgendered or transsexual people were central, for the years 1984–86 and 1994–95. Among other things, we coded the shows for ten different primary themes (topics of sustained discussion, often but not always loosely defined by the producers' frame) such as promiscuity, honesty, the morality of unconventional sexualities and genders, tolerance, telling the difference between male and female or gay and straight, rights and discrimination, mental health and therapy, and so forth. The results offer an interesting snapshot of the talk show field: sex and gender nonconformists sit against a backdrop of extensive, if rarely high-level, moral and political discussion—despite the image of talk shows as hotbeds of amorality and depoliticized pap. Moral themes remain the most common ones to emerge on TV talk shows about sex and gender nonconformity; like political themes, which operate more or less as counterpoints to the moral ones, moral discussions dominate on nearly a fifth of the programs in my sample. While several themes hover at around 10 percent of the programming and a few others at around 5 percent or below, moral discussions were prominent on 17 percent of these shows, and political discussions on 18 percent. (See the appendix for more information about the sample, coding, and results.) Whether or not the shows always have it in mind, and whether they are screaming matches or reasoned arguments, many TV talk shows on homosexuality, bisexuality, or transgenderism turn out to focus on the morality and politics of these statuses. Not all sexual dissidents get the same kind of treatment, we will soon see, and that fact carries a morality and politics of its own, but the breadth of both moral and political discussion on these programs as a whole is undeniable.

Knowing that moral (and political) talk remains commonplace on daytime television does not, however, tell us much about how such talk works. Like everything else on talk shows, they are certainly messy; propositions fly around without much priority, hosts say one thing and then immediately contradict themselves, conversations are nonlinear and sometimes nearly incoherent. Viewed as a whole strip of activity—that is, seen the way viewers encounter them—talk shows are filled with inconsistent moral assertions, which compete without much pressure toward resolution. Yet the shows themselves clearly structure the sorts of discussions that emerge, encouraging certain themes and ignoring others, loosely scripting the program, as we have seen, in an attempt at managed spontaneity. The discussions of the morality of sex and gender nonconformity are a particularly interesting illustration of how the mix of sloppiness and control turns the tables on the antigay right, producing an unusual acceptance of gay and lesbian, and some bisexual and transgendered, people—a tenuous, easily undermined, conditional acceptance, but a rare Band-Aid on the wounds of the past.

The bigot as freak

I wanted to book this guy who says he can make gays straight. Oh, man, I wanted him on. I also wanted the reverend from Kansas— Phelps was his name. We got more mail about that than any other show. I love this guy. I wanted him on in the worst way because my theory was that if you actually had him on with somebody who stayed very calm and asked good questions, that he would hang himself. And I think he did.

FORMER TALK SHOW HOST JANE WHITNEY

Guest: *Well, I came on this program not thinking that this would be a set-up. The audience here has a heavy proportion of gays and lesbians.*

109

*It has a heavy proportion of—if I might continue. You folks had the
first forty minutes. Could I please have an opportunity to present a different viewpoint? (Host: I wish you would make your point. Yeah,
make your point please.) . . . Listen, I didn't interrupt you when you
spoke. Would you at least be respectful and give me five minutes to
your thirty-five minutes? And this audience's reaction, I want the people at home to know that this audience is not typical of you folks at
home. So this is a very unrepresentative—Rolonda, I'm not finished
yet. I didn't even get my five minutes. Give me a chance. These folks
had 35 minutes already. Don't I have a chance to make my point?
Give me five minutes. (Audience member: Excuse me, the microphone
is in my mouth.) . . . Homosexual orientation is not a sin. Homosexual activity is sinful. That is what is wrong. Not the orientation. If you
are an alcoholic, that is not in and of itself sinful. To engage in drink-
ing to excess, it would be wrong. . . . The drug abuse, the poverty, the
violent crime, the educational difficulties, all of these are highly corre-
lated to a breakdown in the family. The American family and Western
civilization families in general are in a state of disarray. . . . Anything
that's wrong with the strong family values is destructive of the family
and is contributing to this problem. (Host: What do you say to people
who say part of my family's values are accepting differences, part of
my family values are accepting the rights of gay people like other people as well?) It's my judgment, and in my judgment homosexuality is a
psychosexual disorder. These people are creatures of God. They are
made by God. They are brothers and sisters of all of us. . . . I would
accept an alcoholic for being an alcoholic. I mean, I love this person,
he's an alcoholic, so what? But I'm not going to encourage him to engage in activity that is destructive to his physical well-being or possibly
to his spiritual well-being. Same way with homosexual behavior.*

AMERICAN FAMILY ASSOCIATION CHAPTER PRESIDENT FRANK RUSSO, ON ROLONDA[3]

The religious opposition to nontraditional sex and gender populations is
very familiar, from so many years of repetition in this culture: God made
things this way, and told us how things should be. Men have penises, women
have vaginas; they are meant to come together to procreate and raise children, which also requires monogamous, committed relationships. Other versions—men with vaginas, women and women together, and so on—are per-
versions of God's plan, wrong and twisted and devilish. They must be turned
around, or at least stopped. As a young white man in a tie summarized it

from *Sally*'s audience, "How come there are two kinds of people, man and woman? Why wasn't the world created with just one kind of body? There's a reason. God has a balance in everything that He does. We have nuts and bolts. They can't go together, these two, there are nuts and bolts for that."[4] Although it is hard to keep it fresh, this position is also often terrific for television, with its familiarity and simplicity, its resistance to proof but not to counterargument, and the fire-and-brimstone, accusatory, hate-filled words with which it is typically delivered. Along with antigay allies from the world of "research," such as the members of the Family Research Council, right-wing religious guests can wake up the crowd, both in the studio and at home. "In particular shows, a producer says we have to have this element of controversy, we have to have somebody like [radical-right psychologist] Paul Cameron," says an associate producer for one of the more moderate shows. "The producer is going to come to you and say, 'This is all fine, but we have to have some kind of rabble-rousing figure, or something that's going to generate the heat.'" Given the programs' reliance on controversy and conflict, the notion that homosexuality is a moral abomination gets tremendous play on talk shows. The rabble-rousers get the mike for the simple reason that they can rouse the rabble.

So we find a white pastor on *Donahue* saying that God teaches that sodomy is "a deviant, vile affections *[sic]* and it's wrong and it's worthy of death" and that "God hates fags," and a black preacher on another *Donahue* explaining why he would march with the KKK against gays, making the argument that homosexuality cannot be a black thing, since slaves with limp wrists would not be bought, and pointing out that "you don't see no drunkards that are asking for special rights." A radio commentator on *Rolonda* decries the "dangers that lurk inside the homosexual lifestyle" and a 15-year-old boy on another *Rolonda* tells "fags" to "turn or burn, you're going to hell for eternity" while his mother Shirley adds, "When they die and they split hell wide open, that won't comfort them any." A young man on *Oprah* ("opposed to Hannah being gay," reads his identifying caption) argues that "it goes against the Bible and it goes against nature"; bearded Christian John Lofton scolds Oprah on another show for wrinkling her nose and saying she knew she was going to hear "what God thought about this and that," since God, Lofton reports, "says this is a vile sin."[5]

Every couple of years, we even find a show on "former homosexuals," such as the scary *Sally*, in which Dan, Lisa, and David, all white, "redeemed homosexual" members of a "Christian fellowship that helps people out of the homosexual lifestyle," sit on a large blue outdoor stage in Phoenix, backed by beautiful mountains and a deep valley that cannot help but remind you of God. (Every once in a while, Sally and others take their show on the road, traveling-circus style.) They get some opposition from the split-opinion, mostly white, well-dressed and -hairdoed audience but very little from Sally herself, and as the only guests on the show, for the whole hour they speak from the platform with what appears to be the program's endorsement of their legitimacy, bringing fundamentalism and pop psychology into a combination that could without much effort be revealed as nutty. David, having mentioned the organization's hotline number, talks in a high, animated voice about how he tells people, "You are forgiven, just get up and keep moving forward," and Lisa, in a foofy dress, explains how as a lesbian she "wasn't into little foofy things." Homosexuality is not an attraction to the same sex, says Dan, but an ambivalence about the same sex; homosexuals are "heterosexual people experiencing homosexuality." Adopting an expert tone, he asserts that there are "three factors" involved with homosexuality: a God-given need for same-sex love that is there from birth, a misinterpretation of those needs as erotic rather than emotional, and a reparative act on the part of the homosexual to meet those needs.[6] A few years later, psychiatry professor Charles Socarides appears on *Geraldo* to argue that "you can cure a person if they're willing to undergo treatment"—that is, if they have not been seduced by the "rewards of the gay life," which he lists as "brilliant, easy access to partners, the promiscuity," the "keeping of their own income to themselves," and "the lack of responsibility in raising children." A central opponent of the successful early-1970s mobilization to remove homosexuality from medicine's list of diseases, Socarides continues to battle in 1995.

> *We psychiatrists and psychoanalysts who treat homosexuals are not really a minority. We're a solid majority that have been cowed into saying nothing because of the media, in certain ways, except this show . . . who, who, who silence us at meetings, at presentations, in publications, in book publications right along the line. We're really a silent majority. We view the, the removal of homosexuality, obligatory homosexuality, as one of the real fiascoes, scientific fiascoes, or con games, of this century. This was done for social, political—through social, political action. And there was never any evidence to prove that homosexuality, of the obligatory kind, was, was, was not a disorder. This was pushed through by fiat and by gay activism within our own organization.[7]*

It is strange to hear such arguments sputtered more than twenty years after their defeat, but talk shows make a little room for even the most retro of arguments, as long as they promise to get some backs up. Thus, although talk radio and news are the right wing's media of choice, daytime TV talk makes a great deal of space for such voices of antigay Christian conservatives and their scientific and political allies. And what they have to say, over and over, is consistent: you are not right, you are not loved, you do not even really exist.

Yet daytime TV is not the most welcoming spot for such views. Talk shows are among the few places where right-wing paranoia about the liberal media is not so far off. ("Gay and lesbian is about tolerance. It's about acceptance," says one executive producer, a line shared by many other producers with whom I spoke.) For one thing, post-*Ricki* talk shows have often simply gone about the business of accepting lesbian, gay, and bisexual people as members of the tribe, integrating them into shows on nongay topics, such as *Jerry Springer*'s "I Love Someone I Can't Have," "Confess, You Liar!" and "I Can't Stand My Sibling," *Ricki*'s "Today I'm Going to Break Up My Ex and His New Chick" and "Surprise! I'm Hooking You Up," *Geraldo*'s "I Saw You on Geraldo and Just Had to Meet You," *Donahue*'s "Is There Life after a Career in Porn?" *Dennis Prager*'s "Comedians against Prejudice," or *Sally*'s "Why I Was Fired."[8] Here it is another identity that defines lesbian, gay, bisexual, or transgendered guests—comic, porn star, vengeful ex, sibling, liar, unrequited lover. There is little room in these shows for complaints that homosexuals are sinners, violators of family values, or sick; these shows are *about* something else, and gay people on them just *are*.

On the many shows that are directly focused on sex and gender nonconformity, moreover, the voices of moral condemnation of homosexuality are almost never endorsed by the show itself, through its host or its overall framing. In general, talk shows fit into four different program types: what I think of as "testimonial" programs, in which a number of people are brought on primarily to tell their interesting stories in what amounts to an interview by the host and audience (what it is like to be a gay teenager, for instance), make up about a quarter of the shows; about another fifth of the shows are organized as "issues" programs, in which guests, host, and audience discuss the political aspects of personal experience, or debate public policy directly (workplace discrimination of sexual minorities, for instance); roughly another fifth of the sample consists of "family conflict" shows, in which relatives, usually of different generations, battle it out for the cameras (for example, parents who don't accept their sons' cross-dressing), and a final fifth concerns "relationship troubles" (men whose wives have cheated on them with other women, for example). Claims that homosexuality is an abnormality and abomination in the eyes of God are made within these program types, usually on programs constructed as political or interpersonal disputes. Morality is always the response, but never quite the question asked by the show.

The *Rolonda* show with the mother and son, for instance, was set up as a discussion of whether teenagers should be allowed school credit for "bashing gays." The *Oprah* show evaluating Hannah's disputed "lifestyle" was arranged as an issue of what sort of schooling gay teens should have, and included progay testimonial statements from lesbian celebrities Melissa Etheridge and Amanda Bearse; the *Oprah* featuring John Lofton was a discussion of gay marriage, and included married bodybuilding sweater guys Bob and Rod Jackson-Paris ("marriage comes from the heart," they say, and "we just got a new puppy, and we have a bird").[9] The God-hates-fags *Donahue* show was an examination of antigay violence, and the black-preacher-against-homosexuals show was a referendum on gay rights, and included black bisexual minister and religion professor Elias Farajaje-Jones ("the problem is that when lesbian, gay, bisexual, transgender people in the African American community have to deal with racism in the dominant culture, as well as with homophobia at home, you know, that makes it all the more painful") and PoMo Afro Homos, an African American gay performance trio ("Brothers, join the struggle. Let's put an end to these demeaning depictions of black gay men as snap-happy sissies perched above the masses. We demand an end, I said an end, to mainstream misappropriation of Negro faggotry!").[10] These are topics seldom drawn from the agenda of the radical right, but instead from, dare I say it, the gay agenda.

Especially since the recent "younging" of talk shows, right-wing antigay voices emerge even more commonly through programs formatted as interpersonal conflicts. As one executive producer explains, it used to always be "right, wrong, Bible thumping," but "that's the old days."

> We don't treat it as a controversial issue. It's not enough anymore. It's like, "Okay, I know there's two sides of an issue." These people are going to repeat the same thing, that if God wanted to create Adam and Adam he would have, blah blah blah. It's all been said and done before, so how are we going to advance it? You never get anywhere. You're never going to change the Bible thumpers. Never. No matter

what you do. So why make that the issue of an hour show? It is one of those issues that people are so entrenched religiously, emotionally. How are we going to maybe change some of their minds? How are we going to maybe create tolerance? The only way you do it is not inherently make that the focus of the hour, not making it a right or wrong issue. It's not like it's right or wrong, it's more like, "Can this mother accept her son's gay lover?" It's like we're taking the assumption that the mother is accepting the son is gay. What you do is take real people that have real family concerns and they in particular want to try to get over it. Or they themselves within the two of them, the son and the mother, want to have some sort of peace. Like, "My mom kicked me out because I'm gay," okay. We're talking about individuals now. We're not talking about the issue of gayness. We're talking about an issue where a son wants to be able to go back into the house because he loves his mother. The mother can't accept the fact that he's gay. That goes beyond saying is gay right or wrong. We have a family in a crisis.

Even for companies less geared toward conflict (such as NBC's *Leeza,* one of the few programs bought by a network, which always wanted a show they could feel was "respectable"), the interpersonal or family framework is useful. "The thing we constantly ask ourselves is, 'Is this something our audience can relate to?' " says *Leeza*'s executive producer, Nancy Alspaugh. For shows on homosexuality that women at home can "relate to," the show typically places the issue in a family context, with families that look like the middle-class, white viewers—hosting Martina Navratilova's ex-lover Judy Nelson and her "all American" sons, for example.

So whereas lesbian issues aren't something that maybe middle America, you know, maybe the housewife with three kids who's in Kansas City isn't that related to, but yet she can understand a mother-son relationship. I think that people can kind of relate to what it must be like to be going through something like that and have to deal with your children. Or like coming out to your parents and friends. It's not necessary that everyone can relate to being homosexual, but people can relate to having to reveal something to your parents, reveal something to your friends, that's going to potentially cause problems.

These production maneuvers, while not necessarily rooted in any vision of a gay-loving world, put moral objections to sexual nonconformity at a bit of a disadvantage, since they are somewhat out of their element. In the

playing fields of rights (be they "equal" or "special") and interpersonal difficulties, the issues near and dear to the radical right are not the central ones:
at the hub is "Is discrimination against gay people acceptable?" or "How
can a mother deal with a cross-dressing son?" not "Is homosexual desire
and behavior right?" Moral evaluations of homosexual status are pushed
to the sidelines. Members of the religious-political right, in these kinds of
shows, are a bit like people who have shown up at the wrong party but jump
right into the fun. Indeed, those audience members who are not commenting
about Adam and Steve often begin their challenges to antigay guests by asking them where they are from. "Where are you from? Are you a Mormon?"
a Latina woman on *Ricki,* to laughter and applause, asks a guest who has
said she will raise her children to believe that homosexuality is wrong.
"No," the woman replies, smiling as though she has been asked if she is from
another planet.[11] Mormons and people who believe that homosexuality is
wrong do not quite make sense on the talk show planet.

How can such a planet exist, we should wonder, in a system that is widely
known to be so risk-averse, money-driven, and ideologically timid? After
all, years of studies of the television industry have documented that commercial and occupational commitments tend to dominate all others.[12] If talk
shows are, as many critics contend, the triumph of the bottom line, why do
they so often seem to let particular ideological leanings guide them? In part,
given that they are so inexpensive to produce and so profitable, Jane Shattuc
points out, talk shows are allowed "an ideological latitude or a certain open
political bias" not allowed in prime time.[13] In part, it is simply because, as
many producers report, many of the current and former hosts, especially
Donahue and the women—Oprah Winfrey, Ricki Lake, Jane Whitney, Sally
Jessy Raphael, Jenny Jones—are "gay-friendly," both politically and personally, and because of the high proportion of gay male production staff.
Yet it is also clear that those individual leanings alone are not enough to
explain the fate of antigay morality on talk shows. As *Leeza*'s Alspaugh
explains, it is mostly just luck if your personal views coincide with the commercial approach of a show.

> *I feel very fortunate that I'm in a position that my personal feelings
> can be reflected in what I do, and I work with somebody who very
> much is on the same wavelength as I am. At the same time, if I were
> a producer of* Hard Copy, *would I make it the best tabloid show it
> could be? Yes. I mean, these companies have goals with their pro-
> grams. They identify a niche. They identify a market, and you have to*

produce into that. If you're going to do it, revel in it and do the best
you can. Just do it and say, "This is entertainment. We're not here to
change the world." We wouldn't do what a lot of the other shows do,
because of Leeza and because of what she wants to do with the show,
and because of the network. But if that was the directive of the com-
pany, I would. I'm just incredibly fortunate.

There is something more at work here than progay staffers doing their bit
for the cause by squeezing religious objections to homosexuality into uncomfortable niches. With television, ideology has to be consonant with commercial and institutional needs. Ideology has to be entertaining.

More general ideological commitments crucial to their commercial niche,
not just the personal inclinations of those putting them together, are what
make talk shows not terribly warm homes for religious conservatives. Talk
shows work not so much with an explicitly progay agenda, but with an
ideology of liberal pluralism: we are all different, live and let live, tolerate
and respect the rights of others to be who they are. "My view is that everybody should be able to tolerate everything," says host Jerry Springer. "It's
only the First Amendment, it's only free speech. The show is crazy and it
is outrageous, but this is a forum for that to happen." Whether or not one
sees this as a heartfelt commitment, it reveals the match between talk shows
and the we're-all-different ideology: the shows depend financially on the
constant display of difference, which in a variety of ways makes the entertainment possible. Add to that what host Rolonda Watts calls "that American thing," freedom of expression, which justifies the high-drama, channel-
surf-resistant social conflict also so prevalent. "I mean," says Ro, misattrib-
uting the words of Voltaire, "as Patrick Henry said, 'I may not agree with
what you say, but I'll defend to the death your right to say it.' " Looking
at one of her guests, the bitter, hatred-filled Shirley, she adds, "May we also
learn understanding and tolerance and let each person speak one at a
time." [14] For TV talk to work, everyone must be allowed to speak, or yell,
regardless of their position; appeals in the name of tolerance, understanding,
and Patrick Henry/Voltaire give this talk at least the appearance of a purpose.

This pluralist tone gets wedded, moreover, to the therapeutic values we
have already seen, which give an extra push toward tolerance. "What we
are trying to tackle in this one hour," Oprah Winfrey once said, "is what
I think is the root of all the problems in the world—lack of self-esteem is
what causes war, because people who really love themselves don't go out

and try to fight other people."[15] This emphasis on individual self-knowledge, self-determination, self-love, and self-improvement allows talk shows to claim a "service" function, to push for money shots of self-revelation, and to pursue postfeminist female audiences with little patience for men who tell them what to do and be. That focus on the individual self is tightly linked to an "essentialist" faith, an assumption that what is inside has always been there, given by nature, and needs to be treated with care and respect; the search is for the true self, whatever it turns out to be. These are important ideological support beams for talk shows' show-and-tell entertainment: we are just uncovering what is there, promoting understanding and self-understanding, which are good, if emotionally difficult, things.

Two-faced as it is, this therapeutic-pluralism-turned-entertainment is much more sympathetic to liberal approaches to sexual nonconformity than to conservative condemnations of it—not only to coming out as a positive act of self-empowerment, but to tolerance, and to the protection from arbitrary prejudices of individuals who are just being who they are.

The result, often, is that the bigot becomes the freak. A 1994 *Jerry Springer* show, for instance, pitted a lesbian couple running a feminist center in Mississippi against townsfolk saying that "we don't want these people being role models," "anyone who is homosexual or lesbian is against what God teaches and has—they have a sick mind," "they have gone against nature," and "they know the judgment of God, and those who do that are worthy of death." The lesbians' daughter argues that "we're governed by the laws of the Constitution of the United States, not by the Bible and not by bigotry," and Springer agrees in his daily "final thought" commentary, which as it always does, conflicts drastically with the outrageousness that came before. Typically, Springer, having hosted a show filled with ridicule, talks about how sexual and gender identities are innate and therefore should not be subject to ridicule. On this day, however, he instead appeals to the American thing, distinguishing himself from the backwoods bigots of Ovett, Mississippi.

> We've spent considerable time today talking about homosexuality: whether it's godly or not; whether one chooses to be homosexual, or by birth simply is; whether it threatens the values of the majority community. And yet in this case none of that may be relevant. Clearly, most folks in Ovett, Mississippi, don't want the camp there, don't want the lesbian lifestyle anywhere near them. And yet, this is America. And though it is the business of each of us to instill a value

*system in our children, it is the business of none of us to impose such
lifestyle, value system, religion, politics, or sexier—sexual orientation
on our neighbors. We may have the right to say, "I don't want a Catholic or a Baptist or a Jew or a Black in my neighborhood." But we
don't have the right to enforce it. It's really very fundamental. If you
can stop someone from living in your town because of what they are,
then one day they can stop you from living where you want because of
what you are. There are places in the world where that is the case. But
they are not called America.*[16]

When the ideology of living the "truth" of the self fades, the rhetoric of
tolerance often renders it irrelevant, and homosexuality is stirred into the
mix of protected differences that make talk shows' bread and butter.
Springer makes explicit the position generally taken by daytime talk shows
themselves: it is those guests who impose antigay morality who are sick,
ungodly, bigoted, un-American freaks.

When guests from the antigay right (religious or not) are prominent, in
fact, the audience, and often the host, tend to turn against them. In 1993,
for instance, *Geraldo* hosted two same-sex couples who had caused controversies by attending their high school proms. In the front row sits dough-
faced Paul Cameron, chairman of the Family Research Institute, whose credibility as a psychologist has already been widely discredited outside of the
talk show circuit; a few people down the row sits one of the founders of
Parents and Friends of Lesbians and Gays, a somewhat frail middle-aged
white woman in glasses who had lost her son to AIDS two weeks earlier.
When Cameron begins to talk about how "depressing" it is that we are
encouraging such mistakes in children, how "irresponsible" it is of the
school system to allow them to enter a "lifestyle that will kill them," and
so on, the show becomes almost a ritualized bashing of Cameron and his
views. One after another, audience members and panelists denounce Cameron, to cheering and applause. Eventually, he begins to talk about AIDS,
using the other guest's son as an example. "This poor woman," he begins,
and she stands up to scream at him. "I am not a poor woman," she shouts
to immediate and long-lasting cheers and applause. "I can hold my head up
high," she continues, the rest of her sentence drowned out by prolonged
clapping. This denunciation of Cameron continues, but he pushes ahead,
until Geraldo, riding the explosive anti-Cameron audience energy, simply
says, "Shut up, I don't want to hear your story."[17]

Or take *Rolonda*'s Shirley, who is roundly demolished over the course of the hour by members of the studio audience, who stand up and make a series of statements: "God loves everybody in the world no matter if they're gay or what," says one; "What right do you have to tell anybody about their sexuality?" another asks; "If anybody should burn in hell," another tells Shirley, "I think it should be you," while still another declares her "an ugly woman, God does not love ugly, and the statements that comes out of your mouth and the nonsense you're teaching these children is wrong." Shirley becomes the ugly one, unloved by God himself, while the audience continually preaches a liberal, individualist politic in which lesbian and gay people are included: "I think in my opinion," as one sums it up to audience applause, "it doesn't matter what sexual orientation, race, creed, or color, you should judge a person, but you should judge a person by what their heart and what their personality is." In the meantime, the screen flashes statistics from the FBI, the National Gay and Lesbian Task Force, and Yankelovich Partners on hate crimes against lesbians and gays, gay teen suicide rates, and gay population percentages.[18] Here, as in many programs in which public attitudes toward homosexuality are central, the claim that homosexuality is immoral, that heterosexuality is the exclusive law of either nature or the Bible, cuts against the show's assumptions and triggers audience hostility. Lesbians and gays are not only victims of bigotry, but also more similar to the audience—more normal, one might say—than those guests seeking to enforce antigay sexual morality. Indeed, the presence of the religious-political right, brought on in the interest of heating things up, creates a narrative in which the need for protection is even more obvious: they are the attackers.

The Ricki Lake Show, often credited with triggering the lowering of talk show standards, has produced some of the most explicitly and unrelentingly progay television via this same programming strategy: arranging bigots like ducks in a row. One 1994 show called "White Men Fight Back" paraded a series of put-upon white men ("African blacks are more violent than white people" and "white men are the minority," they assert) in front of its almost entirely nonwhite, and entirely unsympathetic, audience. In the role of the opposition, with the enthusiastic support of the audience, is Donald Suggs—black, openly gay, and then the public affairs director of the Gay and Lesbian Alliance against Defamation. Suggs recalls "sitting next to this guest who at one point said, 'I think what you sodomites do is disgusting.' And I said exactly what went through my head at the time. I turned to him and said, 'You know what, it would be disgusting if I was doing it with you.'

The audience howled and howled. The audience loved it. I would never say that on a news show, but at this particular setting, it was really the perfect thing to say." Here is the unusual, orchestrated spectacle of an articulate, outspoken, gay man of color leading the charge against white men espousing racial superiority along with complaints about "sodomites," wildly championed by a mob of urban teenagers.[19]

Suggs is not the only gay activist to be brought onto *Ricki* as an expert. Writer, outing-promoter, and ACT UP veteran Michelangelo Signorile, for instance, took the role usually given to a therapist, holding forth from a thronelike chair on a show whose title, "I'm Gay . . . Get over It!" even recalls Queer Nation's "We're here, we're queer, get used to it!" Various family members denounce their gay relatives, refusing, in Lake's terms, "to accept you for who you are": Tammy tells her sister Pam, a butch lift-truck operator from Georgia, that she doesn't know what she's missing ("I know what I'm missin', but I know what I'm a-gittin', too," Pam responds); a cute, bleach-blond gay white 14-year-old's grandmother says she knew there was something wrong with her grandson when he was born ("Not wrong, just different," corrects Lake). "Michelangelo, can you educate her?" Lake says, turning to Signorile. "Michelangelo, enlighten us," which he does, telling this one to love her child and that one that there's nothing she can do about it.[20] Signorile, who had appeared on many shows as an advocate, now with a book to promote, was here the authority.

That made a big difference in the way I was treated by the families, and the audience, I think. You suddenly have so much more authority. I mean, the families, as much as they disagreed, they still looked to me. At one point this girl said, "I'd like to ask the expert a question," as if my answer is going to be what they're going to do. And later after the show, they're asking me questions. I don't know what they thought. When you didn't give them someone on the other side of homosexuality, there wasn't like, "Oh, there's a choice on how to think on this." And if you're going to give me the authority position, I can mediate between these people. I can tell them what I think is right. I said up front to the mother, "What you're feeling is totally okay and normal and nobody expects that you're going to get over this right now or whatever. But you can love your daughter. You can accept your daughter. I'm not saying you have to accept homosexuality today." All I was trying to say was, "You should accept this person in your life." The problem is when they have somebody else who's trying to tell these people what they should do, too, and to do it on the other side.

Not only was there no antigay, don't-accept-your-children "other side" but, in a twist that has some of the sweetness of just desserts, the militant gay activist had become the one dispensing advice to unloving family members—*enlighten us!*—the gay son elevated to the therapist's throne above what might as well be his own confused, damning, narrow-minded mother.

On another 1995 show in which antigay family members confront their gay relatives, Ricki Lake, as always, is openly sympathetic to the gay guests. DJ and Tamarra, a large, many-chinned white couple, both in blue, quickly explain how they moved to another state when they found out her father was gay ("his boyfriend was lower class, really rude"); Jim, the ponytailed, earringed, Birkenstocked father, enters to applause and cheering, and explains how after thirty-five years, he decided to stop hiding from himself. "I praise you for being able to be true to yourself and to live your life the way you want to live it," Lake says, backed by shots of the applauding young audience, "but I can't imagine how it must feel after doing that to have your daughter reject you." If your dad was such a good influence on you, she asks Tamarra, who has expressed concerns for her children ("it would really confuse them"), why wouldn't he be a good influence on your children? "I guess the situation scares me," Tamarra says, to which Lake responds with an impatient whine. "But what's *wrong* with being gay?" The show is organized to answer Lake's question with a big "nothing." Going to commercial, along with the usual statistics (a Gallup poll statistic that 37 percent of Americans prefer that homosexuals stay in the closet) and pro and con statements from men and women on the street, are quotes from a University of Chicago sociologist declaring that "people have this assumption that there are two clearly defined groups of people, heterosexuals and homosexuals, but people can be lots of places on the spectrum," and from an English actor, suggesting that "it's a wonder you have any homosexuals in America, because the children are bombarded with anti-homosexual propaganda daily."

Indeed, this *Ricki* turns out to be counterpropaganda. When Jodie, yet another large woman in a blue dress, is introduced as being concerned that gays "might take it too far and start touching the kids," the audience awws disapprovingly; when she adds that "if they have the attitude that they think they can be gay, who's to say how far they would go with that," Lake pounces immediately. "Does anybody here disagree and think that being gay is not a choice?" After an audience member points out that "anybody can molest your child, that doesn't have to do with sexuality," Lake jumps in. "Let me just read you something, FYI," she says, looking at one of the cards in her hand. "Most pedophiles know their victims and are most often parents who abuse their own, usually female, children. Only a small percentage of them are homosexual. So," she says, hand on hip, looking pointedly at Jodie, "there goes your theory." Like Jodie, the rest of the antigay guests are thrown to the lions, with Ricki Lake leading the charge. Sandy, who wants to protect her 9-year-old son from his gay father's "lifestyle" (he has nightmares, she reports, after visiting his dad), provokes a string of criticism: your children are going to resent you, says one white woman, and as long as they're treating the children well, what they do in the bedroom shouldn't matter, says a black woman; Jesus Christ will decide what's right and wrong, says another; it's not a lifestyle, it's a life, says Lake herself.

After several segments of this, Dina, a young redhead in a leather vest, and her husband Kevin, in a tie and long sideburns, come on to talk about how "homosexuality is wrong and homosexuals should be put to death." Very soon after they have done so, Lake brings out Steve and Phil, "a couple who say that parents like you are dangerous." They are shrill screamers, but compared to Dina and Kevin and the cartoon bigots who preceded them, their anger seems righteous. Phil immediately goes on the attack, and with all the screaming and cheering and egging on from the audience as he does so, it becomes hard to catch more than snippets of his bombast: "First off, that's pure bigotry. . . . You should raise them to base somebody on their inner being, not on their race, not on their sex, not on their religion. . . . The Bible says love thy neighbor." After a few rounds of insult trading, a white woman in her forties stands up in the audience, her red hair piled high on her head, and lets loose her no-nonsense evaluation in a strong New York accent. "I think you better start researching a little more, you got the facts all wrong," she says, waving her hand dismissively at Kevin, who has just suggested that the majority of people with AIDS are homosexual. Then, with barely a breath, she turns to Jodie, pointing. "And you, over there, Miss Homophobia. You got a real problem, because if you're instilling fear and hatred into your children towards gays, what else are you instilling in your children." Like everybody else flattening these guests, she gets a big round of applause, and probably not only because of the brilliant fantasies of a Miss Homophobia pageant (wilted flowers, black sash, tiara made of switchblades) her comment induces. Several minutes later, a black woman in big earrings and a big white sweater adds religion back into the mix, but reverses the usual Adam and Steve logic. "Who told you that homosexuals are going to hell?" she says, pointing directly at the skinny white Bible thumper on stage. "What Bible? How can you get up on television—no, my Bible doesn't tell me that homosexuals are going to hell. *Bigots and people that judge are going to hell.*" Ricki Lake's final word, after a straight woman comes on to praise her gay babysitter, is in keeping with the show's set-up-the-bigots strategy. "Remember," she says to the camera, sitting casually on the steps of the stage as if on a Brooklyn stoop, "children are not born to hate and fear, they are *taught* to hate and fear." Or, as Tempestt says simply to the audience of her own "Get Used to It" show, after a series of young gay people of all colors have told off their friends, "You *have* to learn tolerance."[21]

Although it is not entirely controllable, neither is this kind of show accidental. After all, producers select the cast and write the script, even if unpredictability is written in. One openly gay producer tells of seeing a newspaper story about a small-town mayor who had come out of the closet and then returned from a trip to find "Fag, get out" painted all over his house.

> So what we did was we booked him, and we booked a couple from the town who is dead set against him as the mayor. Like, "We don't want a fag in our town as the mayor," that kind of thing. And we booked people from the town who were very much in support of him. He's a great guy, a great mayor. And then in researching, we found a transsexual who's running for mayor of her town, and we booked her and other people. And that was a great show. It presented these gay people—and you know, this man who was the mayor of this small town was just a nice guy, an upstanding citizen, a normal, very positive gay role model. We also had a transsexual on the show who's like, if you didn't know she was a transsexual, you might think she is just the funniest, neatest, funny lady, classy lady. Just classy, just fun. Part of me feels like, you know, I'd love that everybody in America could see those two role models. And then they saw these people from this town who were so bigoted, who were missing their teeth, who were bigoted. And I thought, to me this was a good show.

The upstanding gay and transsexual citizens are set against the small-town bigots; in a cross-fertilization of gay, lesbian, bisexual, and transgender mainstreaming and talk show class representations, the bigots fare badly not just because of their prejudice, but because of their toothless announcement of small-town poverty in the face of the "classy" people they hate. "We didn't set them up," the producer says. "We didn't go looking for them or anything." But of course the fact that the bigots really have bad teeth and really hate queers does not mean they have not, in a more general sense, been set up to, as the producer puts it, "show America 'don't be so bigoted.' "

The order and presentation of guests, although it is no guarantee of an outcome, can shape audience reaction significantly. I asked another openly gay supervising producer of a similar bigot-bashing program if he had explicitly set up homophobic guests as audience targets. "In a word," he answered quickly, "absolutely." Driven by their own commitments, and even more by the confidence that their young, urban, largely African American and Latino studio audience would, given a structure that moves from strong-willed bigots to we're-not-going-to-take-it victims, rise up against bigotry, the show's producers arranged the story with a clear movement from "bad guys" to "good guys."

I don't think we intentionally tried to villainize people. To me the other side in that story was wrong. And I'm just being a pigheaded asshole, but it's wrong, those people were on the wrong side. And there were people in the audience who certainly stood up and defended them, defended the people who were the bad guy in the story. But for the most part the moral Greek chorus in the audience seemed to fall on the same side, as the younger audience often does, of our feeling putting the show together, that these people were not giving opinions that were fair. They were based on prejudice, they were based on stereotype.

By the time the gay voices emerge, audience sympathy is firmly set against the homo-haters. The moral chorus is conducted, by the show's structure, to sing loud and strong against antigay prejudice, drowning it out with an ethic, sometimes biblical and often not, of love, honesty, and suspension of judgment.

The nice thing about white supremacist sexist homophobic men

Despite a baseline ideology that is sympathetic to self-determination and sexual freedom, it does not take much for a show's tune to change dramatically, so that antigay moralizing is celebrated rather than stigmatized. Ironically, a shift in the way panels are put together, often sought by gay media activists, goes a long way: shows programmed *without* Bible-thumping, moralizing guests often wind up legitimizing Bible-thumping moralizing. When there is no one playing the "bigot" role on the panel—which is increasingly the case, as relationship programs displace issues programs, and as lesbian, gay, bisexual, and transgender guests appear simply to tell their stories unopposed—audience members pick up the slack, inevitably making the "Adam and Eve, not Adam and Steve" and "keep it in the closet" arguments. These audience members meet with much less hostility than "extremist" panelists, and in fact more often meet with strong audience support. In the absence of hateful embodiments of intolerance, audience hatred and intolerance are often fired up.

On a 1993 show on bisexuality, to take just one example among very many, the guests are all openly bisexual people and their families, along with one expert. The usual range of questions and objections are raised by audience members along the way: a young black man wants to know if they are going to make their children gay, a white woman complains of being followed around by two bisexual women at a party who "ruined my evening," a middle-aged white guy smugly suggests that the "young ladies" might "resolve your dilemma" by "dating men who like to dress like women." There are questions about friends' and parents' reactions, pressure from the gay and lesbian community, how early the awakening to sexual difference took place, religious beliefs. The latter question, like most of them, is simply asked and answered: "God is Love," says activist Lani Ka'ahumanu, "and we're talking about loving other human beings here." But it is not until late in the show, when a young black woman in a white shirt and black vest responds to Ka'ahumanu's comment from half an hour earlier, that the show really picks up steam. "God is Love," the woman says, "but God does not condone what you're doing. If he did, Moses and Sarah wouldn't have gotten married, and Jesus himself would have married John the Baptist." The audience explodes into applause, as if their leader has finally spoken. "You are confused," she says, pointing, "yes you are."

The host, Bertice Berry, tries to move the show in other directions, initiating a sort of rap session between the psychologist and the panel, and then interviewing a bisexual-man–heterosexual-woman couple in the audience, but the show has bogged down and the audience is not finished. A light-skinned, middle-aged African American woman (deep red dress, done hair) stands up and tells a young African American woman named Terri (brown vest, backward baseball cap) that she applauds the mother who, having kicked Terri out of the house, prays for her; she talks about "spirit" and "lust of the flesh" and "the truth and the light," while the cameras catch the reaction of the white mothers on the panel. "You have been deceived!" she cries, a charge enthusiastically received by much of the studio audience.[22] The arguments are no different from those made by (typically white) Christian or pseudoscientific right-wing panelists, but the dynamic is nearly turned around; what looks extreme in one case looks mainstream in the other. Ironically, the absence of panelists articulating religious-right rhetoric, combined with the talk show's celebration of the commonsense authority of "ordinary" people, opens up space for the regular folks in the studio to make the moral and political argument that gay, lesbian, and bisexual people are abominable.

And often it is not just *any* ordinary person who stands up to Adam-and-Steve the show. Since talk shows draw on an association of elite authority with whiteness (and everyday authority with darker skin), they often wind up staging encounters between a white moral voice and a moral voice carried by audience members of color. Conservative religious African Americans, often with a good deal of support from the rest of the largely African American and Latino studio audience, issue moral condemnations of white bisexual, gay, lesbian, and transgender guests. This racialized spectacle is quite common, especially now that the *Donahue*-derived format, in which white gay activists face off against white religious denouncers, has been used up. The picture shifts, of course, on those increasingly frequent occasions when there are gay people of color on the panel, and we get what is rarely seen in mainstream media culture: an internal African American cultural dialogue (sometimes including black host, black audience members, and black guests) about sexual morality. But more often than not, on programs directly focused on homosexuality, bisexuality, or transgenderism as *political* issues, a predominantly white panel speaks humanist liberalese while many audience members of color speak traditional conservatese.

In fact, on shows where moral disputes erupt, the racial dynamics can sharply alter the bigot-as-freak phenomenon. As a general rule, when white speakers are bigoted, their racial privilege (and sometimes class privilege as well) undercuts their authority to a large degree; when people of color speak, they speak with the talk show authority of everyday, less powerful folks, less susceptible to the hostility aroused by those who seem to think they're better than everybody else. This has something to do, for sure, with the strength of gender conservatism and homophobia in African American and

Latino cultures; yet that homophobia is easily exaggerated, and many shows with similar audiences and similar topics activate love-and-compassion responses rather than you're-going-to-hell responses, so there is no simple transmission of attitudes going on here. These racialized encounters over sex and gender norms are *structured* by talk shows—unintentionally, really, through the accidents and habits of talk show producing. Inadvertently, talk show producers have stumbled onto an easy, inexpensive way to get the heat of moral condemnation, laced with an also-hot undertone of racial tension, and spiked with the exciting sight of less powerful people challenging the privileged, without ever directly endorsing an antigay conservative agenda.

The Helen factor

It is not just the absence of white bigots that can turn a show's tenor, regardless of the intentions of producers, from accepting and celebratory of sexual freedoms to critical and belittling. The personalizing push of both the television medium and the talk show genre—the emphasis on personality above all else, most centrally—means that a gay person who comes across as *unlikable* can manage to turn a sympathetic studio audience into a nasty one, and that a character demonized in one instance can, paired with the right opposing figures, gain support in another. Television's personality-uber-alles tendency has been pointed out by critics for decades now,[23] and many repeat guests report the discovery that likability, not the particularities of what they had to say, seemed to be the key to getting audience support. Longtime activist Ann Northrop, who had worked as a producer on the *CBS Morning News* and as a writer for *Good Morning, America,* sized up an early *Donahue* appearance as "much too strident and argumentative and angry." Over time, appearing on *Donahue, Geraldo, Rolonda,* and other programs, she came to follow the rules she knew well as a producer.

> *Don't let yourself get angry and out of control because the whole thing is the people want to like you as a person. I can get angry at the drop of a hat, and I don't think that's a winning strategy. What you want to do is ingratiate yourself with an audience, smile a lot, be very lovable, and then you can say anything and they'll go along with it. Smile a lot. Try to stay very calm. Sit up straight. Put the small of your back against the seat because the tendency is to slump and you'll look ter-*

*rible doing that. Speak very calmly. The people in the audience really
don't care what you're saying. They are going to judge you as a person
and whether you are a good person or a bad person. What stays with you
is the sense of whether you liked someone or didn't like someone.*

Breaking these rules can turn the tables. Michelangelo Signorile, for instance, first appeared on *Ricki* opposite Andrea Sheldon of the religious-
right Traditional Values Coalition, "this very demure, attractive, level-
headed, yuppie mom, who looks just like everybody else's mom."

*I just really lost control with her, and I think I wound up coming off
as the shrill one. She was so nice, and she got me going before the
show started by saying "You know, Michelangelo, I just want to tell
you that, you know, we're probably going to see each other on these
shows a lot as time goes on, because this is what I do and this is what
you do, but it doesn't mean we can't be friends." And she went to
shake my hand and I was like, "You are destroying my life. How
could you? This is about my life and about you people taking away
my rights. What are you?" And then we went on in the middle of that.
So I was already furious with her, and at one point I was yelling so
loud I accidentally spit on her. And she said, "You spit on me." And I
was calling her a nut, and I lost it completely. I feel like I blew it, and
she came off as more reasonable.*

Marjorie Garber, a Harvard professor who has written on both cross-
dressing and bisexuality, became something of a "credentialed fad" on talk
shows with her books, appearing on *Geraldo, Oprah, Maury Povich, Sally,
Jane Whitney,* and others. "You have to be civil, charming, understated
rather than overstated, firm, smile, you know," she says, echoing Northrop.
"If they don't love you, especially if they think the topic is an unlovable
topic and they don't love you, they're not going to read your book. If they
think that you are charming, sensible, articulate, well-educated, a little bit
self-abnegating, that's a much better profile. It just doesn't work to go over
the top and say, 'Hey, wait a second, wait a second, you're getting it all
wrong,' or 'You're setting me up.' It's much better to be charming if you
can manage it."

As anyone who has watched a talk show knows, many people do not
come across as charming, calm, sensible, smiley, and lovable. This may be
what experienced talk show guests learn to be, but most guests are not experienced; it may be what strategically oriented guests want to be, but produc-

ers are certainly encouraging most of them to be otherwise. Besides, as most talk show guests attest, there is not much time to be self-conscious: the studio lights are on, the camera is on, everybody's talking, the situation has a life of its own. And when they are not likable—likability and sexual identity are not, these shows amply demonstrate, necessarily linked—or when they make a move toward a particular talk show no-no such as selfishness or bad parenting, they can easily fire up displays of antigay sentiment.

Compare, for example, the *Ricki Lake* show in which guests were trashed for not wanting gays around their kids, to a similar *Ricki* that same year, also involving the issue of gays and children. As with Tamarra and Jodie, at first, so with Lorraine and Karen. Lorraine, a 35-year-old homemaker from Arkansas, is there to tell her friends Stacie and Tammy, twentysomething lovers with a child, that she "doesn't think a child of gay parents can grow up normal." Having lobbed questions at Tammy and Stacie ("So you're saying that it's better that he's being raised by two loving people, whether they're a man or a woman, it doesn't matter?" and "What do your families think?" and "What do you want to say to people who don't agree with it?"), Lake rips quickly into Lorraine, who charges that the child will not know what it is like to have a male figure. "What do you think about a woman who raises a child without a male figure?" she asks, jumping on the double standard. When Lorraine then complains that the kid will not know what is normal, Lake, in a sharp navy pants suit, gets a serious, slightly impatient look on her face, as though she is speaking to a small, somewhat bratty child. "But that's just it, what *is* normal, Lorraine?" (Later, Lake puts "unnatural" and "abnormal" in air quotes.) Asked by Lake why straight couples can sit on the same sofa and hold hands at her house while Stacie and Tammy cannot, Lorraine says she is not ready to explain it to her kids. "What is the difference?" says Lake. "But they love each other. It's not like they're spewing hate everywhere. What *you're* doing is spewing hate telling them it's wrong to love someone." Applause from the audience, shouts of "Go Ricki! Go Ricki!" directed by me toward the TV. Bigots bad, lesbians good.

That is, until a bad lesbian mother shows up. Karen, a 15-year-old heterosexual African American student from Illinois, is there to tell her mother, Helen, and her mother's lover Marie that she thinks "being gay or lesbian is disgusting." Helen, who has seven kids, quickly crosses her arms, and speaks angrily about how this is "something Karen has to deal with," and how "her opinion doesn't matter to me, I'm happy, I made a choice to be with a woman and I'm not ashamed of it." The sympathy, not surprisingly, quickly moves toward the daughter, who confesses to Lake that she was so bothered by her mother's lesbianism that she once tried to take her own life. The audience responds with cooing sympathy, and Helen becomes a lightning rod for audience hostility the rest of the program, while various other guests do their shtick—a lesbian who doesn't think gay people should parent, a gay man with discolored teeth bickering with a straight woman who complains that he goes through his lovers like he changes his underwear, circuit-conservative Paul Cameron, certified homosexual Gabriel Rotello. "I have no problem with your being gay," a black man in the audience says to Helen, to much applause, "but how can you say you don't care about your own child's feelings?" Helen spars with this man ("What society tell her to feel, I don't care"), with Lorraine ("How many daddies have your kids had?"), Paul ("What make you so normal?"), and with her own daughter. "What happens when she tries to kill herself again?" Lake asks. "It happens," Helen responds, to an explosion of booing and hooting. Her arguments are not much different from those of white, college-educated gay activists—"normal" is often a synonym for "in power," homophobia not homosexuality is the social problem, lesbians and gays are as entitled to fulfillment as straight people, and so on—albeit in a different language, and in brief, hard-to-catch outbursts. But her *person* is not sympathetic, she has a *bad attitude,* so her claims are more or less dismissed.

By contrast, Paul Cameron, usually a monstrous lightning rod himself, winds up a sort of hero in this setting, as the opportunistic leader of the attack on Helen. "You've already shown yourself to be a terribly selfish person," he says, as Helen is yelling at him, and the audience, whose cohorts have booed and screamed at Cameron and those like him on other shows, cheers and applauds. Having seized the pro-Karen mood by joining the attacks on Helen's character, he deftly manages to link selfishness, bad parenting, and lesbianism. Being a parent, he says later, "means not being selfish and just saying, 'I feel like being a lesbian today.' " It is not a large step, it turns out, from *this woman is selfish* to *lesbianism is selfishness,* from *this woman is an unfit parent* to *lesbians are unfit to parent.* He more or less wins the fight against Helen—who defeated herself early on, anyway—simply by saying again to the great pleasure of the audience, "You don't care about your children."[24]

It is unlikely that the show's producers thought any differently about the creation of this show than of the progay, antibigot screamfest earlier in the year. Indeed, Lake's closing remarks run along the same lines of acceptance: "It would seem that if a person, straight or gay, was sincere about making the commitment to raising a child with love and compassion, then the issue of their sexuality need not be an issue at all." But given the genre's emphasis on individual character, an unsympathetic homosexual can undermine a show's sympathy for homosexuals in general. The show's structuring mechanisms—a bunch of conflict, a touch of chaos, good guys who can just as easily function as bad guys—make for a very unstable acceptance of gay people. Even an audience that is relatively progay, if it becomes anti-Helen, can turn.

The partitioned garden

Although Helens are no big disappointment for them, it is quite clear that producers for the most part program shows on homosexuality with an emphasis on tolerance and acceptance of nontraditional attachments. They habitually sketch within the lines of a be-true-to-yourself-and-let-others-be-themselves credo. But this framework is quite shaky, despite the habit of stringing up bigots like so many punching bags. It is, moreover, conditional. Producers' interest is certainly not in effecting social change—although that can be a happy by-product of their work—but in attracting audiences. The trick is to simultaneously challenge and affirm the audience's beliefs and experiences; the challenge is engaging, the affirmation comforting. Talk show sexual morality thus becomes a murky brew of political liberalism and cultural conservatism. Nowhere does this become clearer than in a comparison of the fate of homosexuality with that of bisexuality and gender-crossing.

The treatment of same-sex relationships as morally acceptable in fact takes place on the condition that two other norms remain conserved and supported: of gender conformity (men should look and act like "men" and women like "women") and monogamy (people should only couple in exclusive pairs). Some of this setup shows up in a certain division of labor into which sex and gender nonconformists are fed on talk shows, the formats into which, say, transsexuals appear most often as compared to those most common for homosexuals. If same-sex desire is so often morally acceptable in the talk show world, that is partly because it is *not* bisexuality or gender-crossing; put simply, bisexuality is commonly equated with promiscuity and becomes morally suspect, while transsexuality and cross-dressing are routinely placed outside the audience's moral universe.[25] We will see later what this means for normal/abnormal boundaries, but for now a peek can bring into final focus talk shows' wobbling moral support for sexual nonconformity.

For one thing, some kinds of sexual nonconformity barely qualify as even eligible for political and moral disputes. Gay men and lesbians are much more likely than bisexuals, transsexuals, or cross-dressers, for instance, to appear on shows that treat the political issues affecting their lives; while moral questions remain a constant for all kinds of populations, for gay people the controversy and conflict is often exactly over the political consequences of moral disapprobation. In my sample as a whole, about a fifth of the shows are produced in political-issue formats (discrimination, military policy, law, and so on); when we look at the homosexuality-themed shows alone, more than two-fifths are formatted as political issues. Taking another cut, when we look at the shows programmed around political issues, we find the near total elimination of transsexuals, cross-dressers, and bisexuals from the picture; 96 percent of these sorts of shows in my sample involve gay or lesbian topics and guests. Lesbians and gay men, much more often than their bisexual and transgendered colleagues, fit into formats in which theirs is a political status, in which the question of their sameness to or difference from heterosexuals is on the table, in which they are asked to speak up against those who damn them. Moral condemnation takes a place in those shows, but it competes with political support.

Cross-dressers and transsexuals, however, get a program niche that almost entirely shuts down any question of their similarity to those who never "cross" traditional gender lines. First of all, they appear in formats that are largely displays, often sandwiched between conversation, such as pageants or performances. Except for the occasional gay comedians show, display programs exclusively involve gender-crossers, be they transvestites, drag queens, or transsexuals; while only about 7 percent of the sample as a whole involves performances, a full third of the shows on cross-dressing involve these display-yourself formats. At its most extreme, such a show might involve a contest, as when a *Richard Bey* show pitted drag queens against "real women" in such stunts as "Feminine Family Feud" (categories: hair removal, PMS symptoms), nail pounding, and sawing a board in half; more often, it will involve a bit of lip-synching or stripping or a parade of transgendered women in bikinis, as in *Sally*'s transsexual versus nontranssexual women's bikini contest, or the ubiquitous female-impersonator shows.[26]

On the one hand, gender-crossers fare quite well in these display formats, which more or less preclude moral condemnations. But more significantly, they escape such disapproval simply because they are not taken seriously enough to be subject to evaluation one way or the other. Why bother condemning a harmless jester? "I have made at least thirty talk show appearances," says drag queen Miss Understood, whom I met in his boy persona, Alex. "Twenty-three *Richard Bey*s, three *Geraldo*s, two *Rolonda*s, *Gordon Elliott, Mark Walberg, Tempestt.* And I've never actually got to talk about anything." As he tells it, this is just the deal he is offered. "We're there to make it look colorful." That may work for drag queen performers, but for the transsexuals and transvestites reeled into the same format, for example, it means agreeing to be a showthing rather than a person.

Gender-crossers also appear disproportionately in family-conflict formats—kids and parents and siblings arguing with one another. For instance, while transsexualism is a primary topic in roughly 23 percent of my overall sample of gay, lesbian, bisexual, and transgender programming, it is the primary topic in around 36 percent of the family-conflict shows in the sample; similarly, cross-dressing is twice as common a topic in family-conflict formats as it is when all formats are taken together. When they are not called upon to dance or show off, then, gender-crossers and their family members are confronting one another, as on *Maury Povich,* when Stephanie, formerly Roger, Sr., confronted his ex-wife Dixie ("until he has his penis taken off, he'll always be Roger"), and his sons Thomas ("he's not my father, really, because he's like a woman and he has breasts") and Joshua ("there's not much to do at his house").[27] Gender-crossers may not always be freaks, but programming strategies tend to channel them into nooks that exclude political discussion, and emphasize either their laughable difference from other humans or their conflict-causing difference from their families of origin. A nonconforming gender status largely puts transgendered people outside the moral and political realms, implying that gender conformity is a condition for *entry* to a place where freedom and acceptance might, on a good day, even be possible.

Bisexuality and bisexuals get a somewhat different program niche. Political issues shows, compared to the field for homosexuals, are relatively rare when it comes to discussions of bisexuality; in their place, on the one hand, is more testimonial programming, in which the general topic of "what is bisexuality and what's it like to be bisexual" structures a show. (The simple phenomenon and experience of bisexuality, at least for the moment, is still exotic enough to be a stand-alone topic, as homosexuality was in the early days of talk shows.) On the other hand, bisexuality is also more often formatted in terms of the problems it creates in intimate relationships, and especially in terms of a tie to sexual nonmonogamy. While relationship-trouble formats account for about a fifth of the overall sample, for instance, they account for about a third of the shows focused on bisexuality: bisexuals are disproportionate relationship troublers, in the talk show world. Moreover, whereas issues of promiscuity, nonmonogamy, threesomes, and the like are found in just 4 percent of the sample of all bisexual, gay, lesbian, transgender, and cross-dressing shows taken together, they make up more than four times that percentage of the bisexuality-themed shows. Bisexual activists often fight to get monogamous bisexuals (and same-sex couples with a bisexual partner) on talk show panels, but for the most part their efforts have been spurned. "Why take a chance?" says former host Jane Whitney, recounting the logic. "Why go out on a limb and hope that your audience is going to listen to a monogamous bisexual? You know they're going to listen to a promiscuous bisexual. It's about minimizing risks." Not surprisingly, as we will soon see in some detail, these formats use bisexuals to trigger and affirm the morality of monogamy. Bisexuality, then, though it is more likely than other forms of sexual nonconformity to be discussed in a direct, interview-style format, is also more likely to be framed in terms of nonmonogamy and the trouble bisexuality causes in relationships. Again, this niching of bisexuality, while it has many more openings for supportive moral and political voices, also suggests a condition for approval: a renunciation of anything but monogamous pairings.

What goes for gay people, then, does not go for the rest of the crowd of sex and gender nonconformists, who are disproportionately programmed as either amoral outsiders or immoral sexpots. In many ways, bisexuals and transgendered people pay the price for daytime television's progay moral cheerleading. The moral defense of homosexuality, in fact, is shaped by the frequent dismissal of transgendered and bisexual people on TV talk. When same-sex desire is linked to nonmonogamy (as it so often is on programs dealing with bisexuality), or when it is closely associated with gender-crossing (as it consistently is, especially on *Jerry Springer, Richard Bey,* and the other outrageousness-is-our-business shows), we hit a brick wall in the drive toward a morality of love, freedom, and acceptance. The morality that the talk show seems structured to protect is not so much the denunciation of Adam and Steve and Jane and Eve, not so much the moral superiority of heterosexuality, but the moral inferiority of unconventional gender presentation and sexual nonmonogamy: Adams with more than one partner, butch Eves, Janes with a wandering eye, Steves who might be a little bit on the Eve side of things. A step across the wrong line, and the morality of tolerance so strenuously pushed by talk shows is withdrawn.

Conditional love

Like most of what we have been seeing, the conditions under which sex and gender dissidents are subject to moral condemnation and moral defense on daytime television are, above all, *production* conditions, which themselves most often derive from economic ones, as our lives are used to make money in an industry whose morality is profit. The representations emerge through producers' intentions, but even more so through the requirements of the daily production of these kinds of nonfiction dramas.

Sometimes, too, they are shaped by forces above and beyond producers and their everyday routines, since corporate executives have the first and last words. Toward the end of her run, for example, when her show was moved to daytime on NBC, Jane Whitney's special interest in gay and lesbian topics had to be toned down. "Too controversial. 'We don't do abortions, we don't do gay and lesbian rights. Don't want to alienate anybody.' It's a whole lot safer to go with 'two kids who slept on a department store bed' than it is with 'a couple in New York fighting for adoption rights for gays and lesbians.'" Despite her resistance, discussion of homosexuality as a political topic was, at the behest of the network, edged out by discussions of heterosexuality as a purely personal one. The fear that certain kinds of topics would be perceived by advertisers as potentially alienating to viewers was well recognized by William Bennett and others participating in the brief mobilization to "clean up" talk shows. "When you realize that [Jenny] Jones and [Ricki] Lake are two of the leading 'cultural assassins' of trash talk TV," the American Family Association's Donald Wildmon wrote to his troops, "you can see why it's so important for you to write Procter & Gamble today."[28] For some shows—the more outrageous ones such as *Jerry Springer,* for instance, whose advertisers already knew they were sponsoring wrestling-style mania—the chill never came, and for most others, at least those that survived cancellation, the advertiser vigilance wore off after the public attention faded. But for a period, on programs like the one for which Martin Calder was a producer, the word from above was cut back on anything that looked "unclean." Instructively, this list included gay people, black people, drag queens, and risqué dressers.

All the William Bennett stuff came out and advertisers started paying attention to that. So after advertisers started paying attention to that, we were told no more gay guests. "No gay guests." It wasn't just gay guests. It was also certain things about, you know, you can't put them out in low-cut tops. Like you had to watch how they were dressed. If somebody stripped, you know, if somebody got up and started a gyrating dance, edit it out. It was editing out anything that was at all like sex, like dirty. No more drag queens. I did a show that had a Madonna impersonator that was a guy, and that was okay, but no drag queen issues, no more, "I'm a drag queen." It was never written down on paper, but it was clear. It was also like, "Scale back on the number of black shows." We're going to be rerunning a lot of shows. No shows that have openly gay guests will rerun. It sickened me and made me furious, but it's not like I'm in a position of power. I have to pay the bills.

The message from the executive-gods at Paramount, Warner Brothers, Multimedia, and the like demonstrates the ultimate condition of love: give them voice, and do it however you want, unless they threaten profits, in which case, please shut them up.

Such conditions are obvious enough, and as we have seen they are nowhere near the whole story, since talk show producers manage for the most part to routinely use their loose ideologies of self-esteem, truth-telling, tolerance, and personalized authority to make profitable entertainment. There are many people with genuine political commitments here, even in the television industry, and often, when they are consonant with the overriding ideologies of TV talk, their allegiances translate into an active attempt to stage the demolition of religiously and politically driven hatred. But advertisers pay the bills, and major media corporations run the ship—and besides, even when those parties are satisfied or looking the other way a slight change in talk show casting can shift the tide. In a genre so dependent on individual personality and unpredictability, waves of hatred often sweep over the television screen, as audiences join in the bashing, antagonized by a lousy presentational style, or apparent selfishness, or a violation of the ethics of discernible genders and monogamy, or boredom. These waves are a reminder to many of us watching, a repetition of the message many of us, the luckier ones actually, have received elsewhere in our lives: you may be both gay and loved, but it is not the kind of love you want or need. *There are always conditions.* We may take the opportunity to yell back at bigots or to smile calmly as others do it for us, just as we sometimes accept scraps of acceptance because we are so starved. But that does not do nearly enough to heal the wounds of knowing that you are accepted and loved, once again, here again, here where you at least sometimes rule, conditionally.

5 I WANT TO BE MISS UNDERSTOOD

The true Freak . . . stirs both supernatural terror and natural sympathy, since, unlike the fabulous monsters, he is one of us, the human child of human parents, however altered by forces we do not quite understand into something mythic and mysterious, as no mere cripple ever is. . . . Only the true Freak challenges the conventional boundaries between male and female, sexed and sexless, animal and human, large and small, self and other, and consequently between reality and illusion, experience and fantasy, fact and myth.

CULTURAL CRITIC LESLIE FIEDLER[1]

Hearken unto me, fellow creatures. I who have dwelt in a form unmatched with my desire, I whose flesh has become an assemblage of incongruous anatomical parts, I who achieve the similitude of a natural body only through an unnatural process, I offer you this warning: the Nature you bedevil me with is a lie. Do not trust it to protect you from what I represent, for it is a fabrication that cloaks the groundlessness of the privilege you seek to maintain for yourself at any expense. You are as constructed as me; the same anarchic womb has birthed us both. I call upon you to investigate your nature as I have been compelled to confront mine. I challenge you to risk abjection and flourish as well as have I. Heed my words, and you may well discover the seams and sutures in yourself.

TRANSSEXUAL WRITER SUSAN STRYKER[2]

The night I went out for cocktails with seven friends to the Top of the Mark, one of San Francisco's premier tourist spots, I was the only one wearing a wig. Mark packed his tight body into a tight black dress, fishnets, and heels, and with his makeup, pearls, and short hair he looked something like a femme-lesbian bodybuilder on her way to an upscale nightclub. Britt's brown skin was set off nicely by his peach dress, straw hat, purple hoop earrings, subtle eyeshadow; like Irwin, he wore his own hair and beard. Maurice, in sunglasses and a bright lime jacket over his minidress, spiked his hair up a bit with gel and glued on huge false eyelashes, working a chic Liza look. In my borrowed wig, shiny dress, pearls over chest hair, cat-eye glasses, and sneakers, my look was dowdy, someone's aunt on her way home from work in sensible shoes. Even with the wig, like the rest of the crowd my genders were mixed.

The evening was a festival of photo opportunities—makeup session, banister sliding, motorcycle mounting, still life of pumps—but one remains my favorite years later. Maurice (known that night as Pooty) is dancing with Ben (drag name: Rachel) on the bar's small dance floor. They are slow dancing, two fashionably butch women in makeup, gloves, pearls, and heels, with short hair and ten o'clock shadow, arms around each other's waists. In the background several other couples dance, men with women, and behind them a few other couples hold each other on the sidelines. The music is clearly romantic, but no one seems even remotely interested in their partner. All eyes are on Rachel and Pooty, who smile toward the camera. The couples stare blank-faced, mouths slightly open, as though in a trance, overpowered.

Except for the staff, who met us with exaggerated hospitality ("right this way, ladies"), when people awoke from their encounter with the extraordinary, it seemed they did so only in order to press things back into some recognizable, ordinary state. "Now we've really had our San Francisco experience," I overheard one table telling each other. (What's happening is a kooky, regional cultural aberration.) Catcalls from men, envious wardrobe comments from women. (What's happening is a mimicking confirmation of man-oriented femininity.) "Is this a fraternity thing?" an older gentleman asked us as we passed his table. (What's happening is a boyish prank.) "No," skinny, goateed, matronly Irwin immediately replied with a finger snap, "it's a sorority thing." It was only the bride and groom in the elevator, ready to exit into the lounge as we were preparing to board the elevator to leave, who understood. They were in full wedding drag themselves—he in tuxedo, she in gown and veil—and when we all screamed, "Love the dress! Want that dress!" they pushed the close-doors button furiously and fearfully. As the doors closed, we watched them move slowly backward, as though pushed back by some big, invisible, drag queen hand.

Of course, it was a San Francisco thing, a joke, a prank of sorts, but it was also much more than that: *we were there to be misunderstood.* The watchers did not let us down. For the most part we amused ourselves, but it was their inability to take their eyes off of us, their desperate, almost-hostile attempts to make sense of us, to put broken pieces of a worldview back together, that gave the experience real electricity. For a bit, things stopped making sense for them, and began to make sense for us.

Talk shows are often filled with moments like these, mixtures of disruption, confusion, and reassertion of the way things, especially gender things, work. This is especially the case when bisexual, transsexual, or cross-dressing guests appear since, as many cultural analysts have noted by now, these are people who do not always easily fit the either-or categories to which this culture is so fervently attached. Their oddity, their "thirdness," their "dizzying fluidity of bodies, desires, and social statuses," means that, as Judith Lorber writes, they "show us what we ordinarily take for granted—that people have to learn to be women and men."[3] People who in one way or another mix genders, or who express attractions for men and women, pop up throughout contemporary American history and culture: a literary or movie character here, a famous surgical subject or rock star there.[4] On talk shows, as we already know, they are common enough to have become trite. Yet they remain clichés whose presence is a disruption—indeed, that's more or less what they are brought on to be.

More often than not, it is a disruption that goes to show that things are exactly right the way they are, and more often than not, there is little room for actually articulating a coherent challenge to sex and gender categorization. Talk shows are cliché-mongering entertainment, and to suggest that they effect major paradigm shifts would be to overestimate their cultural effects; they display the radically different mostly in ways that reaffirm the normality of the watchers. Yet they throw open little cultural openings that, compared with the rest of commercial, mass-mediated popular culture, look huge. They are like darkened, cracked windows through which tiny cultural bombs can be tossed, disturbing the peaceful, everyday confidence in the simplicity of gay-straight and man-woman difference. The freakier and more monstrous the bomb throwers, the more the boundaries are exposed. Seams and sutures start to pop out.

Most people, including most gay, lesbian, bisexual, and transgendered people, have no interest whatsoever in messing with social categories. As Mary Douglas and others have pointed out, for one thing, "separating, purifying, demarcating, and punishing transgressions"—and defending classifications against the ambiguities and anomalies to which they give rise—are central tasks of any culture. Cultures, simply put, "impose system on [the] inherently untidy experience" of living.[5] Most people's personal identities, and many people's social and political identities, depend on clear, binary categories; they depend on an assumption that the difference between groups is hard, fast, and recognizable. Power and privilege also ride the classifications. In political systems such as this one that distribute power, rights, and resources along gender lines, there is certainly a logic to guarding the clarity of those boundaries: men's elevated status over women's, and the strength of heterosexual social arrangements, rest on the notion that "man" and "woman," and "straight" and "gay," are distinct categories. Claims for women's or gay rights, moreover, also depend on these same lucid, discrete classifications. When those are messed up, when it's not clear just who is and isn't a "woman" or "gay" (or, for that matter, "black"), or when the lines between categories get especially fuzzy, it becomes much harder to argue for "our" rights.[6] So, on talk shows as elsewhere, most everyone works very hard to stitch things back together, to hide the seams and make sure the either-or categories are still intact, and the programs help them along in the task. But talk shows are more remarkable for the degree of category-confounding they seek out and invite, making public exactly the phenomena that bring ambiguities to the fore. People encountering these shows, in the studio or at home, are made to work, as witnesses to a rumpus of wild things: either to scramble for ways to make things fit, or to push the closedoors button.

Figure 6 Phil Donahue, talking with cross-dresser Melody on his show, wears a skirt, November 1988. AP/Wide World Photos.

This story certainly rings with the general cultural ambivalence toward bisexual and gender-crossing people noted by other analysts: they provoke distress and desire, fascination and censure; they disrupt and confirm the gender system's logic.[7] But it adds a bit of a different take. Talk shows do more than allow some underlying, free-floating collective anxiety to make itself more loudly heard, allowing it to find its focus and fanning its flames. Through specific organizational practices, they *structure* and *enact* the opening and closing of sexual and gender boundaries, actively creating a series of popular narratives in which categories are popped open and slammed shut like shutters in a windstorm. Their production needs lead them to amplify a crisis in sexual boundary making, yet also to elicit exaggerated reassertions that the boundaries are intact. These kinds of talk shows, by making a pastime of telling the difference, reinforce both the clarity of sex and gender differences and the worry that they might not be so easily told.

Telling differences

For Rolonda, *it was crazy, a big production. They showed up at about 7:00 in the morning, and I was down in the lobby getting some coffee for Cynthia. And they come storming up there and they said, "Well, where's Linda?" And Cynthia said, "Well, she's down in the lobby." So they come down in the lobby and here's all these other women stumbling around down there and I'm stumbling around with them. And I saw these people with cameras and everything and I said, "Are you looking for Linda Phillips?" "Yeah." And I said, "Well, I'm her." So we went back upstairs and they wanted to take pictures of me putting on my makeup and I said, "You don't understand," I said, "I've had electrolysis. I don't have a beard. I don't have anything to cover up. I use very little makeup." And I tried to explain it to them but they don't want to listen to you. So I said, "You know, you can take pictures of me but you can go out and take pictures of any woman putting on her makeup." So I put my makeup on and this guy stood in the bath tub and took pictures of me putting my makeup on. So then we go out and they took pictures of us, almost all day, I guess. They filmed us going up Fifth Avenue. We did this, we did that. They videotaped us doing everything in the world. We went all over town, and they took pictures everywhere. And then they called us in and they said, "Well, we can't, we're not going to do you because you just look like two women." Too normal. They said, "God, this is, you guys are really great. And it was really great, but it just looks like two women out shopping." I said, "That's right. That's our life."*

TALK SHOW GUEST LINDA PHILLIPS

If Truman Capote were alive and appearing on Jenny Jones, *some eager intern would probably be whispering for him to act a little more flamboyant.*

COMEDIAN JAFFE COHEN[8]

Linda and Cynthia Phillips have been married for some forty years, and for many of those years Linda, male according to anatomical criteria, has lived as a woman. Were you to see them on the street, you would indeed probably take them for a pair of white, middle-aged suburban women out shopping, since that is more or less who they are and want to be. As they found out after shopping with *Rolonda*'s camera crew, that is not always enough for a talk show. For most talk shows, cross-dressers should make a gender mix visible rather than disappearing into one gender or another; they should be walking gender contradictions. Although they have exchanged wedding vows on *Sally* and *Jenny Jones,* and made appearances on *Geraldo* and many other talk shows, the Phillips's gender presentation is far too "normal" for most producers. They pass too well; they do not mix genders well enough; they embrace rather than mess up gender conventions.

When they went on *Sally,* for instance, the producer took one look at Linda and said, "You look just like a woman." Yes, she said, that's the idea. Like many other producers, he wanted Linda to use a male name, either her own or borrowed—Charlie, Marvin, whatever—and a "male voice." She agreed to choose a male name, but insisted that the voice she was using was the only one she had. "Well, uh, can't you make it deeper?" the producer said. "He wanted to make sure that people didn't think it was two lesbians," Linda recalls. "What they really want is some guy about six foot four, that weighs 300 pounds, to come on and dress up like a woman. We just look like two middle-aged women." They want their subjects to arrest the eye, and the attached remote-control finger, by being, in one way or another, unbelievable. The difference must be immediately visible and audible—exactly the complaint of many nonheterosexual viewers interested in assimilation rather than exaggerated difference.

Or, alternatively, producers choose to play the B side of this broken record, by exaggerating the "realness," the ability to pass, of gay people or gender-crossers, in order to initiate games of To Tell the Truth: will the "real woman," or the "real lesbian," please stand up. Difference is rendered temporarily invisible. Miss Understood, for instance, is a drag performer who, with her sometimes multicolored hair and her one-of-a-kind, over-the-top outfits, can hardly be said to pass. "Drag, especially in New York," says Alex, the mister side of Miss Understood, "is so much more about an aesthetic than about trying to look like a woman. Like it's not female impersonation so much. A lot of drag queens don't even use tits. I mean, it's more about a visual. It's about a certain, it's an art form. It's about looking a certain way and being colorful more than it's about female impersonation." This perspective on drag as a genderbending art form mostly sits outside the talk show agenda. When Miss Understood appeared on *Gordon Elliott,* s/he reports, s/he was told by the producer, Daniel ("a big asshole," s/he says after the fact), that *Gordon Elliott* was not like the other shows, that they did not set people up.

And he calls me and goes, "Okay now, can you dress to look like a real woman?" And I go, "No, that's not what I do." I said, "I'll look pretty." He says, "Well, can you look a little kind of real? Because we want to do this thing where we put you up with a real woman and they have to guess who's the drag queen." And I go, "That's nothing like what I do." I mean, I wear a corset and I look leggy and, you know, I have these characteristics of a woman, but I'm very overdone. I wear very heavy makeup and very big wigs and that's my look and that's what I do. Here I'm going on a talk show and he's trying to change what I do to fit his topic. This is the one who went over and over, "We're not like that, we're not like those other shows." Then he goes, "Can we call you Alex? Because Alex sounds like a woman's name." I go, "No. You can tell them my name is Alex but my stage name is not Alex," you know. "I'm coming on there as Miss Understood, that's what I do. I don't present myself and call myself Alex." And then we got there, they do that thing with the real woman, and she kind of did look a drag queen. But most of these guests were not people that try to pass themselves off as real women. They were people who are very character, who aren't trying to like pass themselves off or fool anyone. That was like distorting what we do to begin with to even pretend that that's what we're trying to do.

It was the game of telling-the-difference that the producer wanted—a different version than the announcement of it by lowered voices and male names and gender dissonance, but the same game.

This theme of telling-the-difference between gay and straight, man and woman, is quite common in the talk show world. A less fun, more disquieting implication sometimes tags along with difference-telling games: that the differences are hard to see because the categories are faulty. In the process of announcing "here are people who don't seem to fit," or "here are people whose gender is not what it seems to be," or, less kindly put, "here come the freaks," talk shows intentionally open up the question of sexual and gender boundaries. They tap into the fascination my cocktail-lounge-drag photo captures: since you cannot figure out how to categorize the people you are seeing, and you are compelled somehow to do so, you cannot turn the channel.

On most shows focused on lesbians and gay men alone, the categories of "gay" and "straight" and "man" and "woman" are unproblematic; these just *are* gay people (lesbian cops, gay gang members, lesbian activists, and so on), and that's that. (Sustained discussions of how to distinguish gay from straight appear on only about 3 percent of the programs in my sample.) In part, this is no doubt the fruition of much gay and lesbian organizing of the 1980s: homosexuality has been integrated enough into the cultural fabric to be seen, at least sometimes, as a fact of life. Shows like *Ricki*'s "Back Off Boys! I'm a Lesbian and You'll Never Have Me," in fact, have no discussion of either sexual morality or sexual ambiguity at all. Instead, a series of women—mainly women of color—being as lesbian as can be, assert against the claims of various men that the line between lesbian and heterosexual is firm. "I don't want to respect the sister, I want to uplift her," says Ernest about Vontese, whom he calls a "fine, sexy black queen." "I hear the same thing from my woman, who I love very much," Vontese replies angrily. "I'm in love with my woman." To the usual big applause, Ricki tells Ernest to "stay away from her and her girlfriend and get a real life," and later, a man in the audience tells the men on the panel to "go on with your egos and go on to another quest, since you're pursuing something that's never going to happen."[9] Often, on shows like this, homosexuality is asserted as a category as fixed and sharp as heterosexuality. Movement from one to the other is never going to happen.

But the occasions where the theme of difference telling does emerge on gay-focused shows hold important clues. On the one hand, they seem to suggest that heterosexuality is an extremely unstable state: husbands are suddenly leaving their wives for other men, wives are declaring their desire to sleep with women, friends are turning friends gay, people are turning from gay to straight, and so on. You cannot really tell who is what; people are boundary jumping all over the place, as though heterosexuality can leave the body whenever it wants. Here as elsewhere, the constant questions about children, whom audience members habitually worry are vulnerable to the suggestion of homosexuality ("Are you going to propagandize and brainwash the child into being gay like you?" as Geraldo Rivera summarized the concern on one show), serve as the strongest reminder of heterosexuality's fragility. The children must be protected from "abnormal" sexuality exactly because "normal" sexuality cannot protect itself. In such a state of affairs, even if underneath it all there is a confidence that the *categories* are immutable, the *boundary* between straight and gay appears permeable, and the difference between straight and gay difficult to discern. This is what makes the shows grabby, in fact: a bit of a fear is stirred up that maybe the sexual boundaries are not as natural as they seem.

Although they covered themselves in a prolesbian, antistereotype veneer, for instance, a brief slew of lesbian shows in the early 1990s sought to attract their audiences largely by suggesting that it was no longer possible to pick a lesbian out of the crowd. Typically they reverse the prohibition on passing that Linda and Cynthia encountered, bringing on lesbians whose difference from other women is invisible. But the game of telling-the-difference is the same. The guests eagerly pick up on this, asserting that "we are everywhere"—simultaneously a truth claim and a threat—even when you think we are not. "They're out and coming to a town near you," a 1994 *Geraldo* show on "power dykes" announces in its title, heralding an invasion of lesbians, some of whom look shockingly like other women. "So what is an average lesbian?" Geraldo asks the panel. "There is no average lesbian," Frances Stevens, the publisher and editor of the glossy lesbian magazine *Deneuve* (now *Curve*) answers predictably. "I mean, if you look around, could you decipher who was lesbian and who was not?"[10] And if not, how do you know where the boundary is between you and them?

This is exactly the question animating the occasional "lipstick lesbian" and "gorgeous and gay" talk show. In the middle of his "lesbian chic" show, Geraldo asks his cameraman to pan the panel. "This is what lesbians look like," he says, in his Ripley's-Believe-It-or-Not tone, as the camera moves over repeat-guest Stevens (this time in an Anne Klein suit and Ann Taylor shoes, she has announced, verifying that "everything I have on is women's attire"), comedians Karen Williams ("I'm a mall dyke") and Suzanne Westenhoefer ("we're the last unknown territory"), Olivia Records and Cruises founder and president Judy Dlugacz ("we're just like everybody else"), therapist and writer JoAnn Loulan ("there's thousands of ways to be women and thousands of ways to express that gender"), and two members of the all-woman band Fem to Fem ("just because I look like a woman it doesn't mean I can't enjoy being with a woman"). "You all know lesbians," Dlugacz says, reasserting the show's invisible-threat sales appeal. "You just don't know you know lesbians." That is, *there is no reliable, visible marker of this category.* Loulan sums up the show's logic. "When people say to me, 'Oh, you don't look like a lesbian,' I say, 'Get ready to get—really get scared, because this is what lesbians look like.' And we never—you know, who knows who a lesbian is?"[11] Exactly: you can never know, since the code does not work.

A crisis in difference telling is thus willfully created by the talk show. Yet despite the holes they seem to shoot in the walls between gay and straight, since they cannot risk leaving an audience thrown off, these shows are often programmed to rebuild the walls; the crisis is created only to be averted. The audience does much of the work here regardless of show structures, with the host sometimes leading and sometimes following, always attempting to channel for the mainstream. Often the audience response is simply wild cheering for any declaration of heterosexuality (go team!), or the matter-of-fact assertion that leopards cannot change their spots ("once you gay, baby, you always gay," as a woman on *Jane Whitney* says[12]), or hostile commentary directed at lesbians and gay men. Often, especially when working-class audiences are ruling the studio, reinforcements are brought in from the popular association of effeminacy and male homosexuality (and, less frequently, of masculinity and lesbianism), and a line is redrawn between "gay" and "man." "Don't go hanging around with your gay friends at gay bars and acting gay, and then come home and supposed to snap back into a man," sassy Falisha tells Lance, an African American man whose wife, Falisha's best friend, wants him to stop hanging around his gay friends, since she is worried he may return to an earlier gay life and, of course, has just announced that she is pregnant. The audience applauds and cheers.[13] Here's how we tell the difference: *gay men are women.*

The audience, however, does not work alone here. The show structures pick up on and promote these associations, in order to recoup the threatened loss of difference-telling ability with which they draw an audience. They often provide a more direct opportunity to reassert stable boundaries, to *practice* telling the difference, offering reassurances that the difference is there, if buried. You just need to know how to recognize it. We saw earlier, for instance, how shows on "gay husbands," while fostering the notion that gayness can crop up in any marriage, often include some discussion of "warning signs"—how to tell if your husband is really gay. Difference-telling shows do much the same thing, focusing on the telltale clues.

Bertice Berry's program featuring ostensibly straight people who are mistaken for gay, for instance, takes this routine to the extreme. The show opens with a confusing tell-the-difference question ("Do you think you can spot a gay person even though they're not gay?"), and offers answers that reassert a gendered code of homosexuality through a series of light-hearted, joke-filled segments. A disc jockey named Mo is identified as someone who radio listeners think is gay, and his partner Grego as someone who "defends his radio partner's manhood." The show is an hour-long enactment of this gayness versus manhood idea. When Mo asks Berry to slap a woman who has been rude to him, she asks, "Would you slap her like this?" throwing a limp wrist toward the offending woman. Berry asks Mo to show her his walk, and then announces that "I don't think it's gay." She asks audience members to guess which of two twins is gay (Robby, guesses one man creatively but incorrectly, "from the posture"), and then introduces a "man who has two earrings, wears makeup, he's a hairdresser, and he can't figure out why people think he's gay." The show ends with a Letterman-like list of things you can do if you want people to stop thinking you're gay: "1. Resign as president of the Liberace Fan Club. 2. Learn to spit in public. 3. Get used to dropping your dirty underwear all over the house. 4. Start going to a different bar. 5. Never say 'girlfriend,' unless you have one." [14]

These particular instructions are a joke, but they are part of a more serious set of talk show resolutions to the uncertainty about sexual categories the shows themselves invite. Lesbians and heterosexual women look the same, a gay man cannot be distinguished from a straight one, sexual boundaries are invisible and perhaps permeable, they say, but then quickly return to mark gay difference with cliché (an inability to spit, the posture of a pervert, a certain lightness in the loafers). Discussing the conflation of transvestism and homosexuality—a common, inflated version of *Bertice Berry*'s limp-wrist stereotyping—Marjorie Garber nails this dynamic: "It is as though the hegemonic cultural imaginary is saying to itself: if there is a difference (between gay and straight), we want to be able to *see* it, and if we see a difference (a man in women's clothes), we want to be able to *interpret* it. In both cases, the conflation is fueled by a desire to *tell the difference*, to guard against a difference that might otherwise put the identity of one's own position in question." [15] On talk shows, this is not just some amorphous, free-floating "hegemonic cultural imaginary," however, but a concrete set of actors actively *producing* a situation in which they attract viewers by simultaneously threatening and reassuring them. The requirements of this genre of commercial television entertainment magnify and concretize the cultural game of seeing and interpreting sexual differences; it is the generic media needs, not just the strength of heterosexual hegemony, that make this happen. Deepen your voice a bit, please. Walk gay. In the end, producers cannot afford to allow audiences to think the joke is on them.

Both and neither

Sometimes, I suppose, boredom gives rise to some really good sex. At one never-aired *Maury Povich* taping, I sat in the audience as Jason, a large 18-year-old from a small town in Ohio, declared his lust for Calvin, who was having an affair with Jamie (Jason's twin sister, also the mother of a 3-month-old), who was interested in Scott, who had had sex with, as I recall, both Calvin and Tiffanie. Tiffanie, who walked on stage holding Jamie's hand, had pretty much had sex with everyone except Jamie—during group sex, Tiffanie explained, she and Jamie did not touch each other. "We're not lesbians," she loudly asserted, against the noisy protestations of some audience members.

The studio audience, in fact, was quick to condemn the kids, who were living together in a one bedroom apartment with Jamie's baby. Some of the condemnation and advice was predictably accusatory: you are freaks, some people said; immoral, said others; pathetically bored and in need of a hobby, said others. But much of it struggled to attach sexual labels to an array of partnerships anarchic enough to throw such labels into disarray, as the same-sex partners of openly gay and bisexual teenagers declared heterosexual identities. "If you are not lesbians, why were you holding hands?" one woman asked Tiffanie. "If you are not gay," another audience member asked Calvin, "how is it you came to have oral sex with two young men?" The boys were told to "come to terms with their sexuality" and to "figure themselves out." But it was not just the young people who were confused. Their mix of sexual desires and identities created a situation in which sexual categories were unsettled, up for grabs. It was the audience who needed to come to terms.

While shows focused on gay men and lesbians alone tend for the most part to operate as though the categories of gay, straight, man, woman are self-evident and stable, it is especially on programs focused on bisexuality and transsexualism that categorization gets troubled. On these shows, the categories themselves constitute a disproportionately strong theme: the theme of telling-the-difference appears strongly on 11 percent of the overall sample (when shows on bisexuality, transsexuality, male homosexuality, lesbianism, and cross-dressing are all included); it is prominent, however, in 16 percent of the bisexual shows and 24 percent of the transsexual shows in the sample. This ought not to be surprising, since these are disorganizing identities. Bisexual identity, like transsexual identity, is "an identity that is also *not* an identity, a sign of the certainty of ambiguity, the stability of instability, a category that defies and defeats categorization."[16]

This category defiance runs throughout many shows on bisexuality, in part because bisexual guests get occasional opportunities on these programs to raise the possibility, not just with their presence but sometimes with their words, that sexuality is fluid and that we should not be so confident in the demarcations divvying us up into sexual categories. "We polarize so many things in this culture," Carol, a white bisexual woman in a smart purple pants suit says on *Donahue,* for instance, "where it's either this or that, and the foolishness of this to me is that the world is a both/and place."[17] Translating Foucault and Kinsey and Freud for *Oprah*'s audience, professor and writer Marjorie Garber suggests that "these categories of heterosexual and homosexual are very new" and "we shouldn't be thinking in these compartmental ways," that "bisexuality is the ground of human sexuality," and that if people "looked back over the whole course of their lifetime, they would see these bisexual moments in their lives, whether or not they call themselves bisexual now." Mark, the publisher of a magazine called *Anything That Moves,* raises "this question of purity, whether you're completely one thing or another," also on *Oprah.* "A lot of issues in our society get split right down the line," he argues. "You're either all the way to the left or all the way to the right, and I think that life's a lot more complicated than that, whether it's sexuality or whether it's race." The suggestion that sexual categories are oversimplified, too rigid, that sexuality runs on a continuum that cannot be captured by two compartments, that maybe we could do without them entirely, gets a good deal of play here. "It's not straight or gay," as Oprah Winfrey said, introducing her show "The Secret Lives of Bisexuals." "It's both and neither."[18]

That's the middle-class activist version. The other version is more back-door and, for that reason, arguably harder to dismiss: shows about people who are looking desiringly toward their own sex but do not identify as lesbian, gay, or often even as bisexual. Just what *are* they? people want to know. "If you were put, like, on an island or something and they told you that you had to pick between men or women and you had to pick one, which would you pick?" an audience member asks Darlene ("she likes to sleep with women and her boyfriend doesn't mind") and Pammy ("she makes love to women and her husband doesn't mind") on a 1994 *Donahue*. "I'd pick him," my husband, replies Pammy, who says sex with women "is a completely different situation, a different feeling." "A man," says Darlene, who also desires women. Darlene adds that if her boyfriend told her he'd slept with another man, she'd be "sickened"; Pammy says she "guesses" she's bisexual, but doesn't want anybody to call her a lesbian. Alas, one caller does just that, asserting that "they're just two lesbians who just want a man around the house just to keep a roof over their head and food on the table."[19] That same year, Jerry Springer hosted Chris, who "says his two-year affair with Nancy's best male friend does not make him gay." He was just "curious to what sexuality I really was," he says, and that he "messed up" with this two-year affair and "it is never going to happen again."[20] All of this distancing from homosexuality only threatens to further muddy the categories: if heterosexuals can desire and have sex with people of the same sex, what exactly is the difference between a heterosexual and a homosexual? These square pegs make the standard round holes look like shape shifters. Even without the talk of fluidity and continua, these shows about bisexual desire present sexuality as, at least potentially, both-and rather than either-or.

The possibility that the gay/straight and male/female dichotomies might be unworkable is raised even more strongly on shows featuring transsexuals. "What makes you a man or a woman is basically what other people see you as," says Susan Stryker on *Gabrielle,* while a reaction shot shows a young man putting his head in his hands.[21] At the end of a very respectful, emotional *Rolonda* program on "women who become men," one of the guests, a gay female-to-male transsexual named Shadow, has this to say: "I don't feel I was born into the wrong body. I was given this path for a very specific reason. Even if that [reason] was in today's society to come forward and have everybody question what is gender. What makes a man a man and what makes a woman a woman? We're not the only ones who are dealing with gender issues. All of you are as well. We hear it every day of our lives, as soon as you're born you're handed a pink blanket or a blue blanket. We need to question those things, all of us."[22] At the end of a much less respectful hour with transgender guests, host Jerry Springer sums up the point, sounding more like a slightly muddled gender theorist than the referee of a show often likened to pro wrestling.

Gender's apparently more than what hangs or doesn't hang between one's legs, nor can body parts define what sex one's attracted to. Perhaps we'd like to think there are only two classifications: male and female. But the reality is—considering the myriad genetic, cellular and chemical combinations that make up gender and sexual orientation, the reality is that we are all simply degrees of one or the other: either mostly male or mostly female, mostly man, mostly woman. Picture, if you will, a continuum from one to 100, one being all male, 100 being all female—overwhelmingly masculine or feminine. But many gravitate in their physiological or psychological makeup more to the middle: a man with female characteristics or a woman with male characteristics; perhaps bisexual—in the most extreme cases, the actual body parts of both.[23]

The desire to mess with genital classification, in fact, was what drove Jacob Hale, a philosophy professor and self-described "nerdy academic" with "little sense of what goes on TV," to disclose the details of his own body on the quickly canceled *Gabrielle*. "I went back and forth and back and forth on that. There's a whole cluster of prurient interest that people have in transsexual bodies. I knew it would make me damn uncomfortable. But we decided that yeah, I would go ahead and say that stuff. Partly because it seems to just fuck with people's notions so much to think that I look as I do and operate in the world as a man and don't have a penis. In a vague sense, I wanted to disrupt the notion that this is all about genitals." The show was something of a bust, with a newly married transsexual man overshadowing Hale by "bragging about his dick," cockily assuring the audience that this indeed is all about genitals; but one is hard pressed to find anything resembling Hale's intentional, fleeting interruption of that pervasive discourse anywhere outside of academia.

Statements such as Shadow's, Springer's, and Hale's remain relatively rare, and the "born in the wrong body" or "gender dysphoria" takes on transsexualism are extremely strong in the talk show world, as they are elsewhere in the culture.[24] Talk shows certainly do not manage to *change* what Harold Garfinkel called the "natural attitude" toward gender: there are two and only two genders, which are invariant, natural, and marked by genitals; exceptions must not be taken seriously, and everyone must be classified as one or the other.[25] But in one way or another, the question of what makes a man and what makes a woman is *on the table* in most talk shows featuring transgendered people. After all, these are people claiming to be men with vaginas or women with penises, to have been made into, or to have made themselves into men or women, with or without surgery. These are people who push "men" and "women" into quotation marks. By intentionally promoting the disturbing incongruity between bodies and identities, these shows heighten the threat of a gender-ambiguous world.

In the midst of the bells and gongs of his intentionally over-the-top "drag queens versus real women" show, for instance, Richard Bey aggressively argues with the "real women" about what makes them "real." "All your arguments are fallacious and wrong," he yells, pointing out that there are real women who have hysterectomies or can't have children (it's not the ability to give birth), that some real women don't have real breasts (it's not the body one is born with), and so on. "You're just like a real woman," Bey tells Bambi, a blonde queen in a miniskirt, when she refuses to tell an audience member "what's underneath there." "You always keep a guy guessing."[26] On a 1991 *Donahue* featuring transsexual lesbians, a bland-looking white woman addresses Tala, a long-haired woman in a long-sleeved black dress, whom Donahue reports has "taken hormones, you've had breast implants, and you still have your penis." Why not have genital surgery? audience lady wants to know. "I mean, are you a man, are you a woman, are you an it? What are you?" *Be nice,* Phil says, as Tala is shown laughing it off. "I am a woman," she replies, and "I wanted implants because I wanted to have larger breasts." The woman persists. "Do you want to feel like a woman or like a man? What is the purpose?" Tala remains calm. "I feel like a woman," she says. "You feel like a woman, but you're a man." "No, I'm a woman," Tala insists. At this point, Tala's girlfriend, a 27-year-old redhead, jumps in, pointing both fingers at the audience. "What makes a woman a woman? I dare any five people in this room to agree on that definition."[27] This is exactly the talk show dare that draws them in, but not surprisingly, no one takes the dare.

In a less held-back exchange, Vanessa, a transsexual prostitute on a *Jerry Springer* show chock full of reaction shots of young, white people laughing in disbelief, makes essentially the same point. "Having a penis does not make you a man, honey," she says, dressed in a sequined black strapless dress. "And having a vagina does not make you a woman. Wait a minute—wait a minute, wait, wait, wait," she continues, over noisy audience objections. "Wait a minute, let me explain myself. If that's what it costs, then any man in here for $40,000 can become a woman, but does that actually make you a woman? No, it does not. So it's not a vagina or a penis that makes the sexuality or anything else. It's the person inside of you."[28] That same year, on *Jerry Springer*'s "I Want to Be a Girl," a female audience member offers kind words to Tiffany, a 14-year-old transgendered white southerner who tells of being set on fire by people she thought were her best friends. The woman supports Tiffany not because she is at all likable ("I'll tell you straight up I'm a bitch," Tiffany says), but because she is ladylike compared to 15-year-old Tamika who, according to the woman, is not living up to the claim of womanhood. "Tiffany, I think that you, personally, carry yourself very well as a woman, the way you sit and the way you dress," she says. "But, Tamika" ("Girl," Tamika interjects, "shut the [censored] up"), "I think you need to close your legs. I think you need to close—" Tamika cuts her off. "Bitch," she says. "She's so ugly, the bitch."[29]

These conversations are as much about getting off a plum insult than making any particular point, yet they turn out to be ground-level versions of high-academic theories of gender "performativity" and gender construction:[30] men can be women, especially if they keep their legs closed and carry and dress themselves in certain ways, since this is, after all, how women become women. All of the screaming can only partly drown out the troubling questions raised, verbally and visually. If gender is a continuum, if gender can be made with surgery or clothing, if a woman can have a penis, can gender distinctions be natural occurrences of the body? Are the boundaries between sexes permeable and fluctuating?

Rarely do these questions fly right in, of course; they hover, then here and there poke through the thick cover of ridicule or clinical concern. Some transgender shows are somber considerations of gender transition, others rambunctious discussions of dating or relationships, some simply light, performed translations of the question of telling-the-difference into fashion shows or dance routines, in which transsexual women inevitably appear in bikinis, to hoots and hollers and catcalls. "Can a man be just as glamorous as a woman?" Maury Povich asks his audience before a series of glamorous women walk the show's "runway," on a typical one of these shows. "On our stage today will be some of the most beautiful and talented young women—well, sort of, young women. Actually, some of our guests are men and some are women. Will you be able to know the difference?" The answer, basically, is no, and a series of people profess confusion. "I'm just dazed and confused," says one guy. "I'm getting more unsure. Now I'm confused," says a female audience member. "Why—why is it—why is it, on a show like this, I always seem to stammer?" Povich himself asks, stumbling through the questioning. "I mean, there's something a—I mean, I do—I—I just don't know how to act. I just don't know what to do."[31] *Jerry Springer* and *Sally* founder Burt Dubrow captures the production strategy at work here: "We've done the best transsexual or transvestite fashion shows that you will ever see. Someone came to me and said they wanted to do a transsexual fashion show, and I said, 'Only under one condition. I want to see the most beautiful women in the world.' I said, 'I don't want one person up there that looks like a man dressed as a woman. I want someone that every man in America will think, "I want to fuck that." ' And we did it. These people were beautiful, and it was insane. It was the highest-rated show in the book, I think." It's all in good "fun," of course, but what's being promoted is the kick of gender confusion, of suddenly not being able to tell the difference, and therefore of not knowing how to act, what to do, how to speak, whom to want. You think you can tell the difference between men and women, these shows ask in a variety of ways, but can you?

Beyond the bikini displays—which themselves play with, and candidly eroticize, the assumption that genitals are definitive of gender—on most shows there is some moment in which the discussion, however rowdy and hostile, turns to the utility of labels. "How can you call yourself a straight man if you're messing with a man?" an audience member on *Sally* asks Thomas, the boyfriend of transsexual Deborah. "Is this a man?" Deborah says, standing up (in her bikini, of course). "Does that look like a man to you?" Thomas adds. "It is a man, though," the woman in the audience insists. "You is a man no matter what." Having just defended his girlfriend's womanhood on the basis of the appearance of female parts, Thomas takes the last word by suggesting that gender is in the eye of the beholder. "To you," he says. "To me, she's a woman. That's to you. To me, she's a woman."[32]

This is a very common interchange, in which the confusion about gender status leads to a confusion about sexual identity status. Indeed, ironically, it is exactly because transsexuals alone have become too passé a talk show topic that producers have turned to a strategy that winds up eliciting all sorts of sexual-identity disturbances: bringing on the *partners* of transsexuals. Geraldo Rivera, for instance, follows this line of questioning of Mike, who insists that he sees his preoperative transsexual girlfriend Nikki as female, and who identifies as straight. "Where does the relationship go?" he asks. "Is it like a gay relationship? Are you two gay guys together? Is that what it's like?" An audience member wants to know the same thing. "I don't understand why if the two on the end still have their—well, have their male parts why that's not a homosexual relationship," she says. "I don't understand how that can be anything other than a homosexual relationship."[33]

Jerry Springer's circuslike show, which has made transgendered people a programming staple, nearly always elicits this kind of discussion. In one typical program in 1995, "My Girlfriend Is a Man"—here again, the title tries to blow your mind with a gender oxymoron—Ciro, who "says he is a straight man even though his girlfriend is really a guy," confronts his friend Jason, who "says if Ciro dates guys, he must be gay." Ciro, in the midst of the screaming and yelling, echoes *Rolonda*'s Shadow. "A woman is defined by much more than what—than—than their genitalia that's down there," he says. Later, Kelly, a transsexual woman, having listened to a love poem recited to her by a viewer who had seen her on a previous show, confronts an audience member who says that the only reason the men date "these women" is "because they can't get no real woman like my woman over here." "That's just because you're defining a woman as between—what's between her legs," Kelly says, "and that's not what makes a woman." Ciro's friend Jason sums up the identity conflict elicited over and over by the transsexual presence on talk shows. "This is not a man and this is not a woman, ok?" he says of Mercedes, Ciro's transsexual girlfriend. "On the outside, it's a woman; on the inside, it's a man. It's half and half. *You don't have something like that. As far as I'm concerned, there's just two categories.* This is not a man and not a woman."[34] An audience member on *Sally* is considerably less polite. "I love women, okay?" he says.

First of all, God made Adam and Eve, not Adam and Steve, all right? Number two, any guy that goes out with y'all has to be a homosexual. Because I knew all of y'all was men, the minute I looked at you. You can't fool me, I know you are all men. You look good, that's a man right there, too. [He points to a female audience member, who stands up and begins yelling back at him.] *I know a man when I see a man, you all cannot fool me. I know a man. I know women. I know a woman and I know a man and you are all men. You are a homo and you are a homo. You are nothing but homos.*[35]

This is a common, if uncommonly cocksure, response to a genre that so often makes the scary-funny question of telling the difference between male, female, gay, and straight central to the show.

Like the drag witnesses at the Top of the Mark, in fact, these speakers seem to be in the midst of what Marjorie Garber calls a "category crisis," a "failure of definitional distinction, a borderline that becomes permeable, that permits of border crossings from one (apparently distinct) category to another."[36] Are there more than two sexual categories? Do the labels even work at all? If not, how do I know who I am, and who or what is normal? The ferocity with which some guests and audience members answer that question suggests that the categories are indeed threatened, if only temporarily, on these programs.

Getting rid of the confusing parts

The confidence in categories is, then, on the one hand, destabilized. But leaving it at that would, both for a producer and an analyst, be woefully insufficient. As on the gay shows in which borderlines are discussed, the response to the category challenges implicit or explicit on many bisexual and transgender shows is often impatience, clampdown, and a reassertion that there are two and only two categories. People stumble around for a while (is this a joke? a prank? a kooky New York thing?), but then they generally let the guests have it.

When they have to, the studio audience will always step in to recreate a familiar order from threatening disarray. Over and over, for instance, bisexuals on talk TV are told they need to choose. Aren't you really just homosexual? they are asked. As an older black woman in the audience of the *Geraldo* show on "bisexual teens, the latest rage," puts it, to much applause, "I think you're confused and you're experimenting. You're experimenting, because you'll have to pick one or the other. You have to be one or the other. Either gay or straight. You can't enjoy both. That's impossible." When Leslie, a young bisexual woman, keeps asking her why, the audience member simply repeats herself ("You—you're confused—you're confused"), indicating that while there is confusion here, it is not necessarily Leslie's. Importantly, much like the political division of labor we encountered earlier and will see again soon, the crisis and the response it calls forth bolster not only the sense of heterosexuality as natural, but also of homosexuality as natural. "It's not natural," the audience member finishes, again, to shots of nodding heads and applauding hands. "It's not natural to have—to enjoy both sexes."[37] Arthur, a flamboyant African American gay man brought on to *Ricki* to say "you're either gay or you're straight, there's no in between," tells Ricki that her guests, a white, married, bisexual couple, are "two cans short of a six-pack." He uses himself as a comparison case. "I lived that [bisexual] role for the family's sake," he says. "Baby, I'm out now, and I don't plan on going back in." The crowd explodes.[38] Gay is real, bisexual is false.

The resources with which to reestablish the certainty of the sexual taxonomy are many, and audiences and hosts routinely put them all into play, as guests reject them one by one. You place sexual appetite above fidelity (I am loyal to my partners);[39] you are stuck in a sort of sexual purgatory with, as a *Rolonda* show title put it, "two lives to lead" ("I lead one life, as a 100% bisexual woman");[40] you are confused, you must choose (I am not confused, I have chosen).

On these shows, in fact, this last issue of *choice* makes the most regular appearance, and its deployment is instructive. It is marshaled somewhat differently than on lesbian and gay shows—where it also comes up constantly, as it still does in most everyday discussions of homosexuality—although to the same end. The claim that sexual orientation *cannot* be chosen is typically used to argue against condemnation of homosexuals; if your sexuality is inborn, you cannot be "blamed" for it. Bisexuals, however, are condemned for their unwillingness *to choose* either heterosexuality or homosexuality; in their case, the direction of sexual desire is suddenly something one can and must choose. Using the analogy of buying a brand of cookies and potato chips, gay actor Ant argues that "you pick one, or you're just a big slurpie." " 'Today I like women, yum yum yum, today I like men, yum yum yum,' " he says. "Pick one!" The audience eats it up.[41] These are flip sides of a coin used to purchase the preservation of stable sexual order, of two-and-only-two types: while with gay people it is the lack of choice that preserves, with bisexuals the imperative of choice becomes the preserver. The overriding push for retaining the categories renders the inconsistency in these positions invisible, or at least not terribly bothersome.

Transgender shows, with all their foregrounding of telling-the-difference, maintain the simple differentiation between men and women in part by audience proclamation, as people stand up to insist that transgendered people, like bisexuals, fit into one category or the other. Which bathroom do you use? audience members ask, as irritatingly familiar a question to transgenders as the assertion that God made Adam and Eve is to gay people. Or audience members simply dismiss transsexuals and their partners, often with great hostility, as not "real." "I'm a real man. A real man wouldn't be sitting up there right now like he is," a haughty African American man says from the audience of *Sally,* distinguishing himself, as if someone had asked, from Deborah (a cross-dresser who herself says she likes "a real man" rather than a "gay guy") and her boyfriend. The audience applauds and cheers, and a couple of minutes later, another man stands up to "cosign." "I would have found out in two weeks what you really are," he says, to more cheering and clapping, "and I love women, real women."[42] At the end of the show, a young, slight Asian American man stands up to address these earlier comments. "Hi," he says. "I just wanted to make a comment about the two people over here about defining what real men are. I think people like them, as far as, like, defining what men should be, inhibit people to be themselves. And I think that's totally wrong." Light applause. The audience has voted for real men—that is, straight men with penises who sleep with straight women with vaginas.[43] They have voted, that is, for gender as we know it. There are only male and female, and genitals tell us which is which; there are therefore only two types of couplings, same and opposite sex; anything that suggests otherwise is nonsense, unreal, freakish.

Not that transsexuals mostly choose to be on the other side, really. Much of the repudiation of gender ambiguity comes from transgendered guests themselves, who often have much invested in conserving unambiguous gender categories and meanings, are often "*more* concerned with maleness and femaleness than persons who are neither transvestite nor transsexual."[44] Thus repeated lines like "I didn't like playing with GI Joes, I only liked playing with Barbie dolls and stuff,"[45] and TJ's declaration on *Gabrielle* that "I am no longer a transsexual, I am a man," backed up by his claim that his constructed penis is both convincing and big, a claim further certified by his story of "a very heterosexual man, married, who came up to me and said, 'Hey, I've known you a long time, let me see it,' and he said he was cheated."[46] Thus the ubiquitous "I'm more woman than you'll ever be" line, either in high-glamour, polite-headed form ("true glamour is the ability to be a woman when you're not," says Maya on *Maury Povich*'s are-they-women-or-not beauty pageant show) or in low-rent, nasty-headed form ("I'm a better woman then you're ever going to be," Tiffany says to Paris, the disapproving girlfriend of her cousin, on *Jerry Springer;* "I could take your man if I wanted him—not that I would want him").[47] On one of many transsexual-themed *Sally* shows, it is a nontranssexual audience member who argues that gender is made, and a transsexual guest who argues that it is inborn. "Let me tell you something," says the black woman from the crowd. "Little girls and little boys have to be taught this. I don't know about any feeling about being a little girl. You have to be taught that. I am letting you know, as a woman, I had to be taught that, I wasn't born one." Transsexual Barbara responds with her story. "Excuse me, darling, but I came home crying from school, 'They're calling me sissy, Mom.' My mother tried, put me in baseball practice, put me in basketball. I was still a little girl."[48] *One is born a woman,* even if it takes surgery to get there.

Much of this response is spontaneous, driven by the audience and guests, who of course draw on the existing discourse on gender-crossing and bisexuality. But, more important, it is also *produced:* the talk show formats in which bisexual and transgender issues are typically found, and the themes structured into them, encourage this kind of talk. Producers need the viewers at ease, not so disturbed that they change the channel. Thus talk shows reassure, putting the categories back together again. What the occasional panelist or the questioning host may open up, the show usually manages to shut down hard and fast.

In part, they have set themselves up from the beginning to do so, by continually marking, or announcing, the difference: this is really a man (now let's figure out how you can tell), this is really a homosexual (now let's figure out the signs). Producers, balancing novelty with familiarity, from the outset work against the challenging potential of bisexuality and transsexualism. Marjorie Garber, for instance, when she took her book on the road, found producers often fending off the crisis simply by not hearing the challenge. At *Oprah,* this misunderstanding of bisexuality, the maintenance of an either-or framework in which the gay-straight dichotomy is preserved, led to a miniature production crisis.

The producers had provided Oprah with a set of sound bites ostensibly gleaned from preinterviews with guests. She read these comments—largely truisms about "bisexuality"—from index cards as she opened the show. The problem was that these clichéed observations were, in fact, quite the opposite of what the show's guests had told the producers on the telephone, and each time Oprah read one off ("John describes himself as bisexual because he can't decide whether he's straight or gay") the guest would politely contradict her ("Well, no, that's not the case. There were times in my life when I thought I might be straight, but now I know I'm bisexual"). And Oprah would turn to the next card and the same thing would happen. Finally she tossed away the whole stack and said, with a shrug, "That's what the producers told me." Meantime the producers—who were quite young, college students or recent graduates—were looking agitated, and during the commercial breaks they rushed over to the guests, trying to get them to admit that they had said what was written on the little cards. What had happened, pretty clearly, was that in the telephone interviews the producers had asked questions about bisexuality to which they thought they knew the answers, and had written down what they thought they'd heard—which accorded with what they already believed—rather than the more complicated and nuanced answers given by the interviewees. (I recognized this technique from my own experience with these and several other preinterviews.) The upshot was that the first few moments of the show were chaos, and the producers wound up trying to get the guests to confess to saying what the guests had not in fact said, so that the producers could look good to Oprah.

The producers need to keep their program as close to standard assumptions about sexuality as they can, even as they invite guests precisely because they defy those assumptions. This process is especially tough to fight: the commitment to "bisexuality is fence sitting" is not so much ideological as commercial, since it serves to reassure audiences that there are indeed just two sexual neighborhoods, with a big strong fence at their border. Consciously or habitually, producers suppress the category challenge they encourage.

Despite the "both and neither" introduction to her 1995 bisexuality show, for instance, Oprah Winfrey makes clear throughout the show that she thinks there is no such thing. "I've always thought you were either one or the other," she says at one point. "If you are bisexual and you are married and you are monogamous, then you're not bisexual," she asserts later (which a guest points out is like saying that a heterosexual without a sexual relationship is not heterosexual). "I'm not confused," says a guest, correctly anticipating the common assertion that, rather than an indication that gay and straight do not exhaust sexual possibilities, bisexuality is a bogus state of befuddlement. "That's good you're not confused," says Oprah, "because I really am a little bit by this conversation." The audience applauds; as she often does so skillfully, Oprah taps into audience sentiment—in this case, that either these people have stopped making sense or sense has stopped being made.[49]

The programming of transgender shows tends to facilitate a return to the body, whose gender indeterminacy and ambiguity are the shows' selling point, to reestablish the logic of two distinct sexes. On the lighter shows, they literally ask viewers to distinguish the real woman from the fake one. On top of the come-hither anxiety that they are indistinguishable, this framework builds the comforting assertion that, underneath it all, the body tells the truth, that gender-crossing is gender falsification. By framing transgender as "fake" gender, they foreground a cultural logic in which "bending gender rules and passing between genders does not erode but rather preserves gender boundaries," since transgenders are seen as "only transitorily ambiguous."[50] It's just a matter of *finding those genitals*.

On the serious shows, they twist this logic around a bit, by picking up the essentialist medical discourse of both passing transsexuals (we are people trapped in the wrong body) and doctors treating "gender dysphoria" (the physical body must be brought into line with gender identity). Gender *change* becomes the show frame, through discussions of early childhood cross-gender identification and the ins and outs of surgery. (Jerry Springer, for instance, ends nearly every show with transsexuals with an analogy to birth defects, and an associated plea for tolerance.) In this framework, a mistake has been corrected; it's not categories that need reexamination or correction, but the transsexual body. These shows are often more sedate, with less hostility from audiences, because a category conundrum is more or less ruled out by the show's structure. Genitals are gender.

In an echo of the normalization of homosexual status through the stigmatization of gender-crossing, a final programming structure conserves a two-gender system while stigmatizing both gender-crossing and homophobia. Despite the repetition that gender and sexual identities are distinct, many shows return to the claim that a transsexual may just be a gay man gone too far. This framing of transgender as an extension of homosexuality has the peculiar, backward result of supporting lesbian and gay statuses by treating them as the sane, unassailable stopping point before a crazy, butchering gender change. *No need to go that far. Just be gay.* One major purveyor of this line, Jerry Springer, suggests to a transgendered teenager, in a wondrous display of ignorance, that "the reason you're going through such a drastic change is because you're not comfortable with being gay." The guest, he argues, "doesn't want to take the heat of being gay, so he's willing to consider becoming a woman." Some young boys, he suggests, think, "I'm feeling very effeminate. I'm feeling a little, you know, maybe I'm gay. If I'm having these feelings, it's a lot better to go all the way and be a woman and not get teased than to live life as a gay male as a teen." A transsexual guest, Kitty, allows that this could be true. If it were easier to be gay, Springer suggests, no gender transition would be necessary.[51] In a strange twist, an argument against homophobia is maneuvered, in the midst of programming that equates effeminacy with homosexuality, to imply that transsexualism is homosexuality gone haywire. As the challenge to the gender order is defused by the "homophobia is the problem" rhetoric, the hint of gender complexity is snuffed out.

This is just an especially deranged version of something we have seen all along the way: the cultural commitment to homosexuality-as-abnormal on daytime talk shows is remarkably weak, while the commitment to conventions of gender trumps antigay stigmas. For a time homosexuality was, at least potentially, itself also a category disrupter, suggesting that heterosexuality was not the only natural sexual classification, that people who appeared to belong in one category might actually turn out to belong in some other one. But pushed along by the growth of a vocal movement for lesbian and gay rights, homosexuality has been accommodated, moving much closer to the quasi-normal. As one audience member at a transsexual *Sally* show put it simply, "Gay is fine. I mean, I totally accept it. But *this* is bizarre."[52] There is something desperate in all of this manic hostility toward bisexuals and transgenders, this fascination with genitals, these you-must-choose dicta, this sympathy for gender "disease," this willfully ignorant, selective formulation of transsexualism as the crazy edge of gayness—especially when compared to the relative calm and matter-of-factness with which gay men and lesbians are increasingly treated on daytime TV. It is the mania of people who have lost their footing, who feel the ground moving beneath them and just want to be back on a stationary earth. The Springer twist, and the various other twists and turns taken on shows with bisexuals and gender-crossers, helps clarify why the normalization of homosexuality is so unproblematic on talk shows: it is protection of the *distinctions* between gay and straight and male and female, and not so much of heterosexual superiority, toward which talk shows are so heavily wired.

From the mouths of freaks

Talk shows are like giving Twinkies to a starving person. But I like pushing people's buttons. I think it's good to push people's buttons. I like shaking people up. I mean, personally I get a thrill out of it. But the reason I get a thrill out of it is because I'm rebelling against something. I mean, the personal is political. When I go on those shows, like when I come out for a dating game show, I always make it a point to kiss the guy if I can. If I see he's really nasty, I'll usually sit in his lap and give him a kiss, because for me I think it's funny, but also like I'm kissing a man on television. When you're in drag you can get away with it. When you're in drag, you're very intimidating to people. You can do anything you want, you can get anything you want from people. So I just like being seen as a freak. I'm just the opposite of those people who want to show everyone how normal they are. I'd rather them look to me in awe. I don't want them to say, "Oh, you're just like me." I want them to say, "Wow, you're not like me, you're amazing."

DRAG PERFORMER MISS UNDERSTOOD

When you're a monster, you really are outside of normative constraints in so many ways. And you can say and do very magical things. I was pretty impressed with the level of sophistication with which they manipulated me on the talk show. But still, though, at least what I would hope, although I don't know that this happens, is that there would be things that would slip out of my mouth, you know, that would come through the cracks somehow that would give the audience, whatever audience is seeing it, some glimmer of radical difference. I want to be the monster who's speaking. I want to be the monster that is able to speak, you know, and articulate its monstrosity.

TRANSSEXUAL WRITER AND ACTIVIST SUSAN STRYKER

Standing with freaks never hurt anyone—it's when we agree that we deserve the oppression and ridicule that accompanies the freak's position in the culture—that's when the wound is mortal.

TRANSSEXUAL WRITER AND ACTIVIST KATE BORNSTEIN[53]

I saw the bearded lady on television years ago—*Donahue,* I think it was—long before I had given much thought to blurred categories. *What a sad thing,* I thought, looking at her. *Electrolysis,* I thought. But when she spoke, she seemed eerily familiar, and braver than most people I knew. It turns out, I figured out later, that she must have been Jennifer Miller, a woman with a beard who, according to the *New York Times,* performs "an amalgam of old-time vaudeville and feminist theater" in a group called Circus Amok. " 'I *am* a woman with a beard!' she says, tugging on it to prove it is real. Her voice is playful, insinuating, with the exaggerated delivery of sideshow entertainers. 'A woman with a beard, not "the bearded lady!' " she says. . . . From the moment she appears onstage, she confounds expectations: she parades her beard, forces her audience to look at it, to ask questions."[54] Hers is the spirit of the talking "freak": to confound, to force questions, to live in the in-between. It is the spirit of the woman with a beard, who is both a "normal" human and somehow socially unfathomable, rather than the bearded lady, who is fathomable only because she is somehow inhuman.

Talk shows are particularly adept at showing that the transsexual, or Siamese twin, or whoever it may be, "is one of us, the human child of human parents," in Leslie Fiedler's words, not because they have much interest in social transformation. Their common use of "freaks" to defend cultural categories is not terribly surprising—that's the usual usage. What is remarkable is the way this piece of TV culture does just the opposite at the same time, uprooting the guard rail between the freakish and the normal. The everyday workings of ratings-driven TV production make this happen. The shows freakify to get viewers in the door; they humanize to keep them there. This combination makes them scarily intriguing enough to glue people to the TV set. And the "freaks" don't just sit there on the stage looking pretty and bearded. They talk back. They talk about childhoods, about fears, or about how bad you look in that outfit. They are strange and not-strange, you and not-you, inside and outside of recognizable categories. Talk shows love them for that reason, although not for that reason alone.

This blurring, in fact, is a particularly talk show sort of thing, the way in which, without overblowing their innovativeness, it is useful to think of the talk show as a quintessentially "postmodern" genre. As Wayne Munson writes, talk shows in general "confound our coordinates, the lines on our cognitive maps, our familiar distinctions and stabilities—yet all in a new kind of productivity. . . . [They] juxtapose rather than integrate multiple, heterogeneous, discontinuous elements. Rather than *reconcile*, talk shows (barely) *contain*. Postmodernity, like the talk show, substitutes 'both-and' for modernity's 'either-or.' "[55] Their carnivalesque excess, to borrow from Mikhail Bakhtin, celebrates "temporary liberation from the prevailing truth and from the established order"; their spectacular side, as Susan Harding says of spectacles in general, creates "an irrepressible sense of events-out-of-control, of confusion, disorder, and a constant instability of genres, borders, roles, and rules."[56] The form itself is well-suited to the both-and content of bisexuality and transgenderism, which refuse to easily fit familiar gender distinctions and sexual maps.

Those people who straddle categories, even though for the most part they do not themselves identify as freaks and monsters, do indeed knock open mind doors here and there, as we have seen. The farthest-out of sex and gender nonconformists, the most stigmatized, can cause meaning crises. They awaken in audiences the sneaking, sleeping suspicion that perhaps they do not get it, that the differences they are used to are not making sense, that maybe all brides are drag queens and some females are men. You too are monstrous, they announce, since you and I are the same. Their us-ness makes them potentially potent messengers of new ways of thinking about sex and gender, much more potent than any run-of-the-mill lesbian or regular-guy gay man.

Very few people are willing to embrace the "monster" or "freak" label, even in order to humanize it, since doing so is to put oneself largely outside of social recognition. But the occasional person who does so brings the woman-with-a-beard spirit, buried in even the most normality-seeking bisexual or transgender guests' appearances, to the light. Jordy Jones, a transsexual artist, appeared on a show that he knew from the outset was going to be "presented in this sort of spooky-wooky, 'what an amazing world we live in' and 'look what we have here, these people aren't even one sex or the other' " kind of way. He knew he was being brought in to boost ratings.

I don't necessarily have a problem with that as a presentation, and I don't necessarily see that being presented that way makes it impossible to communicate to the normal side of things, too. Everybody has a

*freaky side. So to that extent, I feel a certain amount of responsibility
as, at least in my own opinion, as somebody with a certain amount of
levelheadedness and articulateness about something that is a monstrosity and is perfectly normal at the same time. So part of it's I feel an ob-
ligation as a diplomat, somebody who can walk in both worlds. I'm
able to sort of get behind people's eyes sometimes. And that's where it
comes down to acknowledging the monster. And also seeing that the
monster is us, it's normal, and yes, it's a monster.*

You think you understand me, but I am here to tell you that you have misunderstood us both.

That challenge is rarely found anywhere else in American media culture.
It is alive and well in certain wings of academia and the avant-garde, as well
as in political- and social-movement discourse, but it is rarely disseminated
in any sustained manner anywhere in mass culture. When it does appear,
it is almost always in fictional form, and either defanged or given a different
set of fangs: in *To Wong Foo, Thanks for Everything, Julie Newmar,* asex-
ual, passing drag queens descend like angels on a town filled with dowdy
women, and teach them how to empower themselves through lipstick and
hairdos; in the much-maligned and very popular *Basic Instinct,* the sex-
crazed bisexual woman famously wields an ice pick. That talk shows actively and repeatedly promote a set of boundary challenges complicates the
charge that they are "freak shows" undermining the goals of movements
for changes in the sex and gender system, since it is because they can rupture
categories that "freaks" and "monsters" are so important for cultural
change. There is a significant trade-off here, which the next chapter expli-
cates: talking monsters open up important cultural opportunities (as the categories on which the current system is based are cut open) while closing
down important political ones (as legitimacy for nonconforming populations is threatened).

From this angle, talk shows may not be quite freaky *enough* since, when
the rubber band snaps back, talk shows tend to effortlessly turn gender-
crossers and bisexuals into dismissible jokes or sickos. Just as the door is
opened, it is shut. Talk shows cannot tolerate a crisis of meaning any more
than the rest of the culture, and without much more than the relatively
thoughtless habits of television, producers do their best to keep things just
as they were. This does not mean that nothing magical happens for the moment the door is opened, or that no glimmers come through the cracks, if
only because on talk shows there are so many, many cracks. Talk shows

offer a popular, unusual walk along the cracks, as for a time things almost come undone, but the road ultimately leads back very close to where it started. It is one of the great miscarriages of the talk show world that the guests who appear the most alien have in some ways the most to say, a great big public place to say it in, and almost no one who really wants to listen. The moment they are understood is the moment they must once again be misunderstood.

6 FLAUNTING IT

People are afraid of us. Straight people are afraid of gay people, that's true, that's what they say. I had a woman totally flip out on me, stood in front of me and goes, "Oh, my God. Well, now that I know that you're a lesbian, I can't get undressed in front of you and stuff." I'm like, "Really, Miss, just take my order."

COMEDIAN SUZANNE WESTENHOEFER[1]

Before the days when my reputation preceded me into the classroom, I used to hold my identity close to my chest, poker-faced and straight-seeming, earning as much respect as I could as a teacher until a day toward the end of the semester when Foucault or some other hook to sexuality was on the agenda. On that day, taking a deep breath, I would walk in, strip off my sweater, and reveal a T-shirt: pink triangle, "Silence = Death," black background. Some students were unfazed, or relieved, having spotted the signs—which I had worked so hard in earlier parts of my life to eliminate—much earlier. The jaws of many others dropped, and eyes glazed over as they tried to assimilate the Superfreak at the head of the table. What does the T-shirt mean? I would ask. Why would I want to wear it here? I would ask. Isn't my sexuality none of your business? I would ask. Many nodded, but I think the elementary lesson got through: sexual identity, like it or not, is all about power; although to me my gay self is increasingly boring, it has become increasingly political; this moment, me standing before you in a T-shirt, is politics. Now I miss those moments. I have used up the charge of my identity.

Disclosure is a power play. In the politics of both governments and everyday lives, it can turn tables and bring down houses. That is the virtue of scandal, for instance, in which disclosure is generally not voluntary: think Jessica Hahn and Jim Bakker, or Watergate. It is also the insight of coming-out strategies. The voluntary unveiling of a stigmatized, sometimes scandalous sexual identity plainly has a political impact, at both the macrolevel (a general awareness of the existence of gay people, an opportunity to organize collectively) and the microlevel (a dramatic shift in the power dynamics of personal relationships).[2] Of course, despite the optimism of much gay coming-out rhetoric, the direction of the impact is not a given; while it can

lead to openings and freedom-enhancing changes, an awareness of gay people can and does set in motion all kinds of repressive governmental activities
(Defense of Marriage Act, ordinances to deny legal protections, taking away
of children) and all kinds of repressive interpersonal activities (family rejec-
tion, community alienation, the wielding of baseball bats), as well. Indeed,
as critics of color in particular have pointed out, white middle-class people
can more easily afford the risks of coming out; those facing racial and economic oppressions have a greater need for the protections often provided
families and communities of origin, and coming out often isolates and, by
making sexual identities primary, forces a false choice over equally important racial identities.[3] Secrets may be safer, but at least one thing is clear:
revelation moves power around.

Sexual identities, especially on talk shows where they are so frequently
made public, are therefore very often chips in power struggles large and
miniature. We have already seen some of the rhetorical battles, between *hate
and outlaw* and *love and include* arguments, and between those who would
limit the appearance of sexual *perversion* on television and those who defend
sexual *diversity* on the grounds of free speech. When we take a closer look
at the politics of talk show sexual identities, we can see a whole slew of
other political divisions playing themselves out. Lesbian, gay, bisexual, and
transgender talk show guests, for one thing, tend to recognize that, as much
as anything they have to say, it is usually just their status as outsiders of
one kind or another that makes them sought-after guests. They not only use
this chip of identity to bargain and negotiate with producers for control
over tidbits of cultural representation, but also often self-consciously treat
their appearances as part and parcel of an ongoing battle for recognition
and rights.

Talk show producers, for their part, unselfconsciously build on and exac-
erbate internal divisions within lesbian, gay, bisexual, and transgender political organizing. In their pursuit of conflict, they sometimes stage clashes
between mainstream and radical approaches to sexual-social change, under-
cutting the alliances between these approaches. Even more important, in
part as a response to the organized control activities of activists, they have
turned to those with little connection to middle-class gay, transgender, bisexual, or lesbian organizing, with little interest or experience in the politics
of representation, giving themselves freer reign as producers and infuriating
many middle-class activists. The production of rowdy outrageousness draws
out and intensifies animosities that divide movements for sexual-social
change, snipping at threads of alliance and coalition: between those who

emphasize assimilation into the "mainstream" and those who emphasize separation and autonomous culture building, and between the various populations (gay men, lesbians, bisexuals, transgendered people) making up the larger movement. Talk shows are surely too money-oriented, capricious, and thin to do much deliberate ideological service, but both their loose liberal-therapeutic dogmas and their everyday pursuits—even, and perhaps especially, when they are fixated solely on the "personal"—lead them nonetheless to sharpen political lines of division. With all their silly profundity and profound superficiality, talk shows move power around.

Talk show viewers dance on and around the dividing lines. The viewers with whom I spoke—nine heterosexual focus groups, three gay and lesbian ones, and a transgender discussion group—illustrate the dance. (Focus-group details are in the appendix.) The middle-class, highly educated gay and lesbian viewers we will hear from, for instance, watch the shows like media monitors, concerned about the political impact of "extreme," "negative" or "unrepresentative" images; heterosexual liberal viewers tend to share this concern, seeing talk shows as damaging, exploitative contributors to the ongoing victimization of sex and gender deviants. Sympathy for the "exploited," however, is often tempered by a sometimes subtle, sometimes brash animosity toward "trash"—those people who will display themselves outrageously, the bad, low-class queers. Thus, right up there next to "leave them alone" is "leave me alone": get out of my face, stop flaunting it. Conservative talk show viewers tend to take this position to the extreme, understanding talk shows as part of a progay publicity apparatus, one of many ways in which, to borrow the charmingly indelicate phrase of choice from a group of viewers with whom I spoke, queer life is "shoved down their throats."

Talk shows on sex and gender nonconformity are experienced, then, largely as funny pieces in the midst of serious culture wars; primarily through the class divisions to which they are beholden, they encourage viewers to separate "bad" gays from "good" ones, and to link the appearances of sexual nonconformists to inappropriate uses of public space. There is, in fact, an important clue here. The various political battles that talk shows elicit, profit from, and amplify, all take a part in a more general war: over the lines between public and private, and over who benefits from changing or conserving current public-private divisions. Talk shows open up these cultural battles not so much through the particular discussions they facilitate, not through anything specific that gets said, but through their simple encouragement of publicly visible sex and gender nonconformity. Symbolic political battles over sex and gender norms energize a bigger whirlwind, and are then sucked right into it. Through talk shows, the storms of class and sex and publicity and gender feed one another.

Dreaming of Donahue

You're given a very tiny little window and you're not told in advance how big your window's going to be. And there are things that you want to put through that window, and it's almost like this thing that's shut and opened and shut and opened, and you have these things that are very important and as the window opens you want to try and get those in. It's almost like throwing out little like pouches of information, pouches of impressions. It's entirely performance and the window can get cut off at any moment. You can get interrupted, they can turn off your mike and someone else can interrupt you—another panelist, the host, a commercial, anything. It's trying to push that little bubble of information through the window before you get interrupted and do it in a way that seems entirely relaxed and calm.

BISEXUAL ACTIVIST AND TALK SHOW GUEST ROBYN OCHS

Lani Ka'ahumanu is not the type to cry at her television set. After all, she has had the grit to seek out and grow into all kinds of incarnations of herself: she has been a housewife and mother married to her high school sweetheart, a bit of a sixties hippie, the first divorcée in her family, a public lesbian, and then an outspoken bisexual organizer.[4] But the night before her first incarnation as a talk show guest, the night of President Clinton's 1993 inaugural address, she wound up surprising herself with sappiness. She used to dream of being on a talk show, and of all shows, on *Donahue;* here she was, flown in from San Francisco, in a fancy hotel, about to be a guest of Phil. Unable to sleep, she ordered room service and watched as Clinton, over and over in clips on CNN, talked about his dream of being president some day. "Just like my dream of being on a talk show," she thought, crying over her room-service meal at two in the morning. "Here I am," she thought, feeling like a princess, courtesy of *Donahue.* It was her moment with Bill, a corny moment of indulgence. Her dream, like his, was coming true.

Ann Northrop had no such response. A former television producer turned activist who had appeared on *Donahue* before, she is all hard edges and impatience when it comes to television in general, and Phil Donahue in particular. "I think he's a pompous ass, and I think he's far too full of himself and doesn't know half of what he thinks he knows," she says. "And he is a condescending son of a bitch." In fact, this "lifelong hatred of Phil Donahue" made her especially eager to get into the ring with him, and her chance came again when she was asked to be the lesbian voice on the *Donahue* show on bisexuality that Lani awaited in her hotel room. The producer, she quickly figured out, wanted to cast her as a lesbian *against* bisexuals. "I'm not a gay person who hates bisexual people," Ann objected. "I don't think we have any argument. We have issues we could discuss and I'm happy to discuss those things but you're not going to get me into a fight with them. You're trying to set up a confrontation here, but it ain't going to be like that." The producer wanted her anyway. "Well, it's your funeral, baby," Ann told her.

For Robyn Ochs, a Boston bisexual teacher and organizer, the *Donahue* call was just one in an ongoing series of calls from talk show producers over the years, and she moved quickly into action, referring the producers to other guests she knew she could trust, in an attempt to have some control over the composition of the panel. The producers told her the show was just a generic bisexuality show, but when a phone call came from a New York gay activist, who told her that *Donahue* producers had been calling around town looking for a gay man or lesbian who did not "believe in" bisexuality, she hit the phones again. ("I resent the presumption that the existence of bisexuality is something negotiable," she says. "They don't do that anymore to lesbians and gay men. My existence is not negotiable.") The show had gotten Ann Northrop, she was told, so Robyn called some people she knew in New York—Northrop is a friend of friends of friends—and called Ann a week before the show. "Hey, you were supposed to be on the show, and we've been told that you're going to be the opposing view," she said. "Can we talk?" Let's not be pitted against one another, she said. Let's work together on the show, and not allow them to divert us from talking about homophobia and biphobia. Ann Northrop, whose allegiances were clear and who relishes a good fight, was more than game.

The show's producers, of course, had made it very clear that they did not want this sort of preshow interaction. "Don't talk to the other panelists," they told Eve Diana, a bisexual woman from Boston who was to appear with her straight husband John. "We don't want you to rehearse and we want you to just be spontaneous and fresh." Eve, who was otherwise quite trusting, saw through that one. "Oh, yeah," she thought, "what a load of bullshit." Like the rest of the guests, Eve simply ignored the edict, and when she and John wound up on the same plane as Robyn, the three of them talked it over a bit. Eve was reassured: it was going to be a strong panel of trusted activists presenting "a united front."

In the interests of uniting the front, Robyn arranged a breakfast meeting the next morning with the various bisexual guests at the hotel where they were all staying, and Ann Northrop joined them. The discussion was basic: no matter what the host did, the guests would keep turning back to the upcoming March on Washington for Lesbian, Gay, and Bisexual Equal Rights, plugging it in front of this audience of millions; the guests would try to control the show so that homophobia, not antibisexual gay people, would be the focus. They charged the meal to *Donahue*.

When the first limousine arrived to take them to the studio, the bunch of guests began to climb in. "No, no," said the driver, stopping them. "This one is just for so-and-so." But we're all here, Eve said, and we're all going to the same place. "Nope, nope," the driver responded. "I have very strict orders." The guests played along. Arriving at the studio, they were introduced to each other, and pretended they had never met; even if they did not fool the producers, they reasoned, they were not about to get thrown off the show at that point. The lesbian got her dressing room, the bisexuals got theirs, but the separation came too late: the secret breakfast meeting had already taken place. The activists had their agenda, *Donahue* had theirs. "We hoped our agenda was similar to Donahue's," Eve Diana recalls, "but we weren't going to subvert our agenda for theirs."

Watching the show a few years later, I can see this skillful assertion of the breakfast-meeting agenda. Phil sets up the show with assertions such as "there are a lot of gay people who are angry at bisexuals," and "gays can be homophobic" and "disdainful of bisexuals." Without denying the truth of these statements, the guests act on their plan to refuse them. "All of us in all categories tend to simplify all categories," Ann says, wearing an ACT UP button. Donahue is left to represent the "gays against bisexuals" view himself, and Robyn explains, with a pasted-on talk show smile, that gay hostility comes from the understandable need for an embattled community to close ranks because of a homophobic society. The guests emphasize the political similarity of homosexuals and bisexuals: Lani explains that Colorado's prodiscrimination Amendment 2 includes bisexuals, Robyn points out that when she received a death threat, the caller did not say he was going to half-kill her. As the conversation drifts toward the staple stereotype of nonmonogamy, Ann grabs the floor, making a lengthy, calm speech. "What we're talking about is the capacity for attraction," she begins, and by the time she has finished, she has brought it all back to heterosexism. "If it's true that there are all these capacities for attraction," she asks, while the television shows shots of the quiet, listening audience, "then why the hell do we have this heterosexist society, which has arbitrarily chosen opposite sex relationships as the only ones that are valid? Who made these rules?" Holding up fliers announcing the March on Washington, Ann announces the march's date. The march's title, which includes bisexuals, she says pointedly, "corrects a little bit of the record on the lesbian and gay community." This is not the only promo of the hour; Lani's book (an edited collection of writings on bisexuality), Robyn's bisexual resource directory, bisexual support groups, and an article on bisexuality by another guest, are all announced.[5] For activists, it is something of a dream come true, a good reason, finally, to well up with tears at the sight of bisexuals on television.

When movement-based guests hit the screens, as they continue to do (although in dwindling numbers), such stories are common. Activists rightly see talk show appearances as continuous with their political organizing, in part because, unless they are gender-crossing activists, they are often brought on for explicitly political discussions, or can transform a more sexualized and personalized topic into a political one. "Our philosophy was, we don't have the luxury of saying no to these people," says activist and writer Michelangelo Signorile. "Until we have our own television station or something."

Our goal as activists, as gay people, is to get a message out there within the context of this mainstream media that controls it. So an opportunity to get on there and talk about gay issues is one that we're not likely to pass up quickly. We're working within the system as activists, as writers, as advocates for gay people. We need that air time to talk about homosexuality. Before we would go on, particularly on the shows about the outing issue, for instance, I would say to people, "They have us here to fight with each other. Why don't we turn that around and just talk about the closet and the dangers of it?" And not even talk about the outing issue or whatever it is they want us to talk about. Let's take their show, you know, from them. *Sometimes that has worked, sometimes you've got gay people who also think you're the enemy, so they don't want to do that. Are you going to make talk shows less sensational? No. But you're going to kind of get them to exploit your issues in a way that helps you. I'm exploiting. I'm using the show. I'm using the talk show hosts, the producers, the air time, the network, whatever, to push my social agenda.*

Even when no precise social agenda is pushed, and even when a show is out of activists' control, activists still often see the shows as effective outreach tools. Angela Gardner of the Renaissance Education Association, a group for cross-dressers, tells of going on the raucous *Morton Downey, Jr., Show,* a 1980s nighttime predecessor to the noisy daytime shows of the early 1990s.

> *Our whole idea when we go on any kind of a television or radio thing is that yeah, we may end up entertaining some people in the general public, but more often what we're doing is just going out there to reach people that need us so that they know they're not alone. When we did Morton Downey, I thought, "We're going to get trashed on this show. We're going to get ripped to shreds." But I still agreed to go on it because I felt it would reach more people. So we took a team of three. I was wearing what I consider to be a demure outfit—just-above-the-knee skirt, a little short-sleeve blouse. But when I walked out the audience was like hoot, hoot, hoot, kind of hubba hubba, kind of catcalls. Then as the interview went on, I could sense these guys saying to themselves, "Well, gee, we were like hooting and whistling at her and she ain't what she seems." And then when the third person came out, the cow pile really hit the fan. She was kind of uptight to begin with, and some girl stood up and said something negative about the way she looked, and so she just hit back at her and said, "You don't look so good yourself." And you could see the whole audience turning against us, and then Mort sensed that and he was fanning the audience because he knew he'd got controversy now. The show was like a root canal without the anesthetic. But we got more membership response from that show than anything we ever did. Every time it ran, and they ran that show like four or five times, we got about fifty phone calls. From all over the country we were getting phone calls for information, we were getting things in the mail. So it was successful, even though it was like a really, really bad experience.*

The recognition that talk shows reach different audiences than most of their other work, moreover, magnifies the self-image of many middle-class activist guests as political ambassadors. "The power of television is amazing," says Cianna Stewart, a "mixed race, mixed culture" bisexual activist who appeared on a *Montel Williams* show about lesbian sex clubs. "We were able to do more education and outreach through that one show to more places that would not normally let us in than any other method I could think of. Even doing our own show would not have gotten that much air time or that particular sampling of people in the U.S." The particular sampling, activists are generally aware, is not the usual middle-class news watcher. "Talk shows reach poor, working-class people whose primary source of information is the television set," says bisexual writer and activist Jill Nagle, describing her reasons for appearing on talk shows. "I'm never going to talk to those people otherwise. And those are the folks who, some of them, may be the ones to go out at night with a white hood on their head to their local white supremacist meeting. Who's going to talk to those folks? I'm not going to go to that meeting, but I'll go on TV." Talk shows "are now pitched toward a youthful audience," adds media activist Donald Suggs, "and that's the audience we really need to reach in terms of stemming the tide of antigay violence. That's the audience that desperately needs information, and desperately needs to see us in human terms."[6]

Movement-based guests, even when they do not succeed in "taking over" a show, generally see talk shows as an opportunity to make sex and gender *mean* differently. Whether or not shows are programmed around social and political "issues," activists seek to tap into the overarching *symbolic* politics of talk shows, in which, regardless of the topic, representations with political significance are circulating, verbally and visually. These might be stigmatizing, devaluing stereotypes (gay men are feminine, bisexuals are promiscuous, and so on), in which the meaning attached to a sex or gender status helps justify physical attacks or political ones. They might be cultural frames that, whatever their complications, serve as defenses against attacks (a transsexual is someone trapped in the wrong body, lesbians are born that way, and so forth) or cultural frames seldom heard outside of social movements or academia (heterosexuality needs homosexuality to define itself against, for instance, or gender is a series of performances). Or they might simply be personal stories, through which abstract political issues become symbolically attached to people's lives.

The personalizing push of talk shows, in fact, is arguably a boon for some political agendas. They advance a goal many gay activists see as crucial: "putting a face" on homosexuality. As Suggs argues, "We have this problem now where gays and lesbians are visible as an issue, but there's still very little information that's out there about our actual daily lives. And talk shows are focused very closely on people's daily lives—I mean, in sensational ways sometimes, but on people's daily lives. And the talk shows really show you lesbians and gay men that talk show audiences see and recognize as members of their community." Indeed, in addition to pursuing meetings with talk show staff, Gay and Lesbian Alliance against Defamation (for which Suggs worked) planned to organize training sessions for potential talk show guests, both around specific issues such as gay marriage, and more general training, in which they would teach people what to expect, how to get their points across, and "how to say no," since, "once people understand that they can say no, they feel empowered to basically manipulate the situation, shape the situation so that they'll be able to say yes." Organizations like GLAAD often serve as guest clearinghouses ("I feel like I'm an amateur talk show booker myself," says Suggs), and they recognize the leverage this gives them, not only for providing prominent community members to talk about issues, but also for providing "man or woman in the street" guests to talk about relationships. "If we can get two or three hundred people, you know, in New York, to come to a training, that's a huge pool of people for them to choose from," Suggs suggests. "And when the talk shows call us, we can have a list of people." People chosen and trained by *us.*

Whether or not they are operating as part of an organization, then, movement-identified talk show guests approach talk shows with a political eye, trying to gain as much control over the symbolic politics as possible, planning according to their own political agenda, and, since it so often conflicts with the shows' entertainment agenda, negotiating with producers. Producers themselves recognize the political significance of shows to activists, in fact, and occasionally use it to their advantage. Linda Phillips, for instance, happened to mention to a producer before a transgender-wedding show that one way to think of her—an anatomical male living as a female with a wife—is as a "male lesbian." The producers loved it, but Linda didn't particularly want to repeat it on the air. She and her companion Cynthia did, however, want to publicize a book about the transgender community written by a friend, which the show refused to do.

> So Cynthia sneaks this book on right after the wedding and says, "If people want to know more about this, they can read this book." They didn't want her to do that, but they traded out during the break. They said, "We won't cut this out if you'll talk about being a male lesbian." So I looked over in the wings and this guy's got a huge banner that he had made up and it says MALE LESBIAN and he's got several exclamation points after it. And I'm thinking, "Oh, boy." So I waited till the very, very last minute—and I still get a kick out of it—and then, "Well, if you want to talk about sexuality, I'm a male lesbian." And blink and that was it.

It is not always so easy to "trade out" with the shows, however. Robyn Ochs tells of her attempt to get a male AIDS expert on a *Geraldo* panel on bisexuals, on which she was to be the bisexuality expert.

I felt that the show was such a horrible setup that going on was dam-
age control. They were having Tom Smith, who wrote a book put out
by a sleazy press about how he's been having sex with men for over
forty years, the entire time he's been married. He was their stereotype
personified. He's a slime. Then I knew there was also going to be a
woman who got AIDS from her husband and didn't find out he had
AIDS until after his death. So I said, "Two people or you'll have to
find yourself someone else," and they said, "Okay." So the person I
found, from California, was sick, and then they started kind of waf-
fling. They said, "We can't afford to have a second expert." I said,
"I'll find you an expert on the East Coast, and it will cost you less
than you already agreed to pay." So I spent three hours on the phone,
and I found three people. When I called them back, they said, "We
changed our mind. We're only having one expert. Are you going to be
it or not?" I said, "You said two," and they said, "Well, are you going
to be it or not?" And then they threatened me. "Honey, if you don't
do the show, we're going to find ourselves another expert, and I can
promise you that it's not going to be anyone who has anything posi-
tive to say about bisexuality." So we buckled.

Once there, whatever the outcome in early negotiations, like movement speakers in news settings,[7] most activist guests treat their appearances as strategic opportunities to frame and reframe the meaning of sexuality or gender. From their experiences elsewhere, they certainly know what they are up against. "They'll tell you, 'Bisexuality is nonmonogamy and cross-dressers are gay,' " says Marjorie Garber, summing up the frustrations of many bisexual and cross-dressing guests. "These are the commonest of cli-chés. And it's not helpful—or accurate—to overstate or overcorrect: some cross-dressers *are* gay and some bisexuals *are* nonmonogamous." At times, the fight is explicitly planned, as when Signorile and his colleagues attempted to transform *Geraldo*'s outing show from an issue of "right to privacy" (good gays versus bad gays) into one of the "dangers of the closet" (gays versus heterosexists), or when the bisexual activists tried to rework *Dona-hue*'s "gays versus bisexuals" into "gays and bisexuals versus homophobia." More often, however, it is a matter of individuals translating a political point, or a cultural disruption aimed at opening up new political space, into a language they think will work for talk show audiences. "I wanted to try, if I had a chance, to challenge the idea that identity is determined by your flesh," Susan Stryker says, describing her appearances on the short-lived *Gabrielle* and *The Other Side*. "I wanted to somehow problematize the easy association of a particular form of embodiment and a particular identity that goes with it, while still talking about the specificities of the experience and the specificities of your sociological situation." Of course, embodiments and identities and specificities and sociological situations have no place whatsoever on daytime TV, as Stryker fully recognized. So, drawing directly from Kessler and McKenna's classic discussion of gender attribution,[8] Stryker simply revised the language. "We don't wear our genitals on the outside of our clothes," she repeated on the shows, refusing to answer questions about her own genital status when no one else was expected to do so. "It's code switching. If I wanted to get on the talk show and do my, you know, transgender theory, poststructuralist, queer-inflected thing, it would not fly. So I found that what worked was telling stories about yourself that have some kind of hook with someone else's experience, like talking with nontranssexual women who are going through menopause or who have fibroid tumors or have their ovaries out for whatever reason, and they're doing these things that alter their body in a way that calls into question their gender identity for themselves."

Although storytelling works well, some particular interventions are nearly impossible to make verbally on talk shows. To put it mildly, too much ideational complexity is more or less precluded by the talk show format: "There's a commercial break, there's someone in the audience who's got a comment, there's someone on the stage who's got a comment," as writer and talk show veteran Eric Marcus says, "so expressing complex thoughts is almost impossible." The point that gender is attributed rather than given by the body, for instance, is tough to get across when everyone around you (including your host) assumes the latter, when you get to speak in seconds-long spurts every once in a while, and when people see you as something other than human, something from "the other side." Even simpler language doesn't always solve the problem. Bisexual activist Loraine Hutchins, for example, tries to use her status as expert on *Geraldo* to translate the notion that sexual categories, and therefore sexual normality, are socially constructed. "Bisexuality is normal," she says. "And there's no such thing as bisexuality, there's no such thing as homosexuality, there's no such thing as heterosexuality. There's *sexuality*. Does that make sense to people?" The audience rumbles, and Rivera answers her question. "Uh, no," he says, and moves on.[9] But activists learn to adjust, using the emotional and visual opportunities of talk shows, not just the verbal, to disrupt cultural politics as usual.

Even getting dressed for a show can therefore be a complex, semipolitical decision, weighted with the awareness that the image you are embodying communicates politically. Ashley Tillis, asked to appear on a *Sally* show on transsexual lesbians with her lover, was told by producers that they wanted to "downplay the politics." She wore her Queer Nation T-shirt, a pair of jeans, sneakers. "They were like, 'Is *that* what you're going to wear?' " The problem was not so much the T-shirt's explicit political statement (incomprehensible to most viewers), but the fact that Tillis did not look the part. "The fact of the matter is, I don't run around particularly femmed up, anyway, and they obviously didn't want something as boring as that we're ordinary people that wear ordinary clothes, and this wasn't going to be a drag show or a fashion deal, so I was deliberately playing it against type." It's a minor act of resistance, but not a meaningless one: acutely aware that the image of transsexual women as hyperfeminine, more-woman-than-you'll-ever-be glamour girls is both politically limiting and the preferred visual for television, Tillis grabbed the opportunity to slash away at it a bit with her outfit. Marjorie Garber, hitting the circuit with her book on cross-dressing, also found herself thinking in great detail about what to wear. For *Jane Whitney*'s cross-dressing show—a sweeps show with extravagantly dressed female impersonators singing, dancing, and explaining themselves—she faced the task of "participating in the cross-dressing rhetoric without trying to steal the show." She chose a double-breasted, man-tailored women's suit, a kind of a femme-gangster suit with white pinstripes. For *Geraldo*'s show on "women who dress as men," Garber was in a bit of a bind: dressing mannishly might make her appear to pass as a cross-dresser, while wearing a skirt could be read as hostile distancing. Her choice was a feminine crossover outfit: silk pants, shirt, and blazer. "We split the difference," Garber says. These are not just fashion choices, of course, but decisions about political self-symbolizing, unspoken negotiations with the shows' agendas. You want me to be the not-fabulous, distanced expert-judge-professor, but I want to demonstrate my allegiance to the big girls in big costumes; you want me to be the woman who dresses as a man, but my point is that gender and clothing are not in any clear, natural relationship. Let's split the difference.

There is no need to exaggerate the political significance of wardrobe decisions in order to see the more general point. Talk show visibility, when it is seen as an important cultural wing of a political project, sets in motion its own localized politics, its own small-scale power struggles. Producers, using the variety of recruiting, prepping, and scripting strategies we have seen, try to control the rough outlines of the show, and to elicit emotional performances; activist guests try to seize control themselves, planning and going over their key points, trading the use of their status as "deviant" for the opportunity to diversify the panel or to turn the show around to their own purposes.

These micro–political exchanges are one obvious element of talk show politics: existing social-movement activists (including, of course, antigay activists as well) competing for control of public-relations opportunities. But, in less obvious ways, they are built on top of already existing political fault lines *within* the politics of sexuality and gender. Talk shows crack open those fault lines, creating craters that swallow up political alliances and solidarities even as they toss new, previously invisible populations into the air.

Foul-mouthed kids and voices of reason

At Tempestt, *there was an 18-year-old girl sitting next to me who was outed by someone she went to school with, who was a loud, obnoxious, drag queen kid who had no place being on that show. The girl next to me was crying hysterically. Then we had one lesbian who was outed by her ex-husband who was, the only way I can describe her is a loud-mouthed woman from the boroughs who just used foul language at every opportunity. I'm not sure that rehashing it on national television does us as gay people any good, does her any good emotionally, does him any good. It's an issue that should have been talked about in the privacy of a psychiatrist's or psychologist's office, not on national television, where someone was playing with the emotions to make money and make ratings. They made it into a circus, and there was no one rational to present gay people in a positive perspective on that show in the beginning, just a bunch of hysterical people screaming and yelling at each other, with Tempestt as a moderator—and a weak one at that. They did put me on after two segments, but all the listeners got for the most part were gay people who had horrible coming-out experiences, who were manipulated by the producers and by Tempestt to put on a circus of a show, screaming and yelling and using four letter words, behavior that is entirely inappropriate for adults in a public setting, with no voice of reason. When I finally did have the op-*

*portunity to speak, I think I tried to put some reason into a situation
that was unreasonable. Unfortunately, a lot of the people on that
show were what the press focuses on—stereotypical, you know, drag
queens. The press already looks at us as freaks, and the more we play
into that with these freak shows that they put on TV, the worse it is
for our movement. The talk shows play into that. They play into all of
the freakish, radical elements of our community.*

OUT *MAGAZINE PUBLISHER AND* TEMPESTT *GUEST HARRY TAYLOR*

*The whole idea of sexual freedom and personal freedom is that no one
else has to find it acceptable. It's your own business. And we shouldn't
be concerned about what the image is. Intellectually, I understand the
anger of militant gays. If I lived in society and all of a sudden heterosexuality was taboo, and I had to live my whole life either not ever being with a woman or if I was with a woman making sure that no one
ever found out, lying about it, having to, you know, marry a man and
go through the motions of that, and sneak out to find a woman to sat-
isfy me, boy would I be militant. I can understand a person being really, really pissed off about something as necessary and vital to a being
as their sexuality. So I don't mind showing the outrageousness and the
anger in all that.*

TALK SHOW HOST JERRY SPRINGER

Although for bisexual shows an antibisexual gay person is often thrown
in for good measure, it is not actually all that common for talk shows to
pit different factions of lesbian, gay, bisexual, and transgender politics
against one another. It's not really worth the bother, after all, since it is a
more risky and inaccessible entertainment tack than letting the audience or
bigoted guests provide the conflict. In a more subtle, less intentional way,
however, talk shows nonetheless push different groups into opposite sides
of the ring. Especially as the "outrageous" shows took off, and the class
(and age) profile of the genre started to shift, middle-class activist guests
found themselves and their political agendas edged out. The gay, lesbian,
bisexual, and transgendered people who have slowly replaced them—often
flamboyant, unaffiliated, untrained in political agendas, and of lower educational, economic, and social status—threaten the mainstreaming agenda of
many in the gay movement. They are foul-mouthed, freakish, radical, loud,
obnoxious, stereotypical, irrational, emotional: that is, they are great talk
show guests. They emphasize, deliberately and not, a queer *difference* from
the mainstream, and not a terribly appealing one, since on these talk shows

it is conflated with "lower class," which is equated with various sorts of ugliness; ugly, rude, peculiar people, especially on talk shows, do not make the best representatives of the argument for tolerance, acceptance, freedom, and rights.

Many middle-class activist guests, who had earlier had a virtual monopoly on the nonheterosexual talk show guest list, are trying to move in exactly the opposite direction: toward the demonstration that gay people (or cross-dressers, or bisexuals, or transsexuals) are regular, civilized, unthreatening, reasonable, conforming folks. Craig Dean, for instance, went on *Donahue* twice—the second time on a show that included a gay wedding.

> *We were going up there to talk. And talk about issues, you know, and I knew the show was a freak show to begin with because of what they were doing. Not only was it a gay black couple, but it was a short black man—it was a freak show. And they wanted us to come on to lend legitimacy to what they were doing. They wanted to use us, you know, and I felt for the good of the gay rights movement, that we needed to be there to present something a little more palatable to the American public. . . . These guys came up, vrooom, they got married. There was no humanization—and people reacted like, "You faggots, look at this shit you're putting in our face." As opposed to "We love each other and we're going to express our commitment to each other." Yeah, there's a really big difference, so I'm pissed at what happened.*[10]

Gay writer Eric Marcus intentionally dresses up as "sort of the boy next door, well-educated, well-groomed, polite, would never get angry at anyone, wouldn't hurt anyone, not a threat at all." By comparison to Paul Cameron ("he's sitting there talking about fecal matter and all the semen that we ingest, and I'm sitting next to him in a blue shirt, nice crisp tie, my hair's combed properly, I'm very polite"), and even to Michelangelo Signorile ("he came across as a nut case"), he looks "sane" and "normal." But increasingly, Marcus promotes his books and his "best possible case for gay people" in an environment in which the polite, well-educated, well-groomed image is an anomaly. While they still help sell his books, the talk shows have started to run counter to Marcus's political agenda. Marcus offers the example of a gay kid at the *Sally* show wearing a midriff T-shirt, elbow-length gloves, pearls, a top hat, and makeup. "If I were in charge, I would say, 'Stay home.' I think of those television talk shows as propaganda that can be used in a very productive way. Someone like that doesn't help further my political agenda. He's on there, I'm on there, so people do get to see that gay people come from all walks of life, but in that moment of the show he created quite an uproar, and the argumentativeness of the show increased because of this kid with the elbow-length gloves and makeup. So the argument is lost because of what he looks like."

And so the monster's two heads again battle it out, although here the twin sisters are queer. We must behave appropriately in public, says one, and work through our ugly stuff in private, in a doctor's office maybe, the way classy people do. Shrink, shmink, says the other, let's go on TV. We are sick of being told what to do and where we can do it, and we're going to take our scary, inappropriate selves as public as we can.

Ironically, it is in part because of the successes and increased savvy of movement activists in the talk show arena that many middle-class organizers now find themselves on the defensive. For one thing, from the point of view of talk shows, they have pretty much had their time: been there, done that. For another, they have trained themselves in the basics of using-the-talk-show-for-our-own-purposes, and their haggling and negotiating and caution makes them sometimes more trouble than they're worth. It is much easier simply to turn to guests with little agenda other than a few minutes of TV fame and an out-of-town trip. "I wish there was a pool of nice gay folks they called on to do these sorts of things," says Marcus, "but these shows thrive on combativeness, on arguments. They don't want reasonable guests, except as so-called experts."

The fact that not-nice, unreasonable people who get crazy are many shows' guests of choice has led some mainstream organizations to simply refuse to assist shows altogether. For the Renaissance Education Association, an organization that provides "education and support to the transgender community and the general public," talk shows had been an important tool for both visibility and outreach throughout the 1980s and early 1990s. By the time I spoke with members in 1996, they had decided to impose a moratorium on talk show appearances by their members, inspired partly by a moratorium call by the executive director of the Sexuality Information and Education Council of the U.S. (SIECUS).[11] Transsexual radio host Cheryl Ann Costa describes similar talk about talk shows in her own circles.

Springer had a person who had a sex change, and they dragged his family on there. His two sons saying, "We ain't going to talk to him anymore." And his little 11-year-old daughter stands up in the audience, says, "I don't want to ever see him again." And Springer stands up with his last five-minute little comment and says, "If you're think-

ing about having one of these things and you brought kids into the world, why don't you just keep your pants on until they're grown up and out of the house and then do what you're going to do." That was an outright attack on our community and we are desperately trying to dry up his supply of transgenders. They'll still find people. They're going to have to find an awful lot of rogue people, though, people that aren't connected, because anybody who's connected with anything, we're going to basically say, "This show is quarantined." We're going to shut him down as far as transsexuals are concerned.

Opting out, of course, is no guarantee of change. "You get people in our own community who are willing to say anything the producers want them to say in order to create that controversy," says a member of the Manhattan Gender Network, a transgender organization. "The problem is, those of us who don't want to have our brains picked on national television, we leave that to those people who will do whatever is necessary, who look to get on every talk show that they possibly can."

The calm, trained, reasonable behavior preferred by middle-class organizers is appropriate for an "expert," however, and figures like Marcus and Signorile, and Ochs and Ka'ahumanu, have been elevated to expert status, sometimes even in place of "relationship experts." But even this promotion pushes them to the side. When you see your agenda as promoting images of cool, rational, middle-class civility, the authority granted you as expert is a small consolation in a losing battle, more of an opportunity to cut losses than to make any progress, as Eric Marcus's *Sally* story captures.

The show was about people who can't accept their gay relatives, and my job was to sort through all of the things that had just been seen on the air and try to come to some sort of understanding. So they brought me in, they gave me a rundown on some of the guests beforehand and sat me in a room. I was supposed to be able to watch on the monitor in this office, but nobody came in to tell me the show had begun. I just happened to be flipping the stations and there was the show, it had started already. So it's about five minutes into the show, and I realize that they have on a collection of the most incredibly dysfunctional people from rural parts of the United States. People who have never been on television before and are saying the most horrific, hateful things to each other. Mother to daughter, lesbian lover to the mother-in-law, half-brother to brother. And I'm watching this thinking, "How am I ever going to go out there and make any sense of any

*of this?" One guy yelled, "The only pussy you've ever seen is the cat
that crawled across the floor in your house," and "my fucking daughter this and that." Every other word was "fuck." Then they introduced a mother and her straight daughter and her lesbian daughter—
they haven't seen each other in I don't know how long—and her
lover. There was screaming back and forth. "You're not my child.
They must have mixed up the babies at the hospital." And the sister
says, "She's ruined her life. They took the children away because of
the lover." Terrible things back and forth. Then they brought out a sister and brother, Hispanic sister and brother. And, "fucking this," and
"fuck that," and "he borrows my clothes and I'm going to get AIDS
from the clothes." And then Sally introduced two boys, sixteen and
nineteen, straight kids from the mountains of Tennessee, who had the
most horrible things to say about gay people. They were there because
their brother was going to be on the show. Well, they introduced the
brother and the lover. They came out holding hands, swish onto the
stage, throw themselves in their chairs and tongue kiss. But they were
worked up too, they were angry and they were told to do whatever,
and they're not going on with any particular agendas. And I thought,
"We're in great shape now."*

Renaissance Education Association organizer Angela Gardner captures the
logic of the Renaissance talk show moratorium, and the internal political
divisions on which it rests, in her account of a disastrous *Charles Perez* show
on "transsexual regrets" for which she was the expert.

*Most of the other people on the show were not leaders of the commu-
nity or anything, they were these people I think they found in New
York night clubs, and they were primarily on this show for their fifteen minutes of fame. And then there was this girl, a total jerk, doesn't
have two brain cells to rub together, and she started like attacking the
audience. There was only one person on the show that I think was a
true transsexual. There were a couple of street-queen types who were
taking hormones and living full-time as females, talking about getting
sex changes. And when they finally brought me out near the end of the
show as the expert, I basically said, "If these people have any regrets
it's because they weren't really candidates for it, and you have to follow the standards of care." And then I got shouted down by somebody else with a comment that they had to make. I was not going to
stand up and start screaming at people so I just sat there demurely for*

the rest of the show and they went ahead and yelled at each other. The thing that really, really came through, you know, was we're being associated with something that we don't want our potential members to see. We don't want them to see this show and equate those people with what the potential member is—wild, yelling at the audience. I mean, they're valid people. But the problem is that if people see something that's really bizarre and strange then they're not going to identify with us. Or they are going to identify but they're going to think, "I don't want to be like that so I'm not going to do anything about my feelings because I don't want to be like those people." You know, it's like real white-trash mentality, and we want to be the voice of reason. I'm all for diverse viewpoints, but on the other hand if you're trying to let people know that there's a community out there that is a community full of people that support each other and also a lot of strife and disagreement, it might be best to just get general information out and keep all the little in-fighting stuff off the air. It's not so much the circus aspect but the low-life circus aspect that makes me really reluctant to go on a show, because I don't want us equated with the fringes of the transgender movement. And we don't want to frighten them with somebody who has pink hair and comes in high heels, you know, who is acting weird. I'll go on a show with somebody who has giant pink hair and six-inch high heels as long as they are an intelligent person making intelligent statements, but not if they're on there saying, you know, bizarre shit.

Talk shows, Marcus notes, "show us in all of our awful diversity": swearing Hispanic homosexuals, tongue-kissing mountain boys, borough broads, dysfunctional Ozark lesbians, guys in pearls and makeup, rogue transsexuals in giant pink hair, gay kids without media training. But many middle-class activists see little advantage to the "awful diversity" of the "low-life circus," which would only seem to increase the stigma they are trying to remove in the pursuit of civil rights. "When you're very different, and people hate you for it, this is what you do," Marshall Kirk and Hunter Madsen write in *After the Ball,* which outlines an unabashedly conservative campaign of "unabashed propaganda" for gay people. "*First* you get your foot in the door, by being as *similar* as possible; then, and only then—when your one little difference is finally accepted—can you start dragging in your other peculiarities, one by one."[12] This is primarily a pragmatic position (we cannot afford these images right now), but one also often tinged with animosity (these people don't know how to behave in public), and the confidence that comes from having long felt entitled to call the shots (these people don't get it). Mainstreaming activists are rightly concerned that talk shows provide a distorted image of gay life—but then again, the image, although more socially acceptable, was no less distorted when it was only white, middle-class, gay movement movers and shakers. Lurking underneath the concern, encouraged by the class dynamics of TV talk, are hints of class, racial, and regional superiority. When gay was just *us,* things were going so well, people seem to want to say. Why did they have to go and give *those* people the microphone?

Talk shows certainly did not *create* the division between moderates with an eye toward assimilation, who want to demonstrate middle-class legitimacy and similarity to heterosexuals, and in-your-face radicals, who use difference from heterosexuals to create space for themselves. This is a long-standing strategic dispute in sex and gender politics, as it is in most social movements. For a good long time, picking up extra steam in the last decade, civil rights strategists favoring integration into the "normal" have met with resistance from others favoring a transgressive, confrontational "queer" politics that pushes at the boundaries of normality.[13] Of course, it takes a somewhat different form here, since most of the antiassimilation imagery comes not from organized radical activists, but from unaffiliated individuals seizing the opportunity for televisual confirmation of their social significance. Talk shows, though, take the line between "fringe" and "center"—a divider that, in my own eyes and the eyes of many others, is neither necessary nor productive for political organizing by sex and gender dissidents—and dig away at it, deepening it into an almost-unbridgeable chasm. (This comes not just from the strategies of outrageousness-selling shows, but also from those like *Oprah,* which create a "respectable" environment in which people from the wrong side of the tracks are excluded.) The structure of the talk show world intensifies the tension over who rightfully represents "gayness," making it nearly impossible for legitimacy-seeking activists *not* to close ranks, dissing and disowning their own.

No snobbery or animosity is required, however, for sensationalized talk to appear threatening. Too much "accuracy," for one, can seem to producers to risk incomprehensibility. Ann Northrop tells of a producer who called looking for a gay man, but was not interested in her suggestion of a black gay guest. "Why not?" she asked. "That's too complicated," he replied. If the goal is "accurate" representation, there is no question that talk shows, which have no particular interest in reflecting all lives, only the most interesting ones, score very low. Even Jerry Springer, who claims that "we don't ever have anyone on that speaks for or is representative of any particular group of people," admits that "the groups of which people are better informed will have a better chance of surviving my show than the groups of which people are less informed. That's a weakness of my show." When I gathered three groups of gay and lesbian talk show viewers in New York— obviously a sophisticated bunch, but typical, I expect, of highly educated gay viewers—I quickly found that many of them watch talk shows like amateur antidefamation leaguers, to see, as Morgan put it in one discussion, "what America is being fed about gay and lesbian people." Often imagining that talk shows are the primary source of information about gay people for "some housewife in Des Moines," or "the people in Missouri," or "people in Iowa who believe what they see," they are worried that only the same old stigmas are getting repeated. Thus, while various advantages to talk shows also emerge (any visibility is good, the shows illustrate the range of gay life, and so on), and while there are clearly all kinds of pleasures in the watching, the strongest theme in these discussions is the damage done by appearances of gay people who aren't "regular."

The concern with accuracy, in these discussions, quickly slides into a desire for moderate, mainstream imagery. The complaint of Jim, for instance, a white artist in his forties, equates "real" and "not extreme." "I want to see somebody that would just look like, you know, the people that we see on the street. But you never seem to see that. I'm hoping it will be just a regular person, but it never is. They always try to pick somebody from a far end of somewhere. There's never any reality to it. It's always a very deep extreme, and there's never any real people." Deborah, a white graduate student in her thirties, speaking in a lesbian discussion group, also decries the lack of "regular" people: "I would like to see some representations of normal lesbian life, instead of these dramas. I mean, people like us, people who do have normal conversations, who go to work, who get up in the morning, who make coffee, you know, not people who are represented as being somehow well outside the bounds of the normal." A member of a transgender discussion brings out the class dimensions of the call for "regular," counterstereotypical images: "I would love to see a show that had a transgender person or a transsexual person who was a doctor, next to someone who was a lawyer, next to someone who was a scholar. Let's say four or five very, very well-dressed people in business clothes, who sounded really intelligent. Even if they had the morons in the audience, they'd have nowhere to go with that. I mean, they just want to see someone wiggle their ass and jump around and say, 'Look, I'm a drag queen.' " It is not the idea that some gay men cross-dress, or that some lesbians do not get up in the morning and go to work, or that some transgendered women wiggle their asses that bothers these viewers, but the idea that, if you only know about us from talk shows, you would think that most gay men do drag, few lesbians have undramatic conversation, and that no transgendered people wear business clothes. You would think, that is, that we are not part of the middle-class mainstream. If these viewers are at all typical, middle-class lesbian and gay viewers feel edged out of talk shows as well, and at odds with most of the guests they see, implicated by imagery that sets them outside the bounds of the normal, a place they decidedly do not want to be.

Liberal heterosexual sympathizers, who invariably talk about exploitation by talk shows, seem to reach their sympathy through a class identification with professional, middle-class gay and lesbian people. "If I were gay," says Caren, a 22-year-old white student in one of my discussions with heterosexual women, "I wouldn't want the people that they put on to be put on, because they kind of put on someone who's like, that has typical 'gay' gestures. I think they take people that have like these extreme gestures that people associate with homosexuals, and if I were gay I wouldn't want that person representing, like, all gay people." Like mainstream-oriented gay and lesbian activists and viewers, many straight liberal heterosexual viewers, in their attacks on the inaccuracy of talk shows, collapse *fair, typical, moderate,* and *professional* into a single heap of desirable imagery. Rachel, a 30-year-old Latina secretary, argues that gay people are misrepresented on the shows.

Like sometimes you'll see a gay person with the spiked hair, which is fine, you know, and the way that they dress if that's the way they want to dress, but they seem to focus on those type of individuals, when you have gay and lesbians that are regular people with regular lives, they're not always into clubbing or piercings or whatever. These people watch these programs, that are home day and night and that's all they do, that's what their lives revolve around, and when they see these people portrayed that way all the time, you know, they don't see them as professionals, you know, as people that live normal lives.

Jill, a 28-year-old white nurse's aide, agrees.

It's a shame, because some people are afraid of that, and then they see a show like that and it just confirms what their own prejudices.

*They're all like flamboyant and extremist. They're using these people
to make people's hatreds go up, you know what I mean, by showing
the extreme examples. And it's a shame where you see everybody believes that it's this extreme part of the population. They don't seem
like normal people, just like individual people. The talk shows, it's not
like anyone I know. Everyone I know is pretty much like a professional. That's like the word I think of when I think of like gay people
who I know, I think of the word "professional."*

Talk shows are bad for gay people, they say, because they work against
the notion that gay people are regular rather than irregular, similar to the
heterosexual mainstream rather than different, on the inside rather than
out—that is, middle-class professionals. The line separating nice gay and
lesbian insiders (victimized by talk shows) and their nasty, extreme, flamboyant outsiders (victimizing themselves on talk shows) is repainted with a
bright, fresh coat.

This is no deliberate divide-and-conquer on the part of talk show producers who, as we have seen, are hardly oriented toward politics in their everyday work lives. The opening up of the center-fringe, or sameness-difference,
fault line is a result of the way producers make their money, and of the
ambivalence built into the talk show genre (high/low class, polite/rude,
rational/emotional). An array of "fringe" characters make it to talk TV because of how they play on screen, and because they are easy to recruit and
easier to manipulate; they say and do things in public that others are not
always willing to say and do. In a genre shot through with class cultural
divisions, in a place where authentic class cultural expression is indistinguishable from its exaggerated display, where "trash" is a synonym for
"lower class," working-class guests (and, through that weird American confusion of race and class, often guests of color as well) are placed directly
against the comfortable calm of the middle-class mainstream; bisexual, gay,
lesbian, and transgender guests who are not middle-class are quite easily
placed in the same trash basket. It is not too surprising that many middle-
class activists and viewers, informed by a sense that political gains are at
stake, are not too excited about joining them there.

Donna wears a jockstrap! Donna wears a jockstrap!

The talk show world rips open existing class divisions within transgender,
bisexual, lesbian, and gay politics, but not only these: it also rips away at

the tenuous alliance among these nonconforming populations, primarily by rewarding some populations with "acceptability," as we saw a bit in the last chapter, at the expense of others. Many mainstream gay activist guests and viewers express the worry not only that images of dysfunctional, angry, and uneducated parts will be taken to represent the whole, but that disproportionate representation of "abnormal" parts will make it harder for all of us to become "normal." The freaks—especially the gender freaks—are giving us all a bad name.

Again, this is a preexisting tension, and the attempt to ally all sorts of sex and gender dissidents under one flag—drag queens, passing transsexuals, guppies, lipstick lesbians, dykes, cross-dressers, queer kids, monogamous and nonmonogamous bisexuals, and so on—is relatively new, complex and extremely hard going.[14] Bisexuals and transgendered people, most notably, have waged difficult battles for recognition and inclusion in organizations and celebrations, and centrist gay men and lesbians argue, with some realpolitikal evidence on their side, that some battles (the Employment Nondiscrimination Act, for instance) are not currently winnable with bisexuals and transgenders on the list of claimants. The talk show world reinforces these divisions not only by using transgendered people as display objects and bisexuals as symbols of promiscuity, but also by offering homosexuals a tempting option: distance yourself from bisexuals and transgendered people, keep your sex and gender practices conservative, and you will be rewarded with acceptance.

Take, for instance, the common "love triangle" structure into which many shows on bisexuality are structured. On a 1992 *Jane Whitney* show on bisexuality, while a white, bearded bisexual guest named Cole is attacking the myth of bisexuality as simultaneous relationships ("I don't have to be in a relationship with both a man and a woman"), a label appears under his image. "Cole," it reads, "intimate with both men and woman." The show, like many others on bisexuality, is structured as a series of triangles: Cole is involved with Hector (who doesn't appear) and with Laura (Latina, bisexual) who is involved with Marcia (African American, lesbian); Jill is involved with both Woody and Rebecca, who has a long-term lover. ("No," says Whitney introducing them, "they're not involved with Laura. They're another bisexual triangle.") Not surprisingly, despite a variety of attempts by panelists to disaggregate bisexuality and nonmonogamy, and to distinguish committed, honest nonmonogamy from sex-crazed disloyalty, commitment and sexual monogamy become the focus of audience questions and attacks. "How do you decide," asks a young white guy with long, rock-star hair, "flip a coin?" to laughter and applause. "They're changing their preferences every day like they're changing their shirts," says an older white man, and soon a young blond man asks, "Why do you have to have sex with all of them?" to which a tie-wearing, buzz-cut man adds, "As a gay man, I think you're doing a disservice, you should be pursuing the one person and not all this free love." Don't you believe in commitment? a series of people asks in a variety of ways. Given the show's Marcia and Laura and Cole and Hector setup, the answers, all of them well articulated, get lost in the applause for monogamy.[15]

What is also lost, though, is any concern with the "abnormality" of same-sex relationships, in place of an attack on nonmonogamous relationships (equated on the show with bisexual ones). Sexual loyalty, whoever its subjects, is what's really being protected here. In fact, audience members and the host express sympathies and concern for the gay boyfriends and lesbian girlfriends of bisexuals, whose partners "can't commit" (as when *Jane Whitney*'s Marcia, for example, the sole lesbian on the panel, is encouraged to stop putting up with being a "third wheel"). In these very common "triangle" shows, where bisexuality functions primarily as a stand-in for promiscuity and is therefore denigrated, monogamous sexuality gets the high ground, taking monogamous *homosexuality* along for the ride. In this cultural setup, from the point of view of gay men or lesbians on the verge of mainstream acceptance and political gains, allying with bisexuals is indeed a risky proposition.

The appearance of cross-dressing on gay-themed shows, which can often lead to the denigration of homosexuality, is a flashy mirror of this process. The early 1990s series of shows on conventionally feminine lesbians, for instance, used the term "lipstick lesbians" as something of a mind-blower and stereotype-breaker, as Maury Povich's introduction, spiked with the straight-porn image of girly-girls going at it, captures. "They are beautiful, they're sexy, glamorous, and successful, so one would assume that they have more men than they can handle. But it's not the men they want. Instead, these stunning beauties prefer other women." (Cut to video of women's bodies putting on lingerie and lipstick and nail polish.) "What about the women who are butch and proud of it?" (Cut to shots of Dykes on Bikes and other butch lesbians in a pride march.)

There is much talk here about debunking stereotypes, many questions about how one can be simultaneously lesbian and conventionally feminine, a gratuitous male guest named Tommy who thinks he can "turn a lesbian straight," and much manly-man ribbing. (Maury to four young guys in front row: "You're not interested anymore, right?" Guy: "No, we've been interested from the start." Maury: "Well, you know, hot blood has no conscience, guys.") But it is the presence of *Village Voice* writer Donna Minkowitz, a broad-faced, short-haired, witty, and somewhat wired woman, that galvanizes the audience. Wearing a red blazer and men's pants and shoes, Minkowitz talks with an impish smile about being attracted to "women in military uniforms, women in LL Bean jackets, women who look like they mean business." Over the course of the show, Minkowitz is pelted with insults. Her violation, it seems, is not being lesbian, but being unconventionally female. Povich asks Tommy, the apparent expert on heterosexual male desire, whether he thinks the two femme women on the panel are attractive (yes), and then if he thinks Donna is attractive (no). Big applause. Several times, the camera pans Donna from toe to head, as if to punctuate the point. Minkowitz explains herself well ("I'm not trying to embody a man, excuse me, I'm trying to embody a butch lesbian, which is something I love, I'm not trying to be a man, I'm trying to be Donna Minkowitz, in all my glory"), but there is not much of a reception for her argument that "sex roles are crazy, they're just a fiction." Instead, she is told she's "a frustrated male, you look like you want to be a man and were born a woman, unfortunate, I guess," and "you like to wear men's clothes, you like to wear a jockstrap?" While her lesbianism is generally unproblematic, or at least goes uncondemned, her gender nonconformity is penalized with vigor.[16] Indeed, a lesbian who is unmarked, unbutch, who obeys the norms of gender conformity, looks exciting, pretty, and normal by comparison. A public alliance between lesbians who "pass" ("stunning beauties") and those who do not ("frustrated males") is rendered more difficult to make; same-sex desire itself comes to seem unremarkable, but only if the coalition of women who "look like women" (hetero and homo) is favored over that of women who love women.

Even a 1992 *Donahue* show, in many ways a typical bigot-bashing political debate about an antigay referendum in Concord, California, manages to set "good," gender-conforming gays against "bad" gays in drag. Pastor Lloyd Mashore and his colleague square off against a young activist named Ken Stanley and another pastor; the antigay activists argue about special rights, the homosexual agenda, family values, picnics and Little League ball games, while the progay activists talk about equal rights, pride, and love; Phil asks, as always, "What do you want to do with these gay people?" The audience takes this side and that one. But what tips the discussion is the presence of Gil Block, in his persona as Sadie, one of the Sisters of Perpetual Indulgence.

Gil as Sadie is dressed to express: in full red, white, and blue drag, with red gloves, a big white wig, one dramatic eye with white stars over blue shadow and the other with red stripes over white shadow. Political theater, he claims, but once a male caller attacks Sadie, the audience lets loose a barrage of hostility. "Oh, get off the stage," another caller says to audience applause, "you're up there on the platform dressed like an idiot, and you expect to be taken seriously." ("Something should be done with them," she continues. "All they seem to do is cause problems. If we all got together and talked about it, maybe we could figure out what could be done with them. I really think they should all go back in the closet and make life peaceful again.") The two gay activists fighting discrimination are fine, says an audience member shortly thereafter, but Gil, who "is making a mockery of what they're trying to do, is just stupid." Gil tries to talk about being a patriotic American, but it doesn't really work. "I don't understand," says a young white man with a Philadelphia accent, "how dressing up like an oversized Captain America is going to help the gay cause." Laughter, applause. ("I think they should keep it to themselves," adds a young southern white woman with hoop earrings. "I don't make a big point that I'm heterosexual.") A male caller finishes him off. "I'm 26 years old, I'm a gay white male, and I'm embarrassed by the man on the end there," he says. "People think I come home from work and put on a dress and swing from the chandeliers because of people like him."[17] The young man captures the political division talk shows amplify and reinforce: between chandelier-swinging, cross-dressing flamboyants and suit-wearing, privacy-loving passers. The political affinities between them—their shared lack of civil rights protections, for example—are overshadowed by the colorful, provocative lines of gender convention so favored by talk shows.

Thus we reach one of the talk show's true political scandals. The scandal isn't so much that talk shows ambush people, or cynically use people's intimate lives to make a buck, or any of that utterly unsurprising and ugly activity. Nor is it even the fact of their drawing of lines that irks; after all, line drawing is one of the things that culture is always about. The scandal is the *kinds* of lines they emphasize, setting apart potentially powerful sets of political and cultural partners, helping to cut the threads tying working-class lesbian to transsexual to drag queen to gay professional to butch lesbian to bisexual to rural gay kid. That's not of course something they do alone, but they are central to the process, partly because they help it along in such unintentional ways, such entertaining ways, and partly because they mix it, to great effect, with pleas for tolerance, enlightenment, and love. Those alliances are critical because we are engaged in a strange, complicated conflict, which talk shows embody but by no means exhaust: a fight over public space.

Deep throats

You know what? Nobody has any business in the bedrooms of any nation or in the closets. If you want to be gay, just be gay, like just be gay and shut up about it.

DONAHUE *AUDIENCE MEMBER*[18]

I'm sick to death of the entertainment industry cramming homosexuality down our throats. It's disgusting and I'm fed up with it.

DONAHUE *CALLER*[19]

"No one's suggesting that you shouldn't be gay," host Jerry Springer tells an 18-year-old gay man in men's pants and sweater, painted nails and high heels, blatantly misrepresenting the sentiments of many in his audience. "If you're gay, you're gay, period. But why is it necessary to just let everybody know all the time?" Having recruited gay male guests on the basis of their effeminacy and cross-dressing—many of whom are treated to hoots and hollers from a ridiculing audience—Springer wonders aloud at the end of his show about "why gays so often seem to flaunt their sexuality, almost an exaggeration of their effeminateness." He understands it, he tells his viewers, just as he told me, since if you put yourself in the position of having your "sexuality constantly repressed or kept in the closet," you would see that "most of us would go crazy." Many gays, he says, are understandably angry, and unwilling to take it any more. "And they're coming out with a vengeance," he says, "suddenly a militancy polite society has never witnessed before."[20]

In the midst of the obvious hypocrisy and the moldy, ignorant equation of male homosexuality and effeminacy, Springer accidentally makes an excellent point: "polite society" is annoyed. His show scripts a backlash against gay visibility (and transgender and bisexual visibility, to a lesser degree) that is quite commonplace, exposing and participating in a culture war that is partly his own creation. "The homosexuals wouldn't have any problem at all if they would just keep it to themselves, and stop trying to act like they're special cause they're gay," says a caller to the *Donahue* show with Reverend Mashore facing off against Sister Sadie, as the camera catches smiling, applauding faces. "Why is there such a need to come out of the closet?" an audience member asks on another *Donahue,* this one on gay cops.[21] Indeed, the talk show structural emphasis on separating "appropriate" gay people (middle-class professionals, especially those who pass as heterosexual) from "inappropriate" (working- and poverty-class people, especially those who do not pass) is powered by an overlapping tension that talk shows manifest: between their push, in alliance with gay people and others, to make "private" matters public, and the various people interested in keeping certain things, such as homosexuality, away from public view.[22] For many in "polite society," it seems, public declarations of lesbian, gay, transgender, or bisexual identity are inherently inappropriate, impolite, nobody's business.

"I really don't have anything against your sexuality," a man tells John and Jerry, who had just kissed each other hello on a "gay and gorgeous" *Jenny Jones* show, for instance. "But the intimacy, the things that men and women that I think should be doing, stroking your hair—I see you guys holding hands and kissing. I'm sorry, but it really, it disgusts me."[23] Why do you have to flaunt it? audience members ask repeatedly on TV talk shows. Why do you have to have parades, and why do you have to go on television announcing it to everybody? Talk shows, as prime purveyors of public visibility of sex and gender nonconformity, are terrific foci for the anxieties and hostilities that a queer presence evokes.

Daytime talk television, in fact, by publicizing the "private," widens yet another fault line in gay and lesbian politics. "Privacy" is already quite a vexed, complex political issue in sexual politics. On the one hand, lesbian and gay political and social life in the past quarter of a century has been built on making sexual identities public, arguing that ours is a political and social status; since everyone is implicated in oppressing us, in part by keeping us invisible and spreading lies about us, it is everybody's business that we are gay. What we do out of bed, not what we do in bed, is what is most relevant about us. Coming out in public, especially through major public institutions such as schools, the workplace, and communications media, is a way of asserting the public relevance of what others deem private—that is, demonstrating and demonstrating against a second-class, stigmatized social status. (The more recent bisexual and transgender movements have followed this same model.) Talk shows, as we have amply seen, are approached by activists in this light.

At the same time, guided by the logic of constitutional claims-making, gay and lesbian activists have long put forward an argument that retains traditional divisions between private and public, in order to pursue protection under the individual "right to privacy."[24] The only difference between homo and hetero, they have said, is what we do in bed, and what we do in bed is nobody's business, and especially not the business of the government. Thus the nods of my students' heads when I suggest that it's odd to bring sexuality into the classroom. Thus comments such as this one, from a 30-year-old Latina secretary, in the midst of a discussion of talk shows with a bunch of women: "I feel like it's none of my business. Whatever you do in your bedroom is no concern of mine, just like what I do in my bedroom is none of your business." This is about sex, sex belongs in private, and personal privacy is protected from public intrusion. (The political right, tellingly, has used the basic elements of this argument to great effect, arguing that homosexuality is indeed private, sexual behavior, and that sexual behavior is not the basis for either minority status or rights.) While the legal argument for privacy is certainly not incompatible with public visibility, talk shows seem to run against the rhetorical gist of privacy claims. Many heterosexual talk show participants and viewers seize hold of this conflict: you keep saying how your sexuality is none of my business, yet here you are again on television chatting and yelling and kissing and getting married and making fools of yourselves. If you want privacy, then keep it private.

Talk shows invite this perspective on themselves, largely because they seem to be the sorts of places where, to many viewers, all kinds of people are doing and saying things that are nobody else's business. Television itself, as Joshua Meyrowitz has pointed out, messes with the public-private lines: it is a "public" space brought into the "privacy" of home.[25] Daytime talk shows, given that they profit from the discussion of taboo subjects, are hotbeds of impropriety and the discussion of impropriety, more or less by definition; these public living rooms, moreover, sit noticeably in your own private one. The discussion and display of atypical sexualities and genders is often filtered through an ambivalence about just who is doing what now in public—and, more fundamentally, just to whom public space belongs. The first clue to this dynamic comes from the common "where do they find these people?" disdain expressed by all kinds of talk show viewers. Many of the viewers with whom I had discussions, even though they often watch the less genteel fare, take offense at the unseemliness of it all, disparaging guests who bring private talk out of the house, airing their dirty laundry in front of God and everybody when they should be down in their own basement washing it. "I can't believe they would air all this stuff on the air, I mean in front of a general public, so to speak," says Barbara, a 56-year-old non-working African American woman in one of my heterosexual discussion groups. "It's so sleazy," Joni, a white woman a few years older, agrees. "Who needs to put that garbage in your head?" Every discussion includes this kind of statement (more often from older participants than younger). "I think it's getting a little, um, past risqué to the point of really just obnoxious and distasteful," says Ed, a 54-year-old African American human resources director in another group, for instance. "Distasteful. Distasteful," he repeats. "It's just very distasteful for people to get on national TV and just tell all of their business."

The divider between inappropriate and appropriate public talk is, moreover, as viewers' conversations capture, a marker of social status; the aversion of middle-class viewers for "sensationalistic," "exploitative" programming expresses an aversion for the déclassé. "It's like middle class and lower class," Judi, a 32-year-old homemaker, explains simply, as discussion turns to the comparison of *Oprah*'s audience with *Richard Bey*'s. Joni responds by explaining why she prefers Oprah: "On one show she did, she said, 'Aren't these a very clean audience?' Because they all looked dressed, they all looked like nice, middle-class people. They didn't look trashy. Everybody looked so nice and clean. And it's true, she gets a better class of people. And if I have to watch something, I'd rather watch that. Oprah has an average American that knows that they don't spit in public, and they don't do certain things in public, and that's how they conduct themselves. Whether it's false or not, it's civilized. That's what we do in America." It is not just spitting in public that we don't do. We don't *display our sexual selves in public*. Judith, a 55-year-old white teacher in another group, makes the connection between class, privacy, and sexuality quite explicit.

> I wouldn't watch all this garbage. Who's sleeping with who, what's going on with this couple because they were two women living together, or whatever. I can't better myself, I can't get more class to me, and I think class is very important. I think a lot of people have lost it. And this is all just—people are entitled to their private lives. It should be private. And anything that's put on display is just garbage. There's nothing wrong with having sexual topics on television. To put it on

display is what's wrong. When it's private, you work with it, but when you put it on television live, it becomes dirt. If you're going to open it up, have a psychologist there, make it a very proper thing.

The public display of "private life," especially sexuality, is not something classy people do. It is improper. It is garbage, dirt. Watching it, one becomes dirtier, less classy. In the eyes of many middle-class talk show watchers, sexual impropriety is really just the most important and obvious version of unsavory uses of public space. "In the quest to attain sanction for the *full* range of who one is," as Jean Bethke Elshtain argues, "one puts one's life on full display, one opens oneself up fully to *publicity* in ways others are bound to find quite uncivil, in part because a certain barrier . . . is blatantly breached."[26] It is not so much the *gayness* that is bothersome, it's the *publicness*.

So, for many viewers, an ambivalence about homosexuality maps quite effortlessly onto an ambivalence about the making public of sexual status, which itself maps onto a more generalized resistance to changes in what they see as their own public territory: a queer presence easily becomes another example of people behaving improperly. Even though very few talk show discussions of homosexuality are discussions of sexual practice, they are easily and commonly swept into the category of "inappropriate." As viewers invariably point out, for one thing, talk shows in recent years have tipped the balance toward sensationalized, exploitative treatments of sex and gender differences, going for the "sleazy," the "circus," the "extreme," and so on—so that homosexuality, bisexuality, and gender-crossing appear largely in the pile marked "distasteful." Moreover, homosexuality and bisexuality are more often than not, even when they are not framed as purely sexual on a show, placed by viewers in the category of "sexual."[27] While viewers often emphasize "tasteful" presentations of sex and gender nonconformists (a focus on individual experience, a respectful conversation), it is nonetheless a short step from the general grouchiness about what are seen as gauche, low-class uses of the public space of television to a specific animosity toward the public visibility of gay people. Talk shows make it especially easy for same-sex desire to slide quickly into the category of things that are not the business of polite, civilized, clean, nice people to hear about. They offer occasions for middle-class social anxieties about changes in public space to come into sharper focus, by attaching to the unruly class cultures and unusual sexual beings who seem to populate the public space of talk shows.

For liberal viewers, this tends to be expressed as a concern for the damage done to decent gay folks by "fringe" gay guests, for instance, who might be taken to represent the whole. The problem with those talk show guests, they say, is that they do not know how to keep it quiet. But listen a bit more closely, and you begin to hear how the charge that people "flaunting it" on talk shows blends smoothly into a general resistance to gayness in public space. Judi, a 32-year-old white homemaker, has this to say, for instance: "My girlfriend's sister is gay, and they're living their lives the way they want to. On TV, they're doing it for the gimmick, they want the attention, whereas my friends aren't like that at all. They don't flaunt it around. If they love each other, that's their problem. They don't sit there and advertise it all the time." Rosanne, a 47-year-old white bookkeeper in another group, has a different starting point, but comes back to a similar punch line: "I don't particularly even like to walk down the street and see a guy and a girl making out, so seeing two guys kiss or two girls kiss, it annoys me just as much to see a guy and a girl carrying on in the middle of the street. I think if everybody believes in what they want to believe in, and don't try to make a big issue out of it, like, 'Oh, you have to let me do this because I'm a lesbian,' or 'You have to let me do this because I'm a gay,' everybody just staying on their own road, whether it's a road of what some people call normal and some people call abnormal." When she continues later, it becomes clear where talk show impropriety fits into Rosanne's picture: keep anything but talking behind closed doors. "Let's educate some people, let people become aware of what's going on, and try to do it in a subtle way that doesn't make everything seem like smut. And if they're doing it behind their private doors, that's their business. If they come out sitting next to each other and talking and everything else, that's fine. If they start lovey-dovey, to me, I don't think it's appropriate for anyone to act that way. Whatever you do in your own home, and everything else, that's fine." For Bobby, a 24-year-old African American interior decorator, it is not just "lovey-dovey" behavior that is the problem, but any public announcement of homosexuality.

> *My understanding on a lot of gay shows is, like gay people have to force their sexuality on you. They want to let you know that they're gay so bad. They have to let you know. I don't have to let a person know that I'm a heterosexual male. I mean, I don't force it on people. We already have rights for men and rights for women. I don't see why it has to be gay rights and all that type stuff. Why do they have to let people know that*

*they're gay and this is what we do? I don't see why. I get annoyed
with it, by them always forcing on you, and they have to be so flamboyant and so gay and so out there. Just keep it to yourself.*

Ask liberal talk show watchers what they think about shows on gay people,
and this is often what comes out of them, right alongside "live and let live":
don't flaunt it, keep it to yourself, stay off my road.[28]

Viewers with conservative views on homosexuality, who often tend to
be more tuned in to the political aspects of homosexuality, demonstrate this
connection most clearly: they tend to see talk shows as part of a damaging
intrusion by the wrong people into public space. Vincent, a 63-year-old
phone-company manager and the most vehement conservative on gay issues
in a group of male conservatives, is very up-front about this. Over the course
of the discussion, he argues against same-sex marriage ("if they do it for
the homosexuals to get married, they're going to have to do the same damn
thing for the Man-Boy Love Association"), the Supreme Court ("talking
about how you can't restrict even porno on the Internet"), gay protests at
the St. Patrick's Day parade, and a New Yorker cover of two male sailors
kissing. "Why can't it be 'don't ask, don't tell?' " he asks. "They don't want
to be satisfied with that today. It's not hatred against them, believe me when
I say I have a feeling for them and what they're going through, but damn
it, don't tell, keep it in the closet." Talk shows, for him and the other men
in that discussion group ("it's sort of like social engineering," says Dave, a
45-year-old engineer), fit into a more general assault by gay people into what
they see as their own public space. "Homosexuals are here to stay," Vincent
says. "The talk shows only brings them to the forefront. They are here to
stay, just like the pornographic shows, where you can go buy tapes and so
forth and so on." In another hint of the way middle-class politeness plays
into a condemnation of gay publicness, he offers the example of a homosexual glee club, whose members were "professional people, they're not running around the streets or anything like that."

*The talk shows gave me the wrong picture of these people. I think if
they want to promote themselves, they should have something like this
choir I saw. They weren't hurting anybody, and they were pretty
damn good singers. Have your own lifestyle. Have your own lifestyle.
Have your own clubs, your own choirs. Don't stick your nose into St.
Patrick's Day parade. Don't stick your nose here and there. In many
instances it's in your face, and I don't think it should be that way.
These people should have their own lifestyle. Don't ask, don't tell.*

Unless you are singing, that is, please keep quiet, or at least keep it away from us. Stick to your own road.

A group of conservative women, talking about how topics get passé after a while, winds up quite close to Vincent's perspective. "It's like, if that's what they want to do, if that's how you want to live, live that way," says Lynn, a 34-year-old white saleswoman. "But it would have been better if they'd stayed in the closet and no one knew. Now it's like, we have to have these rights, gays have to have these rights." "They're pushing," says Peggy, a 59-year-old nonworking woman. "They're pushing too far," Lynn agrees, invoking the privacy argument. "It's not anybody else's business. If you want to be gay, you know, stay in your house with your partner and do what you have to do. But to have to like parade down the street and show everybody, I don't like that." "I don't either," Peggy says. "They're flaunting it." For these women, the visibility of sexual nonconformity on talk shows is continuous with a more general invasion of public space, a sort of tasteless greediness, by gays and lesbians, who parade down streets and now parade on television right into our homes.

The sense that talk shows are part of an invasion, that when they involve gay people they must be battled rather than watched, can be extraordinarily intense. In the midst of a long, heated argument in a male discussion group, Jim ("Rush Limbaugh is my main man"), a 55-year-old retired police officer, puts it as clearly as it can be put.

> I'm not antigay, I just don't want the gays invading my space. I tolerate them, but I don't want them coming in my face. I think the gays and lesbians, it was better when they were in the closet. Now they come out, and they're trying to force their views on us. More and more every day. Lesbians and gays, fine, they want to do their thing, fine, but don't get in my space. Because I have my beliefs, and I don't want them messing with my family, because my family's the way I raised my family. I'm a churchgoer, I'm a father, and I don't want to see this happen to my children, or my grandchildren. And I want them to stay where they are, and don't impose their views on everybody else. I don't want my space invaded, very simply, and I'll fight to keep my space from being invaded. I don't want them in my house, period. They're right in your face, all the time, and the shows don't help. The shows don't help. They have the people right out there, and they're flaunting it. The talk shows make it look like, oh, it's great, it's better than what you might have. I've always tolerated their lifestyle, I just

*don't want them to put it in my face, that's all, and when they do it
on TV, they're putting it in your face.*

Exploitation and propriety are of no concern here, but the elements left are
shared with more liberal, gay-sympathetic viewers: *keep out of my face,
keep out of my space.*

When sex and gender statuses become politicized—when the personal
becomes political—as the feminist movement has dramatically demonstrated, they often meet with this kind of backlash. This makes good sense,
since what under the old rules had seemed like a natural privilege (man
public, woman domestic; heterosexual public, homosexual secret) is now
claimed to be an exertion of power. The political battle becomes, in part,
a battle over ownership of public space. Both talk shows and gay, lesbian,
bisexual, and transgender movements (along with the feminist movement)
have been aggressively moving previously private issues into the public
sphere; television has, moreover, taken the newly public back into the privacy of home. That move, and all the anxieties about changes in the public
sphere that congeal around it, make talk shows politically relevant despite
the hollow twaddle of which they are so often composed.

Privacy and sexual supremacy, daytime talk and the previously private,
talk shows and sex and gender movements—these relationships are undeni-
ably tight. For those with an interest in protecting traditional divisions between public and private, TV talk shows featuring lesbians, gays, bisexuals,
and transgenders thus look and feel like a double whammy. The shows
want, to paraphrase William Bennett, to turn the world upside down, making public space something entirely different, and giving it to people who
have never before made much successful claim on it. Liberal heterosexual
viewers worry about exploitation and propriety, beneath which seems to
lurk a sense that they are losing control of public space; conservative viewers
bring that anxiety to its extreme, watching those shows, when they can stand
to, as though they are holding their fists in front of their faces, ready to fend
off the onslaught. While lesbian and gay activists are waging their small
skirmishes with producers over representational control amidst their larger
struggles for visibility, these viewers are waging their own battle with the
television set. They are blocking their throats from the talk shows' fast and
furious force-feeding of sex and gender deviance. They are wishing these
people would just shut up, not quite understanding why they need to flaunt
it in other people's faces, why they have to use television to stick queer noses
where they don't belong.

7 The Tight Rope of Visibility

We're assumed to consist entirely of extreme stereotypes: men ultra-swishy and ultraviolet, Frankenstein thug-women with bolts on their necks, mustachio'd Dolly Parton wanna-bes, leather-men in boots and whips, ombudsmen of pederasty squiring their ombudsboys — all ridiculous, deranged, or criminal. And when we are finally allowed to rally and march, to lay our case before the cameras of the straight American public, what do we do? We call out of the woodwork as our ambassadors of bad will all the screamers, stompers, gender-benders, sadomasochists, and pederasts, and confirm America's worst fears and hates. You can call it gay liberation if you like: we say it's spinach, and we say to hell with it!

MARSHALL KIRK AND HUNTER MADSEN[1]

Tolerance is the result not of enlightenment, but of boredom.

QUENTIN CRISP[2]

"My son Jon is a normal, loving kid who grew up in small-town America," Allyn Schmitz said of Jonathan Schmitz, who shot Scott Amedure, another normal, loving kid from small-town America, at such close range that a fragment of one shell's casing wound up in Amedure's left lung and wadding from the other shell was found in his heart.[3] The statement is alarming but accurate: murdering a gay person still does not quite seem to put one definitively over the edge into hateful and abnormal. The Michigan jury, offered a diminished-capacity defense based on a history of troubles (manic depression, suicide attempts, a thyroid condition), and offered another potentially responsible party, *The Jenny Jones Show,* which had featured Schmitz and Amedure in a same-sex-secret-crushes taping, convicted Jon Schmitz of second- rather than first-degree murder, concluding that he had not acted with deliberation or premeditation.

Although everyone agreed that Schmitz had bought a shotgun and shells three days after the show, driven to Amedure's mobile home, and killed him with that shotgun and those shells, the verdict was that he was a normal, loving, depressive kid who for a moment wasn't "in his right mind," as one juror put it.[4] He was pushed over the edge briefly by the humiliation of a public suspicion of homosexuality, a result of what his father called "a dirty rotten conspiracy,"[5] or what none other than Schmitz's prosecutor called "Jenny Jones's producers' cynical pursuit of ratings and total insensitivity to what could occur here."[6] To kill for it may be an indicator of not being in your right mind, but finding the implication of homosexuality degrading, so much so that you have murderous impulses, is perfectly normal. Schmitz just took his normality a little too far.

As almost all of the mainstream media coverage focused on the case as "the talk show murder" ("many lives have been ruined by nothing more than bad TV," concluded an MSNBC reporter[7]), buying more or less whole-sale the defense claim that the show's "ambush" and "humiliation" of Schmitz were the key pieces, many gay critics argued that this was a hate crime.[8] "What happened was not about a talk show," the president of a Detroit gay political group argued, "it's about the cold-blooded murder of a gay man."[9] Of course, the truth is in between. This was not just an antigay hate crime; it is not just coincidence that Schmitz murdered Amedure three days after their talk show taping, rather than just murdering some other gay guy some other time. The *publicness* of the declaration of desire, not just the fact of it, was the problem punished by death—much like public declara-tion of homosexuality in the military, not the fact of gay and lesbian people in it, is punished by expulsion. Such public declarations of taboo desires are certainly a major talk show stock in trade. And it was certainly stupid, if typical, that producers either did not research enough to find out, or simply ignored the finding, that Schmitz was a manic-depressive, suicidal man with a thyroid condition—and perhaps also a closeted gay man.[10] They pulled exactly the wrong man for the job.

But neither was this a murder caused by talk show irresponsibility. In fact, *Jenny Jones* had run a secret gay crushes show the previous October, *Maury Povich* and *Jerry Springer* have done similar shows, and *Ricki* rou-tinely includes same-sex admirers on its secret-crushes programs. None of those shows produced a killer, just a leveling spectacle in which anyone can want anyone else, give or take a bit of tittering. The Schmitz-Amedure show, like those, treated homosexuality as incidental, and treated heterosexually identified guests as potential dates of gay guests, projecting a sort of "try it, you might like it, what's the big deal" attitude in which gay-straight mar-gins are porous. Even on the *Jenny Jones* episode in question, clips of which aired nonstop on news programs at the height of the trial, homosexual desire seemed, if not quite acceptable, certainly not disgraceful to either the crusher or the crushee. Jon, sitting next to Scott and their big, mutual female friend, laughs when he finds out it's a man who wants him; after the fact one can read humiliation or disappointment into his smiling "you lied to me" re-sponse, but on the air it just looks like people are giving each other a good-natured ribbing. When Jon amiably declares himself to be "one hundred percent heterosexual," the audience cheers wildly for him. He has the home-court advantage.

That most commentators (and to some degree, the jury) interpreted the event as public humiliation reveals not just blatant, unexamined hetero-sexism—in the assumption that same-sex desire degrades its object, while

Figure 7 Jonathan Schmitz *(center)* looks toward his friend Donna Riley, as he is hugged
by Scott Amedure during taping of *The Jenny Jones Show,* March 1995. AP
Photos/Court TV.

opposite-sex desire flatters it—but also a telling reaction to the integration
of gays and lesbians into public media space. It is not just by "ambushing"
Schmitz that the talk show became so blameworthy in many people's eyes,
but by refusing the premise that the revelation of homosexual desire is
shameful, that such things should be kept behind closed doors. It is not just
the rules of responsible television the show allegedly broke, but the rules of
heterosexual distinction. Of course, the show wants to have it both ways:
if the revelation isn't painted as humiliation, it certainly is produced to be
more titillating and juicy than your standard-issue heterosexual infatuation.
Yet even if the show's producers, as is most likely the case, led Schmitz to
believe his admirer was female, and even if Schmitz, as is most likely the
case, *felt* humiliated by the event, from the perspective of equal treatment
the premise of the show is as responsible as it is cheaply provocative.

The murder of Scott Amedure, large as it looms in the lives of the families
involved, is not an aberration in the history of antigay violence, or even in
talk show history. Talk shows did not create a situation in which publicly

visible homosexual desire is punishable by murder, in which some men would rather kill a gay man than be perceived to be one. They contributed to the murder by doing what they have been doing for a good couple of decades: making same-sex desire as public as can be, simultaneously scandalizing and normalizing. That is unquestionably an explosive mix. With the right hate-soaked people involved—and given the routine sloppiness of guest screening and the emphasis on big emotion, such people make regular appearances—it can ignite dangerous, sometimes lethal fires. But for all their brainless bravado, the talk shows' contribution is neither homophobia nor heterosexual degradation. Their contribution is the *making public* of homosexuality, in a tone that is at once sensational and matter-of-fact—a routine with a long history in the genre. The facile attack on sensationalism makes it easy to miss the fact that it is its opposite, the desensationalizing and normalizing of homosexuality, against which the backlash is really directed.

The *Jenny Jones* murder thus only makes higher drama out of the festival of irony we have been witnessing: a light, laugh-filled, mindless program in which same-sex attraction is at worst amusing triggers an old-fashioned antigay murder; a show that is part of a boom in gay visibility is turned into a message of *shut up or die,* or *don't ask, don't tell.* It was a moment like many others, only bigger, exaggerating the snarled knots at which we have been tugging throughout this whole book. Indeed, talk shows in general, through their unabashed pursuit of the entertaining moment, make high, personalized, thinned-out drama out of deeper social divisions, cultural anxieties, and political struggles. They are like cheap gymnasium amplifiers operated by mediocre deejays, filled with distortion and screechy feedback and indifference to the kind of music coming out of them, so long as people are dancing.

But just because so many people seem to be playing air guitar doesn't mean the sound system is shot. Listening to this scratchy system, one learns a lot about the visibility traps in which transgendered, lesbian, gay, and bisexual people find themselves, and about the dilemmas of media visibility for marginalized populations more generally; about the political, social, and cultural struggles that talk shows amplify, and in which sex and gender nonconformity becomes enmeshed. In the end, one learns a lot about the cultural contest over public space, over the nature and content and ownership of American "public" life, that makes talk shows possible and necessary, and that structures them into such screwy, impossible shapes.

High-wire acts

Some older women I know feel themselves disappearing, as if ever so slowly they are vaporizing far before their time is up. At first, there are small hints that might just be rudeness: a bump on the street without an "excuse me," eyes that quickly move somewhere else. But as the years move on, despite the certainty of their own existence and the youth inside, they began to feel overlooked, invisible, unseen. It is a slow, dull shock. Many people who are not older women may recognize the process, if perhaps as a sort of reversal of their own; some of us are disappeared from the beginning and feel ourselves getting more visible over time. Whichever direction you're headed, the desire is the same: to be recognized, to have people you encounter know your name, to be bumped into as if you are actually there, to be looked at, right where you are, right in the eyes.

On a collective level, this desire is especially powerful for marginalized groups, whose cultural visibility is often so minimal, or distant enough from the way people live their lives to render them unrecognizable even to themselves. Earlier in the century, "passing" was the predominant response to the prohibitions on same-sex desire, for instance, as homosexuals quietly built institutions by moving under the radar of the larger culture; once those institutions were in place and a political movement took shape in the latter part of the century, *public visibility* became a central concern for lesbian, gay, bisexual, and transgender people. Populations who have been subject to the charge that they do not exist, and many of whom, since queerness is not marked on the body, can and do choose to be invisible, did what they could to show up on the radar screens. The positive effects of visibility are quite plain: "Cultural visibility can prepare the ground for gay civil rights protection," as Rosemary Hennessy sums it up, and "affirmative images of lesbians and gays in the mainstream media . . . can be empowering for those of us who have lived most of our lives with no validation at all from the dominant culture."[11] The desires to be recognized, affirmed, and validated, and to lay the cultural groundwork for political change, in fact, are so strong they have tended to inhibit careful analysis of the dynamics of becoming visible. Cultural visibility, especially when it is taking place through commerce, is not a direct route to liberation; in fact, it can easily lead elsewhere. It looks simple—*just see me, here I am*—but, as the talk show world demonstrates, it is as convoluted and treacherous as can be.

Talk shows drag all kinds of unpopular people into the public eye, and in doing so become lightning rods for anxieties about those people *and* about the public eye—not a problem for producers, since lightning attracts viewers. This is not a losing game for the individuals and populations getting TV attention, but neither is it a winning one. If we can take the case studied here as in many ways typical of the process, becoming visible though the commercial media is, for marginalized populations, something like walking a tight rope: dangers await if you fall, some glory if you make it across, and there's not much to keep you in balance. Even as you walk across, with the enthusiasm of a newcomer or the intensity of an old pro, all kinds of people are tugging at the rope, hoping you'll walk the walk they require, or that you'll simply fall into the pit below. There is not much choice, either. It's either the tight rope or no rope at all.

The most obvious rope pullers are those running the show. As we have seen, media organizations and producers have both an interest in and partic- ular routines for shaping visibility, and that interest is, when all is said and done, defined by ratings. There has never been any question that talk shows, and ratings-conscious television entertainment in general, often select the rousing, unusual edges of a population for attention. This can be especially disturbing if that population is not widely understood, since small pieces can come to be taken for the whole; as Vito Russo put it simply, "The exclusive depiction or representation of any group of people by a minority stereotype is called bigotry." [12]

Nor is it a secret that lots of people want to be on television, not only to promote a product or a political message, but just to be on TV, and that producers use this desire to their advantage. For a while now, observers have noted that we live in a time when many people seem to worry that they are nobody, and that television has come to serve as a certification of somebody-ness: [13] they'll go on local TV to proudly announce that their house was closest to the plane crash, or kill for a spot as a weather lady, or go on a talk show and bare their buttocks to the nation. Talk shows, along with television genres (including news) that rely on "real people," encourage and profit from this response to anonymity, invalidation, and voicelessness. This too can be disturbing for populations pushing for public recognition, since it seems that their neediest, most damaged members are the ones getting the most attention—not necessarily the best overall public- ity for the group.

But take these as starting points and you have to leave aside their comfort- ing simplicity for the more vexing complications, dilemmas, and paradoxes involved in the pursuit of media visibility. It is quickly clear, for instance, that on talk shows the exploitation is typically mutual, as those working their way into the public eye negotiate their way through, with various degrees of consciousness and sophistication, trading a piece of personal revelation for a bit of air time. The struggle for self-representation is not one in which talk show guests are simple victims. They do not control the outcome, but they have a strong hand in creating it.

Nor are talk show interests inevitably stacked against sex and gender nonconformists. On the contrary, it is *because* producer and activist interests line up in important ways that talk shows have been such a hot spot for sex and gender nonconformists, including politically oriented ones. Recall, for instance, the conjunction of the "tell the truth" justificatory scheme of most talk shows, their pursuit of the golden moment of spontaneous self-revelation, and the coming-out rhetoric of much lesbian, gay, bisexual, and transgender activism; recall the consonance of "we are everywhere" with the greedy pursuit of hidden populations, and of novel sex and gender variations. It is *because* of the cynical use of "real people," and people who feel themselves to be disrespected and in need of TV affirmation, that talk shows have offered the most diverse visibility for gay and lesbian and bisexual and transgendered people available, that more colors and sizes and classes and regions and ways of speaking are on view here than anywhere in gay media culture. It is *because* of the tension between spontaneity and control in the production process that opportunities to speak more freely and openly about one's life open up for sex and gender outsiders, even if they quickly shut down. It is *because* of the talk shows' marketable distaste for elite, rationality-claiming authority and taste for personal, emotion-based authority that they have been such key places from which to challenge medical and scientific definitions of "perversion" and to put a "human face" on sex and gender nonconformity. All this while media companies make loads of money off our stigma.

All told, in fact, talk shows turn "good publicity" and "positive images" and "affirmation" into especially slippery goo.[14] A glance back at the emphasis on outrageousness that many talk shows have come to promote—the source of much complaining about negative imagery of lesbian, gay, transgender, and bisexual people—makes it hard to hold onto the notion that talk show selection of "the fringes" is necessarily and always a bad thing. This kind of exoticizing imagery certainly makes social acceptability harder to gain by overemphasizing difference, often presented as frightening, pathological, pathetic, or silly; it is annoying and painful for pretty much everybody involved. But at the same time it can push out a space: an emphasis on difference, especially on a scary kind of difference, can keep those watching at a distance. Like the in-your-face radicalism of some recent "queer" organizing, a freaky otherness is useful, for some purposes. When people push away from you, or think of you as harmless and dismissible, they tend to leave you alone, and sometimes being left alone is exactly what is needed for independent political and cultural organizing. As one queer writer put it in the early 1990s, "If I tell them I am queer, they give me room. Politically, I can think of little better. I do not want to be one of them. They only need to give me room."[15] The same might be said of the talk shows' money-driven interest in the more provocative edges of lesbian, bisexual, transgender, and gay populations: while they Other us, they also give us *room*. Of course, this is also exactly the problem many people have with them, since at least the appearance of normality seems necessary to winning political *rights*. It's a tension built into talk show visibility, and into the emergence of other marginalized people into commercial media recognition: the same imagery that is damaging for some kinds of political work (assimilation into the mainstream) is effective for other kinds (the autonomous carving-out of political space). Both kinds of work are necessary. Talk shows, simply through their pursuit of ratings, inadvertently amplify a political dilemma inherent in becoming visible, in which both exaggerating and playing down our collective eccentricity is vital.

As we have seen, in fact, talk shows play up both sides of this visibility trap. Queers, to begin with, are not even the talk show villains of choice: even as the flamboyant fairy continues to be treated as a joke, the outrageous, antigay bigot is routinely vilified. Moreover, the same ratings pursuit that emphasizes the most stereotypical also leads to programming strategies that buck the stereotypes. We have seen ample evidence, for instance, that it is not only the fringes that are selected by talk shows, but, especially on the more genteel versions of the programming, the you'd-never-know-they-were-different-if-they-weren't-on-a-talk-show folks. Be it the femme lesbian, the bisexual expert, or the passing transsexual, there has been a great deal of space made on talk shows for counterstereotypical people. (Of course, these images themselves are composed from hackneyed stereotypes: hyperfeminine transsexual women, hypermasculine gay men, lipstick lesbians, and so on.) In fact, an overall accentuation of *gender conformity*—most often achieved by bringing on those from the gender-nonconforming flanks—has pushed *sexual nonconformity* closer to the "normal." Here again, the outrageous sword is double-edged.

The same risk-averse logic of television that has led to the sensationalizing of sexual and gender nonconformity (the weirder it is, the less the risk that people will change channels), in fact, has made the sensations repeat and repeat (it worked before, or it works for others, so let's keep doing it). The shocking gets less and less preposterous as it is repeated; the selection of a population's stigmatized extremes may hem in the population as a whole, but the habitual selection of extremes may simply deaden the stigma. "It is not the simple statement of facts that ushers in freedom," Quentin Crisp has suggested. "It is the constant repetition of them that has this liberating effect." [16] Over time, the talk shows have managed to do for their audiences what no one else has: to make homosexuality, and even transsexualism and bisexuality, basically dull. The "fringes," as they show up on TV every week, become run of the mill; they become like a desperate Madonna, whose simulated sex and outside-the-clothing lingerie drew yawns after not too long. The critics of talk shows here have a point: talk shows, through their continual exhibition of the most colorful sideshow figures, make "deviance" seem "normal." From the perspective of those resisting a political and cultural system that labels them deviant, this is a good thing: the edges of normality push ever outward. Tolerance, Crisp informs us, is boredom's offspring. [17]

Where exactly is the "positive" in all of this, and where the "negative"? The stories told here suggest that there is no answer, only the tight rope with its heavy balancing rod. The talk show principles of selection normalize by stigmatizing, while also playing normal appearances against stereotypes of difference; they arrange for both the bigot and the gender rebellious to confront an often hostile audience, moving sympathies for passing people to the center, while pushing the fringes ever outward by turning exaggerated difference into the same old thing; they give voice by controlling it. It is not just that talk show visibility is good for some sex and gender nonconformists and bad for others—although on some level that is also true—but that they are good for all by being bad for some, and bad for all by being good for some.

Crossing wires

Lesbians and gay men today wake up to headlines alternately disputing their claim to equality under the law, supporting their right to family status, denying their desire, affirming their social identity. They fall asleep to tv talk shows where generals call them perverts, liberals plead for tolerance, and politicians weigh their votes. "Gay invisibil-

ity," the social enforcement of the sexual closet, is hardly a problem anymore.

NATION *WRITER ANDREW KOPKIND*[18]

The first pair of battling gays consisted of a pudgy young man and his trashy friend who stole wallets from his tricks. The next segment featured a wild queen and his even more flamboyant cousin, who flounced onstage wearing his windbreaker like a feather boa, as he flirted with the audience like Pearl Bailey on speed. These feuding cousins were followed by a young man who complained about his friend's routinely offering fellatio to long distance truckers; and, finally, we had a young lesbian couple who argued about the butch's penchant for dressing up like Pete Rose at company softball games. . . . There were several times when I had the impulse to shout, "There's more to us than what you see here!" but these impulses never coincided with a moment when Ricki asked me to speak, at which times I was so torn between the desire to be funny and the desire to blow up the studio that I was neither charming nor insightful. In fact, I was so sad at first that I might have thrown myself under a camera crane, except that the afternoon contained one tender mercy—the studio audience. Those kids, who had looked so threatening on my way into the building, were actually far less homophobic then they appeared. In fact, I was nothing less than astounded as, one by one, they gave the thumbs up sign to the young queens onstage. This led me to believe that shows like Ricki Lake's—for all their absurdities—may actually be creating a more tolerant future. These shows, however vacuous, may be eroding homophobia by their sheer lack of commitment to any point of view.

COMEDIAN AND RICKI *GUEST JAFFE COHEN*[19]

Not long ago I watched Dan tell Matt he loved him, he was sorry for hitting him, it will never happen again, please meet him for dinner tomorrow night. I've seen Matt through a lot of dates and boyfriends, and through at least one trick at a gay bar, but he really seemed to love Dan. Dan is a handsome doctor, and that night was wearing a suit and tie. Young, handsome-in-a-Los-Angeles-way Matt had a black eye; I have lost track of his profession (something medical, for sure) since he went into rehab a few months back. A couple of days later I watched a black gay city government professional placing bets with his female coworker on the sexual preferences of a cute male focus-group participant. Not long afterward I encountered two attractive men, looking exactly like chiseled soap-opera hunks, discussing their upcoming cohabitation ("it's a big step"), as Trevor, the brother-in-law of one of the gay boys, awkwardly offered his blessing and their friend Mateo bought them drinks to celebrate. No sissies here. Nothing out of the ordinary or stereotypical in the villains-and-victims sense; just good-looking, professional men who happen to be gay. In fact, they are men who, if you lived on *Melrose Place,* or in the New York of *Spin City,* or in *All My Children*'s Pine Valley, could be your next-door neighbors.

By the conventions of much gay and lesbian media advocacy, this is a dream come true. There are still some problems (none of the making out that the straight *Melrose Place* characters get to do all the time, always the bridesmaid and never the bride), but the 1990s have witnessed a storm of "happen to be gay" television, culminating in the much-hyped coming out of *Ellen*'s central character and star. It is as if the clean-cut, only-difference-is-what-we-do-in-bed homosexuals walked off the talk show sets to become characters on *Melrose Place, Roseanne, NYPD Blue, Friends, Ellen,* and *All My Children.* Having made the move from occasional soupy movie-of-the-week issue to soap and sitcom regulars, lesbians and gay men look more or less like everybody else on sitcoms and soaps: clean, with really good apartments.[20] They have gone from troubled double-lifesters in search of familial acceptance to hip lesbian ex-wives with babies, and gay neighbors who, like their straight counterparts, have drug problems and dysfunctional relationships with lovers, and turn from good to evil and back. Their homosexuality is more or less incidental, not much more than a spicy character flip.

This dramatic new visibility in commercial television fiction, and the slower changes in commercial popular nonfiction media[21]—Melissa Etheridge and her lover, for instance, regulars in *People* magazine, were recent cover girls for *Newsweek*'s examination of gay families, months before Ellen DeGeneres came out on *Time*'s cover—is only the spread of the logic and imagery of TV talk shows, which long ago incorporated lesbians, gay men, transgenders, and bisexuals into their daily dramas. Although you won't find a dyke or a queen on *Melrose Place,* the trajectory of talk show and TV-fiction lesbianism and gayness has been similar: from issues to relationships, from isolation to integration.

Yet I find this dreamy integration into TV land a bit disturbing; I crave a drag queen mud fight, or a young Latina lesbian with attitude telling her ex-husband to "talk to the hand." The mostly white, "straight-acting," middle-class professionals taking their place at the tables of episodic TV are certainly a breakthrough in visibility, but they embody a rather specific, narrow version of the collective they wind up symbolizing—much different, and arguably much narrower, than talk show visibility. The undeniable expansion of cultural visibility of lesbians, gays, transgenders, and bisexuals way beyond the limits of talk shows is not so much a cause for celebration as a reminder of the dilemmas of visibility. Indeed, even when the fight to get people to stop denying our existence was the most obvious, consuming one, things were never that simple; even for bisexuals and transgenders, still struggling simply to be publicly recognized, it is not that simple. The process by which sex and gender nonconformity goes public has always been, will always be, about much more than sex and gender alone.

Within the yawning mindlessness of talk shows a deeper set of lessons lurks, one which the genre, built as it is from the tense fibers of class, gender, and racial division, makes especially clear. Strip the tight rope a bit, and you find that the walk is so shaky because it takes place on many ropes at once. We have seen how all kinds of boundaries, symbolic and social, are disrupted when gender and sexual nonconformists move into public space to challenge their own stigmatized status: not only between "normal" and "abnormal," but also between polite middle-class and raucous working- and underclass cultures (and the racial associations they drag with them), between mainstreaming and antiassimilation forces in lesbian, gay, bisexual, and transgender politics, between "public" and "private." Walking the tight rope means moving through the turbulence of these attached conflicts, and the way we become visible is shaped by them. There is no way it can be otherwise.

The clash of class cultures on which talk shows are built, for instance, structures the fate of sex and gender nonconformists' visibility as much as that of anyone else making an appearance. Having discovered the profitable appeal of younger, less educated, more boisterous guests, talk shows have come to feature calm, educated, older guests less and less; they simultaneously appropriate, exaggerate, and give expression to the straightforward, not-afraid-of-conflict emotionalism of some underclass and working-class cultures. At the same time, using the low-risk strategy of class voyeurism, many shows select guests from the bottom of the social barrel. Nearly anyone can feel superior watching people whose speech, dress, bodies, relationships, and accents mark them as "trash." Legitimacy, in talk show land as elsewhere, is associated with symbols of social class (educated speech, calm manner, clean dress); uneducated speech, rambunctious manner, and showy dress signify a dismissible lower status. If talk shows are filled with "trashy" people (many of them people of color), and also with queers, sexual difference is easily conflated with class and racial inferiority; if "classy" white gay people have no monopoly on the conversation, sexual difference can no longer be legitimized by an association with higher educational, racial, and class status. Those seeking mainstream legitimacy therefore avoid the stigma of rowdy, poor and working-class, mixed-color shows, aligning with the polite, middle-class, predominantly white strand of talk shows. The two-headed monster thus not only splits itself, but amplifies the class divisions of the populations on which it greedily feeds.

The class structure of talk shows makes for a double-edged visibility, with greater class diversity and thus with more stereotype shattering *and* more stigma gathering. The long-standing invisibility (both outside and within gay and lesbian communities) of gay, lesbian, bisexual, and transgender people of color, and of those from lower economic statuses, is cracked open by the talk shows; yet at the same time the shows, with their selection of nasty, noisy, exhibitionist, not-great-to-look-at poor and working-class guests, encourage those interested in social acceptability to disown the visibility of some of their own. A predicament already present in the politics of sexual social change is brought to a head: as we make ourselves visible, do those among us with less status get to speak just as anyone else (increasing the risk of further stigma as the price for democratic diversity) or do the more acceptable get the upper hand (reproducing class and racial hierarchies as the price for gaining legitimacy)? Any path to visibility must face down this question.

This question is especially critical in a period when one edge of the sword is increasingly cutting the path. With the recent "discovery" of gay and lesbian markets, it is primarily those with buying power who come to be seen and heard, even in the publications and programs produced by and for gay, lesbian, bisexual, and transgender people. "As the economic logic of national advertising begins to drive publications aimed at the lesbian and gay community," Fred Fejes and Kevin Petrich claim, "the only voice being heard is that of an upper income, urban, de-sexed white male." "The increasing circulation of gay and lesbian images in consumer culture has the effect," Rosemary Hennessy adds, "of consolidating an imaginary, class-specific gay subjectivity for both straight and gay audiences."[22] As affluent, assimilated gays and lesbians are being marketed and marketed to, talk shows, with their restless class cultural mix, are a refreshing reminder. They highlight the unavoidable complications of class in the necessary pursuit of visibility.

The difficulty goes even deeper, though, much deeper than any talk show will ever go. Talk shows accentuate not only the tension between legitimacy-buying and diversity-promoting visibility but also central dilemmas of collective identity. A sense of collective identification—that this is us, that we are each other—is personally and politically critical: it is an anchor, offering the comforts and resources of family and, at least in this political system, a foundation from which to organize and wage political battles. Identity requires stable, recognizable social categories. It requires difference, knowing where you end and where others begin. It thus makes good sense to do as gay and lesbian movements, modeling themselves on civil rights movements, have done: to build a quasi-ethnicity, with its own political and cultural institutions, festivals, and neighborhoods. Underwriting this strategy, moreover, is typically the notion that gays and lesbians share the same sort of essential self, one with same-sex desires.[23] All of this solidifies the social categories of "gay" and "lesbian," clarifying who "we" are and are not, even as it also stabilizes the categories of "heterosexual man" and "heterosexual woman."

At the same time, though, it is exactly through the fixed, dichotomous categorization into apparently distinct species of gay and straight (and male and female) that antigay, antibisexual, and antitransgender oppression is perpetuated. Even as the categories that mark us as different are necessary for claiming rights and benefits, it is only when they are unworkable that we are really safe; if there is no sure way to distinguish gay from straight, for instance, the basis for antigay legislation disappears. From this angle, *muddying* the categories rather than shoring them up, pointing out their instability and fluidity along with their social roots, is the key to liberation. The political advantages of scrambling the code are always also in competition with those of keeping it clear, not only for people who want to retain their status in a sexual hierarchy, but also for people resisting that hierarchy: a coherent sense of collective identity, a cohesive foundation from which to fight, for instance, for rights as gay people.

This tension between a politic that treats the homo-hetero divide as a given and goes about the business of equalizing the sides, and a politic that seeks to *attack the divide itself,* always present in contemporary gay and lesbian politics, has come to the fore most recently with the controversial emergence of "queer" movements in politics and academia. Queer theory and politics, as Michael Warner puts it, protest "not just the normal behavior of the social but the *idea* of normal behavior."[24] Especially with the vocal challenge from transgendered and bisexual people—not so easily fit into the gay-straight and man-woman binary worldview—the question of the unity, stability, viability, and political utility of sexual identities has been called into question. The queer politics of "carnival, transgression, and parody," with its "antiassimilationist" and "decentering" politics, has been met with heavy resistance from those rightly seeing it as a threat to civil rights strategies.[25] The problem, of course, is that both the category strippers and the category defenders are right: fixed identity categories are both the basis for oppression and the basis for political power.

As we have seen, talk shows create much of their sex-and-gender fare, especially when transgender and bisexual people are involved, on exactly this tension. Talk shows, even though they reinstate them, mess up those reassuring dichotomies, turning solid lines into broken ones, steel boundaries into elastic ones. On talk shows, the categories stretch and contract, stretch and contract. Much talk show visibility, for one thing, is "queer," in the meaning of the term favored by academics, spotlighting "a proliferation of sexualities (bisexual, transvestite, pre- and post-op transsexual, to name a few) and the compounding of outcast positions along racial, ethnic, and class, as well as sexual lines—none of which is acknowledged by the neat binary division between hetero- and homosexual."[26] This very proliferation is a challenge, as all of the panicky, hostile stifling of it seems to testify. And over and over, the shows self-consciously create minicrises in telling the difference between male and female, gay and straight. These are anxious, freak-out, sometimes scary moments for many people, like meeting a mutant who claims to be your sister, like having the floor under your feet suddenly drop away.

For lesbian, gay, bisexual, and transgender collectives, in particular, these disruptive moments of visibility are a crisis: both an opportunity to challenge the *cultural* logic of homo-hetero distinction, and a threat to the sense that "we" make the kind of sense we need, *politically,* to make. Talk shows, with their peculiar interest in the out-there and the in-between, tap and bleed this queer dilemma. The ubiquity of people who do not quite fit the simple categories advances an important cultural agenda, by reminding viewers that the "neat binary division between hetero- and homosexual" is not as neat as all that, tarnishing the certainty of clear, natural differences between sexualities and genders. Even with all the attempts to defuse the identity threats housed by these sorts of disruptions, the sense that "normal" and "natural" are distinguishable from their opposites unravels in bits and pieces. Media visibility, talk shows tell us, is riddled with this difficulty—

and the more diverse and democratic it gets, the more the dilemma comes alive. Walking onto the public stage, we have only the horns of this dilemma to keep our balance.

Going public

You know you're in trouble when Sally Jessy Raphael (strained smile and forced tear behind red glasses) seems like your best bet for being heard, understood, respected, and protected. That for some of us the spooky, hollow light of talk shows, and the tinny, high pitch of their microphones, have seemed a safe haven should give us all pause. In a society that has made television such an important arbiter of worth, and where power circulates in part through the televisual certification of political subjects, profiting from those of us starved for voice and affirmation is a cinch; in a society so rigidly committed to the heterosexual-as-normative, so violently uncomfortable with sexual and gender diversity, it is not surprising to find lesbian, gay, bisexual, and transgender people historically confined to the most unserious spaces, or blocked from openly announcing themselves in the more serious ones. In such a place, the petty negotiations and funky crumbs of talk shows look like portentous war plans and extravagant meals. In the end, it is not so much the often trite, hard-to-hear things that get said on talk shows that educate, but the fact and form of their existence: what they say about the society that calls them into existence and makes them happen as strangely and amusingly as they do.

The rope on which bisexuals, transgenders, gays, and lesbians balance as we emerge into visibility gets especially tangled in a time and place where the "public" into which we walk is a space in turmoil; the gusts from struggles over public space make the whole walk a rough one. Talk shows, which make their money through publicizing personal issues, only make this anxiety easier to see. Sex and gender nonconformists participate in, and detonate, an anxiety about the shifting boundaries between public and private— much as they have taken a place in other "moral panics," such as the 1950s equation of homosexuality and communism, where pervasive fears and anxieties attach to sexual "deviants."[27] The very televised presence of gay, lesbian, bisexual, and transgendered people makes public space, to many people, appear to be crawling with indecency. In an environment where public and private have blurred into new forms,[28] gay, lesbian, bisexual, and transgender visibility comes to symbolize a breakdown in the meaning of publicness.

The charge of public indecency is, moreover, a call to get out: this is *my* space, it says, and you do not belong here. Becoming media-visible, especially if your social identity is rooted in a status previously understood to belong to the realm of "private" life, calls the question on who owns public space. The issue of what can and cannot be spoken about and seen in public, which the televised collective coming out of the last twenty years evokes, is really the issue of who is and is not considered a legitimate member of "the public." This ongoing cultural war over public space and public participation is what makes talk shows—even when they are devoid of anything remotely political—socially relevant, and turns them into such zany, vibrant, coarse scenes. In part, they exist to isolate the socially challenging in a discredited space, offering the heady opportunity to be lords and ladies of a vapid kingdom, while the real powerhouses command the rest of the empire. In part, they exist to provide a concrete locale at which the question of just what public space can look like, and under just whose jurisdiction it falls, is kept alive for everybody to look at and toss around. Entering media space means joining this fight, and the other ones attached to it, with these questions and predicaments scribbled on your hand. It means climbing the ladder from the hard ground below, eyes focused on the many fingers fighting each other for the chance to make you fall, and dancing across the tight rope, calmly explaining and zestily hollering, with all proud indecency, that whoever we may be, this place is ours.

Appendix: Methods

Although I am a sociologist by training (and, having gone into the family business, a second-generation one at that), and although this project and the research from which it arises are sociological in nature, *Freaks Talk Back* intentionally does not present its evidence according to strict academic conventions. This appendix, therefore, provides the methodological details necessary to understand and evaluate more fully the conclusions drawn from my research—what sort of data I used, how I got to them, why I did what I did, and the limitations on the information I collected.

The research design is based on a tripartite model of cultural study that, while still not widely applied, is now acknowledged as fundamental: in order to get a strong grasp of a cultural phenomenon, it is necessary to simultaneously study its production (the activities through which it is created), its thematic, narrative, visual, or textual content (what is being said in and through it), and its reception (how those encountering it use and interpret it).[1] I set out, therefore, to find out as much as I could about the way talk shows are put together, the patterns of content they contain, and the way they are understood by those viewing them. Given the book's narrower topic of sex and gender nonconformity, I was particularly interested in what was said through shows with lesbian, gay, bisexual, and transgender topics, how those involved in the production of them behaved and thought, and how audiences saw these particular kinds of shows. What follows is a rundown of my data-collection process and, where appropriate, details of some of the findings that were not included in the body of the book.

Production

I took a three-pronged approach to data collection on talk show production: interviews with production staff, interviews with guests, and participant-observation at talk show tapings. Recruitment of production-staff interviewees was, revealingly, quite difficult; interviews were refused roughly four times as often as they were accepted. Producers still in the industry, in particular, were wary; executive producers were worried about public relations at a time when talk shows were under widely publicized attack, and lower-level producers were worried about their jobs in an industry with very high turnover. Although I made a first pass by sending letters requesting interviews to executive producers on all the national, daytime, topic-oriented talk shows (which yielded only one cooperative response), my strategy for recruitment was mostly to rely on personal contacts, and to let things snowball from there. With a few early leads from a range of people in my own social and professional networks, and with what I can only describe as fairly dogged persistence, I scored a first round of interviews with producers; those interview subjects passed me on to others. After a total of twenty interviews with current and former producers at all levels (executive producers, supervising producers, producers, associate producers), as well as hosts and staff in research and public relations, I was satisfied that I had reached saturation, as stories, descriptions, and answers began to repeat.

Both staff and guest interviews were loosely structured. I covered the same territory in each interview, but also allowed participants to take the conversations in their own directions. Together, these interviews covered work and guest experiences on just about every national, topic-driven talk show (and a number of local talk shows, which I have not listed): *Bertice Berry, Richard Bey, Carnie, Donahue, Gordon Elliott, Gabrielle, Mo Gaffney, Geraldo, Jenny Jones, Ricki Lake, Leeza, Oprah, The Other Side, Charles Perez, Maury Povich, Jane Pratt, Sally Jessy Raphael, Joan Rivers, Rolonda, Jerry Springer, Tempestt, Mark Walberg, Jane Whitney,* and *Montel Williams.* A sample interview schedule and a list of interview subjects follows this discussion.

The interviews certainly provided me with a good deal of information about how producers do and think about their work, but I also wanted to see it in action. Since access to production meetings and other behind-the-scenes activity was restricted, I attended tapings of most of the New York City–area talk shows (and sat in the control room with producers during one other taping) over the course of the 1995–96 season. The object here was both to witness key pieces of the production process as they were taking place (especially the management of the audience and the guests), and to experience the role of audience member from the inside. I treated the tapings as an anthropologist treats the ethnographic encounter with cultural ritual, taking extensive, detailed field notes for later analysis. A list of the programs attended follows this discussion.

Finally, I wanted to understand where guests fit into the production system, how they negotiated their way through it—not just any guests, of course, but lesbian, gay, transgender, and bisexual guests in particular. These interview subjects were initially recruited through a variety of methods: personal contacts, postings on computer bulletin boards (this was especially fruitful for interviews of transgender and bisexual activist guests), newspaper advertisements (in local lesbian and gay newspapers in the South and Midwest, for instance), and organizational contacts (the Gay and Lesbian Alliance against Defamation, Renaissance Education Association, Sexuality Information and Education Council of the U.S., American Educational Gender Information Service). Again, from here I depended on the "snowball method," as participants sent me to others they knew who had appeared on talk shows. A sample interview schedule and list of the forty-four interviews follows this discussion.

Perhaps the most limiting aspect of this study came with these guest interviews. I was able to find people primarily because they were "networked," affiliated with groups of one sort of another (which is how they wound up being recruited by talk shows, as well); these sorts of guests, activist or not, tend to be of relatively high educational attainment, and mostly middle-class. Their motivations for appearing on talk shows, though they varied, tended to be loosely educational. With the switch in talk show recruiting methods, however, and in the overall guest profile of more recent programming—that is, as the shows came to depend largely on people who call in on toll-free numbers—I recognized that these sorts of guests and motivations, while still common, were less and less typical. My considerable efforts to track down unaffiliated, nonactivist guests (through newspaper advertisements and a guest clearinghouse) were largely unsuccessful: only a handful of my interviews were with guests who went on the shows without objectives much broader than the excitement and affirmation of a television appearance. (Programs refused to release guest information, and guests are only rarely identified by their full names.)

The difficulty is unsurprising, since the guests who volunteer themselves are most often not affiliated with organizations or with lesbian, gay, bisexual, or transgender communities, and are quite often geographically isolated—by definition hard to find. While this is a serious gap in data, filled in by secondary accounts and by the accounts of participants in Patricia Priest's study,[2] it is one I have taken self-consciously into account in the writing.

Sample production-staff interview schedule
1. Talk show work history and current position.
2. Pressures and pleasures of the job.
   a. What makes a good producer?
   b. What is the relationship between the show and the corporate owners?
   c. What do you know about the viewing audience? How does that affect your job?
3. Practicalities of producing a show.
   a. What is a "good" show? Does a good show have to have conflict? Does a good show have to have audience participation? What is a "bad" show?
   b. Where do show ideas come from? What makes a good talk show subject? How do you go from idea to implementation? Who decides whether an idea is pursued? Who has to pick up the ball and what do they have to do with it? How is the show structure shaped, and how tightly planned does it need to be?
   c. How are guests recruited? How do you know if they're for real? What makes a "good" guest and what makes a "bad" one? What do guests get for coming on the show? Why do you think they agree to participate?

    d. How do you prepare the guests for their appearances?

    e. Do you use expert guests? Why or why not?

    f. What kind of research is done?

    g. What are you doing and thinking about during the taping? What are various producers and other staff doing during the taping?

    h. What factors most affect how well a particular show goes?

    i. How much editing is done?

    j. Does the fact that the viewing audience is predominantly female affect the way you produce shows? In what ways?

4. Is this "public service" television?

5. Producing shows on sex and gender deviance.

    a. Are there any different considerations, or is producing these just like producing any show?

    b. How do these shows compare in popularity to others?

    c. How would you describe the ways these subjects have been treated? Are there any typical storylines? Audience questions that appear repeatedly? Any changes in the way these topics were treated over your years on the show?

    d. Do you integrate gay men and lesbians into shows that aren't specifically about homosexuality? Why or why not? What about bisexuals? Transsexuals? Cross-dressers?

    e. Do producers and/or the host have a common position on these kinds of issues? Are there any goals beyond doing an interesting show (e.g., promoting tolerance)?

    f. Does the studio audience make any difference for what you can or can't do with these kinds of topics?

    g. Are there any particular pressures or difficulties associated with doing these kinds of shows? Where are the pressures or difficulties from?

6. Stories of producing particular shows.

7. Current talk show scene in general.

    a. What do you think of the newer breed of shows? In what ways are they different from and similar to the older ones?

    b. What do you think of the recent criticisms of talk shows?

8. What do you think viewers are getting out of these talk shows?

Production-staff interview subjects
(Names in quotation marks indicate pseudonyms, given to participants who asked not to be identified.)
Nancy Alspaugh (March 15, 1996), executive producer, *Leeza*
"Martin Calder" (March 12, 1996), television talk show producer
"Bob Danforth" (January 3, 1996), television production-company publicity director
"Rachel Davidson" (October 20, 1995), television talk show producer
"Carl Davis" (June 3, 1996), television research-company executive

Methods

Burt Dubrow (July 10, 1996), executive vice president for programming, Multimedia Entertainment

Steven Goldstein (February 6, 1996), former television talk show producer, *Oprah, Jerry Springer, Montel Williams*

"Brian Jordan" (August 28, 1995), television talk show producer

"Mike Kappas" (October 2, 1996), former television talk show producer

"Lynn Malone" (August 18, 1995), former television talk show producer

"Sarah Merrick" (January 3, 1996), television talk show producer, *Leeza;* former producer, *Maury Povich*

"Janice Morrison" (June 13, 1996), television company research director

TJ Persia (January 5, 1996), former audience booker and coordinator, *Montel Williams, Mo Gaffney, Marilu*

"Lawrence Randall" (January 5, 1996), former television talk show producer

"David Roth" (November 30, 1995), television talk show producer

Jerry Springer (June 28, 1996), television talk show host

"Randy Tanner" (January 2, 1996), former television production-company vice president

Jason Walker (March 29, 1996), producer, *Leeza*

Jane Whitney (May 30, 1996), former television talk show host

"Jennifer Williams" (September 7, 1995), former television talk show producer

Tapings

Richard Bey (May 9, 1996)

Donahue (February 15, 1996)

Geraldo (April 11, 1996)

Gordon Elliott (May 22, 1996)

Ricki Lake (November 16, 1995)

Maury Povich (April 22, 1995; October 13, 1995; March 28, 1996)

Sally Jessy Raphael (February 1, 1996)

Rolonda (March 7, 1996)

Sample guest interview schedule

1. General background: age, work, education.
2. Do you watch talk shows?
3. The story of talk show appearance(s): recruitment, producers' pitch, motivation, preinterview, preparation, taping-day arrival, prepping by show staff, preshow activities, activities during commercial breaks.
4. Impressions of host, audience, other guests.
5. Whom did you imagine you were speaking to (the studio audience, people like you at home, straight people, etc.)?
6. Was the show what you wanted it to be? What you expected it to be?

7. How did you come across, do you think, compared to the way you see your life outside of the show?
8. Would you do it again?

Guest interview subjects
(Names in quotation marks indicate pseudonyms, given to participants who asked not to be identified.)

Ezra Alvarez (December 15, 1995), *Ricki Lake*
Johnny Bonck (December 27, 1995), *Donahue*
Aaron Caramanis (January 18, 1996), *Ricki Lake*
"Sheri Carter" (November 11, 1995), *Gordon Elliott, Mark Walberg*
Cheryl Ann Costa (November 19, 1995), *Charles Perez*
Remy David (November 19, 1995), *Sally Jessy Raphael, Rolonda*
Eve Diana (March 19, 1996), *Donahue*
Terri Flamer (December 31, 1995), *Bertice Berry*
"Kitt Fraser" (November 19, 1995), *Rolonda*
Marjorie Garber (March 14, 1996), *Geraldo, Oprah, Maury Povich, Jane Pratt, Sally Jessy Raphael, Jane Whitney*
Angela Gardner (November 18, 1995), *Donahue, Morton Downey, Jr., Charles Perez, Shirley* (Canada)
James Green (December 29, 1995), *Geraldo, Charles Perez*
Jacob Hale (January 6, 1996), *Gabrielle*
David Harrison (December 22, 1995), *Donahue, Joan Rivers*
Lisa Heft (December 27, 1995), *Donahue*
Eric Jackson (March 7, 1996), *Carmen Jovet* (Puerto Rico)
Hildene Jacobson (June 6, 1996), aspiring talk show guest
Jordy Jones (December 27, 1995), *The Other Side*
Lani Ka'ahumanu (December 22, 1995), *Bertice Berry, Donahue, Leeza, Shirley* (Canada)
"Barry Long" (November 11, 1995), *Mark Walberg*
Danielle McClintock (December 27, 1995), *Bertice Berry*
Eric Marcus (February 16, 1996), *Donahue, Geraldo, Oprah, Sally Jessy Raphael*
Jill Nagle (December 23, 1995), *Maury Povich, Jane Whitney*
"Melissa Nieman" (February 18, 1996), *Geraldo*
Ann Northrop (January 19, 1996), *Donahue, Geraldo, Rolonda*
Robyn Ochs (November 21, 1996), *Donahue, Mo Gaffney, Maury Povich, Rolonda, Shirley* (Canada), *Jane Whitney*
Laura Perez (December 28, 1995), *Jane Whitney, Face to Face* (Spanish language)
Cynthia Phillips (June 17, 1996), *Geraldo, Jenny Jones, Sally Jessy Raphael, Joan Rivers, Jerry Springer, Montel Williams*
Linda Phillips (June 17, 1996), *Geraldo, Jenny Jones, Sally Jessy Raphael, Joan Rivers, Jerry Springer, Montel Williams*

Methods

"Russell Pierce" (December 21, 1995), *Jane Pratt*
Isabelle Richards (February 9, 1996), *Ricki Lake, Oprah, Sally Jessy Raphael, Rolonda, Jerry Springer, Montel Williams*
JoAnn Roberts (November 18, 1995), *Donahue*
Cole Roland (December 21, 1995), *Jane Whitney*
Michelangelo Signorile (February 9, 1996), *Geraldo, Leeza, Ricki Lake*
Bruce Spencer (June 25, 1996), *Donahue*
Stafford (December 27, 1995), *Geraldo*
Cianna Stewart (February 10, 1996), *Montel Williams*
Susan Stryker (October 6, 1995), *Gabrielle, The Other Side*
Donald Suggs (July 20, 1995), *Ricki Lake*
Michael Szymanski (January 4, 1996), *Donahue, Gabrielle, Mo Gaffney, Leeza*
Harry Taylor (December 13, 1995), *Tempestt*
"Ashley Tillis" (July 15, 1996), *Richard Bey, Sally Jessy Raphael*
Miss Understood (March 3, 1996), *Richard Bey, Gordon Elliott, Geraldo, Rolonda, Mark Walberg, Tempestt*
Penelope Williams (June 12, 1996), *Gordon Elliott, Geraldo, Mark Walberg*

Content

In order to get a clear sense of patterns in talk shows with lesbian, gay, bisexual, and transgender content, I turned to both transcripts and videos. With the assistance of interview subjects, the Gay and Lesbian Alliance against Defamation, and my own VCR, I collected as many videotapes on these subjects as I could get my hands on. The 106 hours of programming include *Bertice Berry, Richard Bey, Danny Bonaduce, Carnie, Donahue, Gordon Elliott, Gabrielle, Geraldo, Jenny Jones, Ricki Lake, Leeza, Marilu, Oprah, The Other Side, Charles Perez, Maury Povich, Jane Pratt, Sally Jessy Raphael, Joan Rivers, Rolonda, Jerry Springer, Tempestt, Mark Walberg, Jane Whitney,* and *Montel Williams.*

At the same time, using the three services that sell talk show transcripts (Burrelle's, Journal Graphics, and SOS), I acquired all of the available transcripts from the years 1984–86 (a small bunch, totaling 8) and 1994–95 (a total of 147) in which lesbian, gay, bisexual, and transgender topics and guests were central; occasionally, when an interview subject would mention it, I also ordered transcripts from other years. Not all programs participate in transcription services, but the sample of over 160 transcripts includes *Bertice Berry, Donahue, Geraldo, Jenny Jones, Oprah, Maury Povich, Susan Powter, Dennis Prager, Sally Jessy Raphael, Rolonda, Jerry Springer, Jane Whitney,* and *Montel Williams.* Each transcription company has a different method of searching—one can search full text, the others only show titles and summaries—but each searched using the words *gay, lesbian, bisexual, transsexual, drag queen, homosexual, transvestite, sex change,* and *cross-dresser.* I collected not only shows in which sex and gender nonconformity were explicit topics, but also programs in which they constituted a significant secondary conversation; since only one service could search full texts, I excluded these mixed shows from the cleanest, most formal sample to be coded and analyzed (which totaled 128 transcripts), but used these shows to build my interpretive discussion.

With my research assistant, I developed a set of coding categories with which to conduct an analysis of the content of the transcribed programs. The narrower sample of programs (that is, the shows where a *title or summary* indicated a sex- or gender-nonconformity topic) were coded along the following dimensions:

1. The *type of sex or gender topic or population* under consideration, as defined by the show's title and summary, checked against the guest composition (e.g., gay drag, lesbianism, male-to-female transsexualism, heterosexual cross-dressing, etc.).
2. The *program format,* as defined by the show's title and summary, checked against the transcript as a whole. Categories: family conflict; male-female relationship troubles; same-sex relationship troubles; mixed same-sex and opposite-sex relationship troubles; political issue; makeovers; pageants, displays, contests, or performances; secrets revealed; sexual nonmonogamy; testimonials; other.
3. The primary, secondary, and tertiary *narrative themes or discussion frames.* This, the most subjective of the measures, refers to the main terms of discussion—what is at issue in the program. Themes or frames were ranked according to their centrality to the discussion as a whole, indicated by the length of discussion of its core issues. *Boundary frames:* telling the difference (versus claim that there is none) between "real" man or woman and transsexual; telling the difference between straight and gay, lesbian, or bisexual; telling the difference between gay/lesbian and bisexual. *Causal frames:* choice versus biology as the cause of homosexuality; choice versus biology as the cause of transgender status. *Morality frames:* the morality or immorality of gender change; the morality or immorality of homosexuality. *Sexual fidelity frame:* monogamy versus promiscuity or nonmonogamy. *Honesty frame:* truthfulness versus telling lies. *Therapeutic frame:* acceptance or self-acceptance versus "living a lie." *Political frame:* group or individual rights, claims, or grievances. *Gender display frame:* exhibition of guests before and after gender transition. *Status of gay identity frame:* fixity or reality versus fluidity or impermanence of gay, lesbian, bisexual, or transgender status. *Tolerance frame:* tolerance versus intolerance of differences.
4. Level of *audience participation* (low, moderate, high) as measured by number of comments made by distinct audience members and/or number of sentences in comments.
5. *Guest composition,* based on guests' self-descriptions of their own identities (e.g., heterosexual woman, nontranssexual lesbian, bisexual male expert, heterosexual transsexual woman, etc.).

After coding, we investigated general frequency distributions (the proportion of bi-sexual topics, for instance, in comparison to homosexual ones) and various relationships within the sample: how narrative themes are distributed among different types of program formats (for example, the proportion of family-conflict shows that emphasize therapeutic themes, compared to the same theme in testimonial-style programming); how program types and the population focus interact (for instance, the percentage of bisexuality-focused shows that are about sexual fidelity, compared to that same issue on lesbian-focused programs); how narrative frames and population focus interact (the relative prominence of causal themes, for example, in gay-focused and transsexual-focused programs), and so on.

I have been cautious about using the results of this content analysis to draw much more than broad outlines of talk show content, for three reasons. First, the sample has some limitations: since many more shows were produced in the mid-1990s, it is heavily weighted toward the 1994–95 period, a period of competition and sensationalism; since not all shows are transcribed, it is necessarily incomplete; it is relatively small. Second, although one other study provides something close,[3] there is no solid basis for comparison to the general universe of TV talk show content. My sample gives a picture of this particular subset of show topics, but not of the overlap between gay, lesbian, bisexual, and transgender shows and their heterosexually themed counterparts. Finally, numerically based content analysis simply has built-in limitations. The coding scheme must obviously be invented, which means that the researchers' interpretations of what constitutes a relevant, sensible category are unavoidably already part of the research design; this is less the case for the least interesting things being measured (e.g., guest composition), and more the case for the most interesting aspects (e.g., narrative themes). Counting up aspects of cultural content, moreover, does not give nearly enough information about the *meanings* that inhere in cultural texts. For these reasons, with the coded content analysis as a backdrop, I have relied much more heavily on the patterns revealed by close readings of the collected transcripts and videos. Nonetheless, some of the key results of the coding, presented below, may interest readers.

General frequency distributions
Guests

Heterosexual	44%	($N = 521$)
Gay or lesbian	22%	($N = 255$)
Bisexual	12%	($N = 138$)
Transsexual	10%	($N = 111$)
Cross-dresser	7%	($N = 77$)
Expert	5%	($N = 52$)

Topics

Homosexual topics	43%	($N = 55$)
Transsexual topics	23%	($N = 30$)
Bisexual topics	18%	($N = 23$)
Mixed topics	8%	($N = 10$)
Cross-dressing topics	7%	($N = 9$)

Formats
Guest testimonials	23%	(N = 31)
Relationship troubles	19%	(N = 24)
Political issues	19%	(N = 24)
Family conflict	17%	(N = 22)
Displays	7%	(N = 9)
Violence	7%	(N = 9)
Nonmonogamy	4%	(N = 5)

Primary themes
Political themes	18%	(N = 21)
Morality themes	17%	(N = 20)
Therapeutic themes	12%	(N = 15)
Boundary themes	11%	(N = 14)
Honesty themes	10%	(N = 13)
Sexual fidelity themes	7%	(N = 9)
Identity status themes	5%	(N = 6)
Tolerance themes	5%	(N = 6)

Distributions in interaction

Common formats of lesbian, gay male, and homosexual programs
Political issues	56%	(N = 16)
Family conflict	17%	(N = 5)
Relationship troubles	14%	(N = 4)
Guest testimonials	10%	(N = 3)

Common formats of transsexual and cross-dresser programs
Family conflict	27%	(N = 11)
Testimonials	23%	(N = 9)
Display/performance	21%	(N = 8)
Relationship troubles	13%	(N = 5)
Violence/crime	13%	(N = 5)

Common formats for bisexual programs
Testimonials	40%	(N = 9)
Relationship troubles	30%	(N = 7)
Nonmonogamy	17%	(N = 4)

Common themes on lesbian, gay male, and homosexual programs
Political	21%	(N = 28)
Morality	20%	(N = 24)
Tolerance	14%	(N = 17)
Therapeutic	13%	(N = 16)
Causes of homosexuality	12%	(N = 15)

Common themes on bisexual programs
Morality	21%	(N = 11)
Sexual fidelity	19%	(N = 10)

Causes of bisexuality	16%	$(N = 9)$
Category boundaries	16%	$(N = 9)$
Common themes on transsexual programs		
Category boundaries	24%	$(N = 17)$
Honesty	21%	$(N = 15)$
Morality	17%	$(N = 12)$
Therapeutic	17%	$(N = 12)$

Audiences

With my participation and observation at talk show tapings, I had a good deal of information about studio-audience behaviors and responses. I wanted, however, something more: data about the ways viewing audiences watch and interpret talk shows in general, and talk shows on sex and gender nonconformity in particular. To get at these, I organized thirteen discussion groups, with seventy-nine people grouped according to various dimensions. Discussions, which included between four and eight participants and lasted between one and one-and-a-half hours each, were taped and transcribed. In addition to nine discussions with heterosexually identified viewers (a total of forty-seven participants), I conducted three discussions with gay men and lesbians (a total of twenty participants) and met with a local transgender group, Manhattan Gender Network, for a less formal discussion (a total of twelve participants).

The baseline requirement for participation was regular talk show viewing, defined as watching once a week or more. With the exception of one group (the Manhattan Gender Network discussion), the discussions were organized and run according to a standard focus-group model.[4] Enlisted over the phone by professional focus-group recruiters using a screening questionnaire, potential participants were asked questions about age, family income, educational background, employment status, marital status, children, occupation, self-categorization of occupation (as professional/managerial, technical, blue-collar, or other), spouse's occupation, racial background, gender, and talk show–viewing regularity. Heterosexually identified viewers were also asked four questions that indicate attitudes toward homosexuality: whether they agree or disagree that homosexuality is an acceptable lifestyle, that gay men and lesbians are unjustly denied civil rights, that homosexuals should be allowed to marry, and that they themselves feel comfortable in the presence of lesbians, gay men, or bisexuals. All of these participants were paid at the end of the meeting.

The heterosexual groups met at the offices of a focus-group firm, Field Work East, in Fort Lee, New Jersey; all of the participants were from surrounding New Jersey towns. Some of the groups were mixed (men and women, people from a range of educational, socioeconomic, and racial backgrounds, people with conservative attitudes toward homosexuality, and so forth), while others were grouped along particular dimensions (men, women with college education, people with conservative attitudes toward homosexuality, and so on). The gay and lesbian groups met in an office space in Manhattan; all of the participants were from the New York City area. One group was mixed men and women, one gay men only, the third lesbians only. (Most of the lesbian and gay participants were highly educated. Thus I am reticent to draw firm conclusions about much more than the response of urban, educated lesbians and gay men.) Like the interviews, the discussions were loosely structured, with standard areas covered but room for the conversations to move where discussants wanted to take them. Details of the groups' compositions, along with a discussion protocol, follow.

Focus groups: heterosexually identified viewers

Participant overview. 24 men and 23 women; 18 aged 18–34, 16 aged 35–54, 13 aged 55 and over; 35 white, 8 African American, 4 Hispanic; 24 with high school education, 23 with some college or more; 27 with conservative attitudes toward homosexuality, 20 with liberal attitudes. Occupations: bartender, nurse, bus driver, computer operator, engineer, phone-company manager, security supervisor, home health aide, cafeteria worker, teacher's assistant, secretary, nurse's aide, truck driver, human resources director, paralegal, pie maker, medical assistant, interior decorator, caseworker, painter, stage setter, police officer, data-entry worker, filmmaker, several teachers, several homemakers, several salespeople, 2 bookkeepers, 2 security guards, and 2 Teamsters.

Group overview. Group 1: Men and women (mixed education, income, age, race, attitudes). Group 2: Men and women (mixed education, income, age, race, attitudes). Group 3: White men and women (mixed education, income, age, attitudes). Group 4: Women with high school education or less (mixed income, age, race, attitudes). Group 5: Women with some college education or more (mixed income, age, race, attitudes). Group 6: Conservative women (mixed education, income, age, race). Group 7: Men (mixed education, income, age, race, attitudes). Group 8: Conservative men (mixed education, income, age, race). Group 9: White men with some college education or more, higher income (mixed age, attitudes).

Focus groups: lesbian- and gay-identified viewers

Participant overview. 10 men and 10 women; 13 aged 18–34, 7 aged 35–54; 13 white, 2 African American, 2 Hispanic, 3 Asian American; 2 with high school education, 18 with some college or more. Occupations: bartender, filmmaker, cosmetician, photographer, special-events coordinator, network manager, stage manager, theatrical licenser, volunteer coordinator, artist, word processor, paramedic, restaurant manager, fund raiser, computer analyst, 2 students, and 2 administrative assistants.

Group overview. Group 1: Lesbians (mixed education, race, age, income). Group 2: Gay men, all college educated (mixed race, age, income). Group 3: Gay men and lesbians (mixed education, race, age, income).

Methods

Focus-group discussion guide

1. Talk show watching.
   a. Why do you watch talk shows (learning, entertainment, etc.)?
   b. How do you select a show to watch on any given day (by topic, by host, by convenience)?
   c. What are your favorite shows? Are there shows you won't watch?
   d. What are your favorite kinds of topics? Are there topics you won't watch?
2. Perspectives on talk shows.
   a. Do you think the shows are for real?
   b. Would you ever go on a talk show? Why or why not? What do you think of the people who go on them? Why do you think people go on the shows?
3. How would you categorize the types of shows out there? What are the different categories of show topics (e.g. news, current events, unusual lifestyles, parent-child conflict, relationship conflict, gossip, etc.)?
4. Sex and gender topics on talk shows.
   a. What types of shows that deal with sexuality can you recall or have you noticed? Do any particular shows about sexuality stand out in your mind?
   b. Do you like these kinds of shows? Why/why not?
   c. Where do gays, lesbians, bisexuals, or transsexuals fit most often in the topic types you've listed?
   d. How would you characterize the ways homosexuality comes across on talk shows you've watched? Negatively? Positively? Accurately? What do you think of these portrayals?
   e. How about bisexuals? Transsexuals? Cross-dressers?
   f. Do you think watching talk shows has affected your attitudes toward homosexuals, bisexuals, transsexuals, and so on? (For gay groups: Have talk shows played a role at all in how you understood being gay or lesbian?)

Notes

Chapter 1

1. Vicki Abt and Mel Seesholtz, "The Shameless World of Phil, Sally, and Oprah: Television Talk Shows and the Deconstructing of Society," *Journal of Popular Culture* 28, no. 1 (1994): 211.

2. Howard Kurtz, *Hot Air: All Talk, All the Time* (New York: Times Books, 1996), 52.

3. In *The Advocate*, December 12, 1995, 12.

4. Ruth Bonapace et al., "Is It Time to Turn Off Talk TV?" *First*, June 12, 1995, 90–94.

5. Michel Foucault, *The History of Sexuality,* volume 1 (New York: Vintage, 1990), chapter 1. Readers familiar with Foucault's work will notice his general influence on this book as a whole, in his observations that modern sexuality is organized not around a principle of repression, but through "the wide dispersion of devices that were invented for speaking about it, for having it be spoken about, for inducing it to speak of itself, for listening, recording, transcribing, and redistributing what is said about it" (34); in his questioning of whether increased speech about sexuality offers possibilities for liberation, or rather its reverse; and in his observation that contemporary power operates largely by delineating the normal from the abnormal in myriad ways, most prominently by making visible and stigmatizing the "abnormal." On this sort of "normalizing" power, see also Michel Foucault, *Discipline and Punish* (New York: Vintage, 1979). (For an extension of Foucault's ideas to lesbian and gay politics, see Mark Blasius, *Gay and Lesbian Politics: Sexuality and the Emergence of a New Ethic* [Philadelphia: Temple University Press, 1994], and to AIDS politics, see Joshua Gamson, "Silence, Death, and the Invisible Enemy: AIDS Activism and Social Movement 'Newness,' " *Social Problems* 36, no. 4 [1989]: 351–67.) Foucault was, in the end, perhaps more pessimistic than I, and not especially interested in the mass media as one of the many "regimes of truth" ferreting out sexuality and making it "speak of itself," but I am clearly indebted to basic insights of his writing.

6. Although I use other terms as well (gay, lesbian, bisexual, and transgender; queer; sexual minorities), I work primarily with the somewhat awkward *sex and gender nonconformity* because it calls attention to the social and relational aspects of sex and gender statuses. "Minority" implies a fixed, unchanging shared characteristic, and "gay or lesbian" tends also to imply an essential, stable kind of self; "sex and gender nonconformist" serves as a reminder that sex and gender identities are constructed with reference to, and through exclusion of, those with identities tagged as deviant. I do not mean to suggest that nonconformity is embraced by all lesbians, gays, transgenders, and bisexuals, only that it is their status as outsiders to heterosexual or traditional gender norms, not some innate difference, that is socially relevant.

I use the term *transgender* to encompass the range of people whose presentation, identity, or behavior involves crossing from one gender to another: transsexuals (who live or seek to live in the gender "opposite" to that assigned to them at birth, and typically change their bodies through surgery and/or hormone treatment) and cross-dressers (who change their gender presentation for periods of time, but usually live at least part-time in the gender assigned to them at birth), including drag queens and tranvestites.

7. Chris Bull and John Gallagher, "Talked to Death," *Advocate,* April 18, 1995, 20–22; Michelangelo Signorile, "The *Jenny Jones* Murder: What Really Happened?" *OUT,* June 1995, 26–29, 142–46; Michelle Green, "Fatal Attraction," *People,* March 27, 1995, 40–44.

8. In Janice Kaplan, "Are Talk Shows out of Control?" *TV Guide,* April 1, 1995, 12.

9. Jeanne Albronda Heaton and Nona Leigh Wilson, *Tuning in Trouble: Talk TV's Destructive Impact on Mental Health* (San Francisco: Jossey-Bass, 1995), 129, 144, 252–58.

10. Jill Nelson, "Talk Is Cheap," *The Nation,* June 5, 1995, 801.

11. Abt and Seesholtz, 206.

12. Kurtz, 62.

13. Heaton and Wilson, 127–28.

14. Neal Gabler, "Audience Stays Superior to the Exploitalk Shows," *Los Angeles Times,* March 19, 1995, M1.

15. Kurtz, 62. My own use of the word *freaks* in the title, and throughout the book, is meant to call attention to rather than reproduce the stigmatization of sex and gender nonconformists, and to complicate the notion that talk shows can simply be understood as freak shows. I use the word as neither a pejorative nor a description of how people see themselves—most people seen as freaks, it's safe to assume, view themselves as human rather than as curiosities—but as a description of a stigmatized social status, a label put on certain populations of people who, in radical ways, do not fit what is at any given time perceived as the natural order. (The word itself, according to Leslie Fiedler, is an abbreviation for "freak of nature," itself a "translation of the Latin *lusus naturae,* a term implying that a two-headed child or a Hermaphrodite is ludicrous as well as anomalous" [*Freaks: Myths and Images of the*

Secret Self (New York: Anchor Books, 1978), 19].) The title, in fact, is intended as both description and prescription: the stigmatized *are* talking back, and they *ought to* keep talking back.

16. Heaton and Wilson, 131–32, 163.

17. Kurtz, 63.

18. In Empower America, "Press Conference" (Washington, DC: Federal Document Clearing House, October 26, 1995).

19. In Maureen Dowd, "Talk Is Cheap," *New York Times,* October 26, 1995, A25.

20. In Scotty Dupree, "Targeting Talk TV," *Mediaweek,* October 30, 1995, 4.

21. Empower America.

22. Kurtz, 52.

23. In Kurtz, 67.

24. Kurtz, 63.

25. Heaton and Wilson, 118.

26. Elayne Rapping, "Daytime Inquiries," *Progressive,* October 1991, 37.

27. Sonia Livingstone and Peter Lunt, *Talk on Television: Audience Participation and Public Debate* (London: Routledge, 1994), 102.

28. In Joe Chidley, "Taking In the Trash," *McClean's,* February 19, 1996, 53.

29. For a historical and theoretical treatment of criticisms of mass culture, see Patrick Brantlinger, *Bread and Circuses: Theories of Mass Culture as Social Decay* (New York: Cornell University Press, 1985); for a discussion of the vexed relationship between intellectuals and popular culture, see Andrew Ross, *No Respect: Intellectuals and Popular Culture* (New York: Routledge, 1989).

30. Cable News Network, *Larry King Live* ("Interview with Phil Donahue"), February 5, 1996.

31. In Stephen Seplow, "Seduced and Abandoned," *Philadelphia Inquirer Magazine,* September 24, 1995, 24.

32. ABC News, *Nightline* ("Phil Donahue"), January 26, 1996.

33. Ellen Willis, "Bring In the Noise," *The Nation,* April 1, 1996, 22–23.

34. Donna Gaines, "How Jenny Jones Saved My Life," *Village Voice,* November 21, 1995, 43.

35. In Mark Schone, "Talked Out," *Spin,* May 1996, 74.

36. Kurtz, 61.

37. In Schone, 74.

38. Livingstone and Lunt, 31. Talk shows, for analysts like Livingstone and Lunt, appear as something of a test of the quality and quantity of media-sponsored rational-critical debate, and thus of the nature of the contemporary public sphere. The central theoretical concern in most of these academic approaches is the nature of the "public sphere," and the key figure of reference is Jürgen Habermas, who has written influentially about the conditions "for a rational-critical debate about public issues conducted by private persons willing to let arguments and not statuses determine decisions," suggesting that "a public sphere adequate to a democratic polity

deepens upon both quality and quantity of participation" (Craig Calhoun, ed., *Habermas and the Public Sphere* [Cambridge: MIT Press, 1992], 1–2), and that "public opinion is no longer a process of rational discourse but the result of publicity and social engineering in the media" (Peter Dahlgren, introduction to *Communication and Citizenship,* ed. Peter Dahlgren and Colin Sparks [London: Routledge, 1991], 4). For Habermas's original argument, see Jürgen Habermas, *The Structural Transformation of the Public Sphere,* trans. Thomas Burger (Cambridge: MIT Press, 1991). For critical overviews, see the Calhoun and Dahlgren volumes; and for an assessment from a feminist perspective, see Nancy Fraser, "What's Critical about Critical Theory? The Case of Habermas and Gender," in *Unruly Practices: Power, Discourse, and Gender in Contemporary Social Theory* (Minneapolis: University of Minnesota Press, 1989). Although the general concern over the nature of the public sphere certainly plays into my analysis, I am more interested here in how the pull between rational debate and entertaining display—cultural activities that anyway are never rigidly distinguishable, something Habermas is criticized for overlooking—interacts with the drawing of social boundaries between public and private, normal and abnormal.

39. Gloria-Jean Masciarotte, "C'mon, Girl: Oprah Winfrey and the Discourse of Feminine Talk," *Genders,* no. 11 (1991): 84.

40. Paolo Carpignano et al., "Chatter in the Age of Electronic Reproduction: Talk Television and the 'Public Mind,'" *Social Text,* nos. 25–26 (1990): 35, 52.

41. Masciarotte, 86–87.

42. Livingstone and Lunt, 33.

43. Carpignano et al., 51.

44. In Seplow, 14.

45. Richard Goldstein, "The Devil in Ms. Jones," *Village Voice,* November 21, 1995, 45.

46. Masciarotte, 90–91.

47. Jane Shattuc, *The Talking Cure: TV Talk Shows and Women* (New York: Routledge, 1997), 129.

48. Masciarotte, 90–91.

49. Masciarotte, 83.

50. Wayne Munson, *All Talk: The Talkshow in Media Culture* (Philadelphia: Temple University Press, 1994).

51. This moving around of public-private boundaries (and other social boundaries) is also a more general effect of new media technologies, as Joshua Meyrowitz argues in *No Sense of Place: The Impact of Electronic Media on Social Behavior* (New York: Oxford University Press, 1985).

52. See Joshua Gamson, "Must Identity Movements Self-Destruct? A Queer Dilemma," *Social Problems* 42 (1995): 390–407; Joshua Gamson, "The Organizational Shaping of Collective Identity: The Case of Lesbian and Gay Film Festivals in New York," *Sociological Forum* 11 (1996): 231–62.

53. See, for instance, Cathy Cohen, "Contested Membership: Black Gay Identities and the Politics of AIDS," in *Queer Theory/Sociology,* ed. Steven Seidman (Cambridge, MA: Blackwell, 1996), 362–94; Stephen O. Murray, *Latin American Male Homosexualities* (Albuquerque: University of New Mexico Press, 1995); Audre Lorde, *Sister Outsider* (Trumansburg, NY: Crossing Press, 1984); Essex Hemphill, ed., *Brother to Brother: New Writings by Black Gay Men* (Boston: Alyson, 1991); Dorothy Allison, *Skin: Talking about Sex, Class, and Literature* (Ithaca, NY: Firebrand Books, 1994).

54. See, for example, Henry Abelove, Michéle Aina Barale, and David Halperin, eds., *The Lesbian and Gay Studies Reader* (New York: Routledge, 1993); Donald Morton, ed., *The Material Queer: A LesBiGay Cultural Studies Reader* (Boulder, CO: Westview, 1996); Judith Lorber, *Paradoxes of Gender* (New Haven: Yale University Press, 1994).

55. See, for example, R. Jeffrey Ringer, ed., *Queer Words, Queer Images: Communication and the Construction of Homosexuality* (New York: New York University Press, 1994); Vito Russo, *The Celluloid Closet: Homosexuality in the Movies,* 2d ed. (New York: Harper & Row, 1987); Fred Fejes and Kevin Petrich, "Invisibility, Homophobia, and Heterosexism: Lesbians, Gays, and the Media," *Critical Studies in Mass Communication* (December 1993): 396–422.

56. Gayle Rubin, "Thinking Sex: Notes for a Radical Theory of the Politics of Sexuality," in *The Lesbian and Gay Studies Reader,* ed. Henry Abelove, Michéle Aina Barale, and David Halperin (New York: Routledge, 1993), 10.

57. See Lorber; Edward Stein, ed., *Forms of Desire: Sexual Orientation and the Social Constructionist Controversy* (New York: Routledge, 1992); Steven Seidman, ed., *Queer Theory/Sociology* (Cambridge, MA: Blackwell, 1996).

58. See Jeffrey Weeks, *Sexuality and Its Discontents* (New York: Routledge, 1985); John D'Emilio, *Sexual Politics, Sexual Communities: The Making of a Homosexual Minority in the United States* (Chicago: University of Chicago Press, 1983); Stephen O. Murray, *American Gay* (Chicago: University of Chicago Press, 1996).

59. See John Gagnon and William Simon, *Sexual Conduct* (Chicago: University of Chicago Press, 1973); Ken Plummer, "Symbolic Interactionism and the Forms of Homosexuality," in *Queer Theory/Sociology,* ed. Steven Seidman (Cambridge, MA: Blackwell, 1996), 64–82; Candace West and Don Zimmerman, "Doing Gender," *Gender and Society* 1 (1987): 125–51.

60. Lorber, 6.

61. Steven Seidman, "Identity Politics in a 'Postmodern' Gay Culture: Some Historical and Conceptual Notes," in *Fear of a Queer Planet,* ed. Michael Warner (Minneapolis: University of Minnesota Press, 1993). Some exceptions to this, works taking up the structural or institutional moorings of sexual categories, include D'Emilio; Murray; Verta Taylor and Nancy Whittier, "Collective Identity in Social Movement Communities: Lesbian Feminist Mobilization," in *Frontiers in Social Movement Theory,* ed. Aldon Morris and Carol Mueller (New Haven: Yale University Press, 1992), 104–29.

62. See Diana Crane, *The Sociology of Culture* (Cambridge, MA: Blackwell, 1994).

63. See Todd Gitlin, *Inside Prime Time* (New York: Pantheon, 1983); Herbert Gans, *Deciding What's News* (New York: Vintage, 1979).

64. Fejes and Petrich, 412; Emile C. Netzhammer and Scott A. Shamp, "Guilt by Association: Homosexuality and AIDS on Prime-Time Television," in *Queer Words, Queer Images: Communication and the Construction of Homosexuality*, ed. R. Jeffrey Ringer (New York: New York University Press, 1994), 104; Darlene M. Hantzis and Valerie Lehr, "Whose Desire? Lesbian (Non)Sexuality and Television's Perpetuation of Hetero/Sexism," in Ringer, 118; Larry Gross, "What Is Wrong with This Picture? Lesbian Women and Gay Men on Television," in Ringer, 152. See also Russo; Larry Gross, "Out of the Mainstream: Sexual Minorities and the Mass Media," in *Remote Control: Television, Audiences, and Cultural Power,* ed. Ellen Seiter (New York: Routledge, 1989); Marguerite J. Moritz, "Old Strategies for New Texts: How American Television Is Creating and Treating Lesbian Characters," in Ringer.

65. Russo, 244.

66. Russo, 325.

67. Gross, "What Is Wrong with This Picture?" 143.

68. See, for instance, Jon Cruz and Justin Lewis, eds., *Viewing, Reading, Listening: Audiences and Cultural Reception* (Boulder, CO: Westview, 1994); Joshua Gamson, *Claims to Fame: Celebrity in Contemporary America* (Berkeley: University of California Press, 1994); Oliver Boyd-Barrett and Chris Newbold, eds., *Approaches to Media* (London: Arnold, 1995); Andrea L. Press, *Women Watching Television: Gender, Class, and Generation in the American Television Experience* (Philadelphia: University of Pennsylvania Press, 1991).

Chapter Two

1. Peter Verney, *Here Comes the Circus* (New York: Paddington Press, 1978), 231.

2. See Wayne Munson, *All Talk: The Talkshow in Media Culture* (Philadelphia: Temple University Press, 1994). Munson, and Jane Shattuc in *The Talking Cure: TV Talk Shows and Women* (New York: Routledge, 1997) provide the deepest and most sophisticated histories of the genre, and the outlines of my historical treatment are informed by their work, supplemented by other historical accounts of commercial entertainments, rather than from independent historical research. I am emphasizing here something that talk show historians underplay, however: the mix of class cultures in talk shows' seeds. On the history of talk shows since the rise of electronic broadcasting, see Brian G. Rose, "The Talk Show," in *TV Genres: A Handbook and Reference Guide,* ed. Brian G. Rose (Westport, CT: Greenwood Press, 1985); Jeanne Albronda Heaton and Nona Leigh Wilson, *Tuning in Trouble: Talk TV's Destructive Impact on Mental Health* (San Francisco: Jossey-Bass, 1995), especially chapter 1; Gini Graham Scott, *Can We Talk? The Power and Influence of Talk Shows* (New York: Insight Books, 1996).

3. Heaton and Wilson, 18.

4. Heaton and Wilson, 18.

5. ABC News, *Nightline* ("Phil Donahue"), January 26, 1996.

6. Heaton and Wilson, 25.

7. Heaton and Wilson, 30.

8. ABC News.

9. Heaton and Wilson, 31.

10. Munson, 20. See also Jürgen Habermas, *The Structural Transformation of the Public Sphere,* trans. Thomas Burger (Cambridge: MIT Press, 1991).

11. Munson, 21.

12. Munson, 23–24. See also Amy Beth Aronson, *Understanding Equals: Audience and Articulation in the Early American Women's Magazine* (Ph.D. dissertation, Columbia University, 1996).

13. Munson, 25–26. See also Kathy Peiss, *Cheap Amusements: Working Women and Leisure in Turn-of-the-Century New York* (Philadelphia: Temple University Press, 1986).

14. Munson, 25.

15. Lawrence W. Levine, "William Shakespeare and the American People: A Study in Cultural Transformation," in *Rethinking Popular Culture,* ed. Chandra Mukerji and Michael Schudson (Berkeley: University of California Press, 1991), 165.

16. Levine, 166–68.

17. Levine, 167, my emphasis. Levine describes, for instance, a performance of *Richard III* at New York's Bowery Theater in 1842, where "the holiday audience . . . overflowed onto the stage and entered into the spirit of things. . . . They examined Richard's royal regalia with interest, hefted his sword, and tried on his crown; they moved up to get a close look at the ghosts of King Henry, Lady Anne, and the children when these characters appeared on stage; they mingled with the soldiers during the battle of Bosworth Field and responded to the roll of drums and blast of trumpets by racing across the stage" (168).

18. Levine, 164.

19. John S. Gilkeson, *Middle-Class Providence, 1820–1940* (Princeton: Princeton University Press, 1986), 260.

20. Paul DiMaggio, "Cultural Entrepreneurship in Nineteenth-Century Boston: The Creation of an Organizational Base for High Culture in America," in *Rethinking Popular Culture: Contemporary Perspectives in Cultural Studies,* ed. Chandra Mukerji and Michael Schudson (Berkeley: University of California Press, 1991), 376. See also E. Digby Baltzell, *The Protestant Establishment: Aristocracy and Caste in America* (London: Secker & Warburg, 1965).

21. Verney; Carl Hammer and Gideon Bosker, *Freak Show: Sideshow Banner Art* (San Francisco: Chronicle Books, 1996); Robert Bogdan, *Freak Show: Presenting Human Oddities for Amusement and Profit* (Chicago: University of Chicago Press, 1988).

22. Bogdan, 94.

23. Hammer and Bosker.

24. Leslie Fiedler, *Freaks: Myths and Images of the Secret Self* (New York: Anchor Books, 1978), 24.

25. Verney, 226. See also P. T. Barnum, *Struggles and Triumphs* (Harmondsworth, England: Penguin Books, 1981); Neil Harris, *Humbug: The Art of P. T. Barnum* (Boston: Little, Brown & Co., 1973). In a further echo of the talk show debates, one author of a history of the circus complains that "nowadays sociologists preach of exploitation, and pity has taken the place of revulsion," and that it must not be "forgotten that it is by exhibiting themselves that these 'Very Special People' can best make a living. They find no shame in this. . . . They were exploited, surely, but exploited by mutual consent" (Verney, 229).

26. Hammer and Bosker, 10.

27. Fiedler, 22.

28. Investigative News Group, *Geraldo* ("A Televised Sex Change Operation and Other Transsexual Tales"), January 27, 1995.

29. Investigative News Group, *Geraldo* ("Girly to Burly: Women Who Become Men"), April 18, 1994.

30. Roland Marchand, *Advertising the American Dream* (Berkeley: University of California Press, 1985), 54. See also Regina Kunzel, "Pulp Fictions and Problem Girls: Reading and Rewriting Single Pregnancy in the Postwar United States," *American Historical Review* 100, no. 6 (1995): 1465–87.

31. Shattuc, 17–18, 24. For more on both early and contemporary tabloids, see S. Elizabeth Bird, *For Enquiring Minds: A Cultural Study of Supermarket Tabloids* (Knoxville: University of Tennessee Press, 1992). Tabloids, like talk shows, have been attacked as "degrading, demoralizing villains that pandered to the lowest instincts" (21).

32. Munson, 5, 10–11.

33. Rose, 334.

34. Shattuc, 33–34.

35. Rose, 334.

36. Munson, 1. Television talk show audiences are roughly 80 percent female, while talk radio audiences are around 40 percent female (Shattuc, 8).

37. Munson, 42.

38. Heaton and Wilson, 11. See also James C. Roberts, "The Power of Talk Radio," *American Enterprise*, May–June 1991, 56–61.

39. Rose, 339.

40. Heaton and Wilson, 15.

41. Heaton and Wilson.

42. Phil Donahue & Co., *Donahue: My Own Story* (New York: Simon & Schuster, 1979).

43. Multimedia Entertainment, "The Donahue 25th Anniversary Special," November 15, 1992.

44. Munson, 61.

45. Paolo Carpignano et al., "Chatter in the Age of Electronic Reproduction: Talk Television and the 'Public Mind,' " *Social Text,* nos. 25–26 (1990): 47.

46. Munson, 44.

47. Carpignano et al., 51.

48. Donal Carbaugh, *Talking American: Cultural Discourses on Donahue* (Norwood, NJ: Ablex Publishing, 1989), 21, 37.

49. Robert N. Bellah et al., *Habits of the Heart: Individualism and Commitment in American Life* (Berkeley: University of California Press, 1985).

50. Edward Alwood, *Straight News: Gays, Lesbians, and the News Media* (New York: Columbia University Press, 1996), 96–97.

51. Alwood, 48–50, 86–88.

52. Alwood, 140, 143.

53. Multimedia Entertainment, *Donahue* ("Masters and Johnson"), April 23, 1979.

54. Multimedia Entertainment, "The Donahue 25th Anniversary Special."

55. Multimedia Entertainment, *Donahue* ("Gay Senior Citizens"), January 21, 1985.

56. Vito Russo, *The Celluloid Closet: Homosexuality in the Movies,* 2d ed. (New York: Harper & Row, 1987).

57. This is exactly the symbiosis described by Verta Taylor, who tells a similar story of the relationship between early talk shows and the postpartum-depression self-help movement. Taylor argues that a 1986 *Donahue* show, in fact, was the "single event that [defined] the transformation of a small group of women struggling to come to terms with their own personal agonies into a full-fledged social movement." Like the televised coming out of gay and lesbian activists, postpartum activists also used confessional "truth-telling" as a deliberate political strategy, in their case as a tool to redefine motherhood. See Verta Taylor, *Rock-a-by Baby: Feminism, Self-Help, and Postpartum Depression* (New York: Routledge, 1996), 59. On movements and media more generally, see William A. Gamson and Gadi Wolfsfeld, "Movements and Media as Interacting Systems," *Annals of the American Association of Political and Social Sciences* 528 (July 1993): 114–25; Todd Gitlin, *The Whole World Is Watching* (Berkeley: University of California Press, 1980); Harvey Molotch, "Media and Movements," in *The Dynamics of Social Movements,* ed. Mayer Zald and John McCarthy (Cambridge: Winthrop, 1979); Gadi Wolfsfeld, "The Symbiosis of Press and Protest: An Exchange Analysis," *Journalism Quarterly* 61 (1984): 550–56.

58. Gloria-Jean Masciarotte, "C'mon, Girl: Oprah Winfrey and the Discourse of Feminine Talk," *Genders,* no. 11 (1991): 94, 96.

59. Sally Jessy Raphael, *Sally: Unconventional Success* (New York: Morrow, 1990), 155.

60. Walter Goodman, "3 Queens of Talk Who Rule the Day," *New York Times,* July 29, 1991, C11.

61. Mimi White, *Tele-Advising: Therapeutic Discourse in American Television* (Chapel Hill: University of North Carolina Press, 1992), 22–23. Like the post-

partum-depression activists described by Verta Taylor, lesbian, gay, bisexual, and transgender organizers took advantage of this therapeutic bent, using the emotional language of the shows to undercut the rational authority claimed by representatives of medicine and science, and the personal disclosure to challenge the status-quo definitions of public and private. See Taylor, 59–61, 75–77, 115–17.

62. Cecilia Capuzzi, John Flinn, and Neal Koch, "Pushing the Limits of Talk-Show TV," *Channels,* May 1988, 94.

63. American Broadcasting Companies, *The Oprah Winfrey Show* ("Homophobia"), November 13, 1986.

64. Mark Schone, "Talked Out," *Spin,* May 1996, 68.

65. Schone, 68.

66. Mayer Rus, "Lake Victorious," *OUT,* June 1995, 78.

67. Rus, 78.

68. Rus, 76.

69. Schone, 68.

70. Schone, 67.

71. Schone, 69.

72. Schone, 69.

Chapter Three

1. Multimedia Entertainment, *Sally Jessy Raphael* ("My Husband Left Me because He's Gay"), August 8, 1995.

2. King World, *Rolonda* ("Family Secrets: Straight Women, Gay Husbands"), November 17, 1994.

3. King World, *Oprah* ("The Fallout of a Gay Husband's Affair"), May 4, 1994.

4. Debbie Epstein and Deborah Lynn Steinberg, "Straight Talking on the Oprah Winfrey Show," in *Border Patrols: Policing Sexual Boundaries,* ed. Politics of Sexuality Group (London: Cassell, 1996).

5. King World, *Oprah* ("Straight Spouses and Gay Ex-Husbands"), February 24, 1992.

6. Jeanne Albronda Heaton and Nona Leigh Wilson, *Tuning in Trouble: Talk TV's Destructive Impact on Mental Health* (San Francisco: Jossey-Bass, 1995), 31, 90–91.

7. Jane Pratt, "I Am a Talk-Show-Host Survivor," *Glamour,* September 1995, 173.

8. In Meredith Berkman, "Daytime Talk Shows: Fake Guests Common in Battle for Ratings," *New York Post,* December 4, 1995, 8–9.

9. In Janice Kaplan, "Are Talk Shows out of Control?" *TV Guide,* April 1, 1995, 12.

10. In Laura Grindstaff, "Producing Trash, Class, and the Money Shot: A Behind the Scenes Account of Daytime TV Talkshows," in *Media Scandals,* ed. James Lull and Stephen Hinerman (London: Polity Press, 1997), 8.

11. In Meredith Berkman, "Liars Send in Clowns for Sicko Circuses," *New York Post,* December 4, 1995, 8.

12. Grindstaff, 9.

13. These kinds of risk-reducing manipulative activities, of course, are not unique to talk television, even if they are exaggerated in the genre. See Grindstaff; Joshua Gamson, "Incredible News," *American Prospect*, no. 19 (1994): 28–35.

14. Grindstaff, 2. Grindstaff's participation-observation study of a *Leeza*-like and *Springer*-like show provides the best guide to the day-to-day production of daytime talk shows. For a still largely relevant early study of the production of entertainment-talk, see Gaye Tuchman, "Assembling a Network Talk Show," in *The TV Establishment: Programming for Power and Profit,* ed. Gaye Tuchman (Englewood Cliffs, NJ: Prentice Hall, 1974), 119–35.

15. This coaching is less the case for shows recruited in the older way, by finding a story in a newspaper or magazine and booking those involved, or deciding on an issue to address and tracking down those who have been actively addressing the issue. Nonetheless, although in those cases guests may need less coaching, booking remains a casting job.

16. BBC Radio, "Coming Soon: TV's True Confessions," October 19, 1995.

17. Patricia Joyner Priest, *Public Intimacies: Talk Show Participants and Tell-All TV* (Cresskill, NJ: Hampton Press, 1995), 47.

18. Priest, chapter 5.

19. Grindstaff, 16.

20. In this, they become much like celebrities, operating in a mode I have elsewhere described as "semi-fictional." See Joshua Gamson, *Claims to Fame: Celebrity in Contemporary America* (Berkeley: University of California Press, 1994).

21. Gamson, "Incredible News."

22. Wayne Munson, *All Talk: The Talkshow in Media Culture* (Philadelphia: Temple University Press, 1994), 71, 74.

23. Munson, 45.

24. Shooting over time and editing down, although some shows do it more than others, is not efficient in terms of money or time. Thus much energy goes into pre-structuring the program, so that the content can be roughly predicted and controlled; dividing it into segments of an estimated length and sticking relatively close to them with an eye to the overall length of the show; directing camera shots during the taping. Ideally, shows are taped to be as close as possible to the final product (rather than rolling tape and multiple cameras and then editing, like a film, a final product), both because of resource considerations and because of the need for a "live," unedited feel.

25. Grindstaff, 6.

26. Perpetual Notion, Inc., *Marilu* ("Gay and Lesbian Parents"), April 4, 1995.

27. Multimedia Entertainment, *Donahue* ("Bisexuals Discriminated Against by Gays and Heterosexuals"), January 21, 1993.

28. Jenny Jones Show, *The Jenny Jones Show* ("Teenage Lesbians Defend Their Orientation"), February 23, 1993.

29. See Jane Shattuc, *The Talking Cure: TV Talk Shows and Women* (New York:

Routledge, 1997), chapter 5; Janice Peck, "TV Talk Shows as Therapeutic Discourse: The Ideological Labor of the Televised Talking Cure," *Communication Theory* 5, no. 1 (1995): 58–81; Franny Nudelman, "Beyond the Talking Cure: Listening to Female Testimony on *The Oprah Winfrey Show*," in *Inventing the Psychological: Toward a History of Emotional Life in America*, ed. Joel Pfister and Nancy Schnog (New Haven: Yale University Press, 1997), 297–315. For a discussion of the code of honesty on *Donahue*, see Donal Carbaugh, *Talking American: Cultural Discourses on Donahue* (Norwood, NJ: Ablex Publishing, 1989), chapter 7.

30. Patricia Hill Collins, *Black Feminist Thought: Knowledge, Consciousness, and the Politics of Empowerment* (New York: Routledge, 1991), 208. African American women, Collins suggests, make a distinction "between knowledge and wisdom, and the use of experience as the cutting edge dividing them, has been key to Black women's survival. . . . Knowledge without wisdom is adequate for the powerful, but wisdom is essential to the survival of the subordinate" (208). Moreover, "for Black women new knowledge claims are rarely worked out in isolation from other individuals and are usually developed through dialogues with other members of the community" (212), and "the theme of talking with the heart taps the ethic of caring, another dimension of an alternative epistemology used by African American women," which "suggests that personal expressiveness, emotions, and empathy are central to the knowledge validation process" (215). Other feminists make similar claims about concrete, firsthand experience as a central ground for "women's ways of knowing" (Mary Field Belenky et al., *Women's Ways of Knowing* [New York: Basic Books, 1986]). Despite the problems some of these analyses involve—most notably, fairly simplistic notions of gender categories and of the shared experiences of women from radically different backgrounds—they do point to an important cultural buoy for the experiential emphasis of talk shows. The use of personal "truth-telling," moreover, has been a central feminist movement organizing strategy, and one put to use directly on talk shows by women's self-help organizations (see Verta Taylor, *Rock-a-by Baby: Feminism, Self-Help, and Postpartum Depression* [New York: Routledge, 1996]).

31. Shattuc, 98.

32. "Essentialism," widely discussed in feminist and lesbian/gay studies in opposition to "constructionism," is basically the belief in a fixed, stable core housed in the self (be it soul, body, or psyche). When it comes to sexuality, this translates into the belief that there are simply different types of sexual essences (formed psychodynamically in early childhood, or present at birth in genes, chemistry, or the brain) and therefore different types of sexual beings. This becomes tied to political liberalism through the claim that innate differences such as these should not be the basis for discrimination. For more on these ideas, see the discussions in Edward Stein, ed., *Forms of Desire: Sexual Orientation and the Social Constructionist Controversy* (New York: Routledge, 1992). For an overview of the search for biological roots of sexual orientation, see Chandler Burr, *A Separate Creation: The Search for the Biological Origins of Sexual Orientation* (New York: Hyperion, 1996).

33. Paramount Pictures, *Ricki Lake* ("Listen, Family, I'm Gay . . . It's Not a Phase . . . Get over It!"), November 20, 1995; Columbia-Tristar Television, *Tempestt* ("I'm Gay, Get Used to It!"), July 31, 1996. Janice Peck makes a similar point about the use of therapeutic talk show discourse to define racism as a disease, in "Talk about Racism: Framing a Popular Discourse on Race on *Oprah Winfrey*," *Cultural Critique* 27 (spring 1994): 89–126.

34. Together, themes of "therapy" and "honesty" make up about a fifth of the shows in my sample. For more on the sample, the coding, and the distribution of themes within the sample, see the appendix.

35. Multimedia Entertainment, *Sally Jessy Raphael* ("My Teen Son Wants to Be a Woman"), June 27, 1995.

36. Investigative News Group, *Geraldo* ("Secret Lives Revealed"), August 21, 1996.

37. Investigative News Group, *Geraldo* ("You're Not the Man I Married"), February 14, 1994.

38. Multimedia Entertainment, *Sally Jessy Raphael* ("I Was Fooled"), May 17, 1994.

39. Multimedia Entertainment, *The Jerry Springer Show* ("My Boyfriend Turned Out to Be a Girl"), December 27, 1994.

40. Munson, 10–11.

41. Nudelman, 304.

42. All American Television, *Richard Bey* ("Coffee, Tea, or Death"), October 22, 1993.

43. Gloria-Jean Masciarotte, "C'mon, Girl: Oprah Winfrey and the Discourse of Feminine Talk," *Genders*, no. 11 (1991): 86.

44. Nudelman, 305.

45. Paramount Pictures, *Ricki Lake* ("You're Gay, How Dare You Raise a Child"), April 27, 1995.

46. Michel Foucault, *The History of Sexuality*, volume 1 (New York: Vintage, 1990), 61, 18, 33, 35.

47. "This emphasis on individual opinions, rights, and experience, however, places liberal discourse in a double bind," writes Janice Peck, discussing racial discourse on *Oprah*. "It becomes difficult to justify the liberal call to correct racially based inequities among different social groups' rights if racism is primarily a problem of and for individuals. Thus, the code of the individual cuts both ways: it can be used to criticize racial stereotyping (defined as a failure to recognize people as individuals), and it can be used to refute the argument that racism is based on, practiced by, and directed at social groups" ("Talk about Racism," 99).

48. Tribune Entertainment Co., *The Joan Rivers Show* ("Confusing Sexual Stories"), October 4, 1993. A few years later, Feinberg came out with a book version of this resistance to others' definitions. See Leslie Feinberg, *Transgender Warriors: Making History from Joan of Arc to RuPaul* (Boston: Beacon Press, 1996).

49. See Ronald Bayer, *Homosexuality and American Psychiatry* (New York:

Basic Books, 1981); Steven Epstein, *Impure Science: AIDS, Activism, and the Politics of Knowledge* (Berkeley: University of California Press, 1996). Epstein notes that activists not only claimed professional expertise, but also often invoked the authority of experience as well, in a mix that echoes talk show strategies of authority.

50. Tribune Entertainment Co.

Chapter Four

1. Multimedia Entertainment, *The Jerry Springer Show* ("Update: Teen Transsexuals"), July 22, 1994.

2. The Michigan State University study of talk show content, conducted somewhat differently from my own on a more general sample (transcripts of eighty different episodes from June–July 1995, videotapes from ten episodes of the eleven top Nielsen-rated shows of July–August 1995), provides interesting results for comparison. The study found that family relations and sexual activity were the major topics of discussion, that sexual propriety was the most common "proposition" under consideration, at issue in 50 percent of their sample, and that sexual orientation was a discussion topic on 11 percent of their sample. On average, they also found, sixteen personal disclosures are made per episode (42 percent by the guest about him or herself, 30 percent about another guest, and 28 percent by the host about a guest), with one of them disclosure of sexual orientation. See Bradley Greenberg et al., *The Content of Television Talk Shows: Topics, Guests, and Interactions* (Lansing: Michigan State University, November 1995).

3. King World, *Rolonda* ("Teen Secrets: Kids Who Are Gay"), March 2, 1994.

4. Multimedia Entertainment, *Sally Jessy Raphael* ("Former Homosexuals"), date unavailable.

5. Multimedia Entertainment, *Donahue* ("When Hatred against Gays Turns Deadly"), February 21, 1995; Multimedia Entertainment, *Donahue* ("Black Preacher Says I'll March with the KKK against Gays"), November 4, 1994; King World, *Rolonda* ("No Gays in My Town"), January 18, 1994; King World, *Rolonda* ("Bashing Gays for School Credit"), January 10, 1995; King World, *Oprah* ("School for Gay Teens"), October 24, 1994; King World, *Oprah* ("Gay Marriages"), December 19, 1989.

6. Multimedia Entertainment, *Sally Jessy Raphael* ("Former Homosexuals").

7. Investigative News Group, *Geraldo* ("Gay Today . . . Straight Tomorrow"), October 18, 1995.

8. Multimedia Entertainment, *The Jerry Springer Show* ("I Love Someone I Can't Have"), October 18, 1995; Multimedia Entertainment, *The Jerry Springer Show* ("Confess, You Liar!"), December 7, 1995; Multimedia Entertainment, *The Jerry Springer Show* ("I Can't Stand My Sibling"), December 19, 1995; Paramount Pictures, *Ricki Lake* ("Watch Me! Today I'm Going to Break Up My Ex and His New Chick"), July 29, 1996; Paramount Pictures, *Ricki Lake* ("You Both Have No Clue

Why You're Here . . . Surprise! I'm Hooking You Up"), September 15, 1995; Investigative News Group, *Geraldo* ("I Saw You on Geraldo and Just Had to Meet You"), October 10, 1995; Multimedia Entertainment, *Donahue* ("Is There Life after a Career in Porn?"), March 1, 1995; Multimedia Entertainment, *The Dennis Prager Show* ("Comedians against Prejudice"), August 11, 1995; Multimedia Entertainment, *Sally Jessy Raphael* ("Why I Was Fired"), April 13, 1994.

9. King World, *Oprah* ("Gay Marriages").

10. Multimedia Entertainment, *Donahue* ("Black Preacher Says I'll March with the KKK against Gays").

11. Paramount Pictures, *Ricki Lake* ("Get It Straight: I Don't Want Gays around My Kids"), June 15, 1995.

12. See, for example, Todd Gitlin, *Inside Prime Time* (New York: Pantheon, 1983); Robin Andersen, *Consumer Culture and TV Programming* (Boulder, CO: Westview, 1995); Herbert Gans, *Deciding What's News* (New York: Vintage, 1979).

13. Jane Shattuc, *The Talking Cure: TV Talk Shows and Women* (New York: Routledge, 1997), 66.

14. King World, *Rolonda* ("Bashing Gays for School Credit").

15. In Barbara Grizzuti Harrison, "The Importance of Being Oprah," *New York Times Magazine,* June 11, 1989, 130.

16. Multimedia Entertainment, *The Jerry Springer Show* ("Misssissippi Violence over Lesbian Camp"), February 14, 1994.

17. Investigative News Group, *Geraldo* ("Gay Teenagers at the High School Prom"), June 25, 1993.

18. King World, *Rolonda* ("Bashing Gays for School Credit").

19. Paramount Pictures, *Ricki Lake* ("White Men Fight Back: I'm Sick of Being Discriminated Against"), February 23, 1994.

20. Paramount Pictures, *Ricki Lake* ("Listen, Family, I'm Gay . . . It's Not a Phase . . . Get over It!"), November 20, 1995.

21. Paramount Pictures, *Ricki Lake* ("Get It Straight: I Don't Want Gays around My Kids"); Columbia-Tristar Television, *Tempestt* ("I'm Gay, Get Used to It!"), July 31, 1996.

22. Bertice Berry Show, *The Bertice Berry Show* ("Parents and Their Bisexual Kids"), November 16, 1993.

23. See Richard Schickel, *Intimate Strangers: The Culture of Celebrity* (New York: Fromm International, 1985); Andersen.

24. Paramount Pictures, *Ricki Lake* ("You're Gay, How Dare You Raise a Child"), April 27, 1995.

25. At issue here are the *formats* into which certain populations tend to appear—testimonials, which are more or less group interviews and storytelling, or family conflicts, or political issues, or relationship troubles, or displays such as pageants and makeovers. The way producers format a show does not always mean that *conversation* sticks within these particular boundaries, of course.

26. All American Television, *Richard Bey* ("Drag Queens vs. Real Women"),

August 24, 1995; Multimedia Entertainment, *Sally Jessy Raphael* ("Women Who Are Really Men"), April 17, 1995.

27. Paramount Pictures, *Maury Povich* ("Dad Wants to Be a Woman"), May 3, 1994.

28. American Family Association, *Action! Page,* January 1996, newsletter.

Chapter Five

1. Leslie Fiedler, *Freaks: Myths and Images of the Secret Self* (New York: Anchor Books, 1978), 24.

2. Susan Stryker, "My Words to Victor Frankenstein above the Village of Chamounix," *GLQ* 1 (1994): 240–41.

3. Judith Lorber, *Paradoxes of Gender* (New Haven: Yale University Press, 1994), 95, 18.

4. See Marjorie Garber, *Vested Interests: Cross-Dressing and Cultural Anxiety* (New York: HarperPerennial, 1992); Marjorie Garber, *Vice Versa: Bisexuality and the Eroticism of Everyday Life* (New York: Simon & Schuster, 1995).

5. Mary Douglas, *Purity and Danger: An Analysis of Concepts of Pollution and Taboo* (New York: Praeger, 1966), 4.

6. See Joshua Gamson, "Must Identity Movements Self-Destruct? A Queer Dilemma," *Social Problems* 42 (1995): 390–407; Joshua Gamson, "Messages of Exclusion: Gender, Movements, and Symbolic Boundaries," *Gender and Society* 11, no. 2 (1997): 178–99.

7. See Lorber; Garber, *Vested Interests;* Garber, *Vice Versa;* Judith Shapiro, "Transsexualism: Reflections on the Persistence of Gender and the Mutability of Sex," in *Body Guards,* ed. Julia Epstein and Kristina Straub (New York: Routledge, 1991).

8. Jaffe Cohen, "Land O' Lake," *Harvard Gay and Lesbian Review,* fall 1995, 36.

9. Paramount Pictures, *Ricki Lake* ("Back Off Boys! I'm a Lesbian and You'll Never Have Me"), October 24, 1995.

10. Investigative News Group, *Geraldo* ("Power Dykes: They're Out and Coming to a Town near You"), June 3, 1994.

11. Investigative News Group, *Geraldo* ("Beautiful, Bright, and Sexy, and for Women Only: Lesbian Chic"), January 17, 1994.

12. Unitel Video, *Jane Whitney* ("My Husband's Friends Are Making Him Gay"), April 2, 1993.

13. Unitel Video, *Jane Whitney* ("My Husband's Friends Are Making Him Gay").

14. Bertice Berry Show, *The Bertice Berry Show* ("Everyone Thinks I'm Gay, but I'm Not"), May 19, 1994.

15. Garber, *Vested Interests,* 130.

16. Garber, *Vice Versa,* 70.

17. Multimedia Entertainment, *Donahue* ("The Bisexual Dating Game: Is It for Love or for Sex?"), September 21, 1995.

18. King World, *Oprah* ("The Secret Lives of Bisexuals"), September 20, 1995. The reference to the complexity of race in Mark's comment is an important reminder that the dynamic I'm discussing is not specific to sex and gender. Talk shows have the same habits when it comes to race, although the discourse from which they draw differs: many shows take categories for granted or focus directly on racial difference (black and white are absolutely distinct), then program shows on biracial or multiracial issues (calling attention to the instability and fluidity of racial classifications).

19. Multimedia Entertainment, *Donahue* ("Loves Husband but Rather Make Love to Women"), January 17, 1994.

20. Multimedia Entertainment, *The Jerry Springer Show* ("My Husband Is Attracted to Men"), October 5, 1994.

21. Twentieth Century–Fox, *Gabrielle* ("Switching Sexes"), October 5, 1995.

22. King World, *Rolonda* ("Transsexuals: Women Who Become Men"), July 8, 1994.

23. Multimedia Entertainment, *The Jerry Springer Show* ("What Am I?"), January 30, 1995.

24. For critical perspectives on this issue, see Shapiro; Lorber; Martine Rothblatt, *The Apartheid of Sex: A Manifesto on the Freedom of Gender* (New York: Crown Publishers, 1995); Sandy Stone, "The Empire Strikes Back: A Posttranssexual Manifesto," in *Body Guards: The Cultural Politics of Gender Ambiguity,* ed. Julia Epstein and Kristina Straub (New York: Routledge, 1991), 280–304.

25. Harold Garfinkel, *Studies in Ethnomethodology* (Englewood Cliffs, NJ: Prentice Hall, 1967); see also Suzanne J. Kessler and Wendy McKenna, *Gender: An Ethnomethodological Approach* (Chicago: University of Chicago Press, 1978); Kate Bornstein, *Gender Outlaw: On Men, Women, and the Rest of Us* (New York: Vintage, 1994).

26. All American Television, *Richard Bey* ("Drag Queens vs. Real Women"), August 24, 1995.

27. Multimedia Entertainment, *Donahue* ("Transsexual Lesbians"), April 29, 1991.

28. Multimedia Entertainment, *The Jerry Springer Show* ("Transsexual Call Girls and Their Men"), May 15, 1995.

29. Multimedia Entertainment, *The Jerry Springer Show* ("I Want to Be a Girl"), December 15, 1995.

30. See Lorber; Judith Butler, *Gender Trouble: Feminism and the Subversion of Identity* (New York: Routledge, 1990); Candace West and Don Zimmerman, "Doing Gender," *Gender and Society* 1 (1987): 125–51.

31. Paramount Pictures, *Maury Povich* ("Men Who Are Glamorous Women"), May 5, 1995.

32. Multimedia Entertainment, *Sally Jessy Raphael* ("Women Who Are Really Men"), April 17, 1995.

33. Investigative News Group, *Geraldo* ("Teen Boys Tell Their Moms, 'I Want to Be a Woman'"), July 28, 1995.

34. Multimedia Entertainment, *The Jerry Springer Show* ("My Girlfriend Is a Man"), October 31, 1995.

35. Multimedia Entertainment, *Sally Jessy Raphael* ("He's So Beautiful He Became a Girl"), December 12, 1995.

36. Garber, *Vested Interests,* 16.

37. Investigative News Group, *Geraldo* ("Bisexual Teens: I'm in Love with the Boy and Girl Next Door"), January 18, 1994.

38. Paramount Pictures, *Ricki Lake* ("S/He Says 'I'm Bi,' but I Don't Buy It"), June 1, 1995.

39. Bisexuals are certainly not the only talk show guests subject to an assault for lack of fidelity or for promiscuity: heterosexual "sluts" and "cheaters" are routinely attacked on the shows, as well, which make a great deal of noise about sexual fidelity in general. The difference, of course, is that bisexual status is usually enough to bring on this attack, whereas heterosexual status does not automatically subject a guest to the charge of infidelity and out-of-control sexuality.

40. King World, *Rolonda* ("Two Lives to Lead: Bisexual Women"), September 20, 1994.

41. Paramount Pictures, *Leeza* ("Not Gay, Not Straight: Bisexual and Proud"), September 7, 1995.

42. Here as elsewhere, discussions of sexual and gender difference seem to make dominant identities congeal, as heterosexual or "real man/woman" identities are made explicit in response to challenge. Jonathan Ned Katz, in fact, has made this argument about the historical emergence of heterosexuality more generally. See *The Invention of Heterosexuality* (New York: Dutton, 1995).

43. Multimedia Entertainment, *Sally Jessy Raphael* ("Women Who Are Really Men").

44. Garber, *Vested Interests,* 110.

45. Multimedia Entertainment, *The Jerry Springer Show* ("I Want to Be a Girl").

46. Twentieth Century–Fox, *Gabrielle* ("Switching Sexes").

47. Paramount Pictures, *Maury Povich* ("Men Who Are Glamorous Women"); Multimedia Entertainment, *The Jerry Springer Show* ("I Want to Be a Girl").

48. Multimedia Entertainment, *Sally Jessy Raphael* ("He's So Beautiful He Became a Girl").

49. King World, *Oprah* ("The Secret Lives of Bisexuals").

50. Lorber, 21.

51. Multimedia Entertainment, *The Jerry Springer Show* ("I Want to Be a Girl").

52. Multimedia Entertainment, *Sally Jessy Raphael* ("My Teen Son Wants to Be a Woman"), June 27, 1995.

53. Bornstein, 81.

54. Dinitia Smith, "Step Right Up! See the Bearded Person Who Stars in Circus Amok!" *New York Times,* June 9, 1995, C1.

55. Wayne Munson, *All Talk: The Talkshow in Media Culture* (Philadelphia: Temple University Press, 1994), 10.

56. Mikhail Bakhtin, *Rabelais and His World* (Cambridge: MIT Press, 1968), 10; Susan Harding, "The Born-Again Telescandals," in *Culture/Power/History: A Reader in Contemporary Social Theory,* ed. Nicholas B. Dirks, Geoff Eley, and Sherry B. Ortner (Princeton: Princeton University Press, 1994), 549.

Chapter Six

1. King World, *Rolonda* ("Gay Comics"), January 31, 1994.

2. For discussions of the impact of "coming out" on politics, see John D'Emilio, *Sexual Politics, Sexual Communities: The Making of a Homosexual Minority in the United States* (Chicago: University of Chicago Press, 1983); Stephen O. Murray, *American Gay* (Chicago: University of Chicago Press, 1996); and, more generally, John I. Kitsuse, "Coming Out All Over: Deviants and the Politics of Social Problems," *Social Problems* 28 (1980): 1–13. For a discussion of the impact on interpersonal relationships, see Gilbert H. Herdt, *Gay Culture in America* (Boston: Beacon Press, 1992); and, more generally, Erving Goffman, *Stigma: Notes on the Management of Spoiled Identity* (Englewood Cliffs, NJ: Prentice Hall, 1963).

3. See, for instance, Essex Hemphill, ed., *Brother to Brother: New Writings by Black Gay Men* (Boston: Alyson, 1991); Cherrie Moraga, *Loving in the War Years* (Boston: South End Press, 1983).

4. Ka'ahumanu is the co-editor of a widely used anthology of bisexual writing. See Loraine Hutchins and Lani Ka'ahumanu, eds., *Bi Any Other Name: Bisexual People Speak Out* (Boston: Alyson, 1990).

5. Multimedia Entertainment, *Donahue* ("Bisexuals Discriminated Against by Gays and Heterosexuals"), January 21, 1993.

6. For more on "strategic self-disclosure" and "disclosure as a social movement tactic" on talk shows, see Patricia Joyner Priest, *Public Intimacies: Talk Show Participants and Tell-All TV* (Cresskill, NJ: Hampton Press, 1995). On media activism in general, see Charlotte Ryan, *Prime-Time Activism* (Boston: South End Press, 1991); on organizing focused on prime-time television, see Kathryn C. Montgomery, *Target: Prime Time* (New York: Oxford University Press, 1989); on gay media activism, see Montgomery, chapter 5, and Edward Alwood, *Straight News: Gays, Lesbians, and the News Media* (New York: Columbia University Press, 1996).

7. See William A. Gamson and Gadi Wolfsfeld, "Movements and Media as Interacting Systems," *Annals of the American Association of Political and Social Sciences* 528 (July 1993): 114–25.

8. See Suzanne J. Kessler and Wendy McKenna, *Gender: An Ethnomethodological Approach* (Chicago: University of Chicago Press, 1978).

9. Investigative News Group, *Geraldo* ("Bedding Down with Bisexuals"), September 11, 1992.

10. In Priest, 117.

11. Debra W. Hafner, "Talk Show Chaos," *Renaissance News and Views,* September 1995, 6, 16.

12. Marshall Kirk and Hunter Madsen, *After the Ball: How America Will Conquer Its Fear and Hatred of Gays in the 90s* (New York: Plume, 1989), 146.

13. See D'Emilio; Urvashi Vaid, *Virtual Equality: The Mainstreaming of Gay and Lesbian Liberation* (New York: Anchor Books, 1995); Joshua Gamson, "Must Identity Movements Self-Destruct? A Queer Dilemma," *Social Problems* 42 (1995): 390–407; Michael Warner, ed., *Fear of a Queer Planet* (Minneapolis: University of Minnesota Press, 1993); Steven Seidman, ed., *Queer Theory/Sociology* (Cambridge, MA: Blackwell, 1996).

14. See Vaid.

15. Unitel Video, *Jane Whitney* ("Bisexuality"), December 17, 1992.

16. Paramount Pictures, *Maury Povich* ("Lipstick Lesbians"), May 29, 1992.

17. Multimedia Entertainment, *Donahue* ("Concord Anti-Gay Referendum"), February 13, 1992.

18. Multimedia Entertainment, *Donahue* ("What, They're Gay? Lipstick Lesbians and Gorgeous Gay Guys"), September 12, 1995.

19. Multimedia Entertainment, *Donahue* ("Concord Anti-Gay Referendum").

20. Multimedia Entertainment, *The Jerry Springer Show* ("Please Act Straight!"), October 23, 1995.

21. Multimedia Entertainment, *Donahue* ("Gay Cops"), June 9, 1994.

22. As Jeff Weintraub points out, there are quite a few overlapping meanings of the distinction between "public" and "private." Most generally, one version contrasts "what is hidden or withdrawn" with "what is open, revealed, or accessible," and another version contrasts "what is individual, or pertains only to an individual" with "what is collective, or affects the interests of a collectivity of individuals" ("The Theory and Politics of the Public/Private Distinction," in *Public and Private in Thought and Practice: Perspectives on a Grand Dichotomy,* ed. Jeff Weintraub and Krishan Kumar [Chicago: University of Chicago Press, 1996], 5). While on talk shows certainly both versions are being negotiated, the first seems primarily to be at play, and it is this hidden/revealed distinction that therefore informs my analysis most.

23. Jenny Jones Show, *The Jenny Jones Show* ("Gorgeous and Gay!"), March 21, 1995.

24. See Richard Mohr, *Gays/Justice: A Study of Ethics, Society, and Law* (New York: Columbia University Press, 1988).

25. See Joshua Meyrowitz, *No Sense of Place: The Impact of Electronic Media on Social Behavior* (New York: Oxford University Press, 1985), chapter 6.

26. Jean Bethke Elshtain, "The Displacement of Politics," in *Public and Private in Thought and Practice: Perspectives on a Grand Dichotomy,* ed. Jeff Weinberg and Krishan Kumar (Chicago: University of Chicago Press, 1996), 176.

27. There are many ways to make sexuality public: talking about sex and sexual identity, having sex in places considered public, performing real or simulated sex in front of others (as in strip clubs), building public places that function in part as sexual meeting places. On talk shows, and in discussions with talk show viewers,

the first meaning of "publicness"—announcing sexual identity—often seems to imply some or all of the others. This is exactly why there is such pressure from some gay quarters to behave "respectably," especially by taking a desexualizing approach to public presentation.

28. In the discussion groups, as on the shows, someone usually offers some version of the standard retort: heterosexuals don't *have* to parade, since pretty much the whole culture is one big heterosexual parade.

Chapter Seven

1. Marshall Kirk and Hunter Madsen, *After the Ball: How America Will Conquer Its Fear and Hatred of Gays in the 90s* (New York: Plume, 1989), 144.

2. Quentin Crisp, *The Naked Civil Servant* (New York: Penguin, 1997 [1968]), 204.

3. Keith Bradsher, "Talk-Show Guest Is Guilty of Second-Degree Murder," *New York Times,* November 13, 1996, A14.

4. In Bradsher, A14.

5. In Richard Jerome, "Playing with Fire," *People,* October 21, 1996, 58–61.

6. In Marc Peyser, "Making a Killing on Talk TV," *Newsweek,* March 20, 1995, 30.

7. In "Media Alert," *IN Newsweekly,* December 1, 1996, 30.

8. The media coverage, for instance, consistently described Schmitz as a "man" or a "talk show guest" and Amedure as "a gay admirer" (in one case, as "a gay male admirer [who] revealed that he fantasized about filling the defendant's shorts with whipped cream") or a "man who revealed a homosexual crush" ("Media Alert," 30–31).

9. In Chris Bull and John Gallagher, "Talked to Death," *Advocate,* April 18, 1995, 22.

10. This claim is made by Michelangelo Signorile, "The *Jenny Jones* Murder: What Really Happened?" *OUT,* June 1995, 142.

11. Rosemary Hennessy, "Queer Visibility in Commodity Culture," *Cultural Critique,* winter 1994–95, 31–32.

12. Vito Russo, *The Celluloid Closet: Homosexuality in the Movies,* 2d ed. (New York: Harper & Row, 1987), 177. See also Richard Dyer, "Stereotyping," in *Gays and Film,* ed. Richard Dyer (New York: Zoetrope, 1984), 27–39.

13. See, for instance, Richard Schickel, *Intimate Strangers: The Culture of Celebrity* (New York: Fromm International, 1985); Stuart Ewen, *All Consuming Images: The Politics of Style in Contemporary Culture* (New York: Basic Books, 1989); Joshua Gamson, *Claims to Fame: Celebrity in Contemporary America* (Berkeley: University of California Press, 1994). From the audience side, this seems to also often mean that a television appearance becomes more interesting than the "freak" status that made it possible. Guests often report that people stop them on the street not to comment or insult them on their status, or on the content of the show, but simply

to say that they saw the guest on television. They approach the guest, that is, like a minor celebrity. "After the show," says Stafford, who appeared on a *Geraldo* show about female-to-male cross-dressers, "people who, if they sat down next to us in a restaurant before they'd seen the show would have gone 'Eeeooo!' and maybe beat us up, now they were saying 'Can we have our pictures taken with you?' "

14. "What is a 'positive' representation of a gay or lesbian character?" Jane Schacter asks of cultural images more generally. "Is it any image that avoids the harshest stereotypes? Is it a highly assimilated image that makes it impossible to 'tell' whether someone is straight or gay? Is it an image that attributes transgressive gender roles to a gay character—an 'effeminate' man or 'masculine' woman—but does so from a 'sympathetic' perspective? Is it simply any such 'transgressive' image, available for a potentially empowering appropriation by lesbian or gay viewers, irrespective of the ways in which nongay viewers might react? These are highly charged normative questions that do not yield singularly correct responses. Moreover, the answers depend in large part upon what underlying theory of equality has been adopted—one that prizes assimilation or transformation, sameness or difference" ("Skepticism, Culture and the Gay Civil Rights Debate in Post-Civil-Rights Era," *Harvard Law Review* 110 [January 1997]: 727–28).

15. Alexander Chee, "A Queer Nationalism," *Out/Look* (1991), 15.

16. Crisp, 204.

17. Clearly, as I have indicated, there is more room in this genre than in others for the repetition of controversial, norm-breaking images and subjects. Homosexual, bisexual, and transgender subjects are still hardly uncontroversial in Hollywood film and television. But as the response to the coming out of sitcom character Ellen Morgan and sitcom star Ellen DeGeneres indicates, the repetition of these controversial images dulls their edge rather quickly: while audiences tuned in to watch the "coming-out" *Ellen* in large numbers, and the usual suspects (Jerry Falwell, Donald Wildmon) decried the "promotion of homosexuality," there was so much commentary, amidst months of media hype for the event, that by the time Ellen and Ellen came out, nobody was anywhere near shocked. Through repeated publicity, her shocking revelation became mundane.

18. Andrew Kopkind, "The Gay Moment," *The Nation,* May 3, 1993, 1.

19. Jaffe Cohen, telling of his appearance on *Ricki*'s "I'm Gay and You're Gay— but You Give Gays a Bad Name!" in "Land O' Lake," *Harvard Gay and Lesbian Review,* fall 1995, 37.

20. On cable television, where the financial stakes are lower and audiences are more narrowly targeted, the picture is more like daytime talk shows—sometimes even raunchier: drag queen–singer RuPaul can kiss drag queen–basketball star Dennis Rodman, all kinds of people can do all kinds of things, including get naked, on cable access, and so forth.

21. See Edward Alwood, *Straight News: Gays, Lesbians, and the News Media* (New York: Columbia University Press, 1996). For a reminder that media industries are still largely enforcers of the closet, see Michelangelo Signorile, *Queer in America:*

Sex, the Media, and the Closets of Power (New York: Anchor Books, 1993), which argues, in the tradition of most gay media studies, that "the Trinity of the Closet" (the New York news industry, the Washington political system, and the Hollywood entertainment system) conspires to keep "most truths about homosexuals . . . from the public" while forcing "the public to know *everything* there is to know about heterosexuals who are public figures," and "by distorting and demonizing homosexuals depicted in the products of mass culture—or by keeping them completely invisible—this power structure makes sure that negative and often violent reactions to gays persist" (xvi–xvii).

22. Fred Fejes and Kevin Petrich, "Invisibility, Homophobia, and Heterosexism: Lesbians, Gays, and the Media," *Critical Studies in Mass Communication* (December 1993): 411; Hennessy, 32. For an argument about the ways "gay sensibility is now either entirely indistinguishable from the mainstream or has been pasteurized into total consumer-culture irrelevance," resulting in "a Stepford sensibility," see Daniel Mendelsohn, "We're Here! We're Queer! Let's Get Coffee!" *New York,* September 30, 1996, 25–31.

23. See John D'Emilio, *Sexual Politics, Sexual Communities: The Making of a Homosexual Minority in the United States* (Chicago: University of Chicago Press, 1983); Steven Epstein, "Gay Politics, Ethnic Identity: The Limits of Social Constructionism," *Socialist Review* 17 (1987): 9–54; Steven Seidman, "Identity Politics in a 'Postmodern' Gay Culture: Some Historical and Conceptual Notes," in *Fear of a Queer Planet,* ed. Michael Warner (Minneapolis: University of Minnesota Press, 1993).

24. Michael Warner, ed., introduction to *Fear of a Queer Planet* (Minneapolis: University of Minnesota Press, 1993), xxvii.

25. Arlene Stein and Ken Plummer, " 'I Can't Even Think Straight': 'Queer' Theory and the Missing Sexual Revolution in Sociology," in *Queer Theory/Sociology,* ed. Steven Seidman (Cambridge, MA: Blackwell, 1996), 134. See also Joshua Gamson, "Must Identity Movements Self-Destruct? A Queer Dilemma," *Social Problems* 42 (1995): 390–407; Steven Epstein, "A Queer Encounter: Sociology and the Study of Sexuality," in *Queer Theory/Sociology,* ed. Steven Seidman (Cambridge, MA: Blackwell, 1996), 145–67.

26. Hennessy, 34. This kind of proliferation and sexual indeterminacy is also taking shape in other media arenas, some of which do very little to put the categories back together again. Discussing advertisements that take a "dual market approach," targeting homosexual and heterosexual markets simultaneously, for instance, Danae Clark points out that such ads often use models who "bear the signifiers of sexual ambiguity or androgynous style" and "employ representational strategies that generally refer to gays and lesbians in anti-essentialist terms," depicting them as not inherently different from heterosexuals. See Danae Clark, "Commodity Lesbianism," in *The Lesbian and Gay Studies Reader,* ed. Henry Abelove, Michéle Aina Barale, and David Halperin (New York: Routledge, 1993), 188, 195.

27. On "moral panics," see Jeffrey Weeks, *Sex, Politics, and Society: The Regula-*

tion of Sexuality since 1800 (New York: Longman, 1981); Gayle Rubin, "Thinking Sex: Notes for a Radical Theory of the Politics of Sexuality," in *The Lesbian and Gay Studies Reader,* ed. Henry Abelove, Michéle Aina Barale, and David Halperin (New York: Routledge, 1993), 3–44. On the conflation of homosexuality and communism during the McCarthy era, see D'Emilio.

28. Joshua Meyrowitz, *No Sense of Place: The Impact of Electronic Media on Social Behavior* (New York: Oxford University Press, 1985).

Appendix

1. See Chandra Mukerji and Michael Schudson, "Introduction: Rethinking Popular Culture," in *Rethinking Popular Culture,* ed. Chandra Mukerji and Michael Schudson (Berkeley: University of California Press, 1991), 1–61; Joshua Gamson, *Claims to Fame: Celebrity in Contemporary America* (Berkeley: University of California Press, 1994), 197–212.

2. Patricia Joyner Priest, *Public Intimacies: Talk Show Participants and Tell-All TV* (Cresskill, NJ: Hampton Press, 1995).

3. Bradley Greenberg et al., *The Content of Television Talk Shows: Topics, Guests, and Interactions* (Lansing: Michigan State University, November 1995).

4. David L. Morgan, *Focus Groups as Qualitative Research* (Newbury Park, CA: Sage Publications, 1988).

Works Cited

ABC News. 1996. *Nightline* ("Phil Donahue"). January 26.

Abelove, Henry, Michéle Aina Barale, and David Halperin, eds. 1993. *The Lesbian and Gay Studies Reader.* New York: Routledge.

Abt, Vicki, and Mel Seesholtz. 1994. "The Shameless World of Phil, Sally, and Oprah: Television Talk Shows and the Deconstructing of Society." *Journal of Popular Culture,* 195–215.

All American Television. 1993. *Richard Bey* ("Coffee, Tea, or Death"). October 22.

———. 1995. *Richard Bey* ("Drag Queens vs. Real Women"). August 24.

Allison, Dorothy. 1994. *Skin: Talking about Sex, Class, and Literature.* Ithaca, NY. Firebrand Books.

Alwood, Edward. 1996. *Straight News: Gays, Lesbians, and the News Media.* New York: Columbia University Press.

American Broadcasting Companies. 1986. *The Oprah Winfrey Show* ("Homophobia"). November 13.

American Family Association. 1996. *Action! Page.* January. Newsletter.

Andersen, Robin. 1995. *Consumer Culture and TV Programming.* Boulder, CO: Westview.

Aronson, Amy Beth. 1996. *Understanding Equals: Audience and Articulation in the Early American Women's Magazine.* Ph.D. dissertation, Columbia University.

Bakhtin, Mikhail. 1968. *Rabelais and His World.* Cambridge: MIT Press.

Baltzell, E. Digby. 1965. *The Protestant Establishment: Aristocracy and Caste in America.* London: Secker & Warburg.

Barnum, P. T. 1981. *Struggles and Triumphs.* Harmondsworth, England: Penguin Books.

Bayer, Ronald. 1981. *Homosexuality and American Psychiatry.* New York: Basic Books.

BBC Radio. 1995. "Coming Soon: TV's True Confessions." Radio broadcast, October 19.

Belenky, Mary Field, Blythe McVicker Clinchy, Nancy Rule Goldberger, and Jill Mattuck Tarule. 1986. *Women's Ways of Knowing.* New York: Basic Books.

Bellah, Robert N., Richard Madsen, William M. Sullivan, Ann Swidler, and Steven M. Tipton. 1985. *Habits of the Heart: Individualism and Commitment in American Life*. Berkeley: University of California Press.

Berkman, Meredith. 1995a. "Daytime Talk Shows: Fake Guests Common in Battle for Ratings." *New York Post*, December 4, 8–9.

———. 1995b. "Liars Send in Clowns for Sicko Circuses." *New York Post*, December 4, 8.

Bertice Berry Show. 1993. *The Bertice Berry Show* ("Parents and Their Bisexual Kids"). November 16.

———. 1994. *The Bertice Berry Show* ("Everyone Thinks I'm Gay, but I'm Not"). May 19.

Bird, S. Elizabeth. 1992. *For Enquiring Minds: A Cultural Study of Supermarket Tabloids*. Knoxville: University of Tennessee Press.

Blasius, Mark. 1994. *Gay and Lesbian Politics: Sexuality and the Emergence of a New Ethic*. Philadelphia: Temple University Press.

Bogdan, Robert. 1988. *Freak Show: Presenting Human Oddities for Amusement and Profit*. Chicago: University of Chicago Press.

Bonapace, Ruth, Herma M. Rosenthal, Alison Sloane-Gaylin, and Tom Toolen. 1995. "Is It Time to Turn Off Talk TV?" *First*, June 12, 90–94.

Bornstein, Kate. 1994. *Gender Outlaw: On Men, Women, and the Rest of Us*. New York: Vintage.

Boyd-Barrett, Oliver, and Chris Newbold, eds. 1995. *Approaches to Media*. London: Arnold.

Bradsher, Keith. 1996. "Talk-Show Guest Is Guilty of Second-Degree Murder." *New York Times*, November 13, A14.

Brantlinger, Patrick. 1985. *Bread and Circuses: Theories of Mass Culture as Social Decay*. New York: Cornell University Press.

Bull, Chris, and John Gallagher. 1995. "Talked to Death." *Advocate*, April 18, 20–22.

Burr, Chandler. 1996. *A Separate Creation: The Search for the Biological Origins of Sexual Orientation*. New York: Hyperion.

Butler, Judith. 1990. *Gender Trouble: Feminism and the Subversion of Identity*. New York: Routledge.

Cable News Network. 1996. *Larry King Live* ("Interview with Phil Donahue"). February 5.

Calhoun, Craig, ed. 1992. *Habermas and the Public Sphere*. Cambridge: MIT Press.

Capuzzi, Cecilia, John Flinn, and Neal Koch. 1988. "Pushing the Limits of Talk-Show TV." *Channels*, May, 94–95.

Carbaugh, Donal. 1989. *Talking American: Cultural Discourses on Donahue*. Norwood, NJ: Ablex Publishing.

Carpignano, Paolo, Robin Andersen, Stanley Aronowitz, and William DiFazio. 1990. "Chatter in the Age of Electronic Reproduction: Talk Television and the 'Public Mind.'" *Social Text*, nos. 25–26: 33–55.

Works Cited

Chee, Alexander. 1991. "A Queer Nationalism." *Out/Look,* no. 11 (winter): 15–19.

Chidley, Joe. 1996. "Taking In the Trash." *McClean's,* February 19, 50–53.

Clark, Danae. 1993. "Commodity Lesbianism." In *The Lesbian and Gay Studies Reader,* edited by Henry Abelove, Michéle Aina Barale, and David Halperin, 186–201. New York: Routledge.

Cohen, Cathy. 1996. "Contested Membership: Black Gay Identities and the Politics of AIDS." In *Queer Theory/Sociology,* edited by Steven Seidman, 362–94. Cambridge, MA: Blackwell.

Cohen, Jaffe. 1995. "Land O' Lake." *Harvard Gay and Lesbian Review,* fall, 36–37.

Collins, Patricia Hill. 1991. *Black Feminist Thought: Knowledge, Consciousness, and the Politics of Empowerment.* New York: Routledge.

Columbia-Tristar Television. 1996. *Tempestt* ("I'm Gay, Get Used to It!"). July 31.

Crane, Diana. 1994. *The Sociology of Culture.* Cambridge, MA: Blackwell.

Crisp, Quentin. 1997 [1968]. *The Naked Civil Servant.* New York: Penguin.

Cruz, Jon, and Justin Lewis, eds. 1994. *Viewing, Reading, Listening: Audiences and Cultural Reception.* Boulder, CO: Westview.

Dahlgren, Peter, and Colin Sparks, eds. 1991. *Communication and Citizenship.* London: Routledge.

D'Emilio, John. 1983. *Sexual Politics, Sexual Communities: The Making of a Homosexual Minority in the United States.* Chicago: University of Chicago Press.

DiMaggio, Paul. 1991. "Cultural Entrepreneurship in Nineteenth-Century Boston: The Creation of an Organizational Base for High Culture in America." In *Rethinking Popular Culture: Contemporary Perspectives in Cultural Studies,* edited by Chandra Mukerji and Michael Schudson, 374–97. Berkeley: University of California Press.

Donahue, Phil, & Co. 1979. *Donahue: My Own Story.* New York: Simon & Schuster.

Douglas, Mary. 1966. *Purity and Danger: An Analysis of Concepts of Pollution and Taboo.* New York: Praeger.

Dowd, Maureen. 1995. "Talk Is Cheap." *New York Times,* October 26, A25.

Dupree, Scotty. 1995. "Targeting Talk TV." *Mediaweek,* October 30, 4.

Dyer, Richard. 1984. "Stereotyping." In *Gays and Film,* edited by Richard Dyer, 27–39. New York: Zoetrope.

Elshtain, Jean Bethke. 1996. "The Displacement of Politics." In *Public and Private in Thought and Practice: Perspectives on a Grand Dichotomy,* edited by Jeff Weinberg and Krishan Kumar, 166–81. Chicago: University of Chicago Press.

Empower America. 1995. "Press Conference." Washington, DC: Federal Document Clearing House, October 26.

Epstein, Debbie, and Deborah Lynn Steinberg. 1996. "Straight Talking on *The Oprah Winfrey Show.*" In *Border Patrols: Policing Sexual Boundaries,* edited by Politics of Sexuality Group. London: Cassell.

Epstein, Steven. 1987. "Gay Politics, Ethnic Identity: The Limits of Social Construc-tionism." *Socialist Review* 17:9–54.

———. 1996a. *Impure Science: AIDS, Activism, and the Politics of Knowledge.* Berkeley: University of California Press.

———. 1996b. "A Queer Encounter: Sociology and the Study of Sexuality." In *Queer Theory/Sociology,* edited by Steven Seidman, 145–67. Cambridge, MA: Blackwell.

Ewen, Stuart. 1989. *All Consuming Images: The Politics of Style in Contemporary Culture.* New York: Basic Books.

Feinberg, Leslie. 1996. *Transgender Warriors: Making History from Joan of Arc to RuPaul.* Boston: Beacon Press.

Fejes, Fred, and Kevin Petrich. 1993. "Invisibility, Homophobia, and Heterosexism: Lesbians, Gays, and the Media." *Critical Studies in Mass Communication* (De-cember): 396–422.

Fiedler, Leslie. 1978. *Freaks: Myths and Images of the Secret Self.* New York: Anchor Books.

Foucault, Michel. 1979. *Discipline and Punish.* New York: Vintage.

———. 1990. *The History of Sexuality.* Volume 1. New York: Vintage.

Fraser, Nancy. 1989. "What's Critical about Critical Theory? The Case of Habermas and Gender." In *Unruly Practices: Power, Discourse, and Gender in Contempo-rary Social Theory,* edited by Nancy Fraser, 113–43. Minneapolis: University of Minnesota Press.

Gabler, Neal. 1995. "Audience Stays Superior to the Exploitalk Shows." *Los Angeles Times,* March 19, M1.

Gagnon, John, and William Simon. 1973. *Sexual Conduct.* Chicago: University of Chicago Press.

Gaines, Donna. 1995. "How Jenny Jones Saved My Life." *Village Voice,* November 21, 41–43.

Gamson, Joshua. 1989. "Silence, Death, and the Invisible Enemy: AIDS Activism and Social Movement 'Newness.' " *Social Problems* 36, no. 4: 351–67.

———. 1994a. *Claims to Fame: Celebrity in Contemporary America.* Berkeley: Uni-versity of California Press.

———. 1994b. "Incredible News." *American Prospect,* fall, 28–35.

———. 1995. "Must Identity Movements Self-Destruct? A Queer Dilemma." *Social Problems* 42:390–407.

———. 1996. "The Organizational Shaping of Collective Identity: The Case of Les-bian and Gay Film Festivals in New York." *Sociological Forum* 11:231–62.

———. 1997. "Messages of Exclusion: Gender, Movements, and Symbolic Bound-aries." *Gender and Society* 11, no. 2: 178–99.

Gamson, William A., and Gadi Wolfsfeld. 1993. "Movements and Media as Inter-acting Systems." *Annals of the American Association of Political and Social Sci-ences* 528:114–25.

Gans, Herbert. 1979. *Deciding What's News.* New York: Vintage.

Works Cited

Garber, Marjorie. 1992. *Vested Interests: Cross-Dressing and Cultural Anxiety.* New York: HarperPerennial.

———. 1995. *Vice Versa: Bisexuality and the Eroticism of Everyday Life.* New York: Simon & Schuster.

Garfinkel, Harold. 1967. *Studies in Ethnomethodology.* Englewood Cliffs, NJ: Prentice Hall.

Gilkeson, John S. 1986. *Middle-Class Providence, 1820–1940.* Princeton: Princeton University Press.

Gitlin, Todd. 1980. *The Whole World Is Watching.* Berkeley: University of California Press.

———. 1983. *Inside Prime Time.* New York: Pantheon.

Goffman, Erving. 1963. *Stigma: Notes on the Management of Spoiled Identity.* Englewood Cliffs, NJ: Prentice Hall.

Goldstein, Richard. 1995. "The Devil in Ms. Jones." *Village Voice,* November 21, 44–45.

Goodman, Walter. 1991. "3 Queens of Talk Who Rule the Day." *New York Times,* July 29, C11, C14.

Green, Michelle. 1995. "Fatal Attraction." *People,* March 27, 40–44.

Greenberg, Bradley, Sandi Smith, James Ah Yun, Rick Busselle, Lynn Rampoldi Hnilo, Monique Mitchell, and John Sherry. 1995. *The Content of Television Talk Shows: Topics, Guests, and Interactions.* Lansing: Michigan State University, November.

Grindstaff, Laura. 1997. "Producing Trash, Class, and the Money Shot: A Behind the Scenes Account of Daytime TV Talkshows." In *Media Scandals,* edited by James Lull and Stephen Hinerman. London: Polity Press.

Gross, Larry. 1989. "Out of the Mainstream: Sexual Minorities and the Mass Media." In *Remote Control: Television, Audiences, and Cultural Power,* edited by Ellen Seiter, 130–49. New York: Routledge.

———. 1994. "What Is Wrong with This Picture? Lesbian Women and Gay Men on Television." In *Queer Words, Queer Images: Communication and the Construction of Homosexuality,* edited by R. Jeffrey Ringer, 143–56. New York: New York University Press.

Habermas, Jürgen. 1991. *The Structural Transformation of the Public Sphere.* Translated by Thomas Burger. Cambridge: MIT Press.

Hafner, Debra W. 1995. "Talk Show Chaos." *Renaissance News and Views,* September, 6, 16.

Hammer, Carl, and Gideon Bosker. 1996. *Freak Show: Sideshow Banner Art.* San Francisco: Chronicle Books.

Hantzis, Darlene M., and Valerie Lehr. 1994. "Whose Desire? Lesbian (Non)Sexuality and Television's Perpetuation of Hetero/Sexism." In *Queer Words, Queer Images: Communication and the Construction of Homosexuality,* edited by R. Jeffrey Ringer, 107–21. New York: New York University Press.

Harding, Susan. 1994. "The Born-Again Telescandals." In *Culture/Power/History:*

A Reader in Contemporary Social Theory, edited by Nicholas B. Dirks, Geoff Eley, and Sherry B. Ortner, 539–56. Princeton: Princeton University Press.

Harris, Neil. 1973. *Humbug: The Art of P. T. Barnum.* Boston: Little, Brown & Co.

Harrison, Barbara Grizzuti. 1989. "The Importance of Being Oprah." *New York Times Magazine,* June 11.

Heaton, Jeanne Albronda, and Nona Leigh Wilson. 1995. *Tuning in Trouble: Talk TV's Destructive Impact on Mental Health.* San Francisco: Jossey-Bass.

Hemphill, Essex, ed. 1991. *Brother to Brother: New Writings by Black Gay Men.* Boston: Alyson.

Hennessy, Rosemary. 1994–95. "Queer Visibility in Commodity Culture." *Cultural Critique,* no. 29 (winter): 31–75.

Herdt, Gilbert H. 1992. *Gay Culture in America.* Boston: Beacon Press.

Hutchins, Loraine, and Lani Ka'ahumanu, eds. 1990. *Bi Any Other Name: Bisexual People Speak Out.* Boston: Alyson.

Investigative News Group. 1992. *Geraldo* ("Bedding Down with Bisexuals"). September 11.

———. 1993. *Geraldo* ("Gay Teenagers at the High School Prom"). June 25.

———. 1994a. *Geraldo* ("Beautiful, Bright, and Sexy, and for Women Only: Lesbian Chic"). January 17.

———. 1994b. *Geraldo* ("Bisexual Teens: I'm in Love with the Boy and Girl Next Door"). January 18.

———. 1994c. *Geraldo* ("Girly to Burly: Women Who Become Men"). April 18.

———. 1994d. *Geraldo* ("Power Dykes: They're Out and Coming to a Town near You"). June 3.

———. 1994e. *Geraldo* ("You're Not the Man I Married"). February 14.

———. 1995a. *Geraldo* ("Gay Today . . . Straight Tomorrow"). October 18.

———. 1995b. *Geraldo* ("I Saw You on Geraldo and Just Had to Meet You"). October 10.

———. 1995c. *Geraldo* ("Teen Boys Tell Their Moms, 'I Want to Be a Woman' "). July 28.

———. 1995d. *Geraldo* ("A Televised Sex Change Operation and Other Transsexual Tales"). January 27.

———. 1996. *Geraldo* ("Secret Lives Revealed"). August 21.

Jenny Jones Show. 1993. *The Jenny Jones Show* ("Teenage Lesbians Defend Their Orientation"). February 23.

———. 1995. *The Jenny Jones Show* ("Gorgeous and Gay!"). March 21.

Jerome, Richard. 1996. "Playing with Fire." *People,* October 21, 58–61.

Kaplan, Janice. 1995. "Are Talk Shows out of Control?" *TV Guide,* April 1, 10–15.

Katz, Jonathan Ned. 1995. *The Invention of Heterosexuality.* New York: Dutton.

Kessler, Suzanne J., and Wendy McKenna. 1978. *Gender: An Ethnomethodological Approach.* Chicago: University of Chicago Press.

Works Cited

King World. 1989. *Oprah* ("Gay Marriages"). December 19.
———. 1992. *Oprah* ("Straight Spouses and Gay Ex-Husbands"). February 24.
———. 1994a. *Oprah* ("The Fallout of a Gay Husband's Affair"). May 4.
———. 1994b. *Oprah* ("School for Gay Teens"). October 24.
———. 1994c. *Rolonda* ("Family Secrets: Straight Women, Gay Husbands"). November 17.
———. 1994d. *Rolonda* ("Gay Comics"). January 31.
———. 1994e. *Rolonda* ("No Gays in My Town"). January 18.
———. 1994f. *Rolonda* ("Teen Secrets: Kids Who Are Gay"). March 2.
———. 1994g. *Rolonda* ("Transsexuals: Women Who Become Men"). July 8.
———. 1994h. *Rolonda* ("Two Lives to Lead: Bisexual Women"). September 20.
———. 1995a. *Oprah* ("The Secret Lives of Bisexuals"). September 20.
———. 1995b. *Rolonda* ("Bashing Gays for School Credit"). January 10.
Kirk, Marshall, and Hunter Madsen. 1989. *After the Ball: How America Will Conquer Its Fear and Hatred of Gays in the 90s.* New York: Plume.
Kitsuse, John I. 1980. "Coming Out All Over: Deviants and the Politics of Social Problems." *Social Problems* 28:1–13.
Kopkind, Andrew. 1993. "The Gay Moment." *The Nation,* May 3, 1.
Kunzel, Regina. 1995. "Pulp Fictions and Problem Girls: Reading and Rewriting Single Pregnancy in the Postwar United States." *American Historical Review* 100, no. 6: 1465–87.
Kurtz, Howard. 1996. *Hot Air: All Talk, All the Time.* New York: Times Books.
Levine, Lawrence W. 1991. "William Shakespeare and the American People: A Study in Cultural Transformation." In *Rethinking Popular Culture,* edited by Chandra Mukerji and Michael Schudson, 157–97. Berkeley: University of California Press.
Livingstone, Sonia, and Peter Lunt. 1994. *Talk on Television: Audience Participation and Public Debate.* London: Routledge.
Lorber, Judith. 1994. *Paradoxes of Gender.* New Haven: Yale University Press.
Lorde, Audre. 1984. *Sister Outsider.* Trumansburg, NY: Crossing Press.
Marchand, Roland. 1985. *Advertising the American Dream.* Berkeley: University of California Press.
Masciarotte, Gloria-Jean. 1991. "C'mon, Girl: Oprah Winfrey and the Discourse of Feminine Talk." *Genders,* no. 11: 81–110.
"Media Alert." 1996. *IN Newsweekly,* December 1, 29–31.
Mendelsohn, Daniel. 1996. "We're Here! We're Queer! Let's Get Coffee!" *New York,* September 30, 25–31.
Meyrowitz, Joshua. 1985. *No Sense of Place: The Impact of Electronic Media on Social Behavior.* New York: Oxford University Press.
Mohr, Richard. 1988. *Gays/Justice: A Study of Ethics, Society, and Law.* New York: Columbia University Press.
Molotch, Harvey. 1979. "Media and Movements." In *The Dynamics of Social Movements,* edited by Mayer Zald and John McCarthy, 71–93. Cambridge: Winthrop.

Montgomery, Kathryn C. 1989. *Target: Prime Time*. New York: Oxford University Press.

Moraga, Cherrie. 1983. *Loving in the War Years*. Boston: South End Press.

Morgan, David L. 1988. *Focus Groups as Qualitative Research*. Newbury Park, CA: Sage Publications.

Moritz, Marguerite J. 1994. "Old Strategies for New Texts: How American Television Is Creating and Treating Lesbian Characters." In *Queer Words, Queer Images: Communication and the Construction of Homosexuality*, edited by R. Jeffrey Ringer, 122–42. New York: New York University Press.

Morton, Donald, ed. 1996. *The Material Queer: A LesBiGay Cultural Studies Reader*. Boulder, CO: Westview.

Mukerji, Chandra, and Michael Schudson. 1991. "Introduction: Rethinking Popular Culture." In *Rethinking Popular Culture*, edited by Chandra Mukerji and Michael Schudson, 1–61. Berkeley: University of California Press.

Multimedia Entertainment. Date unavailable. *Sally Jessy Raphael* ("Former Homosexuals").

———. 1979. *Donahue* ("Masters and Johnson"). April 23.

———. 1985. *Donahue* ("Gay Senior Citizens"). January 21.

———. 1991. *Donahue* ("Transsexual Lesbians"). April 29.

———. 1992a. *Donahue* ("Concord Anti-Gay Referendum"). February 13.

———. 1992b. "The Donahue 25th Anniversary Special." November 15.

———. 1993. *Donahue* ("Bisexuals Discriminated Against by Gays and Heterosexuals"). January 21.

———. 1994a. *Donahue* ("Black Preacher Says I'll March with the KKK against Gays"). November 4.

———. 1994b. *Donahue* ("Gay Cops"). June 9.

———. 1994c. *Donahue* ("Loves Husband but Rather Make Love to Women"). January 17.

———. 1994d. *The Jerry Springer Show* ("Misssissippi Violence over Lesbian Camp"). February 14.

———. 1994e. *The Jerry Springer Show* ("My Boyfriend Turned Out to Be a Girl"). December 27.

———. 1994f. *The Jerry Springer Show* ("My Husband Is Attracted to Men"). October 5.

———. 1994g. *The Jerry Springer Show* ("Update: Teen Transsexuals"). July 22.

———. 1994h. *Sally Jessy Raphael* ("I Was Fooled"). May 17.

———. 1994i. *Sally Jessy Raphael* ("Why I Was Fired"). April 13.

———. 1995a. *The Dennis Prager Show* ("Comedians against Prejudice"). August 11.

———. 1995b. *Donahue* ("The Bisexual Dating Game: Is It for Love or for Sex?"). September 21.

———. 1995c. *Donahue* ("Is There Life after a Career in Porn?"). March 1.

————. 1995d. *Donahue* ("What, They're Gay? Lipstick Lesbians and Gorgeous Gay Guys"). September 12.

————. 1995e. *Donahue* ("When Hatred against Gays Turns Deadly"). February 21.

————. 1995f. *The Jerry Springer Show* ("Confess, You Liar!"). December 7.

————. 1995g. *The Jerry Springer Show* ("I Can't Stand My Sibling"). December 19.

————. 1995h. *The Jerry Springer Show* ("I Love Someone I Can't Have"). October 18.

————. 1995i. *The Jerry Springer Show* ("I Want to Be a Girl"). December 15.

————. 1995j. *The Jerry Springer Show* ("My Girlfriend Is a Man"). October 31.

————. 1995k. *The Jerry Springer Show* ("Please Act Straight!"). October 23.

————. 1995l. *The Jerry Springer Show* ("Transsexual Call Girls and Their Men"). May 15.

————. 1995m. *The Jerry Springer Show* ("What Am I?"). January 30.

————. 1995n. *Sally Jessy Raphael* ("He's So Beautiful He Became a Girl"). December 12.

————. 1995o. *Sally Jessy Raphael* ("My Husband Left Me because He's Gay"). August 8.

————. 1995p. *Sally Jessy Raphael* ("My Teen Son Wants to Be a Woman"). June 27.

————. 1995q. *Sally Jessy Raphael* ("Women Who Are Really Men"). April 17.

Munson, Wayne. 1994. *All Talk: The Talkshow in Media Culture.* Philadelphia: Temple University Press.

Murray, Stephen O. 1995. *Latin American Male Homosexualities.* Albuquerque: University of New Mexico Press.

————. 1996. *American Gay.* Chicago: University of Chicago Press.

Nelson, Jill. 1995. "Talk Is Cheap." *The Nation,* June 5, 800–802.

Netzhammer, Emile C., and Scott A. Shamp. 1994. "Guilt by Association: Homosexuality and AIDS on Prime-Time Television." In *Queer Words, Queer Images: Communication and the Construction of Homosexuality,* edited by R. Jeffrey Ringer, 91–106. New York: New York University Press.

Nudelman, Franny. 1997. "Beyond the Talking Cure: Listening to Female Testimony on *The Oprah Winfrey Show.*" In *Inventing the Psychological: Toward a History of Emotional Life in America,* edited by Joel Pfister and Nancy Schnog, 297–315. New Haven: Yale University Press.

Paramount Pictures. 1992. *Maury Povich* ("Lipstick Lesbians"). May 29.

————. 1994a. *Maury Povich* ("Dad Wants to Be a Woman"). May 3.

————. 1994b. *Ricki Lake* ("White Men Fight Back: I'm Sick of Being Discriminated Against"). February 23.

————. 1995a. *Leeza* ("Not Gay, Not Straight: Bisexual and Proud"). September 7.

————. 1995b. *Maury Povich* ("Men Who Are Glamorous Women"). May 5.

————. 1995c. *Ricki Lake* ("Back Off Boys! I'm a Lesbian and You'll Never Have Me"). October 24.

————. 1995d. *Ricki Lake* ("Get It Straight: I Don't Want Gays around My Kids"). June 15.

———. 1995e. *Ricki Lake* ("I'm Gay, Accept It"). November 20.

———. 1995f. *Ricki Lake* ("Listen, Family, I'm Gay . . . It's Not a Phase . . . Get over It!"). November 20.

———. 1995g. *Ricki Lake* ("S/He Says 'I'm Bi,' but I Don't Buy It"). June 1.

———. 1995h. *Ricki Lake* ("You Both Have No Clue Why You're Here . . . Surprise! I'm Hooking You Up"). September 15.

———. 1995i. *Ricki Lake* ("You're Gay, How Dare You Raise a Child"). April 27.

———. 1996. *Ricki Lake* ("Watch Me! Today I'm Going to Break Up My Ex and His New Chick"). July 29.

Peck, Janice. 1994. "Talk about Racism: Framing a Popular Discourse on Race on *Oprah Winfrey.*" *Cultural Critique* 27 (spring): 89–126.

———. 1995. "TV Talk Shows as Therapeutic Discourse: The Ideological Labor of the Televised Talking Cure." *Communication Theory* 5, no. 1: 58–81.

Peiss, Kathy. 1986. *Cheap Amusements: Working Women and Leisure in Turn-of-the-Century New York.* Philadelphia: Temple University Press.

Perpetual Notion, Inc. 1995. *Marilu* ("Gay and Lesbian Parents"). April 4.

Peyser, Marc. 1995. "Making a Killing on Talk TV." *Newsweek,* March 20, 30.

Plummer, Ken. 1996. "Symbolic Interactionism and the Forms of Homosexuality." In *Queer Theory/Sociology,* edited by Steven Seidman, 64–82. Cambridge, MA: Blackwell.

Pratt, Jane. 1995. "I Am a Talk-Show-Host Survivor." *Glamour,* September, 173, 273.

Press, Andrea L. 1991. *Women Watching Television: Gender, Class, and Generation in the American Television Experience.* Philadelphia: University of Pennsylvania Press.

Priest, Patricia Joyner. 1995. *Public Intimacies: Talk Show Participants and Tell-All TV.* Cresskill, NJ: Hampton Press.

Raphael, Sally Jessy. 1990. *Sally: Unconventional Success.* New York: Morrow.

Rapping, Elayne. 1991. "Daytime Inquiries." *Progressive,* October, 36–38.

Ringer, R. Jeffrey, ed. 1994. *Queer Words, Queer Images: Communication and the Construction of Homosexuality.* New York: New York University Press.

Roberts, James C. 1991. "The Power of Talk Radio." *American Enterprise,* May–June, 56–61.

Rose, Brian G. 1985. "The Talk Show." In *TV Genres: A Handbook and Reference Guide,* edited by Brian G. Rose, 329–52. Westport, CT: Greenwood Press.

Ross, Andrew. 1989. *No Respect: Intellectuals and Popular Culture.* New York: Routledge.

Rothblatt, Martine. 1995. *The Apartheid of Sex: A Manifesto on the Freedom of Gender.* New York: Crown Publishers.

Rubin, Gayle. 1993. "Thinking Sex: Notes for a Radical Theory of the Politics of Sexuality." In *The Lesbian and Gay Studies Reader,* edited by Henry Abelove, Michéle Aina Barale, and David Halperin, 3–44. New York: Routledge.

Rus, Mayer. 1995. "Lake Victorious." *OUT,* June, 75–80, 148.

Russo, Vito. 1987. *The Celluloid Closet: Homosexuality in the Movies*. 2d ed. New York: Harper & Row.

Ryan, Charlotte. 1991. *Prime-Time Activism*. Boston: South End Press.

Schacter, Jane S. 1997. "Skepticism, Culture, and the Gay Civil Rights Debate in Post-Civil-Rights Era." *Harvard Law Review* 110 (January): 684–731.

Schickel, Richard. 1985. *Intimate Strangers: The Culture of Celebrity*. New York: Fromm International.

Schone, Mark. 1996. "Talked Out." *Spin*, May, 66–75, 118.

Scott, Gini Graham. 1996. *Can We Talk? The Power and Influence of Talk Shows*. New York: Insight Books.

Seidman, Steven. 1993. "Identity Politics in a 'Postmodern' Gay Culture: Some Historical and Conceptual Notes." In *Fear of a Queer Planet*, edited by Michael Warner, 105–42. Minneapolis: University of Minnesota Press.

———, ed. 1996. *Queer Theory/Sociology*. Cambridge, MA: Blackwell.

Seplow, Stephen. 1995. "Seduced and Abandoned." *Philadelphia Inquirer Magazine*, September 24, 12–14, 24–28.

Shapiro, Judith. 1991. "Transsexualism: Reflections on the Persistence of Gender and the Mutability of Sex." In *Body Guards: The Cultural Politics of Gender Ambiguity*, edited by Julia Epstein and Kristina Straub, 248–79. New York: Routledge.

Shattuc, Jane. 1997. *The Talking Cure: TV Talk Shows and Women*. New York: Routledge.

Signorile, Michelangelo. 1993. *Queer in America: Sex, the Media, and the Closets of Power*. New York: Anchor Books.

———. 1995. "The *Jenny Jones* Murder: What Really Happened?" *OUT*, June, 26–29, 142–46.

Smith, Dinitia. 1995. "Step Right Up! See the Bearded Person Who Stars in Circus Amok!" *New York Times*, June 9, C1, C23.

Stein, Arlene, and Ken Plummer. 1996. "'I Can't Even Think Straight': 'Queer' Theory and the Missing Sexual Revolution in Sociology." In *Queer Theory/Sociology*, edited by Steven Seidman, 129–44. Cambridge, MA: Blackwell.

Stein, Edward, ed. 1992. *Forms of Desire: Sexual Orientation and the Social Constructionist Controversy*. New York: Routledge.

Stone, Sandy. 1991. "The Empire Strikes Back: A Posttranssexual Manifesto." In *Body Guards: The Cultural Politics of Gender Ambiguity*, edited by Julia Epstein and Kristina Straub, 280–304. New York: Routledge.

Stryker, Susan. 1994. "My Words to Victor Frankenstein above the Village of Chamounix." *GLQ* 1:237–54.

Taylor, Verta. 1996. *Rock-a-by Baby: Feminism, Self-Help, and Postpartum Depression*. New York: Routledge.

Taylor, Verta, and Nancy Whittier. 1992. "Collective Identity in Social Movement Communities: Lesbian Feminist Mobilization." In *Frontiers in Social Movement Theory*, edited by Aldon Morris and Carol Mueller, 104–29. New Haven: Yale University Press.

Tribune Entertainment Co. 1993. *The Joan Rivers Show* ("Confusing Sexual Stories"). October 4.

Tuchman, Gaye. 1974. "Assembling a Network Talk Show." In *The TV Establishment: Programming for Power and Profit,* edited by Gaye Tuchman, 119–35. Englewood Cliffs, NJ: Prentice Hall.

Twentieth Century–Fox. 1995. *Gabrielle* ("Switching Sexes"). October 5.

Unitel Video. 1992. *Jane Whitney* ("Bisexuality"). December 17.

———. 1993. *Jane Whitney* ("My Husband's Friends Are Making Him Gay"). April 2.

Vaid, Urvashi. 1995. *Virtual Equality: The Mainstreaming of Gay and Lesbian Liberation.* New York: Anchor Books.

Verney, Peter. 1978. *Here Comes the Circus.* New York: Paddington Press.

Warner, Michael, ed. 1993. *Fear of a Queer Planet.* Minneapolis: University of Minnesota Press.

Weeks, Jeffrey. 1981. *Sex, Politics, and Society: The Regulation of Sexuality since 1800.* New York: Longman.

———. 1985. *Sexuality and Its Discontents.* New York: Routledge.

Weintraub, Jeff. 1996. "The Theory and Politics of the Public/Private Distinction." In *Public and Private in Thought and Practice: Perspectives on a Grand Dichotomy,* edited by Jeff Weintraub and Krishan Kumar, 1–42. Chicago: University of Chicago Press.

West, Candace, and Don Zimmerman. 1987. "Doing Gender." *Gender and Society* 1:125–51.

White, Mimi. 1992. *Tele-Advising: Therapeutic Discourse in American Television.* Chapel Hill: University of North Carolina Press.

Willis, Ellen. 1996. "Bring In the Noise." *The Nation,* April 1, 19–23.

Wolfsfeld, Gadi. 1984. "The Symbiosis of Press and Protest: An Exchange Analysis." *Journalism Quarterly* 61:550–56.

Index

Italic indicate pages on which illustrations appear

Abt, Vicki, 2, 7, 8
activists as guests, 177–84
Allen, Steve, 42
Alspaugh, Nancy, 115, 116–17, 230
Alwood, Edward, 47
Amedure, Scott, 6, 209–12, *211*, 261n.8
American Psychological Association, 3
Ancier, Garth, 58, 59
Ant (comedian), 71, 72, 159
appropriate versus inappropriate talk, 200–207
Araki, Gregg, 2
assimilation: conflict over, 191; positive images of gays and lesbians, 262n.14; queer politics as opposed to, 223; talk show visibility damaging, 216
audience (studio): antigay attitudes in, 125–28; class cultures of, 63, 202; criticism of, 7; on difference-telling shows, 148; of Donahue, 44–45; gender breakdown, 248n.36; of Gibbons, 30; impatience with transgender, 158–65; Lake's younger, 32, 57, 59–60; as less tolerant than the host, 56; in nineteenth-century the-

ater, 34–35, 247n.17; as playing themselves, 88, 251n.20; as representative, 15; warming up, 87–88; Whitney's New York, 61–62; of Winfrey, 55, 202; younger audiences' style of expression, 64–65
authority: associated with race, 127; as contested on talk shows, 99–105; expert guests, 100–101

Bakhtin, Mikhail, 167
Barnum, P. T., 37
bearded lady, 166
Bearse, Amanda, 114
Bellah, Robert, 47
Bennett, William, 9, 136, 207
Berrill, Kevin, 56
Berry, Bertice: bisexuality show, 126–27; straight people mistaken for gays show, 149
Bey, Richard: on audience as representative, 15; audience compared with Winfrey's, 202; as Donahue mutation, 58; drag queens versus real women show, 133, 154; homosexuality debate show, 100; same-sex desire linked to nonmonogamy, 135

Bieber, Irving, 48

bisexuals: audience impatience with, 158–65; audience opposition to, 126–27; as confused, 158–60; deception in Walberg show on, 74–75; as disorganizing identity, 151–52; as fence sitting, 162; and gay-straight dichotomy, 222–23; Gibbons show, 70–72; homosexuals contrasted with, 195; homosexuals versus bisexuals shows, 70–72, 174–77, 181; love triangle shows, 195; as nonmonogamous, 134–35, 195–96; producers maintaining gender categories, 161–62; program niche for, 134–35; Rivera shows, 181, 182–83; shows on homosexuality compared with, 132–35; stereotype of, 181; as unfaithful, 159, 196, 258n.39; as unnatural, 159; Winfrey show, 151–52, 161–63

Bledsoe, Tempestt: "I'm Gay, Get Used to It!" show, 97, 124; as Lake clone, 59; outing show, 184–85; on tolerance, 124

Block, Gil, 198

Bonaduce, Danny, 59

Bonck, Johnny, 50

Bornstein, Kate, 103–4, 166

Brothers, Joyce, 44

Buchwald, Art, 12

Burke, Alan, 43

cabaret, 34

cable television, 32, 262n.20

Calder, Martin, 136–37, 231

camera shots, 92, 251n.24

Cameron, Paul, 101, 111, 119, 131, 186

Carbaugh, Donal, 46–47

Carpignano, Paolo, 15, 16, 45, 46

Carson, Johnny, 42

cart calls, 60, 81

Carter, Sheri, 74–75

Carteris, Gabrielle: as Lake clone, 59; transsexuals show, 152, 153, 160–61

Cathcart, Kevin, 52

Cavett, Dick, 48

celebrity variety shows, 44

censorship, of Donahue, 44

Clark, Danae, 263n.26

class: of audiences, 63, 202; and coming out, 172; entertainment segregated by, 36; gendered programming styles mapping onto, 43; of guests, 63, 185–86, 193–94; public life and class cultures, 32–42; and sexuality and privacy, 202–3; talk shows drawing from different class cultures, 30, 32–33, 40, 42, 194, 220–21; of viewers, 179

coffeehouses, 33

Cohen, Jaffe, 144, 218

collective identity, 222

Collins, Patricia Hill, 95, 252n.30

coming out: DeGeneres show, 219, 262n.17; and Donahue philosophy, 50; by gay husbands, 70; outing, 181, 184–85; as power play, 171–72, 259n.2; public relevance of, 200; truth-telling rhetoric and, 104

commercial entertainment, 34–36

constructionism, 19–20, 155, 252n.32

Costa, Cheryl Ann, 187–88

Crane, Les, 43

Crisp, Quentin, 208, 217

cross-dressers: defined, 242n.6; Donahue show, 50, 142; Downey show, 178; drag queens and female impersonators contrasted, 145; on gay-themed shows, 196; as gender contradictions, 144; homosexuality conflated with, 149–50; program niche for, 133–34; Rivera show, 183; shows on homosexuality com-

pared with, 132–35; stereotype of, 181; Whitney show, 183
culture wars, 13, 173, 225

Dabney, Charles. *See* Perez, Charles
Dean, Craig, 186
DeGeneres, Ellen, 219, 262n.17
Diana, Eve, 175–76
DiMaggio, Paul, 36
dime museums, 36
Dlugacz, Judy, 148
Donahue, Phil, 44–47; antigay guests, 111, 114; audience, 44–45; bisexuality show, 152; cancellation, 32, 61; censorship of, 44; conflict-and-taboo strategy, 31, 61; as controversial, 44, 47; on critics of talk shows, 14; cross-dressing show, 50, *142;* as explicit about sex, 44; as gay-friendly, 116; gay wedding show, 186; homosexuals as guests, 47–54, 93–94, 197–98; homosexuals versus bisexuals show, 174–77, 181; integrating homosexuals into shows with non-gay topics, 113; liberal individualism as code for, 46–47; Masters and Johnson appearance, 44, 49–50; middle-class public talk as model, 33, 45, 47; postpartum-depression show, 249n.57; respect as norm for, 46, 47; stereotype bashing, 53; in talk show development, 30–32; on talk shows empowering women, 16; topics, 12; town meeting staged by, 45; on transgender issues, 48–49; transsexual lesbians show, 154–55; unpredictability handled by, 93–94; Winfrey compared with, 31, 54; women given a voice by, 31, 45; women's and men's programming mixed by, 44
Douglas, Mary, 141
Douglas, Mike, 44

Downey, Morton, Jr., 43, 178
drag queens. *See* cross-dressers
Dubrow, Burt, 61, 156, 231

800 (toll-free) numbers, 60, 81
elitism: elite authority associated with whites, 127; high culture created by elites, 36; in talk show criticism, 14
Elliott, Gordon: audience singing during break, 62; as Donahue mutation, 58; Miss Understood appearance, 145; warming up the audience, 87
Elshtain, Jean Bethke, 203
Empower America, 9
Epstein, Steven, 254n.49
essentialism, 96, 118, 222, 252n.32
Etheridge, Melissa, 114, 219
Evans, Arthur, 48
expert guests: and authority on talk shows, 100–101; middle-class guests as, 187, 188; relationship experts, 4, 70, 96, 188

Falwell, Jerry, 219, 262n.17
Farajaje-Jones, Elias, 114
Feinberg, Leslie, 103, 253n.48
Fejes, Fred, 221
feminism: private made public by, 207; talk shows as rooted in, 16; truth-telling as strategy of, 252n.30
Fem to Fem (band), 148
Fiedler, Leslie, 37, 138, 166, 242n.15
First (magazine), 3
Foucault, Michel, 4, 102, 241n.5
Fox, Rick, 55–56
Francis, Arlene, 44
freak shows, 36–40; "boy change to girl" sideshow banner, *41;* as exploitation, 248n.25; freaks on exhibit, *39;* the freaks talk back, 165–69; the true freak for Fiedler, 138; Two-Headed Girl, 28
free speech, 95–96

Gabler, Neal, 8
Gaines, Donna, 15
gang girls, 92
Garber, Marjorie: on bisexuality as ground of human sexuality, 151; on category crises, 158; dressing for talk show appearances, 183; on guest demeanor, 129; on producers resisting challenge of transgender, 161–62; on stereotypes of transgender, 181; on telling the difference, 149–50
Gardner, Angela, 178, 189–90
Garfinkel, Harold, 154
Gay Activist Alliance, 48
Gay and Lesbian Alliance against Defamation (GLAAD), 180
gays. *See* homosexuals
gender: conservatism of people of color, 127–28; discussion of difference congealing dominant identities, 160, 258n.42; and genitals, 97, 110–11, 153–58, 160, 163; as learned, 140, 161; mixing genders as disruptive, 140; natural attitude toward, 154; power and privilege as related to, 141; producers maintaining categories of, 161–62; social construction of, 19–20, 155; talk shows opening and closing boundaries of, 143, 146, 223. *See also* sex and gender nonconformists; sexuality
gender dysphoria, 154, 163
Gerbner, George, 3
Gibbons, Leeza: bisexuality versus homosexuality show, 70–72; as Donahue mutation, 58; family framework of shows, 115; guests and audience of, 30
Gilkeson, John, 36
Goldstein, Richard, 16
Goldstein, Steven, 76, 77, 89, 231
Goodman, Walter, 54
Green, James, 85

Griffin, Merv, 44
Grindstaff, Laura, 77, 86, 92, 251n.14
Gross, Larry, 21–22
guests: activists, 177–84; as ambushed, 6; antigay guests, 109–25; celebrity status of, 261n.13; class cultures of, 63, 185–86, 193–94; coaching, 77–79, 86–87, 251n.15; compensation for, 77; conned by producers, 66, 70–72, 83–86; counterstereotypical people, 56, 216; dress, 183; "evangelists," 86; fraudulent, 73–77; fringe rather than mainstream, 184–95, 215–17; of Gibbons, 30; homosexuals, 47–57, 63–64; interviews for this study, 228–29, 231–33; of Lake, 59, 60; likability as essential, 128–32; "moths," 81; as playing themselves, 88, 251n.20; sex and gender nonconformists, 4–5, 8–13, 21, 172; trading out with producers, 180–81; as trailer-park trash and ghetto kids, 29; "trash," 220. *See also* expert guests; recruitment of guests

Habermas, Jürgen, 243n.38
Halberstam, David, 12
Hale, Jacob, 153
Harding, Susan, 167
Harrelson, Don, 52
Harwood, Gean, 51
Hatterer, Lawrence, 48
Heaton, Jeanne, and Nona Wilson: on abnormality exaggerated on talk shows, 9; on Donahue, 31; gladiatorial contests compared with talk shows by, 8; on just about every truth as having been covered, 32; on nothing as sacred on talk shows, 31; on talk shows as bad therapy, 7; Winfrey and Donahue compared by, 31
Heft, Lisa, 50

Henner, Marilu, 92–93
Hennessy, Rosemary, 213, 221, 263n.26
homophobia, 55–56, 96
Homosexuality in Perspective (Masters and Johnson), 49–50
homosexuals: activists as guests, 177–84; antigay audiences, 125–28; antigay guests on talk shows, 109–25; appropriate versus inappropriate, 200; bisexuals versus homosexuals shows, 70–72, 174–77, 181; children as vulnerable to, 147; conservative response to flaunting it, 205–6; as crammed down peoples' throats, 199, 204; and deception, 67–72; divisions exacerbated on talk shows, 194–99; Donahue show, 47–54, 93–94, 197–98; former homosexuals shows, 111–12; fringe individuals chosen as talk show guests, 184–95, 215–17; gay husbands shows, 67–70, 149, 181; gender-conforming versus bad gays in drag, 197–98; gender-crossing normalizing status of, 163–65, 195; as guests on talk shows, 47–57, 63–64; Henner show on gay parents, 93; Lake show on gay parents, 101, 130–31; liberal response to flaunting it, 204–5; as a market, 221; Masters and Johnson on, 49–50; media representation of, 20–22, 47–48; as natural compared with bisexuals, 159; New Homosexuals, 56; passing, 213; as political topic, 136; positive images of, 262n.14; publicly flaunting it, 199–207; queer theory, 222–23; relatives of gays on Raphael show, 188–89; shows on bisexuality and gender-crossing compared with, 132–35; on shows with nongay topics, 113–16; Stonewall riots, 48; straight people as afraid of, 170; talk shows as forum for, 16; talk shows as progay publicity, 173; on television soaps and sitcoms, 218–20; transsexuals as gay men gone too far, 164; transvestism conflated with, 149–50; truth-telling as therapy for, 95–97; as unproblematic category, 146–47; Winfrey show, 55–56. *See also* coming out; lesbians

Hook, Cheryl, 56
Hot Air (Kurtz), 8
Hutchins, Loraine, 182–83

identity: collective, 222; personal, 141. *See also* gender; sexual identity
impropriety, 108, 201–7
inappropriate versus appropriate talk, 200–207
individualism, liberal, 46–47
infotainment, 90
Irving, Washington, 34

Jackson-Paris, Bob and Rod, 114
Johnson, Virginia, 44, 49–50
Jones, Bill, 52
Jones, Cleve, 56
Jones, Jenny: as cultural assassin for Wildmon, 136; as Donahue mutation, 58; as gay-friendly, 116; homosexuals flaunting it, 200; moment of truth on lesbian teenagers show, 94; Schmitz-Amedure affair, 6, 91, 209–12, *211*, 261n.8; younging her show like Lake, 60
Jones, Jordy, 167–68

Ka'ahumanu, Lani: bisexuality anthology, 259n.4; Donahue homosexuals versus bisexuals show, 174, 176, 177; Gibbons homosexuals versus bisexuals show, 71; on religion and bisexuality, 126

Kappas, Mike, 81, 82–83, 231
Katz, Jonathan Ned, 258n.42
Kessler, Suzanne J., 182
Kirk, Marshall, 190, 208
Knudsen, Gunilla, 31
Kopkind, Andrew, 218
Kurtz, Howard, 8, 9, 12, 15

Lake, Ricki, 57–60; and Ancier, 58; audience as younger, 32, 57, 59–60; as authority, 99; bisexuals shows, 159; clones of, 59; coaching guests, 77–78; as cultural assassin for Wildmon, 136; as gay-friendly, 116, 120–24; gay parents shows, 101, 130–31; guests of, 59, 60; "I'm Gay . . . It's Not a Phase . . . Get over It" show, 96, 121–22; integrating homosexuals into shows with nongay topics, 113; lesbian shows, 146; number of viewers, 58; personal relationships as focus, 59; recruiting of guests, 60; secret gay crushes shows, 210; tolerance created by, 218; warming up the audience, 87
leisure, 34
Leitsch, Dick, 48
lesbians: Lake show on lesbian mothers, 130–31; Lake shows, 146; lipstick lesbians, 147, 196–97, 216; as a market, 221; moment of truth on Jones lesbian teenagers show, 94; passing, 197, 213; positive images of, 262n.14; Rivera show, 147–48; Springer show, 118–19; straight people as afraid of, 170; telling the difference shows, 147–48; transsexual lesbians shows, 154–55, 183; Williams show on sex clubs, 178–79
Levine, Lawrence, 34, 35, 247n.17
liberalism: individualism, 46–47; pluralism, 117–18; response to homosexuals flaunting it, 204–5; talk show

sexual morality as politically liberal, 132
Lieberman, Joseph, 9
Limbaugh, Rush, 58
lipstick lesbians, 147, 196–97, 216
Livingstone, Sonia, 13, 15, 243n.38
Lofton, John, 56, 106, 111, 114
Long, Barry, 74–75
Lorber, Judith, 20, 140
Loulan, JoAnn, 148
Lunt, Peter, 13, 15, 243n.38

Mack, Ted, 42
Madsen, Hunter, 190, 208
magazines: "true confession" magazines, 40, 54; women's magazines, 33
Magid, Frank N., Associates, 90
Manhattan Gender Network, 24, 188, 237
Marcus, Eric, 182, 186–87, 188–89, 190
Masciarotte, Gloria-Jean, 15, 16, 54, 100
Mashore, Lloyd, 197
mass culture. See popular (mass) culture
Masters, William, 44, 49–50
McClelland, David, 3
McKenna, Wendy, 182
media: homosexuals as represented in, 20–22, 47–48; movements and, 249n.57; tabloids, 40, 248n.31. See also magazines; radio; television
Mendelsohn, Daniel, 263n.22
Mero, Bruhs, 51
methodology of this study, 22–24, 227–39; audience focus-groups, 237–39; coding of programs, 234–35; content analysis, 233–37; interviews of guests, 228–29, 231–33; interviews on production, 227–33; transcripts and videos of shows,

233–34; tripartite model of cultural study, 227

Meyrowitz, Joshua, 201

Michigan State University study, 108, 254n.2

Miller, Jennifer, 166

Minkowitz, Donna, 197

Miss Understood, 134, 145, 165

monogamy: bisexuals as nonmonogamous, 134–35, 195–96; sexual fidelity, 159, 196, 258n.39

morality, sexual. *See* sexual morality

moral panics, 224

Mother Teresa, 3

movements: activists as guests, 177–84; and media, 249n.57

Munson, Wayne, 17, 33, 40, 42, 90, 167, 246n.2

Musser, John, 69

Nagle, Jill, 179

Nelson, Jill, 7–8

Nelson, Judy, 115

New Homosexuals, 56

Northrop, Ann, 128–29, 174–75, 176–77, 191

Nudelman, Franny, 99, 100

Nunn, Ray, 73

Ochs, Robyn, 174, 175–76, 181

Ornstein, Rich, 74

outing, 181, 184–85

Parr, Jack, 42

Peck, Janice, 253nn. 33, 47

Peo, Roger, 104

Perez, Charles: conflict in shows, 76; deception in transsexuals show, 83–85; fraudulent guests, 73; as Lake clone, 59; on talk shows as democratic, 14; transsexuals regrets show, 189–90

personal identity, 141

Petrich, Kevin, 221

Phillips, Linda and Cynthia, 66, 143–44, 180

pluralism, liberal, 117–18

polite society, 199–200

PoMo Afro Homos, 114

popular (mass) culture: criticisms of, 14, 243n.29; high culture distinguished from, 36. *See also* freak shows; radio; television

postmodernism, 42, 99, 167

postpartum-depression movement, 249n.57

Poussaint, Alvin, 3

Povich, Maury: as Donahue mutation, 58; gender-crossers and their families show, 134; lipstick lesbian show, 196–97; secret gay crushes shows, 210; teen bisexuals show, 150–51; topics, 12; transsexual glamour show, 156, 161; warming up the audience, 88

Power, Tyrone, 35

Prager, Dennis, 113

Pratt, Jane: and Ancier, 58; on fraudulent guests, 73; and Perez, 59

preinterviews ("blind dates"), 76, 86

Priest, Patricia, 81, 86, 229

privacy, 200–207

production of talk shows: camera shots, 92, 251n.24; content influenced by, 23–24; deception by producers, 73–80; divisions among gender nonconformists exacerbated by, 172–73, 194–99; gay staff, 116–17; gender categories maintained in, 161–62; guests trading out, 180–81; as high-pressure work, 78–79; methodology of this study, 227–33; moments of truth as goal of, 24–25, 90–95; order and presentation of guests, 125; performance and dishonesty as built into, 89; taping as close to final product as possible,

production of talk shows (*continued*)
251n.24; tolerance emphasized in
programs on homosexuality, 132; visibility shaped by, 214. *See also* recruitment of guests
propriety, 108, 201–7
public indecency, 225
public sphere: boundary with private
as contested, 173; class culture and
public life, 32–42; gay and lesbian
movement on the private and, 199–
207; Habermas on, 243n.38; leisure
in public settings, 34; making sexuality public, 260n.27; overlapping
meanings of public/private distinction, 260n.22; sex and gender nonconformists breaking down, 224–25;
talk shows wreaking havoc with, 18,
244n.51; television disturbing
public/private distinction, 201;
women redefining relationship between private sphere and, 46. *See
also* visibility
Pyne, Joe, 43

Queen for a Day (television show), 43
queer theory, 222–23

race: authority associated with, 127;
complexity of, 257n.18; gender conservatism of people of color, 127–28
racism, 253nn. 33, 47
radio: listener-participation shows of
1930s and 1940s, 42; talk radio, 43,
248n.36
Randall, Lawrence, 79, 231
Raphael, Sally Jessy: Araki on, 2;
coaching guests, 77; former homosexuals show, 111–12; fraudulent
guests, 73; as gay-friendly, 116; gay
husbands show, 67–68; integrating
homosexuals into shows with nongay topics, 113; Linda and Cynthia

Phillips appearance, 144; relatives of
gays show, 188–89; Isabelle Richards appearance, 100–101; style of,
54; on tabloid talk shows, 2; therapy
and confession on, 54; transsexual
lesbians show, 183; transsexuals
shows, 97, 98, 160, 161; transsexual
versus nontranssexual women's bikini contest, 133, 156; warming up
the audience, 87
Rapping, Elayne, 13
recruitment of guests: cart calls, 60,
81; as casting, 75–76; difficulties of,
79–80; 800 numbers, 60, 81; homosexuals on Donahue, 52–53; by
Lake, 60; "leading the witnesses,"
82; preinterviews, 76, 86; pursuing
guests, 80–83
relationship experts, 4, 70, 96, 188
Renaissance Education Association,
178, 187
respect: on Donahue show, 46, 47; on
Lake show, 57
Richards, Isabelle, 100–101
Rivera, Geraldo: bisexuals shows, 181,
182–83; bisexual teens show, 158–
59; Cameron appearance, 119; confrontational style of, 54–55; cross-
dressing show, 183; fraudulent
guests, 73; guests conned, 66; integrating homosexuals into shows with
nongay topics, 113; lesbian chic
show, 147–48; outing show, 181;
partners of transsexuals show, 157;
power dykes show, 147; on protecting children from homosexuality,
147; as sideshow barker, 37, 40; Socarides appearance, 112; topics, 12;
transsexuals shows, 40, 75–76, 97,
157
Rivers, Joan, 103–4
Rivers, Melissa, 58
Robinson, Marty, 48

Rodman, Dennis, 262n.20
Rose, Brian, 43
Rotello, Gabriel, 101, 131
Roth, David, 59, 60, 62, 64–65, 231
Rubin, Gayle, 19
RuPaul, 262n.20
Russo, Frank, 110
Russo, Vito, 21, 214

Sarris, Cathy, 56
Schacter, Jane, 262n.14
Schmitz, Jonathan, 6, 91, 209–12, *211*, 261n.8
Schone, Mark, 59
Seesholtz, Mel, 2, 8
Senior Action in a Gay Environment (SAGE), 52
sensationalism: in sideshows, 40; in talk show development, 31
service talk shows, 44
sex and gender nonconformists: accuracy in representing, 191–92; activists as guests, 177–84; and "clean up" movement, 136–37; countersterotypical people, 56, 216; divisions exacerbated on talk shows, 172–73, 194–99; and early talk shows as made for each other, 49; as embodying secrets, 102; and freaks, 242n.15; fringe individuals chosen as talk show guests, 184–95, 215–17; media visibility of, 21; opposing arguments on talk shows, 106–37; as political issue, 127, 133, 207; postmodernist contradictions in, 42; publicly flaunting it, 199–207; public/private distinction blurred by, 224–25; public visibility as central concern, 213; religious opposition to, 110–12; shifting boundaries with normality, 18–19; on talk shows, 4–5, 8–13, 21, 172; talk shows discussing morality of, 108–9; tasteful presenta-

tion of, 203; term's use, 242n.6; and therapeutic aspect of talk shows, 54; truth-telling as therapy for, 95–98. *See also* bisexuals; homosexuals; lesbians; transgender
sexual fidelity, 159, 196, 258n.39
sexual identity: disclosure as power play, 171–72; gay and lesbian movement making public, 200–201; power and privilege related to, 141, 171, 172; transgender creating disarray in, 150–58. *See also* gender
sexuality: and class and privacy, 202–3; Donahue as explicit about, 44; essentialist view of, 96, 252n.32; Hutchins on categories of, 182–83; making it public, 260n.27; normal sexuality as vulnerable, 147; queer theory on proliferation of, 223, 263n.26; social construction of, 19–20; talk show approach to, 102–3; truth and sex, 102. *See also* sex and gender nonconformists
Sexuality Information and Education Council of the U.S. (SIECUS), 187
sexual morality: African American dialogue on, 127; as politically liberal and culturally conservative on talk shows, 132; and talk show ideology, 25; as talk show theme, 108–9
Shakespeare, William, 34, 35–36, 247n.17
Shales, Tom, 3–4
Shattuc, Jane, 40, 96, 116, 248n.31
Sheldon, Andrea, 129
Shore, Dinah, 44
sideshows, 36–40, *41*
Signorile, Michelangelo, 121–22, 129, 177, 181, 186, 262n.21
Simmermon, Robert, 4
Smith, Tom, 181
Socarides, Charles, 48, 112
Spencer, Bruce, 53

Springer, Jerry: on accuracy in representing groups, 192; on anger of gay militants, 185; bisexuality show, 152; and "clean up" movement, 136; as Donahue mutation, 58; fraudulent guests, 73; on gays publicly flaunting it, 199; on gender, 153; integrating homosexuals into shows with nongay topics, 113; lesbian couple show, 118–19; same-sex desire linked to nonmonogamy, 135; secret gay crushes shows, 210; teen transsexuals show, 98, 104, 155, 161; on tolerance, 117; transsexuals shows, 155, 157, 163, 164, 187–88; on trash, 13, 15; younging his show like Lake, 60–61

"spur posse," 83

Stanley, Ken, 197

Stasi, Linda, 12

Steinberg, Gail, 58

Steinem, Gloria, 31

Stern, Howard, 43

Stevens, Frances, 147

Stewart, Cianna, 178–79

Stonewall riots, 48

Strassberger, Fred, 3

Stryker, Susan, 75–76, 138, 152, 165, 182

studio audience. *See* audience

Suggs, Donald, 120–21, 179–80

Susskind, David, 43, 48

Szymanski, Michael, 72

tabloids, 40, 248n.31

talk radio, 43, 248n.36

talk shows: antigay arguments on, 106–37; authority on, 99–105; as bad for you, 3–4; breakeven barrier for, 58; "clean up" movement, 136–37; conflict as requirement, 75, 76; criticisms of, 6–13; deception on, 66–105; as democratic, 13–19; as exploitative, 7, 215; as freak shows, 8, 36–40, 63, 165–69, 242n.15; history of, 28–65, 246n.2; ideology of, 25; incitement to discourse on, 4; number of, 32; personality as central in, 128; precursors of, 42–44; as progay publicity, 173; program types, 113–14; as pruriently addictive, 8; sex and gender boundaries opened and closed on, 143, 146, 223; as show business, 7; social effects of, 7–8; on telling the difference, 25; truth as imperative and impossible, 70; as woman-oriented, 16, 30–31, 45–46. *See also* audience; guests; production of talk shows; viewers

Tanner, Randy, 82, 231

Taylor, Harry, 185

Taylor, Verta, 249n.57

Teena, Brandon, 97

television: as arbiter of worth, 224; cable television, 32, 262n.20; celebrity variety shows, 44; homogenization of, 20; homosexuals on soaps and sitcoms, 218–20; infotainment, 90; people wanting to be on, 214, 261n.13; personality as central in, 128; power of, 178–79; public/private distinction disturbed by, 201; reality television, 90; service talk shows, 44; women as target audience of daytime, 45; women's programming, 44. *See also* talk shows

Texas cheerleaders, 80–81

therapy: talk shows and, 7, 8, 54, 96, 249n.61; truth-telling as, 95–98

Tillis, Ashley, 183

toll-free (800) numbers, 60, 81

Tonight Show, The (television show), 42–43

transgender, 138–69; audience impatience with, 158–65; as both and neither, 150–58; as deceptive, 97–98;

defined, 242n.6; Donahue show, 48–
49; as fake gender, 163; gender
ambiguity repudiated by, 160–61;
homosexual status normalized by,
163–65, 195; male lesbians, 180;
and man-woman dichotomy, 222–
23; producers maintaining gender categories, 161–62; as programming staple, 157; shows on homosexuality
compared with, 132–35. *See also*
cross-dressers; transsexuals
transsexuals: deception in Perez show
on, 83–85; as deceptive, 97–98; defined, 242n.6; as disorganizing identity, 151, 152–58; as gay men gone
too far, 164; as not real, 160; partners of, 157; Perez show on transsexual regrets, 189–90; program niche
for, 133–34; Raphael show, 97, 98,
160; Rivera show, 40, 75–76, 97;
Rivers show, 103–4; scientific authority medicalizing, 103–5; shows on
homosexuality compared with, 132–
35; Springer shows, 155, 157, 163,
164, 187–88; Springer teen transsexuals show, 98, 104; transsexual lesbians shows, 154–55, 183
transvestites. *See* cross-dressers
Trollope, Frances, 34–35
"true confession" magazines, 40, 54
True Story (magazine), 40
Truth or Consequences, 42
Tuning in Trouble (Heaton and Wilson), 7

Verney, Peter, 248n.25
viewers: class status, 179; daytime TV
target viewer, 45; gender breakdown, 248n.36; interviews with, 24,
237–39; reactions to gender nonconformist shows, 173; as skeptical of
talk shows, 89–90; urban viewers,
58

visibility, 208–25; as balancing act,
213–17; dilemma of, 217–24; gender nonconformists flaunting it,
199–207; invisibility as the enemy,
21; older women becoming invisible,
213; paradoxes of, 19. *See also* coming out
Vox Pop (radio show), 42

Walberg, Mark: deception in bisexu-
ality show, 74–75; as Lake clone, 59
Walker, Jason, 76, 231
Warner, Michael, 222
Watts, Rolonda: antigay guests, 111,
114, 119–20; bisexuals shows, 159;
gay husbands show, 68; Linda Phillips appearance, 143–44; and Russo,
110; on tolerance, 117; women who
become men show, 152–53
Weaver, Sylvester "Pat," 42
Weintraub, Jeff, 260n.22
Westenhoefer, Suzanne, 148, 170
Westheimer, Ruth, 44
White, Mimi, 54
Whitney, Jane: audience on homosexu-
ality show, 148; bisexual love trian-
gle show, 195–96; cross-dressing
show, 183; as Donahue mutation,
58; as gay-friendly, 116, 136; on
man who claims to cure gays, 109;
on monogamous bisexuals, 135;
New York audience changing show,
61–62
Wildmon, Donald, 136, 262n.17
Williams, Karen, 148
Williams, Montel: as Donahue muta-
tion, 58; fraudulent guests, 73; les-
bian sex club show, 178–79
Willis, Ellen, 14–15
Wilson, Carnie: and Ancier, 58; as
Lake clone, 59
Wilson, Nona. *See* Heaton, Jeanne,
and Nona Wilson

Winfrey, Oprah: antigay guests, 111,
114; audience, 55, 202; bisexuality
shows, 151–52, 161–63; conflict in
shows, 76; as democratic, 15, 17;
Donahue compared with, 31, 54;
fraudulent guests, 73; as gay-
friendly, 116; gay husbands shows,
68–70; as her own guest, 54; hetero-
sensibilities of, 69; homophobia
show, 55–56; number of viewers,
58; personal-and-taboo strategy, 31;
personal intimacy as style of, 53–54;
respectable environment created,
191; therapy and confession on, 54;
on tolerance, 117–18
women: Donahue giving a voice to, 31,
45; older women becoming invisible,
213; as percentage of talk show audience, 248n.36; programming style
for, 43, 44; public and private
spheres redefined by, 46; talk shows
as oriented toward, 16, 30–31, 45–
46; as target viewer of daytime TV,
45. *See also* feminism; lesbians
women's magazines, 33